822GRA

THE DEFINIT...

THE DEFINITIVE
SIMON GRAY
III

faber and faber
LONDON · BOSTON

This collection first published in 1993
by Faber and Faber Limited
3 Queen Square London WC1N 3AU

Photoset by Parker Typesetting Service, Leicester

Printed in England by Clays Ltd, St Ives plc

Quartermaine's Terms was first published in 1981 by Eyre Methuen Ltd
The Rear Column was first published in 1978 in a volume entitled *The Rear Column
and other plays* by Eyre Methuen Ltd
Close of Play was first published in 1979 in a volume entitled *Close of Play and Pig
in a Poke* by Eyre Methuen Ltd. Revised edition first published in 1980 by Eyre
Methuen Ltd.
Stage Struck was first published in 1979 by Eyre Methuen Ltd. Revised edition
first published in this collection.
Tartuffe: An Adaptation was first published in 1990 in a volume entitled *The Holy
Terror/Tartuffe* by Faber and Faber Ltd.
Screenplay *A Month in the Country* was first published in 1990 in a volume entitled
Old Flames and A Month in the Country by Faber and Faber Ltd.

A CIP record for this book is available from the British Library
ISBN 0-571-16453-6

1 3 5 7 9 10 8 6 4 2

CONTENTS

Quartermaine's Terms

For Beryl

Quartermaine's Terms was first presented by Michael Codron on 28 July 1981 at the Queen's Theatre, London. The cast was as follows:

ST JOHN QUARTERMAINE	Edward Fox
ANITA MANCHIP	Jenny Quayle
MARK SACKLING	Peter Birch
EDDIE LOOMIS	Robin Bailey
DEREK MEADLE	Glyn Grain
HENRY WINDSCAPE	James Grout
MELANIE GARTH	Prunella Scales
Director	Harold Pinter
Designer	Eileen Diss
Lighting	Leonard Tucker

The Set

The staff-room of the Cull-Loomis School of English for foreigners, Cambridge, or rather a section of the staff-room – the last quarter of it. On stage are french windows, a long table, lockers for members of the staff, pegs for coats etc., and a number of armchairs; on the table a telephone, newspapers and magazines. This is the basic set, to which, between scenes and between the two Acts, additions can be made to suggest the varying fortunes of the school. Off stage, left, a suggestion of hard-backed chairs, and off left, a door to the main corridor of the school, where the classrooms are.

The period: early 1960s.

ACT ONE

SCENE I

Monday morning, spring term. The french windows are open. It is about 9.30. Sunny.

QUARTERMAINE is sitting with his feet up, hands folded on his lap, staring ahead. From off, outside the french windows, in the garden, the sound of foreign voices excited, talking, laughing etc., passing by. As these recede ANITA comes through the french windows carrying a briefcase.

ANITA: 'Morning, St John.

QUARTERMAINE: Oh hello Anita, but I say, you know – *(getting up)* you look – you look different, don't you?

ANITA: Do I? Oh – my hair probably. I've put it up.

QUARTERMAINE: Well, it looks – looks really terrific! Of course I liked it the other way too, tumbling down your shoulders.

ANITA: It hasn't tumbled down my shoulders for three years, St John.

QUARTERMAINE: Oh. How was it then before you changed it?

ANITA: Back in a pony tail. *(She indicates.)*

QUARTERMAINE: That's it. Yes. Well, I liked it like that, too.

ANITA: Thank you. Oh by the way, Nigel asked me to apologize again for having to cancel dinner. He was afraid he was a little abrupt on the phone.

QUARTERMAINE: Oh Lord no, not at all – besides, it's lucky he *was* abrupt, you know how Mrs Harris hates me using the phone, she stands right beside me glowering, but I managed to understand exactly what he was getting at, something to do with – with a lecture he had to prepare, wasn't it.

ANITA: No, it was the new magazine they're starting. The first issue's coming out shortly and they still haven't got enough material so they had to call a panic editorial meeting – it went on until three in the morning –

QUARTERMAINE: Oh. Poor old Nigel. But it sounds tremendously – tremendously exciting –

ANITA: Oh, yes. Well, they're all very excited about it, anyway,

5

they're determined it shouldn't just be another little Cambridge literary magazine, you know, but they want to preserve the Cambridge style and tone. Anyway, I'm sorry we couldn't have the dinner, and at such short notice. Did you find anything else to do?

QUARTERMAINE: Oh yes, yes, I was fine, don't worry, tell Nigel, because just after he phoned, old Henry phoned, to invite me around.

ANITA: What luck. For dinner?

QUARTERMAINE: No, to baby-sit, actually.

ANITA: To baby-sit. But their oldest – Susan isn't it? – must be nearly fourteen.

QUARTERMAINE: Yes, but apparently she's working away for her O levels – she's very bright – taking it years in advance and all that, so they wanted her not to have to worry about the young ones, you see – in fact, they really hadn't meant to go out, and then they discovered that there was some film they wanted to see at the Arts, some old German classic they seem to be very fond of, about – about a child-murderer as far as I could make out from what Henry told me. So that was all right.

ANITA: You enjoyed it, then?

QUARTERMAINE: Oh Lord yes, well children you know are such – such – it took me a bit of time to get them used to me, of course, as the smallest one, the one they call little Fanny – very charming, very charming – cried when she saw me – she hates it when Henry and Fanny go out, you see – and then the boy – my word, what a little devil, full of mischief, told me little Fanny had drowned in the bath and when I ran in there she was – lying face down – hair floating around – and I stood there thinking, you know, (laughs) Lord, what am I going to say to Henry and Fanny particularly when they get back, especially after seeing a film like that – but it turned out it was only an enormous Raggidy Anne doll, and little Fanny was hiding under her bed – because Ben had told her I was going to eat her up – (laughs) but I got them settled down in the end, in fact it would have been sooner if Susan hadn't kept coming out of her room to scream at them for

interrupting her studying – and anyway Henry and Fanny
came back quite early. In about an hour, as a matter of fact.

ANITA: Well, at least you had a bit of an evening with them then.

QUARTERMAINE: Oh rather – except that Fanny had a terrible
headache from straining to read the subtitles, that's why
they'd had to leave, a very poor print apparently – then Henry
got involved in a – an argument with Ben, who'd got up when
he heard them come in so I felt, you know, they rather wanted
me out of the way –

(*The sound of the door opening, during the above. Footsteps.*)

Oh hello Mark, top of the morning to you, have a good weekend?

(SACKLING *appears on stage. He is carrying a briefcase, is
unshaven, looks ghastly.*)

ANITA: (*Looking at him in concern*) Are you all right?

SACKLING: Yes, yes, fine, fine. (*He drops the briefcase, slumps into a
chair.*)

ANITA: Are you growing a beard?

SACKLING: What? Oh Christ! (*Feeling his chin.*) I forgot!

ANITA: But there must be several days' stubble there.

SACKLING: Haven't been to bed you see. All weekend.

QUARTERMAINE: Ah, been hard at it, eh?

SACKLING: What?

QUARTERMAINE: Hard at it. The old writing.

(SACKLING *grunts.*)

Terrific!

ANITA: Oh, I've got a message from Nigel, by the way, he asked me
to ask you to hurry up with an extract, they're desperate to get
it into the first issue, he says don't worry about whether it's
self-contained, they can always shove it in as 'Work in
Progress' or something.

SACKLING: Right.

ANITA: You look to me as if you've overdone it – are you sure
you're all right?

QUARTERMAINE: I say, how's old Camelia?

SACKLING: (*Barks out a laugh*) Oh fine! Just – fine!

QUARTERMAINE: Terrific, and little Tom too?

SACKLING: Tom too, oh yes, Tom too.

QUARTERMAINE: The last time I saw him he was teething,

7

standing there in his high chair dribbling away like anything, while Camelia was sitting on old Mark's lap making faces at him with orange peel in her mouth –

(SACKLING *bursts into tears*. ANITA *goes to* SACKLING, *puts her hand on his shoulder*.)

QUARTERMAINE: What? Oh – oh Lord!

SACKLING: Sorry – sorry – I'll be all right – still – still digesting.

QUARTERMAINE: Something you had for breakfast, is it? Not kidneys – they can give you terrible heartburn – especially with mushrooms –

(ANITA *shakes her head at him*.)

Mmmm?

ANITA: Do you want to talk about it?

SACKLING: I don't want anyone – anyone else to know – especially not Thomas or Eddie – don't want them dripping their – their filthy compassion all over me.

QUARTERMAINE: What?

ANITA: We're to keep it to ourselves, St John.

QUARTERMAINE: Oh Lord yes. Of course. What though?

SACKLING: She's left me.

QUARTERMAINE: Who?

ANITA: Camelia, of course.

QUARTERMAINE: What! Old Camelia! On no!

SACKLING: Taking Tom – taking Tom with her.

QUARTERMAINE: Oh, not little Tom too!

SACKLING: Tom too.

ANITA: Well, did she – say why?

SACKLING: (*Makes an effort, pulls himself together*) She – she – (*He takes an envelope out of his pocket*.) I was upstairs in the attic – writing away – as far as I knew she was downstairs where she usually is – in the kitchen or – ironing – with the television on. And Tom in bed, of course. So I wrote on and on – I felt inspired, quite inspired, a passage about – about what I'd felt when I saw Tom coming out of her womb – so shiny and whole and beautiful – a wonderful passage – full of – full of my love for her and him – and when I finished I went downstairs to her – to read it to her – as I always do when it's something I'm burning with – and she wasn't there – the house was very still,

empty, but I didn't think – never occurred to me – so I went
up the stairs and into our bedroom and – all her clothes – the
suitcases everything – gone – and this – this on the pillow.
(*He hands the note to* QUARTERMAINE. *He takes it, opens it,
makes to read it. Stops. Shakes his head.* ANITA *makes a small
move to take it from him.*)

QUARTERMAINE: (*Not noticing*) No, we can't – can we, Anita –
really – I mean it's from her to you so – so – (*He hands it back.*)

SACKLING: (*Takes it back*) 'I'm sorry darling, so sorry oh my
darling, but it seems after all that I wasn't cut out to be a
writer's wife. I can't stand the strain of it, the lonely evenings,
your remoteness, and most of all the feeling that your novel
means more to you than Tom and I do. Perhaps that's what
being an artist is. Not caring about those who love you. I'm
going back to mother's, I'll take the car' – yes, taken the car –
she'd take that all right, wouldn't she! – 'as you don't drive,
and begin proceedings as soon as I've got a lawyer. Take care,
my love, look after yourself, I wish you such success and I
know that one day I'll be proud to have been your first wife,
just as Tom will be proud to be your father.'
(*There is a pause.*)

QUARTERMAINE: Um, son, surely.

SACKLING: What?

QUARTERMAINE: Um, Tom's your son. Not your father. You read
out that he was your father. Not your son.

SACKLING: Oh, if only I'd been able to read her that passage – she
would have understood my feelings, she'd have known – but
what do I do, I can't give up now, not when I'm so close to
finishing – my fourth draft – my penultimate draft – I *know* it's
the penultimate – then one final one – and – and – so what do I
do – I can't think – can't think –
(LOOMIS *enters through the french windows. He walks
awkwardly, has thick glasses, is carrying a file.*)

LOOMIS: Good-morning, good-morning, Anita my dear, Mark. I
trust you all had a good weekend?

QUARTERMAINE:
ANITA: } Yes, thank you Eddie.
SACKLING:

9

LOOMIS: I'm just on my way through to do my little welcome speech, with a small dilation this time on the problems of our Cambridge landladies, we've just heard that our faithful Mrs Cornley is refusing to take any of our students except what she calls traditional foreigners, all over some dreadful misunderstanding she's had with those three really delightful Turks we sent her, over the proper function of the bathroom – such a nuisance, Thomas has been on the phone to her for hours – but still, I suppose the problems of a flourishing school – nine Japanese have turned up, by the way, instead of the anticipated six, and as it was three last time we can hope for a round dozen next – Mark, is it these fast-fading old eyes of mine, or did you forget to shave this morning, and yesterday morning, even?

SACKLING: No, no – I'm thinking of growing a beard, Eddie.

LOOMIS: Alas! And what saith the fair Camelia to that?

SACKLING: (*Mutters*) I don't think she'll mind.

LOOMIS: Mmmm?

SACKLING: I don't – I don't think she'll mind, Eddie.

LOOMIS: Good, good – Anita, my dear, may I pay you a compliment?

ANITA: Yes please, Eddie.

LOOMIS: I like your hair even more that way.

ANITA: Well, thank you Eddie, actually I put it up for a dinner party we had last night – and thought I'd give it a longer run – it was a sort of editorial dinner, you see – (*Realizing.*)

LOOMIS: Ah! And the magazine's progressing well, or so we gathered from Nigel. We bumped into him on the Backs, on Saturday afternoon, did he tell you?

ANITA: No. No, he didn't.

LOOMIS: He was having a conference with one of his co-editors, I suppose it was.

ANITA: Oh. Thomas Pine.

LOOMIS: No no, I don't think Thomas Pine, my dear, but co-editress I should have said, shouldn't I, one can't be too precise these days.

ANITA: Oh. Was she – blonde and – rather pretty.

LOOMIS: Oh, very pretty – at least Thomas was much smitten, you know what an eye he's got.

ANITA: Ah, then that would be Amanda Southgate, yes, I expect he
was trying to persuade her to take on all the dog-bodying – you
know, hounding contributors, keeping the printers at bay –
she's terrifically efficient. She's an old friend of mine. I used to
go to school with her sister. (*A little pause.*) She's smashing,
actually.

LOOMIS: Good good – now St John, what was it Thomas asked me
to tell you – or was it Henry and Melanie I'm to tell what to?
Oh yes, this of course. (*He hands him a postcard from the file.*)
We couldn't resist having a look, postcards being somehow in
the public domain, one always thinks. At least when they're
other people's. (*He laughs.*) Do read it out to Mark and Anita,
don't be modest, St John.

QUARTERMAINE: Um, I must writing to thanking you for all
excellent times in your most heppy clesses, your true
Ferdinand Boller. Lord! (*He laughs.*)

LOOMIS: And which one was he, can you recall?

QUARTERMAINE: Oh. Well, you know a – a German –

LOOMIS: Postmarked Zurich, I believe, so more likely a Swiss.

QUARTERMAINE: Oh yes, that's right, a Swiss, a – a well, rather
large, Eddie, with his hair cut en brosse and – round face – in
his forties or so, and –

LOOMIS: – and wearing lederhosen, perhaps, and good at
yodelling, no no, St John, I don't think I quite believe in your
rather caricature Swiss, I suspect you must have made rather
more of an impression on Herr Ferdinand Boller than he
managed to make on you, still I suppose that's better than the
other way around, and his sentiments are certainly quite a
tribute – would that his English were, too, eh? But do try to
remember them St John, match names to faces. (*He laughs.*)
And on that subject, you haven't forgotten Mr Middleton
begins this morning, have you?

QUARTERMAINE: Who, Eddie?

LOOMIS: Middleton. Dennis Middleton, St John, Henry told you
all about him at the last staff meeting, he wrote to us from Hull
expressing such an intelligent interest in the techniques of
teaching English as a foreign language that Thomas invited
him for an interview, and was so taken by the genuineness of

his manner that he offered him some teaching – only part-time
to begin with, of course, until we see how things go – anyway,
he should be here any minute, so whilst I'm making the
students welcome perhaps you would be doing the same for
him, and tell him that either Thomas or I will be along before
the bell to introduce him to his first class, which is, I believe
Intermediary Dictation – Mark?

SACKLING: Mmm?

LOOMIS: Middleton, Mark.

SACKLING: (*Blankly*) Yes. Yes. Right, Eddie.

LOOMIS: See you all at the bell then – (*He walks off, stage left. Then
sound of him stopping. A slight pause.*) Oh Mark, there is one
other thing – if I could just have a quick private word –

SACKLING: What? Oh – oh yes – (*He gets up. As he goes over:*)

LOOMIS: (*Takes a few necessary steps to be on stage. In a lowered
voice*) Nothing important, Mark, merely Thomas wanted me
to mention, in a by-the-way spirit, one of our French students
Mlle Jeanette LeClerc, do you recall her?

SACKLING: Oh. Yes. I think so. Yes.

LOOMIS: She's written complaining that you forgot to return two
or three pieces of her work, an essay and two comprehension
passages I believe she listed, as I say, not cataclysmic in itself,
but as Thomas always points out, so much of our reputation
depends on Jeanette passing on to Lucien what Lucien then
passes to Gabrielle, so do make a note of which students are
leaving when and make sure of getting every item back before
they go. Mark?

(SACKLING *tautly nods.*)

Good, good, and may I put in my personal plea against the
beard, I do think they make even the handsomest chaps
red-eyed and snivelly looking, I don't want to end up begging
Camelia to be Delilah to your Samson, eh, and think of poor
little Tom too, having to endure Daddy's whiskers against his
chubby young cheeks at cuddle-time –

(SACKLING *rushes past him out of the door.*)

But – but – what did I say? A little professional criticism – it
can't have been about the beard, I couldn't have been more
playful.

QUARTERMAINE: Oh, it's not your fault, Eddie, is it Anita, you see
the poor chap's had a – a horrible weekend –

ANITA: (*Warningly, cutting in*) Yes, up all night, working at his
novel. I'll go and see if he's all right. (*She goes off, left.*)

LOOMIS: I see. Well that's all very well, after all nobody could
respect Mark's literary ambitions more than Thomas and
myself, but we really can't have him running about in this sort
of state, what on earth would the students make of it if he were
to gallop emotionally off in the middle of a dictation –
(MEADLE *appears at the french windows.*)

MEADLE: Um, is this the staff room, please?
(*He is hot and flustered, wearing bicycle clips, carrying a briefcase,
and mopping his brow.*)

LOOMIS: Yes, what do you want – oh, of course, it's Mr Middleton,
isn't it? Our new member of staff.

MEADLE: Well, yes – well, Meadle, actually, Derek Meadle.

LOOMIS: Yes, yes, Derek Meadle, well, I'm Eddie Loomis, the
Principal. One of two Principals, as you know, as you've met
Mr Cull of course, and this is St John Quartermaine who's
been with us since our school started, and you've come down
to join us from Sheffield, isn't it.

MEADLE: Yes sir, well Hull actually.

LOOMIS: Hull, good good – and when did you arrive?

MEADLE: Yesterday afternoon.

LOOMIS: And found yourself a room?

MEADLE: Yes, yes thank you, sir.

LOOMIS: Good good, and found yourself a bicycle too, I see.

MEADLE: (*Who throughout all this has been standing rather
awkwardly, keeping face-on to* LOOMIS) Yes, sir. My landlady –
I happened to ask her where could be a good place to buy a
second-hand one, not being familiar with the shops, and she
happened to mention that her son had left one behind in the
basement and I could have it for two pounds so I –

LOOMIS: (*Interrupting*) Good good, most enterprising – at least of
your landlady. (*He laughs.*) But Mr Meadle I've got to have a
little talk with the students, and Mr Cull is still looking after
enrolment, but one of us will be back at the bell to introduce
you to your first class – intermediary comprehension isn't it –

MEADLE: Dictation sir.

LOOMIS: So I'll leave you in St John's capable hands –

MEADLE: Yes sir. Thank you.

LOOMIS: Oh, one thing, though, Mr Meadle – sir us no sirs, we're very informal here – I'm Eddie, Mr Cull is Thomas, and you're Dennis.

MEADLE: Oh, well thank you very much –

LOOMIS: (*As the sound of students' voices is heard off, crossing the garden*) Ah, and here they are – (*He goes off, left.*)

QUARTERMAINE: Well, I must say – jolly glad to have you with us – I think you'll enjoy it here – the staff is – well, they're terrific – and the students are – well, they're very interesting, coming from all quarters of the globe, so to speak – but look, why don't you come in properly and sit down and – and make yourself at home.

MEADLE: Yes, thanks, but – well, you see, the trouble is I've had an accident.

QUARTERMAINE: Really? Oh Lord!

MEADLE: Yes, I didn't want to go into it in front of Mr Loomis, – Eddie – not quite the way to start off one's first day in a new job – but – well – here – you'd better see for yourself. (*He turns. His trousers are rent at the seat.*) How bad is it, actually?

QUARTERMAINE: Well – they're – they're – a bit of a write-off, I'm afraid. How did it happen?

MEADLE: Oh, usual combination of unexpected circumstances, eh? (*He laughs.*) For one thing the bicycle – I suspected there might be something wrong with it for two pounds, but I checked everything – the brakes, the mudguards, the wheels, the inner tubes, even the pump and the dynamo. The only thing I didn't examine meticulously was the seat. There was the minutest bit of spring sticking up, and I suppose it worked its way into my trousers as I was pedalling here. The worm in the apple, eh? (*He laughs.*) But even so I'd probably have been all right if it hadn't been for a little pack of Japanese coming up the school drive. They were laughing and chattering so much among themselves – not the usual idea of Japanese at all – You know, formal and keeping a distance from each other – (*laughs*) didn't hear my bell until I was almost on top of them,

and then a big chap with a bald head – I didn't realize they
came in that sort of size either – stepped right out in front of
me – I was going pretty quickly, I have to admit – wanted to be
in good time, you see for my first day – and of course I lost
control on the gravel and skidded and had to leap sideways off
the bike. But with my trousers snagged I only half-made it.
They were very tactful about it, by the way. Averted their eyes
to show they hadn't seen it, and went on into the office. What
they call saving face, I believe. My face, in this case. Oh,
except for the big balld one. I had the impression he found it
rather amusing – but of course the question is what do I do
about it? I mean I don't really want to spend my first day going
about like this, do I? People might get the impression it's my
normal attire. (*He laughs. But this speech should be delivered to
convey a simmering rage and desperation behind the attempt at an
insouciant manner, and of a natural North Country accent held in
check under stress.*)

QUARTERMAINE: Well, you know old chap, I think the best thing
would be to go back and change. Don't worry about being late
– I'll explain what happened –

MEADLE: Ah, yes, but into what is the question.

QUARTERMAINE: Well – into another pair of trousers, I – I suppose.

MEADLE: Yes, but you see, I haven't got another pair is the
problem. An elderly gentleman on the train yesterday spilt his
chocolate out of his thermos right over the pair I happened to
have on, so the first thing I did when I got in – irony of ironies
– was to take them to the cleaners. And my trunk, which I'd
sent on from Hull and which contained my suit and my other
two pairs, hasn't arrived yet. So there it is. Hot chocolate, a
broken spring, a pack of unusually gregarious Japanese and
British Rail, all working together in complete harmony to
bring me to my first day of my new job looking like Oliver and
Hardy. What do I do? Any suggestions? I mean if I pull them
really high – like this – (*pulling them up*) and leave my clips on –
does it still show?

QUARTERMAINE: Well, just a little – well, not really – well, I say,
I'll tell you what – if you can get your jacket down just a
fraction –

MEADLE: (*He pulls it down*) – but if I keep my hands in – (*putting them in the pockets, and pushing down*) what about it?

QUARTERMAINE: How does it feel?

MEADLE: (*Laughs*) Well – unnatural. Extremely unnatural. (*Taking a few steps.*)

QUARTERMAINE: Actually, you look rather – rather formidable actually.

MEADLE: (*Taking another step or so*) No no – (*Exploding into a violent rage*) Bloody hell, I'm meant to be teaching, I can't go round like this all day, everybody will think I'm some sort of buffoon – this is the sheerest – the sheerest –
(WINDSCAPE *enters through the french windows. He is carrying a briefcase; wears bicycle clips, smokes a pipe.*)

WINDSCAPE: Hello, St John.

QUARTERMAINE: Oh – oh hello Henry – um, come and meet our new chap – (*To* MEADLE) Henry's our academic tutor – syllabus and all that –

WINDSCAPE: (*Comes over*) Oh yes, of course, very glad to have you with us, Merton, isn't it?

QUARTERMAINE: Middleton, actually.

MEADLE: Meadle, as a matter of fact.

QUARTERMAINE: That's right. Sorry. Dennis Meadle.

WINDSCAPE: Well, whatever yours happens to be –

MEADLE: Derek. Derek Meadle.

WINDSCAPE: – mine is Windscape. Henry Windscape. How do you do?

MEADLE: (*He gets his hand out of his pocket, they shake hands,* MEADLE *replaces his hand*) How do you do?

QUARTERMAINE: I say, how were they in the end, Susan, little Fanny and old Ben – and Fanny's headache?

WINDSCAPE: Oh fine thank you, St John, fine – I didn't get Susan to bed until midnight of course (*To* MEADLE) she's studying for her O levels – a couple of years in advance – and – and Fanny had rather a bad moment when she went into the lavatory because of Raggidy Anne sitting there – and dripping – she thought it was little Fanny, you see – (*Laughing.*)

QUARTERMAINE: Oh Lord, I forgot –

WINDSCAPE: St John was good enough to come over and sit with

our three last night – we went to see *M* you know – such a fine film – so delicate and human in its treatment of a – a sexual freak and Peter Lorre – unfortunately the print was a trifle worn – but still – memorable – memorable – but isn't it interesting – on another subject – this English thing about names, how we forget them the second we hear them. Just now, for instance, when St John was introducing you. Unlike Americans for instance. (*He puffs and pulls on his pipe throughout this speech.* MEADLE *nods and chuckles tensely.*) I suppose because we – the English that is – are so busy looking at the person the name represents – or *not* looking, being English (*laughs*) that we don't take in the name itself – whereas the Americans, you see, make a point of beginning with the name – when one's introduced they repeat it endlessly. 'This is Dennis Meadle. Dennis Meadle, why hello Dennis, and how long have you been in this country Dennis, this is Dennis Meadle dear, Dennis was just telling me how much he liked our fair city, weren't you Dennis . . .' (*All this in an execrable imitation of an American accent.*) And – and so forth, and in no time at all they've learnt what you're called by even if not who you are (*laughs*) while we, the English, being more empirical, don't learn your name until you yourself have taken on a complicated reality – you and your name grow, so to speak, in associated stages in our memories, until what you are as Dennis Meadle and the sounds Dennis Meadle are inseparable which is actually – when you think about it – a radical division in ways of perceiving that goes back to the Middle Ages in the Nominalists – the name callers – calling the name preceding the object, so to speak, and the realists –
(*During this,* MELANIE *has entered through the french windows. She puts her briefcase on the table.*)
– who believed the object preceded the name – but one could go on and on; there's Melanie, Melanie come and meet our new chap –

QUARTERMAINE: Hello Melanie, have a good weekend?

MELANIE: Yes thanks, St John, you're in top form for a Monday morning Henry, how do you do, I'm Melanie Garth.

MEADLE: Meadle. Derek Meadle.

MELANIE: And you've come to reinforce us, well we certainly could do with you, Thomas was just telling me about the enrolment chaos, you'll be getting a lot of over-spill from my groups, I can tell you.

WINDSCAPE: Melanie's our Elementary Conversation specialist, by the way.

MELANIE: Oh, I don't know about specialist, Henry. Henry's our only real specialist here, he specializes in – well, everything, doesn't he, St John, from pronunciation to British Life and Institutions, but what I enjoyed most about the sight of you two philosophizing away here was that you both still had your bicycle clips on – as if you'd met on a street corner –

WINDSCAPE: (*Laughing*) Good heavens, so they are. Thank you for reminding me, my dear, whenever I forget to take them off I spend hours after school hunting for them – (*He bends to take them off.*)
(MEADLE *grinning and distraught, makes a gesture towards taking his off.*)

QUARTERMAINE: (*Taking this in*) I say – I say, Melanie, how's – um, how's mother?

MELANIE: Top form, thanks, St John, her left leg's still giving her bother, and the stairs are a dreadful strain, you know, because of this sudden vertigo, but yesterday she managed to hobble down to the corner-shop all by herself, and was halfway back by the time I came to pick her up.

QUARTERMAINE: Oh, that's terrific! Melanie's mother's just recovering from a thingmebob.

MELANIE: Stroke, if you please, St John. She insists on the proper term, she hates euphemisms.

WINDSCAPE: Not surprisingly, as Melanie's mother was Cambridge's first lady of philology – the first woman ever to hold the chair in it – I had the honour of being supervised by her in my second year as an undergraduate – and although she's retired she was still very much a behind-the-scenes force on the Faculty until she had her – little upset a few months ago. And will be again, I suspect, as she appears to be coming to terms with her condition in a characteristically – characteristically indomitable –

MEADLE: I have an aunt who had a stroke a year ago. She was the active sort too. Of course not a professor but – very active. In her own way. She went in for jam.

MELANIE: And how is *she* coping?

MEADLE: Well, she was doing splendidly until she had the next. Now she's pretty well out of it altogether, my uncle has to do virtually everything for her. But then that's one of the usual patterns, they said at the hospital. First a mild stroke, followed by a worse stroke, and then, if that doesn't do the job – (*He gestures.*) But in a sense it's worse for my uncle, he's an independent old fellow, used to leading his own life –

MELANIE: Yes, well, Mr Meadle, I'm sorry for your aunt – and for your uncle – but sufficient unto the day, sufficient unto the day – if you'll excuse me, I haven't sorted out my first hour's comprehension – (*She picks up the briefcase, goes to her locker.*)

WINDSCAPE: Of course that's only *one* of the possible patterns – there are many cases of complete – or – or more than merely partial recovery – if I might – might just – Melanie puts on a remarkably brave front, but don't be led astray, she's an intensely feeling person who knows very well the likely outcome of her mother's – her mother's – she's deeply attached to her, as you probably gathered, isn't she, St John.

QUARTERMAINE: Oh Lord yes!

WINDSCAPE: I hope you don't mind my saying it?

MEADLE: No, no. Thank you. Thank you.

WINDSCAPE: Good man! (*He puts his hand on* MEADLE'*s shoulder.*) Well, I'd better unpack my own – (*He goes over to his locker, looking towards* MELANIE, *who is standing still by hers.*)

MEADLE: (*Smiling tightly, and in a low voice*) Don't think I can stand much more of this. Hardly know what I'm saying – really put my foot in it –

QUARTERMAINE: Well, why don't you just tell them – I mean, it's only a torn pair of bags –

MEADLE: It's too late now, I've left it too late. I can't just clap my hands for attention, oh by the way, everybody, come and look at my trousers, ha ha ha, what I need is safety pins – and then a few minutes in the toilet – can you get me some?

QUARTERMAINE: I'll nip over to the office –

MEADLE: Well, take me to the toilet first.

LOOMIS: (*Comes through the french windows*) Good-morning Melanie, my dear, good-morning Henry – good weekend, I trust?

MELANIE:
WINDSCAPE: } Yes thanks, Eddie.

LOOMIS: All well with mother, I trust.

MELANIE: Yes thanks Eddie. Top form.

LOOMIS: Good, good – and Fanny and the children?

WINDSCAPE: Yes, thanks Eddie – all splendid.

LOOMIS: Good good –

(*As* ANITA *and* SACKLING *enter from the right:*)

Ah, and here you are, you two, and quite composed again Mark, I trust –

ANITA: Well Eddie, actually I'm not sure that Mark –

(SACKLING *feebly gestures silence to* ANITA.)

LOOMIS: And Mr Meadle, I don't know which of you have had the chance to meet him yet, but those who haven't can make their separate introductions, in the meanwhile I'll say a welcome on all our behalves, we're delighted to have you with us – I see you've still got your clips on, by the way, perhaps you'd better remove them or you'll create the impression that you're just pedalling through – (*He laughs.*)

(MEADLE *bends to take them off.*)

– now as we're all here and there are a few minutes before the bell, I'd like to say a few words, if I may. As you've no doubt realized, we have an exceptionally high enrolment for the month, the highest in the school's career, as a matter of fact. (*Little murmurs.*)

QUARTERMAINE: I say, terrific!

LOOMIS: Yes, very gratifying. You all know how hard Thomas has worked for this. Though he'd loathe to hear me say it. But what he wouldn't mind hearing me say is that in his turn he knows how hard you've worked. I think we all have a right to be proud of our growing reputation as one of the best schools of English – not one of the biggest but one of the best – in Cambridge. Which, when it comes down to it, means in the country. Well and good. Well and good. But success will bring – has already begun to bring – its own problems. (*He gestures to* MEADLE.) As Mr Meadle's presence here testifies. But even with Mr Meadle – or Dennis, as I've already told him I intend to call him – with Dennis to help us, there is going to be a considerable strain on our resources. Perhaps a few too many students to a classroom, more work to take home and correct, more difficulties in developing personal contact – that so crucial personal contact – with students many of whom are only here for a short time – well, as I say, you've already become familiar with the problems, the problems, as Thomas remarked 'midst the chaos this morning, of a flourishing school – but please remember, I'm reminding *myself* too when I say this, how important it is if we are to continue to flourish – (SACKLING *faints.* ANITA *cries out, tries to catch him, half supports him, as* WINDSCAPE *gets to him,* QUARTERMAINE *attempts to.*)

WINDSCAPE: There – there old chap – I've got you – out of the way, everyone – while I lower him – (*He does so.*) The thing is to keep his head up.

QUARTERMAINE: Yes, right.
(*He makes to go round, as* ANITA *runs over, takes* SACKLING'S *head, then sits down, gets his head into her lap.*)

WINDSCAPE: Mark – Mark – can you hear me? (*He slaps his cheeks.*) He's right out. (*He puts his hand on* SACKLING'S *heart.*) It's very faint. (*Massaging his heart.*) Somebody better telephone for an ambulance.

QUARTERMAINE: Right! (*He makes to go to the telephone.*)
(LOOMIS *goes to the telephone, dials.*)

WINDSCAPE: And chafe his wrists – and something to put over him – your coat – (*To* MEADLE) Hurry man!
(MEADLE *hesitates, takes off his coat as* QUARTERMAINE *struggles out of his.*)
Come around – put it over him – over his chest –
(MEADLE *does so, as* QUARTERMAINE *stands, jacket half off.*)
There – now – now – now –
(LOOMIS *finishes speaking, puts the telephone down, comes over, stands looking anxiously down. The bell rings.*)

QUARTERMAINE: (*Also looking down*) Oh Lord! Oh Lord!
(*Lights.*)

SCENE 2

*Some weeks later. Friday afternoon, a few minutes before 5 p.m. The
french windows are open. It's a sunny day.*

QUARTERMAINE *is putting books and papers away. He is humming to
himself. He closes his locker, does a few elegant dance steps, and then
goes into a tap dance, at which he is surprisingly adept.* LOOMIS *enters
through the french windows, watches* QUARTERMAINE.

QUARTERMAINE: (*Sees* LOOMIS, *stops.*) Oh Lord! (*He laughs.*)
Hello Eddie.

LOOMIS: You're in sprightly mood, St John.

QUARTERMAINE: Yes, well Friday evening and off to the theatre
and all that – you know.

LOOMIS: And what are you going to see?

QUARTERMAINE: Oh that – that Strindberg, I think it is. At the
Arts.

LOOMIS: I believe it's an Ibsen, *Hedda Gabler* I believe, but tell me
– the bell's gone then, has it, I didn't hear it – but then these
old ears of mine – (*He laughs.*)

QUARTERMAINE: Ah yes, well I let them out a little early, you see,
Eddie.

LOOMIS: Why?

QUARTERMAINE: Well, it was the special Life and Institutions
lecture, you see, and I chose Oxford Colleges with slides – to
give them the other point of view, for once (*laughs*) but of
course the old projector broke –

LOOMIS: It's the newest model.

QUARTERMAINE: Yes, I think that's the trouble, all those extra
bits to master – anyway one of the colleges went in upside
down and wouldn't come out so I had to – to abandon
technology and do it all off my own bat – you know,
reminiscences of my time at the House and – and anecdotes –
and – you know – that sort of thing. The personal touch. But
of course I ran out of steam a little, towards the end. I'm
afraid. (*Laughs*).

LOOMIS: And how many turned up?

QUARTERMAINE: Oh well – about a handful.

LOOMIS: A handful!

QUARTERMAINE: A good handful.

LOOMIS: But there are meant to be twenty-three in the group that that special lecture's designed for.

QUARTERMAINE: Yes, well I think you know – it's being Friday and – and the sun shining and the Backs so lovely and the Cam jam-packed with punts and – but the ones who came were jolly interested – especially that little Italian girl – you know um – um – almost midget sized, the one with the wart –

LOOMIS: If you mean Angelina, she happens to be Greek. Her father's an exceptionally distinguished army officer. Thomas will be very disappointed to hear about all this, St John, he devised that lecture series himself, you know, it's quite an innovation, and if you can't keep attendances up – and then there's the question of the projector, I only hope you haven't done it any damage –

(*The sound of a door opening, footsteps hurrying.*)

and you know very well how important it is to keep classes going until at least the bell – ah, hello my dear, you've finished a trifle on the early side too, then?

ANITA: (*Enters, slightly breathless*) Oh, isn't it past five?

LOOMIS: Well, the bell hasn't gone yet, even in your part of the corridor – intermediary dictation, wasn't it, and how was your attendance?

ANITA: Oh, nearly a full complement, Eddie, they're a very keen lot, mostly Germans, in fact that's why I thought the bell had gone, one of them – Kurt – said he'd heard it.

LOOMIS: Good, good. (*He is not convinced, perhaps.*)

(ANITA *makes to go to her locker.*)

My dear, have I told you what I think about your sandals?

ANITA: No, Eddie.

LOOMIS: Well, when I first saw you in them I wondered if they were quite *comme il faut*, Thomas and I had quite a thing about them –

QUARTERMAINE: I think they're smashing.

LOOMIS: But I've been quite won around, I've come to the view that they're most fetching. Or that your feet are. Or both. (*He laughs.*)

ANITA: Thank you, Eddie.

LOOMIS: And Nigel's still in London, is he, with his co-editress?

ANITA: Yes, he comes back on Saturday or Sunday.

LOOMIS: Quite a coincidence Thomas seeing them on the train like that, he's scarcely been out of his office this many a month, as you know – and it's all working out all right, is it?

ANITA: Yes, she's been absolutely wonderful, quite a surprise really, because when I first met Amanda at a party a few years ago I thought she was – well, absolutely charming, of course, but rather – rather feckless, if anything. But the girl who gave the party's a great friend of mine and she's always said Amanda had a good tough brain. Her boyfriend's being a great help too. He's invaluable.

LOOMIS: How odd, I had an idea you went to school with her?

ANITA: (*Slight hesitation*) No no – with her sister. Seraphina.

LOOMIS: Ah yes – but I was really asking about the magazine itself, how that was coming?

ANITA: Well, they're still having to delay publication because of these printers letting them down, but now they've found a new one in London – and they're getting in some really decent articles and things and – oh, they've finally settled on a title. It's going to be called *Reports*.

QUARTERMAINE: Terrific!

(*The bell rings*.)

LOOMIS: *Reports, Reports*, mmm, well, tell Nigel when he gets back that Thomas has decided to take out *two* subscriptions, one for ourselves and one for the student common room, so we'll be showing a great personal interest –

ANITA: Oh thank you, Eddie, Nigel will be so pleased –

(*From the garden, the sound of* WINDSCAPE.)

WINDSCAPE: (*Off*) I can't stay too long, I'm afraid, just to start you off and explain the rules – but first let's get the mallets and balls –

(*The voices recede*.)

LOOMIS: (*Going to the window*) Ah, the croquet's under way again, good, good, – and who's playing – ah, Piccolo and Jean-Pierre, Gisela – Teresa – Okona – Liv and Gerta – you know, I always feel that if ever our little school had to justify itself, we could do it by showing the world the spectacle of an Italian, a

Frenchman, a German, a Japanese, a Swedish girl and a
Belgian girl, all gathered together on an English lawn, under
an English sky to play a game of croquet –
(ANITA *through this has gone to her locker.*)

QUARTERMAINE: Absolutely, Eddie, absolutely – croquet – I must
try my hand again – haven't for years – my aunt had such a
lawn, you know, and I remember, oh Lord, (*shaking his head,
laughing.*) Oh Lord, I say, I forgot, Thomas told me to tell you
he was looking for you.

LOOMIS: Thomas? When?

QUARTERMAINE: Oh, just at the end of my lecture – he popped his
head in.

LOOMIS: Really, St John, I wish you'd mentioned it straight away,
it would have to be something urgent for Thomas to interrupt
a class – was he going back to the office?
(SACKLING *enters, during this, carrying books, etc.; he sports a
moustache.*)

QUARTERMAINE: He didn't say, Eddie.

LOOMIS: Mark, have you happened to glimpse Thomas –

SACKLING: Yes. I think he and Melanie were going up to your flat –

LOOMIS: Oh. Well, if he should come down here looking for me,
tell him I've gone upstairs – and that I'll stay there so that we
don't do one of our famous boxes and coxes – (*Goes out right.*)

SACKLING: Right Eddie. (*Going to his locker.*)
(ANITA, *during the above, has finished packing and is leaving.
There is an air of desperate rush about her.*)

QUARTERMAINE: Phew! He'd pretty well stopped showing up in
here before the bell – wasn't he in a dodgy mood – but I say,
where shall we meet, Anita, shall Mark and I come and pick
you up at your place, or shall we go to Mark's place, or the
foyer, or – or we could go to The Eagle – or you two could
come to my place –

ANITA: Oh, I'm sorry, St John, I completely forgot – you see I'm
going to London. It suddenly occurred to me that as Nigel
can't get back until tomorrow or Sunday, why not pop down
and spend the weekend with him.

QUARTERMAINE: Oh what a good idea, spend the weekend in
London with Nigel, much more fun than some old Ibsen thing –

SACKLING: Shouldn't you phone him first? I mean, he may be going out or – you know.

ANITA: I haven't got time. Anyway, I don't mind waiting for him – look, I've got to dash if I'm going to make the five thirty – damn Eddie!

SACKLING: Oh – Anita, would you apologize to him again for my letting him down, I'll really try for the second issue –

ANITA: (*Rushing off*) Yes, right, I'll tell him –

SACKLING: Oh Christ! Poor old Nigel!

QUARTERMAINE: Mmmm?

SACKLING: Well, surely you know?

QUARTERMAINE: What?

SACKLING: About Nigel and Amanda Southgate. They're having a passionate affair. He only started the magazine because of her – she's got literary ambitions.

QUARTERMAINE: Oh Lord – oh, Lord, poor old Anita! But they always seemed so happy –

SACKLING: You know, St John, you have an amazing ability not to let the world impinge on you. Anita's the unhappiest woman I know, at the moment. And has been, ever since she met Nigel. Amanda's his fifth affair in the last two years, even if the most serious. But she covers up for him, pretends it isn't happening, or tries to protect a reputation he hasn't got and probably doesn't want anyway, she's had three abortions for him to my knowledge, three, although she's desperate for children – haven't you had the slightest inkling of any of that?

QUARTERMAINE: No, but good Lord – how do *you* know? I mean –

SACKLING: Well, Nigel told me most of it, as a matter of fact. But I'd still have thought it's perfectly obvious there was something amiss – but what I don't understand is why she's suddenly gone down to confront him. She's only survived so far by not daring to have anything out with him – she's never once mentioned even the most blatant of his infidelities, actually that's one of the things about her that drives him mad. But perhaps the thought of the two of them in London while she has to spend the weekend here – anyway, there's nothing we can do about it, is there? I haven't even got his number, so I can't warn him.

QUARTERMAINE: Don't you like Anita?

SACKLING: Of course I do. Far more than I like Nigel, as a matter of fact.

QUARTERMAINE: Oh. Oh well it all seems – all seems – I mean these things between people – people one cares for – it's hard to bear them – but, but I say, what about this evening then, I wonder if they'll take her ticket back or – anyway, how would you like to play it? Eagle or –

SACKLING: As a matter of fact, St John, I'm going to have to bow out of the theatre, too.

QUARTERMAINE: Oh. Oh well –

SACKLING: To tell you the truth, I couldn't face it. You see, last night I went back to it again. My novel. The first time since Camelia left. And there was the old flame aflickering as strongly as ever. And if I don't get back to it again this evening – I'll – I'll – well, anyway, I'll have a rotten evening. And give you one, too, probably. Look, you haven't actually bought the tickets, have you?

QUARTERMAINE: (*Makes to say yes, changes his mind*) No, no, never any need to at the Arts, so don't worry about that but – but it's terrific, that you've started writing again, that's far more important than going to see some – some old Ibsen thing.

SACKLING: Thanks. And St John, thanks also for your companionship these last weeks. It must have been bloody boring for you, having me grind on and on in my misery.

QUARTERMAINE: Lord no. I've enjoyed it enormously. Not your misery I don't mean but your – your – I say, did you get that letter, though?

SACKLING: Yes, this morning. She's allowing me a few hours tomorrow afternoon. With my son. Which is another reason I must spend this evening at the typewriter –

QUARTERMAINE: But that's wonderful, Mark. A breakthrough at last – look, when will you be back?

SACKLING: Tomorrow evening, I suppose.

QUARTERMAINE: Well, perhaps we could have lunch on Sunday or dinner or meet for a drink – and you could tell me how things went with little Tom – I'd really love to know.

(*During this, the sound of a door opening and closing, followed by a yelp.*)

MEADLE: (*Off*) Blast!

QUARTERMAINE: You all right, old man!

MEADLE: (*He is wearing a blazer and flannels, and has a bump on his forehead, covered by a piece of sticking plaster.*) Yes, yes – (*Rubbing his hand.*) It's that doorknob, a bit too close to the door-jamb – at least for my taste – (*He laughs.*) I'm always scraping my knuckles on it – hello, Mark, haven't seen you around for a bit, I suppose because you're usually gone before I finish.

SACKLING: Don't worry, I do my time. Right to the bell.

MEADLE: Oh, I didn't mean any reflection – (*He laughs.*) Good God, I only meant that I always seem to get caught by students who want to practise their English after hours too – of course it doesn't help to be carrying a conversation piece around on your forehead – 'What 'appen 'ead, Mr Mittle?' 'Whasa matter weet de het, Meester Meetle?' 'Mister Mittle vat goes mit der hed?' (*Laughing.*) Up the corridor, down, in the classroom, in the garden – by the time I'd gone through all the details, with pantomime, landlady calling to the telephone, toe stubbing in cracked linoleum, body pitching down the stairs and bonce cracking down on tile I'd have settled for serious internal injuries instead.

SACKLING: (*Smiles*) Goodnight, see you both Monday. (*He goes out through the french windows.*)

QUARTERMAINE: (*Who has been laughing with* MEADLE) Oh, night old man, but oh, just a minute, we haven't fixed our meeting – (*Goes to the french windows and stares out.*)

MEADLE: (*Who has registered* SACKLING's *manner*) He's a hard chap to get to know, isn't he?

QUARTERMAINE: Who? Old Mark? Lord no – oh, well perhaps to begin with but once you do know him you can't imagine a – a better friend.

MEADLE: Oh. Well, I'll keep working on it then.

QUARTERMAINE: And of course he's been through a very bad time – and with his – his particular talent –

MEADLE: By the way, you haven't seen Thomas, have you?

(*Going to his locker.*)

QUARTERMAINE: I think he's with Eddie, anyway they're looking for each other.

MEADLE: Oh. (*He nods.*)

QUARTERMAINE: I say, I've managed to get hold of some tickets for the theatre tonight. They're doing an Ibsen! Would you like to come?

MEADLE: To tell you the truth, Ibsen's not quite my cup of tea, thanks, but anyway as a matter of fact Oko-Ri's taking me out to dinner tonight with the rest of the boys.

QUARTERMAINE: Oko – what?

MEADLE: Ri. Oko-Ri. My Japanese chum.

QUARTERMAINE: Oh, old baldy, you mean? Taking you out to dinner – well, that's – that's – I didn't know you'd hit it off so well with them, after that business –

MEADLE: Well, I never thought they'd made me skid deliberately – and we've had lots of good laughs about it since – now that I'm on their wavelength – Oko-Ri's got a splendid sense of humour. Loves a drink too, I gather, from some of their jokes.

QUARTERMAINE: Oh, well, you'll have a good evening then –

MEADLE: It's really just to say thank you for all the extra hours I've put in with them. They left it to me to decide where we'd go, and I've chosen that French place that's just opened opposite Trinity, Eddie and Thomas were saying it's very good – I'm a bit worried about that, though, I hope it's not too expensive – I had a feeling they hesitated slightly or Oko-Ri did, he's very much the man in charge. One has to keep sensitive to these things – but of course once I'd asked for it, it was too late to change – but I'd better get back if I'm going to meet them later – did I tell you my landlady's just offered me another room as a bedroom letting me keep the bedroom I've got now as a study-cum-sitting-room, so I'm virtually ending up with a little suite of my own, and all for just another twenty-five shillings, for five pounds in all.

QUARTERMAINE: Good Lord. And to think I'm paying six pounds for my pokey little room – how on earth did you manage that, Derek?

MEADLE: I think it's because I remind her of her son, being the same age almost, and he never bothers to write or come to visit, as far as I can make out.

QUARTERMAINE: Golly, I should have a go at Mrs Harris, see if I can remind her of her son, if she has one, although if he's anything like her I hope I don't, eh? Anyway, you certainly do land on your feet, old man, don't you?

MEADLE: Well – (*laughs*) sometimes on my head, eh? Anyway, I'd better get back, (*putting on his bicycle clips*) I've asked Oko-Ri and his boys to initiate my suite, with a bottle of whisky, before our dinner, and I've still got some furniture to move – I'd ask you to come along too, but it's not really my invitation –

QUARTERMAINE: Oh – (*He gestures.*)

(*The sound of a door opening and closing; feet.*)

MEADLE: (*Going out*) Oh. Here. Let me give you a hand with those, Melanie –

MELANIE: (*Off*) No, it's quite all right, I've got them –

MEADLE: (*Off*) Well, let me just take this one –

MELANIE: No, no, really – there's no need –

(*The sound of books dropping on the floor.*)

MEADLE: (*Off*) Oh, sorry, Melanie –

MELANIE: (*Irritably*) Oh – really! I had them perfectly well – and Thomas has just lent me that one with great warnings to be careful, it's a rare edition –

(MEADLE *comes on stage, carrying a distinguished volume.*)

(*Coming on stage, carrying a briefcase, exercise-books and further books*) If you could just put it on the table –

MEADLE: What, here do you mean?

MELANIE: Have either of you seen Eddie? Thomas has been looking for him.

QUARTERMAINE: Now what did Eddie say – oh yes, that he was going to wait for Thomas in the – in the office, it must have been.

MELANIE: Oh, well that's where Thomas has gone – he took me down into the cellar to find the book – it took him longer than he thought and he got worried that Eddie would go into one of his panics, and be in and out of every room in the school – you know how clever they are at just missing each other – so you're the last two then, are you?

QUARTERMAINE: Yes, well apart from old Henry, that is, he's playing croquet –

MELANIE: Is he? Jolly good! (*She goes to her locker.*)

MEADLE: (*Who has been looking through the book*) No, no damage done, Melanie – (*He looks at his watch*) so Thomas is in the office, is he?

MELANIE: Yes, why, what do you want him for?

MEADLE: Oh – well – well actually he said something about seeing if he could get me some extra pronunciation classes – my rent has just gone up, you see, so I really rather need the extra bobs. (*He laughs.*)

MELANIE: I wouldn't go disturbing him now, if I were you, he's had a particularly fraught day. He's got a dreadful headache. The only person he'll want to see is Eddie.

MEADLE: Oh. Well, in that case – goodnight, Melanie.

MELANIE: Goodnight – oh, that reminds me, I'd be very grateful if you'd stop putting your bicycle against the wall just where I park my car – there's not enough room for both.

MEADLE: Oh, sorry about that – right Melanie – well, see you Monday then.

QUARTERMAINE: See you Monday, old man.

(MEADLE *goes out through the french windows.*)

MELANIE: I really think I'd get on much better with Mr Meadle if he didn't try so hard to get on with me. Still, I really had no right to stop him from seeing Thomas – not my business at all. It's just that he's spent the whole afternoon on the telephone because of that wretched Jap – the big, bald one, you know – apparently he got drunk and ran amok in that new French restaurant last night, and the owners are demanding damages and threatening to call the police, if he shows up again, and then one of the other Japanese turned up at lunch-time to book a table for tonight – Goodness knows what's going to happen if the bald one appears too.

MEADLE: (*Meanwhile, off*) 'Night, Henry, see you Monday.

WINDSCAPE: (*Off*) Oh. 'Night Derek. Have a good weekend.

MEADLE: (*Off*) Thanks, Henry – same to you.

MELANIE: (*Listens alertly to this*) Still, apparently he works very

31

hard at his teaching, from all accounts, Thomas and Eddie are both rather thrilled with him – well, St John, and what are your plans for the weekend, something on the boil, I'll bet!

QUARTERMAINE: Oh, well I thought I might take in a show tonight – that Ibsen thing at the Arts –

MELANIE: Isn't it *The Cherry Orchard*?

QUARTERMAINE: Oh, is it? Well – something like that. And then a bite of supper, I suppose. I might try that French place in fact. Might be rather – rather amusing. (*He laughs.*)

MELANIE: It must be jolly nice being a bachelor and having the weekend before you. Especially in Cambridge. Well, I'd better get on with this. I don't think Thomas really wants me to take it off the premises. (*She pulls book towards her.*)

QUARTERMAINE: Oh. Righto. (*He begins to wander up and down, gaze out of the French windows etc.*)
(MELANIE *is writing, glancing occasionally at him. She is, in fact, anxious for him to be gone. There are occasional cries and sounds of* WINDSCAPE*'s voice from the garden, to which* MELANIE *responds by lifting her head, or stopping writing.*)

QUARTERMAINE: I say, Melanie – do you like *The Cherry Orchard*?

MELANIE: Loathe it.

QUARTERMAINE: Oh. Why?

MELANIE: All that Russian gloom and doom and people shooting themselves from loneliness and depression and that sort of thing. But then mother says I don't understand comedy. I expect she's right.

QUARTERMAINE: How is mother?

MELANIE: Oh, top hole, thanks. (*Automatically.*)

QUARTERMAINE: Well, if there's ever anything I can do – you know – if she wants company when you want to go out –

MELANIE: That's very thoughtful of you, St John, thank you.

QUARTERMAINE: No, no – I'd enjoy it. I say, that is an impressive tome old Thomas has lent you, what are you copying out exactly?

MELANIE: Recipes. This one's for roasted swan.

QUARTERMAINE: Oh. For a dinner party?

MELANIE: No, no, St John, it's for my British Life and Institutions lot, to give them some idea of a medieval banquet. Swans are protected birds, you know, these days.

QUARTERMAINE: Oh yes, of course they are. (*He laughs*.) Fancy thinking you'd give them for a – a – oh Lord! But aren't they the most – most beautiful creatures. I was looking at one – oh, just the other day, you know – on the Cam – drifting behind a punt – and they were all shouting and drinking champagne and – and it was just drifting behind them – so calm – and I remember there used to be oh! a dozen or so – they came every year to a pond near my aunt's – when I was – was – and I could hear their wings – great wings beating – in the evenings when I was lying in bed – it could be quite – quite frightening even after I knew what was making the noise – and then there they'd be – a dozen of them or so – drifting – drifting around the next morning – and it was hard to imagine – their long necks twining and their way of drifting – all that – that power – those wings beating – I wonder where they went to. I'd like to know more about them really. Where they go, what they – they –

MELANIE: St John, please don't think me fearfully rude, but I must try and finish this and I can't write and talk at the same time, you see.

QUARTERMAINE: What? Oh – oh sorry, Melanie, no, you're quite right, I can't either. Anyway, I ought to be getting on –

MELANIE: Yes, with such a full evening. I do hope you enjoy it.

QUARTERMAINE: Well – well, 'night Melanie, see you Monday. And don't forget about your mother – any time –

MELANIE: I won't, St John, goodnight.

(QUARTERMAINE *goes*. MELANIE *sits, not writing, as*:)

QUARTERMAINE: (*Off*) I say, Henry, any chance of a game?

WINDSCAPE: (*Off*) Actually, I'm just finishing I'm afraid – perhaps next week.

QUARTERMAINE: (*Off*) Right, I'll hold you to that. See you Monday. Oh, by the way, if you want any baby-sitting done during the weekend, I'll try and make myself available –

WINDSCAPE: (*Off*) Righto, I'll put it to Fanny – I know she's quite keen to see the *Uncle Vanya* at the Arts – perhaps tomorrow night –

QUARTERMAINE: A votre disposition. (*Off*) 'Night.

WINDSCAPE: 'Night.

(MELANIE, *during this, has got up, and gone to the french windows.*)

(*Off*) Oh, well played, Piccolo, well played Jean-Pierre – beautiful lies both – I have to go now I'm afraid, but you're obviously learning very quickly all of you – don't forget to put the mallets and the balls back in the sheds – goodnight, goodnight.

(*Replies, in the appropriate accents, of: 'Goodnight, Mr Windscape', etc.* MELANIE, *during the latter part of this, hurries back to the table, sits down, pretends to continue transcribing.* WINDSCAPE *enters through the french windows. He stops on seeing* MELANIE, *braces himself, then enters properly, jovially.*)

WINDSCAPE: Hello Melanie, my dear, I thought everyone had gone.

MELANIE: How are they taking to the croquet?

WINDSCAPE: At the moment they find it a bit sedate, I think, but another time or two around and they'll discover just how much – how much incivility is possible on our tranquil English lawns – but – but what are you up to? (*Coming to look over her shoulder.*) Isn't that Cussons' *A Culinary History of England*? I've only seen it in a library before, and what are you transcribing – roasted swan, for British Life and Institutions, is it? But you know Melanie, that's rather a good idea – as a way of teaching them some social history I mean – you'll be able to compare dishes from different strata of society at the same period, and then at different periods – why, you could work through a whole chronology of meals, from medieval banquets of – of roasted swan and no doubt boar and venison and guinea fowls right up to – to the modern dinner of frozen hamburgers, frozen chips and frozen peas – and – and – thus illustrating one aspect of our culture's advance, eh, from a very few eating splendidly to almost everybody getting hideously fed – and – and – why good heavens, see where it takes you – a consideration of meals as symbolic functions and domestic rituals – you could bring D. H. Lawrence in there, as *Sons and Lovers* is a set text, isn't it – and – and not forgetting of course all the semantic fun, the differences in meaning between lunches, luncheons, teas, high teas,

suppers, dinners – and of course what they indicate as a kind
of code about class – and – and – the illustrations, not only
literary, Shakespeare alone – Banquo's ghost – *Antony and
Cleopatra* – *Titus Andronicus*! almost every play, and the novels
– but also paintings, lithographs, Hogarth – (*he checks himself
from going on*) good gracious you've really hit on something
there, Melanie.

MELANIE: (*Who has been gazing at him adoringly*) And all I thought
I'd hit on was a way of attracting a little interest – especially
from those three rather scowly French girls – but then how
like you, Henry, to take up my copying out an old recipe and
turn it into an intellectual adventure.

WINDSCAPE: (*Laughs, embarrassed*) Oh just a few – just a few
thoughts – letting myself get carried away as usual, and I really
ought to be sorting myself out – I promised Fanny I'd be home
by six – now where's my briefcase – ah, yes – and a pile of
unseens I seem to remember – (*going to his locker*) to be marked
by Monday –

MELANIE: How is Fanny?

WINDSCAPE: Oh, very well thanks, very well – a bit tired in the
evenings, what with the children on the one hand and her two
hours voluntary with the OAPs – but she's enjoying every
minute of her day –

MELANIE: Good! – And the children – all well?

WINDSCAPE: Oh yes – they're fine! Susan's a little tense at the
moment, actually, with her O levels – a pity she's taking them
so early, I think, but she insists – she's in with a particularly
bright lot and doesn't want to fall behind or let herself down so
she works away until all hours. Quite often after Fanny and I
have gone to bed. But she's developing quite an interest in – in
– well, philosophical speculation, I suppose it is, really – the
other evening – (*bending during this to put on his clips*) she
suddenly insisted – in the middle of supper – she'd been very
quiet until then – she suddenly insisted that we couldn't prove
that other people existed – and that perhaps when we thought
about them or remembered them or saw and heard them even
– we were actually just making them up – and of course I took
her up on this and attempted to explain how it is we do know

that other people exist, including people we don't even know
exist, if you follow – (*laughing*) and she kept saying 'But you
can't prove it, Daddy, you can't actually prove it!' until I
found myself getting quite tangled in my own arguments –
and trying to remember whether there is an irrefutable answer
to solipsism – Fanny had to rescue me in the end by calling me
up to read to little Fanny and Ben –

MELANIE: I've always thought she was the one who takes most
after you.

WINDSCAPE: Yes, yes – perhaps she does, perhaps she does – I'm
afraid I rather like to think so anyway – (*laughs*) but you
haven't seen them for ages have you, you really must come
over sometime soon – Fanny would love to see you again. We
all would.

MELANIE: That would be lovely.

WINDSCAPE: I'll get Fanny to give you a ring over the weekend or –

MELANIE: Good.

WINDSCAPE: Right – well, oh, by the way, I've been meaning to
ask – how is the day-nurse working out, Nurse – Nurse – with
the name out of Dickens.

MELANIE: Grimes. Well enough so far – she seems a very efficient,
cheerful, little soul – a little too cheerful for my taste perhaps,
as apparently she belongs to one of those peculiar revivalist
sects that seem to be springing up all over the place now – you
know, meeting in each other's homes and chanting prayers
and dancing about in their love of God – at least that's how she
describes it – but Mother seems to like her.

WINDSCAPE: Well, that's the main thing, isn't it?

MELANIE: Yes. Yes it is.

WINDSCAPE: Well do give her my – my very best – see you
Monday, Melanie, my dear.

MELANIE: See you Monday Henry.

(WINDSCAPE, *carrying papers, books, etc., goes off left. The
sound of the door closing.* MELANIE *sits. She lets out a sudden
wail, and then in a sort of frenzy, tears at the page of the book from
which she's been copying, sobbing. She checks herself, as: the
sound of the door opening.*)

WINDSCAPE: (*Laughing*) What on earth can I be thinking of – going

36

off with all these in my arms and leaving my briefcase behind –
I do that sort of thing more and more now – perhaps it's
premature senility – (*entering, going to the briefcase, shovelling
the papers and books in*) or did I get switched on to the wrong
track and think I was going off to teach a class – I must have as
I went out that way – (*Looks at her smiling. A little pause.*)
Melanie – Melanie – (*He hesitates, then goes to her, leaving the
briefcase on the desk.*) Is something the matter?

MELANIE: I'm sorry – I'm sorry – but I've got to talk – talk to
someone –

WINDSCAPE: What is it?

MELANIE: She hates me, you see.

WINDSCAPE: Who?

MELANIE: Mother.

WINDSCAPE: Oh Melanie, I'm sure that's not – not – why do you
think she does?

MELANIE: She says I've abandoned her. Betrayed her. When I
come back in the evenings she won't speak to me. She sits
silent for hours, while I prepare supper and chatter at her, and
then when I've got her to the table she refuses to eat. Since that
second attack she can only work one side of her mouth, but
she can eat perfectly well. She says Nurse Grimes feeds her
and so I should too, but when I try she lets the food fall out of
her mouth, and – and stares at me with such malevolence,
until suddenly she'll say something – something utterly – last
night she said 'It's not my fault you've spent your life in my
home. I've never wanted you here, but as you're too stupid to
make an intelligent career, and too unattractive to make any
reasonable man a wife, I was prepared to accept the
responsibility for you. And now you refuse to pay your debt.
Oh, sharper than a serpent's tooth . . .' And coming out of the
side of her mouth, in a hoarse whisper, like a – like a gangster
in one of those films. And she wets herself too. From spite.
She never does it with Nurse Grimes, of course. Only with
me. She says that as I'm behaving like a neglected parent,
she'll behave like a neglected child. The only child I'll ever
have. And she gives Nurse Grimes things – things that belong
to me or she knows I love that we've had for years – the

buttons from Daddy's uniform or the other day a silly
lithograph of a donkey that's hung in my room since I was ten
– of course Nurse Grimes gives them back but – but and the
worst thing is I'm beginning to hate her, to hate going home or
when I'm there have such dreadful feelings – because the
thought of years – it could be years apparently – years of this –
and so wishing she would have another attack and die now –
too dreadful – too dreadful – almost imagining myself doing
something –

WINDSCAPE: You mustn't blame yourself for that, Melanie, you
mustn't. It's only natural – and healthy, probably, even. But
I'm so sorry she's – I had no idea – what can one say? I know –
we both know – what a remarkable woman she was, and I
suppose that the indignity of finding herself increasingly
incapacitated and the – the fear of what's going to happen to
her – I suppose when it comes to it, when we come to our ends
some of us are – well, all the anger and despair turn to cruelty –
and of course you're the only one –

MELANIE: I know. But I can't give up my teaching, Henry, I can't.
Your getting me this job was the best thing that ever happened
to me – of course she always despised it – even when she was
well she thought it – thought it – having been a professor
herself – but I love it and – and I've got to think of myself now.
Haven't I?

WINDSCAPE: Yes. Yes, of course you have. Finally, one always
must. I wish I could give you some comfort, my dear.

MELANIE: You do, Henry. Your just being here and my knowing
that you – that you care about me makes all the difference. All
the difference. It always has (*She begins to cry.*) Oh what a fool
I was not to – not to marry you when you asked me – all those
years ago – I keep thinking of it now – and what Mother said
about your being too young and not knowing what you were
doing – and – and blighting your career – of course I'm happy
that you're so happy – I wouldn't have been able to make you
as happy, but even then she was my enemy – my real enemy –
I'm sorry, I'm sorry – (*Sobbing.*)

WINDSCAPE: (*Hesitates, then with reluctance puts his arms around
her*) There there, my dear, there there – mustn't think of the

38

past – it's the – the future – the future – there there –
(*The telephone rings.*)
(*After a moment*) Perhaps I'd better – perhaps I'd better – um –
(*Releasing himself, he picks up the telephone.*) Hello. Oh Hello
Nigel, yes it is! No she's gone I'm afraid – at least I think she
has – have you seen Anita in the last half hour –
(MELANIE, *now handkerchiefing her tears, shakes her head.*)
Melanie hasn't seen her either so I'm fairly sure – yes, of
course I will. (*He listens.*) You're phoning from Liverpool
Street and you're about to catch the 6.13 so you'll be home
before eight, right, got that but as I say – have you tried her at
home – oh, well, if she's going to the theatre perhaps she's
gone straight there, eh? but if Melanie or I do see her by any
unlikely – yes, right, goodbye – and oh, Nigel, good luck with
your first issue, Fanny and I and everybody we know are so
looking forward to it – have you decided what you're going to
call it by the way? Really? Well, that sounds – that really
sounds most – most – yes – goodbye. (*He hangs up.*) That was
Nigel – for Anita – as you probably realized and – and anyway
she's certainly left, hasn't she – Nigel says she said she was
going to the theatre – so – so – I suppose the Arts – *The Three
Sisters*, isn't it? – such a beautiful play although not – not my
favourite – which will always be *The Seagull*. Apparently
they're going to call the magazine *Reports*, by the way, I'm not
sure I care too much for *Reports*, do you? (*He stares hopelessly
at* MELANIE, *who has somewhat recovered herself.*) You must
come around, Melanie and have a real – a real talk with Fanny
– take you out of yourself – away from your problems –
MELANIE: Thank you, Henry.
WINDSCAPE: No, we'd love to see you, I'll get her to ring you. All
right? And now I must – I really must – (*Looking at the clock.*) I
promised Susan I'd help her with her maths, and then I've got
to listen to Ben doing a Chopin piece, he's going to perform it
at the school concert, really rather too advanced, but still, and
there's little Fanny's bed-time read – I'm trying to get her on
to Walter De La Mare but he hasn't really taken yet – so – so –
MELANIE: Yes, you must get back.
WINDSCAPE: Yes. See you Monday, my dear.

MELANIE: Monday, Henry.

(WINDSCAPE *looks around vaguely for a moment, then goes out through the french windows.* MELANIE *stands for a moment, then sees the briefcase, registers it, takes it to* WINDSCAPE's *locker, puts it in, goes back to the book, looks down at it, tries futilely to sort it out, pressing the page flat with her hand, then goes to collect her briefcase, etc. As she does so, the sound of violent quarrelling, in assorted tongues, off, over the croquet: 'No, you cannot—Mr Windscape said . . .' etc.* MELANIE *pauses to listen, then as the voices continue, then fade, the sound of the door, off left, opening.*) Oh, hello Eddie! (*Brightly.*)

LOOMIS: He's not here then—I can't make it out—I've been everywhere, everywhere, up to the flat, all the classrooms and in the office—and the phone going all the time about some of our Japanese and that French restaurant, and they're not even French, it turns out, they're from Wiltshire—and I don't know what Thomas has said to them, I didn't even know about it—he knows I can't deal with that sort of thing—and he's booked a table for the two of us tonight at their request, forcing us to take responsibility, I don't see what it's got to do with the school if a few Japanese can't hold their drink, I don't know why he agreed—it really is all too—

MELANIE: Now Eddie. Now. (*Going to him.*) You mustn't worry. You'll make yourself ill, and it's not worth it. Why don't you go upstairs to the flat and have a rest, I'm sure it'll all sort itself out, you know Thomas, he'll get it completely under control, he always does, in the end.

LOOMIS: Yes, yes, of course you're right, my dear, thank you, thank you. And a little rest—and I'll try and make Thomas have one, too—

MELANIE: That's right, Eddie, you both need it—oh, and would you give this back to him when you see him, and tell him I'm terribly sorry (*as she collects her briefcase and hands* LOOMIS *the book*) a page of it seems to have got torn—our Mr Meadle insisted on snatching it out of my hands and then dropped it—he was only trying to be helpful of course—but you know how clumsy he is—

LOOMIS: Oh—oh dear, Cussons—one of our favourite books,

Thomas will find it hard to forgive Meadle – well – have a good weekend my dear, and bless you. (*They go off.*)

MELANIE: Thank you Eddie. (*Off.*)

LOOMIS: (*Footsteps off, then he stops*) Oh, and by the way, how's mother?

MELANIE: Oh, top hole, thanks Eddie.

LOOMIS: Good, good. (*The sound of the door shutting.*)

(*There is a pause.* QUARTERMAINE *enters through the french windows. He looks around him, stands for a moment, then sweeps his left leg, vaguely, as –*
Lights. Curtain.)

ACT TWO

The following year, towards summer. It is a Monday morning,
about 9.30.
There have been a few improvements, different perhaps; a record-
player, with a record-rack consisting of poetry readings and
Shakespeare plays. There is also a large new tape-recorder,
sophisticated for the period.
QUARTERMAINE *is seated, with his feet up, staring ahead.*
WINDSCAPE *enters through the french windows, carrying a briefcase,*
smoking a pipe, wearing bicycle clips.

WINDSCAPE: Hello St John. (*He goes to his locker.*)

QUARTERMAINE: (*Doesn't respond at first, then takes in*
WINDSCAPE) Oh, hello – um (*thinks*) Henry.

WINDSCAPE: (*Turns, looks at him*) Deep in thought?

QUARTERMAINE: Mmmm? Oh. No no – just – just – you know.

WINDSCAPE: Ah. Did you have a good half-term?

QUARTERMAINE: Oh. Yes thanks. Yes.

WINDSCAPE: What did you do? Did you go away? (*Going to his*
locker.)

QUARTERMAINE: Well, I – I no, I stayed here.

WINDSCAPE: Here!

QUARTERMAINE: Yes.

WINDSCAPE: Oh, in Cambridge, you mean? Just for a moment I
thought you meant actually *here* – in this room – I think
perhaps because the last time I saw you, you were sitting in
exactly the same place in very much that position – as if you
haven't moved all week.

QUARTERMAINE: Oh. (*He laughs.*) But I say – good to be back,
isn't it?

WINDSCAPE: Well, I could have done with a little longer myself.

QUARTERMAINE: (*Watches* WINDSCAPE *at the locker*) I say,
Henry, what did you do for the half?

WINDSCAPE: Mmmm? Oh nothing very exciting really, we
packed ourselves into the caravan and took ourselves off to

42

a spot we'd heard about in Norfolk –

QUARTERMAINE: That sounds terrific!

WINDSCAPE: Yes – yes – well, the trouble was that it rained fairly
    steadily – all week, in fact – so we didn't get out as much as
    we would have liked – a shame really as among other things
    we were hoping that a few jaunts would cheer Susan up.

QUARTERMAINE: Oh – is she a bit low then?

WINDSCAPE: Yes yes – well she's still brooding over her O level
    results – we keep telling her that at her age six positive passes
    – I mean Bs and Cs – is jolly good – but she seems to feel
    she's let herself down – but I'll tell you what we did see – it
    really was most – extraordinary – one morning at about six it
    was, I was up trying to plug the leak – it was right over little
    Fanny's bunk – and so she was awake and so was Ben – and
    Susan hadn't slept at all – so it was all rather – rather fraught.
    With tempers fraying – but Fanny she'd gone outside to the
    loo, as a matter of fact – and suddenly she called us – all of us
    – told us to put on our wellies and macs and come out and
    look – and we did – and there – silhouetted against the sky
    was the most – the most –
    (MEADLE *enters through the french windows in bicycle clips,*
    carrying a briefcase.)

MEADLE: Greetings, Henry, St John.

QUARTERMAINE: Hello, old chap.

WINDSCAPE: Hello, Derek. Have a good holiday?

MEADLE: Yes, thanks, Henry, very, very good indeed. What
    about you? (*Goes to his locker, taking off his clips, etc.*)

WINDSCAPE: Yes, I was just telling St John, we went to Norfolk,
    a little wet, but there really was one very remarkable – well,
    moment is all it amounted to really. In temporal terms.

MEADLE: Sounds marvellous. Thomas isn't around yet, is he?

WINDSCAPE: He wasn't in the office when I came through, have
    you seen him, St John?

QUARTERMAINE: Mmmm?

WINDSCAPE: Thomas. Have you seen him?

QUARTERMAINE: No no – but I expect he's here somewhere. Up
    in their flat or – or down in their office but I say – I say,
    Dennis, did you have a good holiday?

43

MEADLE: Who's Dennis, St John? (*He laughs.*)

QUARTERMAINE: Mmmm?

WINDSCAPE: You said Dennis, instead of Derek. And he's already said he had a very good holiday.

QUARTERMAINE: Oh. What did you do?

MEADLE: I went to Sheffield, as a matter of fact.

WINDSCAPE: Sheffield, I know it well, Fanny and I went there the year before Susan was born, we were doing a tour of out-of-the-way urban domestic architecture, I've got great affection for Sheffield, what were *you* doing there?

MEADLE: Um – oh. Attending my aunt's funeral, as a matter of fact.

QUARTERMAINE: What?

WINDSCAPE: Oh Derek, I'm so sorry. How upsetting for you.

MEADLE: Yes, it was. Very. Very.

WINDSCAPE: But actually when I asked you earlier, you did say – I suppose it was merely social reflex – that you'd had a good half-term –

MEADLE: Yes, well actually I met someone there I used to know. And I managed to see quite a lot of her. That was the good part of it. Not my aunt's death, I need hardly say. (*He laughs.*)

WINDSCAPE: Ah.

QUARTERMAINE: Who was she?

MEADLE: Oh, just a girl St John, – we were at Hull University together, as a matter of fact, she was doing the library course but we – we lost contact, for various reasons. Although I hadn't forgotten her. And when I was in Sheffield I had to take back all my poor aunt's books. And there she was. Behind the counter.

QUARTERMAINE: What was she doing there?

MEADLE: Well, stamping the books in and out of course. What do you think she was doing? (*With a mitigating laugh.*)

WINDSCAPE: Oh don't worry about St John, one of his absent days, eh St John, but how nice for you to bump into her like that, especially under those circumstances, eh?

MEADLE: Yes, I can't tell you what a – a blessing it turned out to be. As soon as she was off work she'd come over and sit with

me and my uncle, and on a couple of evenings when I had to
go out and console some of my aunt's friends, she came and
sat with him anyway, by herself. He's very keen on football,
but he can't follow it in the newspapers as his eyesight's
nearly gone and they're too quick for him on the radio. So
she'd read out all the teams and their scores. Which was very
tiring for her, as she's got quite a serious speech impediment.

WINDSCAPE: What a nice girl she sounds, eh, St John?

QUARTERMAINE: What, Henry?

WINDSCAPE: What a nice girl Derek's friend sounds.

QUARTERMAINE: Oh – oh yes, terrific, terrific. Um, tell me – tell
me – what – what are her legs like?

MEADLE: What!

WINDSCAPE: Good heavens, St John, what an extraordinary
question!

QUARTERMAINE: Oh yes, – oh – I'm sorry – I was just trying to
imagine – I have a sort of thing about girls' legs, you see. (*He
laughs apologetically.*) I can't stand them if they're dumpy or
– (*thinks*) stumpy.

MEADLE: Well, let's just say, shall we, St John, (*manifestly
exercising smiling control*) that Daphne's legs happen to be my
sort of legs. Will that help you to imagine them?

QUARTERMAINE: Your sort of legs. (*He looks at* MEADLE'*s legs.*)

MEADLE: The sort of legs I happen to like. But I don't want to
dilate on the subject of Daphne's legs (*laughs*) at least just at
the moment – look, St John, I wonder if you'd mind, there's
a matter I was very much hoping to have a conversation with
Henry about. As a matter of fact, it's rather urgent.

QUARTERMAINE: Oh. No. Sorry. Go ahead.

MEADLE: Well the thing is, St John, it's – it's of a confidential
nature.

QUARTERMAINE: Oh – oh well, I'll go and have a little stroll then,
in the garden. (*Getting up.*) To tell you the truth my head
feels a little – a little – as if it could do with some air.

MEADLE: Thanks very much, St John, very decent of you.

QUARTERMAINE: (*Going off*) Oh, not at all – but I say – I say –
(*Going out*) what a beautiful morning! (*He goes.*)

MEADLE: (*Smiling*) You know, I can't help wondering sometimes about old Quartermaine. I can't imagine a more charming fellow but from the students' point of view – do you know what one of the advanced Swedes was telling me just before half-term –

WINDSCAPE: (*Interrupting*) I think it would be better really – really much better – if we didn't find ourselves talking about a colleague and a friend – I know that your concern is entirely – entirely disinterested, but – but – these little conflabs *can* do unintended harm. I hope you don't mind my – my – pointing it out.

MEADLE: Not at all, Henry, you're quite right, one can't be too careful, needless to say I meant no – no slur on St John –

WINDSCAPE: I know you didn't, I know you didn't. But now. You said you had something urgent –

MEADLE: Yes, well, the thing is – well look, I've been here a year now, Henry, and Thomas said when I started that it wouldn't be long before I was made permanent – and yet here I am, you see, still on part-time. The only one of the staff on part-time, as it happens. (*He laughs.*)

WINDSCAPE: And part-time isn't really very satisfactory for you, then?

MEADLE: Well, no, it isn't, Henry, frankly. I get paid one pound two and sixpence for every hour I teach.

WINDSCAPE: But surely Dennis –

MEADLE: Derek. (*He laughs.*) Quartermaine seems to have started you off on Dennis –

WINDSCAPE: Oh good heavens, I'm so sorry, *Derek* – but one pound two and sixpence an hour isn't such a bad rate, is it?

MEADLE: Ah yes, Henry, but you see I don't get paid during the vacations, you see. I only get paid by the hour for the hours I'm allowed to do, while the rest of the staff get paid an annual salary. So even though I'm currently doing twice as many hours again as everybody else, I in fact get slightly less than half of what everybody else gets, over the year. I mean, take this half-term we've just had, Henry, a week of paid holiday for everybody else but a week of no money at all for me, it was just luck that my aunt died in it, or I might have had to miss an earning week to go to her funeral and sort out my uncle you see. – And last Christmas, well, I've kept this very quiet, Henry, but last Christmas I had to be a post-man. (*He laughs.*)

WINDSCAPE: Oh dear!

MEADLE: Yes, and let me tell you it wasn't simply the work, Henry – being up at six, and trudging through the snow and sleet we had the whole of those three weeks – it was also the sheer embarrassment. Twice during my second round I nearly bumped into some students. I only got away with it because I kept my head lowered and once Thomas himself went right past me in the car – it was a miracle he didn't see me, especially as I'd slipped on some ice and I was actually lying on the pavement with the letters scattered everywhere – and now the summer holiday's looming ahead – I simply don't know how I'm going to get through that. Or at least I do. I've already sent in my application to be an Entertainments Officer at one of those holiday camps in Hayling Island.

WINDSCAPE: Oh dear!

MEADLE: Yes. And now that Daphne's back in the picture – well you probably gathered from what I said that we're pretty serious about each other – and I don't want to keep her waiting around with a long engagement – there's been a lot of tragedy in that family, Henry.

WINDSCAPE: Oh dear!

MEADLE: Yes, I won't go into it, if you don't mind. Not that Daphne tries to conceal it. She's too straightforward for that.

WINDSCAPE: Well, she really does sound a most – a most remarkable –

MEADLE: Yes, I consider myself a very, very lucky man. So what do you think, Henry – I know how much Eddie and Thomas respect you – I'm going to try and nab Thomas for a few minutes this morning – how should I go about it, with him?

WINDSCAPE: Well, Derek, I think there's no doubt that you have a very strong case. Very strong. And as we all know, Thomas and Eddie are very fair, always. I know they'd respond most sympathetically – most sympathetically – to all that you've told me about yourself and Deirdre –

47

MEADLE: Daphne, actually. (*Smiling.*)

WINDSCAPE: Daphne – I'm sorry, Daphne of course –
(*The sound of the door opening: footsteps.*)

SACKLING: (*Off*) 'Morning. (*He enters somewhat jauntily, his
moustache now accompanied by a beard.*) Henry – Derek –

WINDSCAPE: Oh hello, Mark, good holiday?

MEADLE: You didn't notice if Thomas was in his office as you
went by, did you?

SACKLING: Yes, he was. Just come down. I like the chin. A
comparatively unexplored area, isn't it, if we exclude the
puffy nose from falling over the croquet hoop just before
summer, how did you come by it, not shaving, I trust.

MEADLE: (*Who has been getting up*) Oh, I'd forgotten about that –
no, no, not shaving, don't worry – (*Attempting a chuckle.*) I'll
tell you all about it later – and thanks, Henry, for your
advice. It was most helpful –

WINDSCAPE: Oh, not at all, I'm glad if – if –
(MEADLE *goes out, during this, and as the door closes:*)
Oh – oh good heavens – Derek! Oh –

SACKLING: What's the matter?

WINDSCAPE: I think we had a slight misunderstanding – he's
under the impression that I was advising him to go and see
Thomas about being put on a more – a more permanent basis
– and the truth is I was going on to explain to him that in
spite of the – the strong claim he has – he should – well, in
my view anyway – hold his horses for the moment – Thomas
is under a bit of strain, you see, with all the recent renovation
expenses and now the sudden drop in student in-take – this
business of the Japanese suddenly deserting has really hit us
very hard – so in fact it's the worst possible moment for
Meadle – I was going to try and divert him to Eddie – I do
sometimes feel, strictly between ourselves, that it *is* hard on
him as the only part-time teacher – and we must be careful in
the staff-room not to show any – any – well, make fun of him
more than is perhaps – under the circumstances – if you see,
Mark.

SACKLING: Oh, I shouldn't worry about Meadle. (*He's been at the
locker during all the above.*) Even St John's observed that he's

one of those people who always lands on his feet – even if he damages a toe in the process. The thing is to make sure it's his and not yours. Well, Henry, peace-maker, apostle and saint, what sort of half did you have?

WINDSCAPE: Oh, we did the usual sort of thing, took the caravan to a spot near the Broads. The weather wasn't too splendid but as I was telling – St John, I think it was – there was one rather exceptional experience. To tell you the truth I've never seen anything quite like it. Fanny actually wrote a small sort of prose poem about it.

SACKLING: Really? I didn't know Fanny wrote! But on that subject – listen – I must tell you. I've finished.

WINDSCAPE: Finished?

SACKLING: My novel, old cheese.

WINDSCAPE: Oh Mark – well, congratulations, congratulations!

SACKLING: Thanks Henry. I knew *you'd* know what it means to me, I'd rather you kept it to yourself for the moment – for superstitious reasons, as it's still only the first draft. But the point is I feel – in my guts – that it's the first draft of the final version and damned near the thing itself, actually. Because of the way it happened, you see. What I did was – I put everything I'd previously written – a total by the way of 3,643 pages – into a box and lugged it into the cellar and started again. Completely from scratch. Just me, the typewriter and a carton of paper. I was actually quite – quite frightened. But it was all perfectly simple. No strain. No effort. Almost no thought. Just a steady untaxing continuous flow of creation. For a whole week. It was the nearest I've come, will probably ever come, to a mystical experience.

WINDSCAPE: I envy you. I once tried to write a novel – but as Fanny said my forte – if I have a forte – (*He laughs.*)

SACKLING: The thing is, though – the thing is – it proves to *me* that I'm a novelist. The doubts I've had since Camelia left – and worst of all, the envy! I'd read the reviews and see the photographs of other novelists – the real ones, who'd been published – some of them people I knew, had been up with – God, there's a man at Trinity – an absolute imbecile – his *second* novel came out last month, well received too – and

when I saw his face in the middle of some interview he'd
given – the same imbecile face, with a smirk added – that I
used to see opposite me in Hall I – I – well, I'd better not go
into what I wanted to do to him. And all those women that
are getting published everywhere – everyone, everyone but
me, that's what I began to think – as if they'd got something,
through some genetic accident – like an extra gland or double
joints – that I hadn't. And so they could do it, again and
again – while I was working away like some – some drudge –
some lunatic drudge who'd given up his wife and child and
hours and hours of his life – and would go on and on
drudging, through thousands and thousands of pages, not
one of them publishable, to the end of my life – so I suppose
that what I've discovered at last is my – well, let's use the
word. My talent. Perhaps it's been growing down there, in
the dark, all this time – until finally it's strong enough to take
over, eh? Anyway, now all I've got to do is a bit of pruning,
no doubt some tightening up – correct the spelling and the
typing mistakes, and float an extract or two in Nigel's
currently fashionable little magazine – I've been promising
him for years – (*He laughs.*)

(QUARTERMAINE *enters through the french windows.*)

QUARTERMAINE: All clear, then? Hello, Mark!

WINDSCAPE: What – oh good heavens, St John – yes, yes, I forgot
that you were still out there.

QUARTERMAINE: Oh no – I enjoyed it – to tell you the truth it
seems to have cleared my head – I was feeling a bit – a bit odd
before – Hello Mark!

SACKLING: Hello, St John, have a good holiday?

QUARTERMAINE: Yes – yes – terrific thanks! Terrific! And how
were they?

SACKLING: Who?

QUARTERMAINE: Camelia. And little Tom too. Weren't you
going to see them over half-term?

SACKLING: Oh, that's right. Actually, as it turned out, they were
unavailable. Tom was getting over mumps, or so at least
Camelia claimed, so she decided to take him to a friend of her
mother's, in Wales, to convalesce. They have a cottage by

the sea, and of course I couldn't offer him that, could I? Even though this half-term was mine, according to the agreement.

(WINDSCAPE, *during this, goes to his briefcase, takes out books, puts them on top of the tape-recorder, puts his briefcase and other books in the locker, etc.*)

QUARTERMAINE: Still, perhaps it did him some good – I mean, the beach and the valleys and hills and – and – I mean if poor little Tom's been ill –

SACKLING: St John, I'd be grateful if you'd stop referring to him as little Tom, and *poor* little Tom too, it makes him sound like something out of the workhouse, and he's anyway not so little any more, the last time I saw him he must have weighed in at a good five stone –

QUARTERMAINE: What? Oh – oh right. (*A little pause.*) Five stone, eh? (*He whistles.*) Um – but what a pity I didn't know you were stuck in Cambridge over the half, we could have got together – but perhaps you got some writing done –

SACKLING: Yes – well some – as always –

(ANITA *enters through the french windows.*)

Hi, Anita!

QUARTERMAINE: Hello, Anita!

WINDSCAPE: Anita, my dear –

(ANITA *takes off her coat. She is pregnant.*)

SACKLING: – you're swelling along pleasantly. Rapidly too.

(ANITA *laughs.*)

QUARTERMAINE: But you look – you look – (*Gazing at her in a sort of reverence.*) I mean (*He gestures.*) in just a week, good Lord!

ANITA: Well, it's taken a bit longer than a week, St John.

QUARTERMAINE: No, no, but I mean –

WINDSCAPE: Just like Fanny, nothing shows for ages and then one day there it is – for the world to see –

SACKLING: And how's Nigel getting on in New York?

ANITA: Oh, he decided not to go. He suddenly became convinced – had a dream, or something – that I'd spawn prematurely, so he stayed at home and mugged up on all the texts – Spock for practicals, and Blake and D. H. Lawrence and some

Indian writer he's discovered and is going to publish, for
significance – which was lovely for me as I didn't have to go
to my parents, I spent most of the time in the bath reading
thrillers. It was lovely.

QUARTERMAINE: Oh, I wish I'd known you were here, so was
Mark, as it turned out, weren't you Mark, we could have got
together – but I say, it's good to be back in a way, isn't it – I
mean, after a good holiday of course –

SACKLING: Tell him I'm going to give him a ring, will you – (*To*
ANITA)
(*The sound of the door opening, and closing, during this.*)
– there's something I've got for him. At last.

ANITA: Oh Mark, really! He'll be so thrilled – he keeps refusing
to phone you because he says it's like soliciting –

QUARTERMAINE: Hello, Derek, have you had a good half – ?
(MEADLE *enters.*)
(*Laughing*) But of course I've seen you already, I'm sorry if I
was a bit – off-colour, don't know what was the matter with
me – but oh Lord, what have you done to your cheek – I
didn't even notice it before, you do get in the wars, though,
don't you, old man. Was it shaving?

ANITA: Are you all right, Derek? You don't look –

MEADLE: Yes, yes thanks – well – (*laughs*) apart from just finding
out that I won't be joining you as a full-time member of the
staff. In fact, my hours are going to be cut. By over a
quarter. Which won't give me enough money to survive on.
Furthermore, unless there's a sudden swing upwards in
enrolment, I may not have any hours at all next month. So
I'll – I'll probably be leaving you then.

QUARTERMAINE: Leave! Oh no! That's rotten!

WINDSCAPE: I'm very sorry Dennis. I blame myself. I should
have explained more fully. But you were out of the room so
quickly –

SACKLING: Look, we must have a word with Thomas, with Eddie
– we can't allow Derek just to be chucked out – Henry,
perhaps you could speak to Eddie and Thomas on behalf of
us all –

ANITA: Yes. Henry, you will, won't you?

WINDSCAPE: Of course I'll – I'll do my best. But you see the
financial situation – it's not at all good, at the moment, is it?
The school can only afford what it can afford. But whatever
happens, Dennis – it's no reflection on your teaching. None
at all.

MEADLE: Oh, I know that. It's Derek, by the way, Henry.
(*Laughing.*) But that's life, isn't it? That's the joke. How
hard I've worked. I mean, old Quartermaine here – well,
according to one of the Swedes I'm not allowed to mention
because it's a fraction on the unethical side to speak ill of a
colleague – well, he sometimes sits for a whole hour not
speaking. Even in dictation classes. Or if he does condescend
to speak, goes off into little stories about himself they can't
make head or tail of.

(*There is a pause.*)

QUARTERMAINE: What, a Swede, did you say? What does he
look like?

MEADLE: Oh, what does it matter? Everybody knows that for you
one Swede is like another German, one Greek is like another
Italian, you can't tell them apart and you don't know what
they're called – unlike me, you see – because do you know
what I do? I memorize their names before their first class,
and then study their faces during it, and then when I go
home I close my eyes and practise putting the two together so
that by the second class I know every one of my students
personally, and do you know what else I do, I keep a look-out
not only in term-time but also in my holidays – my *unpaid*
holidays – for any item that might interest them for British
Life and Institutions and actually make a note of them – here
– in my notebook, which I always keep especially in my
pocket (*wrestling with it with increasing violence, jerking it out
of his pocket, tearing his pocket as he does so*) along with any of
the out-of-the-way idioms and interesting usages I might
happen across – and do you know what *else* I do – I – but
what does it matter what else I do, that's what I mean by joke
or life or whatever it is, because I'm the one that's facing the
push, and you're the one that's on permanent. (*During this
speech* MEADLE's *accent has become increasingly North*

Country.) Not that I begrudge you – it's just that I reckon that I've earned it. Look – look, I don't mean – I don't mean – the last thing I mean is – (*He turns away, possibly in tears*.) (*There is silence, into which* MELANIE *enters, through the french windows*.)

QUARTERMAINE: Oh hello, Melanie, have a good half?

WINDSCAPE: Hello Melanie, my dear.

SACKLING: Melanie.

ANITA: Hello Melanie.

(MELANIE *goes to the table, puts down her briefcase, takes off her coat*.)

QUARTERMAINE: Um – um – how's your mother?

WINDSCAPE: Yes, how – how is she?

MELANIE: She's dead. She died last Tuesday.

(*There is silence*.)

WINDSCAPE: Oh Melanie – I'm so sorry – so sorry –

(*Murmurings from the others*.)

Was it another attack, my dear?

MELANIE: No. She fell down the stairs and broke her neck. We don't quite know how it happened as it was after I'd gone to bed. Nurse Grimes found her there in the morning, I still hadn't got up, the first I knew of it was Nurse Grimes calling me – and – and – that's really all there is to tell. I'd be grateful if we could dispense with condolences and that sort of thing, because what I really want most of all is to get on in the usual fashion, without any – any fuss. I shall tell Thomas and Eddie, naturally, straight away –

(*The sound of the door opening: footsteps, rather odd, though*.)

LOOMIS: Hello everybody, hello, all rested up I trust, welcome back, welcome back – but first, is Melanie here, ah there you are, Melanie my dear. (*Appearing on stage. He has a stick, his glasses are tinted, and his voice and manner are frailer*.) There are a couple of policemen in the office with Thomas, who want a word with you. They refuse to say what about, but not to worry, not to worry, because I asked whether it was illness or accident, and they assured me it wasn't, so your mother's perfectly all right, my dear, which is the main thing, isn't it, it's probably some nonsense to do with your

54

car, anyway if you'd go along to the office and flirt with them
– and whatever you do, don't let Thomas lose his temper.
(*He laughs*.)
(MELANIE *stands for a moment, then braces herself and walks
off, left, as:*)
Really! Our Cambridge bobbies, they always have to make
such a solemn meal out of the most trivial business –
pursuing their inquiries on information received, as they put
it – goodness knows how they'd behave if they had
something truly serious – Anita, my dear, how blooming you
look, how blooming – and how did Nigel find New York?

ANITA: Oh fine, thank you Eddie, fine –

LOOMIS: Good good good, well tell Nigel how much we're
looking forward to the first Anglo-American edition, and
how sorry we are we've had to cut back to just the one
subscription but *semper fidelis*. Henry, what sort of half-term
did you have – one of your adventurous caravan treks, where
to this time?

WINDSCAPE: Yes Eddie – to Norfolk.

LOOMIS: Weather all right, I trust?

WINDSCAPE: Oh yes, Eddie, yes, lovely thank you, except when
it rained and – and even then we had one – one amazing
moment at sunrise –

LOOMIS: Good, good, especially for Fanny, little Fanny, Ben and
Susan eh – and how did Susan get on with her O levels,
results as expected?

WINDSCAPE: Yes, Eddie, thanks, lots of – of Bs and – and – Cs
and – and so forth.

LOOMIS: I'm not surprised, with you and Fanny behind her, give
her our congratulations do, and Mark – if that is Mark I see
behind a week's further fuzzy-wuzzy, lots of tap, tap,
tapping?

SACKLING: Oh, well, yes – yes, a little, thanks Eddie.

LOOMIS: Well keep at it, we know that one day – ah, there's our
Derek, but I've already said my welcomes to him, haven't I
Derek, in the corridor – I gather you found Thomas?

MEADLE: Yes thank you, Eddie, yes yes.

LOOMIS: And that you got whatever it was you were so anxious to get sorted out, sorted out, at least Thomas seemed very pleased with the fruits of your deliberations.

MEADLE: Well – well yes, thank you, Eddie, all sorted out, yes.

LOOMIS: Good, good – and St John, now what was I going to say to you – oh, I remember – in spite of this tired old brain of mine – yet another postcard for you in the office, from that fervent fan your Swiss, I hope you don't mind my having a peek, but I always think postcards – what's his name?

QUARTERMAINE: Um, Muller isn't it –

LOOMIS: Boller, I think it is. Ferdinand Boller. How lucky that you don't have to recall his name to his face, or he might not go on being so devoted to you, anyway, he's hoping to see you when he's in England on business late this year, or next or some time or never, that is, if I understand him correctly, his English actually seems to get worse from postcard to postcard, though we can't hold you responsible for that, can we, at this stage – (*laughs*) now, now there's something I'd like to take the opportunity of saying to you, just between ourselves, and a little behind Thomas's back, so to speak, I expect you've all noticed the very distinct drop in student enrolment these last few months. Thomas is slightly more worried than perhaps he's let any of you realize, we all know how dedicated he is to the future of the school – and to the future of the staff –

QUARTERMAINE: Hear, hear!

LOOMIS: – we've long thought of you as part of a family, I think you all know that we do our best to care for you in that spirit –

QUARTERMAINE: Absolutely!

LOOMIS: – and I'm sure you're all wondering what you can do to help us through this little rough patch – and the answer is, to go on giving of your very best to your teaching, and to show what students we've got that while we may not be as grand as some schools in Cambridge, we yield to no school in the country in the thing that matters most, our devotion to their devotion to their learning of our language.

QUARTERMAINE: (*Amid murmurs*) Hear, hear!

LOOMIS: That's how we can best serve our school at this time of

slight crisis, and as I say, this is strictly *entre nous*, without
reference to Thomas. Thank you everybody and bless you all
– the bell will ring in a minute or so I believe, so – (*He
gestures.*)

(*And as all except* QUARTERMAINE *move to their lockers, etc.*:)

QUARTERMAINE: Eddie that was – that was terrific!

LOOMIS: St John, a word of warning, I'm afraid there have been a
number of complaints about your teaching – Thomas, I
regret to say, received a round robin before half-term.

QUARTERMAINE: Oh Lord, that Swede, you mean?

LOOMIS: What Swede?

(*During this, the sound of the door opening: footsteps.*)

Ah – Melanie, my dear, you've cleared it up, have you, what
was it all about?

MELANIE: Oh yes, Eddie. All too preposterous. Apparently a
group of French girls – from my intermediary Life and
Institutions got hold of the wrong end of the stick. They
didn't realize my recipe for roasting swan was for a medieval
banquet, and actually tried to kill one on the Cam, can you
believe it! Club one to death from a punt, with the intention
of taking it back to their rooms and cooking and eating it!
And then when they were reported to the police, blamed me.
I'm glad to say that the swan, being a swan, survived. And
gave one of them a badly bruised arm. Typically French.
(*She goes to her locker.*)

(*Amidst laughter from all except* WINDSCAPE *the bell rings.
They all move towards the door, with books, etc., except for*
QUARTERMAINE, *who goes to his locker, stands before it looking
puzzled, takes out one or two books, slightly confused.*)

QUARTERMAINE: If it's not dictation it must be comprehension.
Or – or – oh Lord!
(*Lights.*)

SCENE 2

A Friday evening, some months later. The french windows are open.
QUARTERMAINE *is asleep in an armchair, papers and books on his*

lap. He is visible to the audience, but not to anyone on stage who doesn't look specifically in the armchair.

QUARTERMAINE *suddenly groans. There is a pause.*

QUARTERMAINE: (*In his sleep*) Oh Lord! (*A pause.*) I say! (*A pause. He laughs, sleeps.*)

(*The sound of the door opening: footsteps.* MELANIE *enters from the left. She goes to her locker, puts her books in.*

QUARTERMAINE, *not heard, or perhaps half heard, by* MELANIE, *lets out a groan.* MELANIE *takes an overnight bag out of her locker.*)

QUARTERMAINE: (*Lets out another groan, rises to his feet*) Oh, Lord!

MELANIE: (*Starts, turns, sees* QUARTERMAINE.) St John! (*She goes towards him.*) Are you all right?

QUARTERMAINE: (*Blinks at her*) Oh – oh yes thanks – um – Melanie – next class, is it?

MELANIE: Heavens no, we've finished for the day. For the week, in fact.

QUARTERMAINE: (*Clearly confused*) Oh, I – I didn't hear the bell.

MELANIE: It hasn't gone yet. Don't worry, Eddie's having one of his very out-of-sorts days, poor lamb, and Thomas is in the office. We're safe.

QUARTERMAINE: Oh. Oh yes – I suppose I must have let them go early – always restless on a Friday, aren't they, and then sat down and – and –

MELANIE: St John, what are you doing tonight?

QUARTERMAINE: Oh – usual – nothing very –

MELANIE: Then I'd like to introduce you to some very special friends of mine. Would you like that?

QUARTERMAINE: Well yes – yes – thank you, Melanie.

MELANIE: I'm sure you'll enjoy it – we always end up with singing and dancing, the food's delicious and the people are – well you'll see for yourself.

QUARTERMAINE: Well, it sounds – sounds terrific!

(*The sound of the door: footsteps.*)

MELANIE: Right, you wait for me here, and I'll come and collect you when I'm ready – Oh hello Derek, you too – what a bunch of skyvers we're all turning out to be, eh?

MEADLE: Yes, well, it's only a few minutes off – besides Daphne's coming down for the weekend, I don't want to miss her train –

MELANIE: (*Going out*) Jolly good – give her my love –

MEADLE: Right, Melanie, right – but I had a bloody near one in the corridor I can tell you. I was sloping past the office – terrible din coming from it, sounded like a gang of Germans all bellowing away and Thomas trying to calm them down – anyway I'd just got past the door when Eddie came round the corner.

QUARTERMAINE: Phew!

MEADLE: Yes. I began to mumble some nonsense about wanting to check on a student – you know – but thinking I'd better wait until Thomas was freer – but he didn't see me – went right on past – I mean, we were like that! (*Showing*.)

QUARTERMAINE: Oh Lord! (*Laughing*.) Still, I hope he's all right – I mean for him not to notice –

MEADLE: Oh, by the way, I've got an invitation for you. You know Daphne and I are engaged – not that we haven't been from the moment I walked into the library and saw her again. But now that I've got my permanency, we might as well make it official. We'll get married on the first day of the summer vac, and I'm going to ask Thomas and Eddie to be best man. I mean, let them decide which – I don't want to upset one by choosing the other.

QUARTERMAINE: Congratulations! Terrific! And then off on your honeymoon, eh?

MEADLE: Yes. We've settled for Hayling Island. Not very exciting, I know, but there may be a way to pick up a little money as well as having a good holiday ourselves. Daphne's keen to start saving for a house – you know how it is, there's a very practical head on those little shoulders of hers. There's a good chance she might even come and do a bit of teaching here – to replace me as the part-time, you see. I've already dropped a little hint to Thomas – I think he was worried by her speech impediment, but I pointed out that in some respects that could be an asset – with the elementary groups, for instance, and especially the Japs – that she understands the problems of pronunciation from inside, so to speak.

QUARTERMAINE: Absolutely – and she'd be – a great asset here, wouldn't she, in the staff-room, I mean – she's a wonderful girl, Derek.

MEADLE: Yes, well, I think you'll like her even more when you meet her. Because frankly she's – she's – (*He shakes his head.*) And I'll tell you something – I don't know whether you've noticed but since she came back I've stopped having all those ridiculous accidents. They were the bane of my life, even though I was always trying to make light of them. I suppose it's – it's something to do with needing – well, well, the right person, eh? Love. Let's face it. Love. Oh, I'd better get going. So see you at seven. It'll be nothing special, but my landlady wants to put on a celebration supper – she's already very fond of Daphne, by the way – and she said if I wanted to ask along a friend – and there's nobody I'd rather have –

QUARTERMAINE: Derek, I'm very – I'm very honoured –

MEADLE: Actually, you'd better make it six thirty, as it'll be more on the lines of a high tea. And if you could bring along a couple of bottles of wine –

QUARTERMAINE: My dear chap, I'll bring – I'll bring *champagne* – and – and – oh Lord, I'd forgotten! Oh no! I've already accepted an invitation for this evening.

MEADLE: Oh. What to?

QUARTERMAINE: Well, I can't make out, quite – I was in a bit of a haze when Melanie asked me, but she said something about friends and singing and dancing –

MEADLE: And you accepted?

QUARTERMAINE: Well yes. She seemed so – so anxious – and anyway –

MEADLE: But it's – it's – one of those evenings. What they sing is hymns and dancing is up and down and around and about and then that Nurse Grimes declares for Jesus – and then the rest of them follow suit, and then they all stand around and wait for you to do it – at least, that's how it went the night she got me along. She's trying to convert you.

QUARTERMAINE: Oh Lord – oh Lord –

(*The bell rings.*)

MEADLE: But I told you all about it –

QUARTERMAINE: Yes, but I'd forgotten – I mean she didn't mention Jesus –

MEADLE: Well, she won't let you get out of it now. (*During this, he has been getting ready to go, putting on his bicycle clips, etc.*) (*Off, from the garden, foreign voices, laughing, calling out, etc., some of them Japanese; among them* SACKLING's, *calling out goodnights, in the distance. Then:*)

SACKLING: (*Closer*) No, sorry, I really can't – I'm in a hurry – and anyway – most of the mallets are broken and there aren't enough balls – so goodnight – goodnight – (SACKLING *enters, as* MEADLE *speaks.*)

MEADLE: Well, I'll get you and Daphne together very soon – don't worry – (*Making to go.*) Here, Mark, guess what St John's got himself into – one of Melanie's evenings.

SACKLING: (*In a hurry, with books etc.*) Christ, you haven't, have you? (*He is clean-shaven, by the way.*) You *are* a chump, St John, you must have heard her going on about her dark night of the soul, after her mother died, and how Nurse Grimes introduced her to her sect and redeemed her – she's talked about nothing else for months and – and anyway I remember telling you how she tried it on me – don't you take anything in!

QUARTERMAINE: Yes, yes I did, but – but –

SACKLING: But you didn't know how to say no. Which, if I may say so, is both your charm and your major weakness.

QUARTERMAINE: Well, you never know – it may be – may be quite interesting – one has to – has to have a go at anything really – and I wasn't doing anything else this evening.

SACKLING: (*Who is now ready to go*) This evening! Yes, you bloody *are* doing something else this evening. You're going out to dinner.

QUARTERMAINE: What – where?

SACKLING: At my place – oh Christ! Don't say I forgot to invite you. Well you're invited. So there you are, saved from salvation. All you have to do is to tell Melanie that you'd forgotten –

QUARTERMAINE: Oh, this is terrible. You mean I'd be having dinner with you?

SACKLING: You *are* having dinner with us. It's obligatory. For one thing, I told Camelia I'd asked you – she's counting on you – we all are – even Tom, I promised him he could stay up an extra half-an-hour to see you again – you're always going on about looking forward to seeing him – (*He is putting on bicycle clips. The first time in the play.*)

QUARTERMAINE: But what about Melanie? I promised her –

SACKLING: Oh, to hell with Melanie! It's all a load of pathetic nonsense – and probably blasphemous, too, if one believed in God. Look, speaking as one of your best and oldest and dearest etc. – it's *crucial* that you come. Of the greatest importance. To me. You see. OK? Look, I've got to dash, I'm picking Tom up from school –
(*The sound of the door opening: footsteps.*)
Make sure (*to off*) that he turns up tonight, won't you? He's got himself into one of his usual messes – see you both at eight. (*He goes as:*)
(ANITA *enters. She has a look of weariness about her, is subtly less well-turned out than in previous scenes.*)

QUARTERMAINE: Oh don't say you and Nigel are going to be there too – oh – oh –

ANITA: Why can't you come?

QUARTERMAINE: Well I fell into one of those dozes again – you know how they keep coming over me suddenly – for a minute or so – and – and when I came out of it, there I was, right in the middle of this – this Melanie business.

ANITA: Poor St John.

QUARTERMAINE: But I can't just turn round to her now – she was so – well her eyes – I can't explain – very – well – and anyway I can't just turn round now and say sorry Melanie, something much better's turned up – oh, if only Mark hadn't forgotten! – but I suppose he knows I'm usually free – and – thought he had – or – but what do I do, Anita, Mark seems so – so determined, too. What do I do?

ANITA: I don't know. But come if you can. It's meant to be a reconciliation dinner, and you know how they usually turn out. So you'd be a great help, as the perfect outsider.

QUARTERMAINE: Well, you know I'd do anything – anything – to make sure that old Mark and his Camelia and little Tom too, of course, stay together.

ANITA: Oh, it's not them that need reconciling. They already are.

QUARTERMAINE: Oh.

ANITA: It's Mark and Nigel. Hasn't Mark told you anything about that?

QUARTERMAINE: No. Nothing. You mean old Mark and old Nigel – oh, Lord, but they're such friends, what happened?

ANITA: Oh, it was all a couple of months ago. They had the most appalling row, because Nigel turned down an extract from Mark's novel. About seven extracts, actually.

SACKLING: Oh no. Oh, poor Mark!

ANITA: Well, Nigel made everything worse by deciding to be completely honest for once. I suppose he thought Mark, being an old friend, had it coming to him. What he said was that everything Mark had sent him was imitative and laboured, and anyway who really cared any more about the mysteries of sex, the wonders of childbirth, the delicacies of personal relationships – it had all been done and done and done to death, there were far bigger issues.

QUARTERMAINE: Oh Lord, oh Lord! Are there?

ANITA: So of course when the magazine folded, and Nigel was going through his rough patch, with the printers threatening to sue and various other things, Mark wrote him a gloating letter saying how delighted he was as *Reports* had never been interested in serious literary values, only in pandering to the top names – or trying to – and added a PS about the old Amanda Southgate affair, claiming to be indignant on my account, I must say, I rather wish he'd resisted that.

QUARTERMAINE: But still – but still – he has asked Nigel to dinner –

ANITA: Oh, that was probably Camelia. She never took literature seriously, and now that Mark's sworn off writing – at least for the time – the important thing for her is that we had them to dinner just before she left Mark, and now she's come back she's realized she owes us the return. I loathe the thought of it – for one thing we haven't been able to find a baby-sitter, so we'll have to bring Ophelia in her carry-cot – she's still got

six weeks colic, after four months – so it would be nice if you
came, St John, you'd make the whole thing more bearable.

QUARTERMAINE: Oh, I'd love to – and to see Ophelia – I've only
seen her the once, in hospital – what hair she had!

(ANITA *laughs. Is in fact crying slightly.*)

Oh Anita – what is it – oh, Lord, I hate to see you unhappy –
more than anyone else – (*He makes a move towards her, checks
himself, makes a move again.*) Oh Lord! (*He stands before her,
helplessly.*)

ANITA: I'm all right, St John, honestly – it's just that – oh, the way
things go, I mean. Or don't go. Nothing seems to come out
right. All the years I adored him and he couldn't bear me. And
now he adores me and I can't bear him. You see. (*She looks at
him.*) What a – what a nice man you are. (*She begins to cry
again.*) I'm tired, I expect, tired – (*Turning away, blowing her
nose, wiping her eyes, etc., as:*)

(*The sound of the door opening: footsteps.*)

QUARTERMAINE: (*Turning*) Oh – oh hello Henry, you've finished –
finished late – um –

WINDSCAPE: (*Appearing rather heavily*) Yes, I got into a bit of a
tangle with my Intermediary British Life and Institutions,
over our parliamentary system. Usually it's perfectly clear to
me but this time it all came out rather oddly. Or it must have
done, as I had the whole lot of them dismissing it with
contempt – the three or four from the Eastern bloc, all the
ones from Fascist countries, the Spanish, the Portuguese, the
South Americans – the French were the loudest, as always –
but even the Japanese – normally such a polite, reticent man –
and I don't see quite how it happened or what I said, but it was
rather hard being lectured at on – on political decencies – and
shouted at by – by – still, I suppose it's better they should all
join up for a wrangle with me than with each other – although
to tell you the truth I found it rather hard to keep my temper
(*sitting down*) but I think I managed to – with the result that
I've got a – a slight headache. After all, I was only *explaining*
our constitution, not boasting about it. I've got my own – own
distinct reservations – no system's perfect, as I kept having to
say to Santos. His father's a Bolivian cabinet minister.

ANITA: (*Who has been discreetly composing herself during the above*)
It's awful when they get like that, isn't it? I always make
them explain our politics to me, and then just correct their
English, whatever they say – one of the advantages of being
female, I suppose – (*she attempts a little laugh*) well,
goodnight, Henry, see you Monday –

WINDSCAPE: 'Night, Anita, my dear. Best to Nigel, and little
Ophelia –

ANITA: And St John, see you later I hope. Do, if you can.

QUARTERMAINE: Yes, well – I'll – I'll – right, Anita. Right. If I
can.

(ANITA *goes out through the french windows. There is a pause.*
WINDSCAPE *is sitting in the chair, stroking his forehead.*)
(*Is standing in a state of desperation*) I say, Henry – I say – I
wonder if you could give me some advice.

WINDSCAPE: Mmmm?

QUARTERMAINE: I'm in a bit of a pickle, you see.

WINDSCAPE: Oh. Oh good heavens, St John, that reminds me –
I'd completely forgotten – is there any chance you could
come over tonight?

QUARTERMAINE: What?

WINDSCAPE: I'm sorry it's such short notice, it wouldn't have
been if I'd remembered. The thing is that Fanny's really very
down in the dumps, very down, she really does need an
evening out. So do I, come to that. It's Susan, you see. She's
taken a turn for the worse.

QUARTERMAINE: Oh – oh –

WINDSCAPE: Oh, it's probably just withdrawal from all the
tranquillizing drugs they put her on, in hospital, and then
her friends would keep coming over in the evenings and
talking about their plans and their blasted A levels and of
course there's no possibility that Susan – at least for a few
years – anyway, last night, she laughed at something on
television, a good sign, Fanny and I thought, the first time
she's laughed since her breakdown, so we didn't realize until
we were in the living-room that what we were laughing at
was a news flash to do with some particular hideous atrocity
in – in – (*he gestures*) and what followed was a bit of a

nightmare, especially for Ben and little Fanny – it ended
with the doctor having to sedate her – almost forcibly, I'm
afraid – so – so I noticed *La Règle du Jeu* at the Arts, one of
our favourite films, so decent and – and humane – and then a
quiet dinner afterwards at the French place – just the two of
us – if you could manage it. You're the only person Susan
will allow to baby-sit, you see. She seems to feel some – some
reassurance from you. And of course little Fanny and
Benjamin love it too, when you come.

QUARTERMAINE: I'd love to, Henry – love to – but could it be
Saturday?

WINDSCAPE: No, Saturday's no good – we have our family
therapy session in the afternoon and we all feel so – so
exhausted afterwards. Demoralized, really. I've still to be
persuaded that they serve a – a useful – though of course one
mustn't prejudge –

QUARTERMAINE: Sunday, then?

WINDSCAPE: Unfortunately Fanny's mother's coming on
Sunday. Rather against our inclinations as – as she's rather
insensitive with Susan – advises her to pull her socks up –
that sort of thing – you can't manage this evening then.

QUARTERMAINE: Well, I – I – you see the problem is – I can't –
(*The sound of the door opening: footsteps.* MELANIE *appears.
She has changed her dress, is wearing high-heeled shoes, some
make-up, and has taken much trouble with her hair.*)

MELANIE: Well, there we are then, St John – sorry to have been
so long – oh, hello, Henry, I didn't know you were still here.

WINDSCAPE: Hello Melanie (*Slightly awkward.*) Oh, I've been
meaning to say all day how much I like that dress.

MELANIE: (*Smiles*) Thank you. I'm taking St John to one of my
evenings –

WINDSCAPE: Oh. Oh yes. I'm so sorry that Fanny and I have
been unable to come so far –

MELANIE: Oh, I know how difficult things are for you at the
moment – as long as you both realize that any time you want
to come along, I've been thinking that perhaps Susan
might –

WINDSCAPE: Yes, yes, thank you, Melanie. (*Cutting her slightly.*)

MELANIE: Are you all right, you look a little fraught.

WINDSCAPE: Oh just tired, Friday eveningish, that's all.

QUARTERMAINE: And a bit of a headache – eh Henry?

MELANIE: Oh? Where?

WINDSCAPE: Well – in my head.

MELANIE: Yes, but which part?

WINDSCAPE: Well, it seems to be – just here – (*Rubbing his brow.*)

MELANIE: Ah, well then it's a tension headache, Nurse Grimes showed me a marvellous trick for dealing with that, let me have a go at it. (*She comes over to* WINDSCAPE, *behind the chair.*) Now put your head forward – right forward – (WINDSCAPE *does so, with perceptible lack of enthusiasm.*)

MELANIE: There. Now. (*She proceeds to knead her fingers into the back of* WINDSCAPE'*s neck.*)

QUARTERMAINE: So that's how they do it – looks jolly relaxing, anyway –
(WINDSCAPE *endures for a few seconds, then suddenly lets out a cry, leaps up. There is a pause.*)

WINDSCAPE: I'm – Melanie, I'm sorry – I – don't know quite what –

MELANIE: I expect I hurt you, pressed the wrong nerve or – I still haven't quite got the trick of it, with my clumsy –

WINDSCAPE: Well – well actually it feels a little better. (*He tries a laugh.*) Thank you.

MELANIE: (*Smiles*) Well, St John, we'd better be on our way. It's quite a drive. Goodnight, Henry, and rest yourself during the weekend, won't you?

WINDSCAPE: Yes, yes – the same to you (*a slight hesitation*) my dear. Goodnight, St John, see you Monday.

QUARTERMAINE: See you Monday Henry and – oh, if it turns out that Saturday or Sunday – well, I'm sure I'll be free –
(WINDSCAPE *smiles, nods. As they go out through the french windows there is the sound of the door opening and feet, a stick.*)

WINDSCAPE: Oh hello Eddie, I didn't know you were about today.

LOOMIS: (*Enters. He is much frailer than when last seen.*) Well, there was a frightful schmozzle in the office – and Thomas asked me to come down – but was that St John's voice I heard just now?

WINDSCAPE: Yes. His and Melanie's –

LOOMIS: Ah. Well, I would have quite liked a word with our St
John. He's caused us quite an afternoon. He appears to have
missed his class entirely. His students waited doggedly
through the whole hour for him to turn up, and then went to
the office and berated poor Thomas – they were mostly
Germans, and you know what they're like if they think
they're not getting their money's worth of syllabus.

WINDSCAPE: Oh dear.

LOOMIS: Though I doubt whether they'd get much more sensible
English from St John present than from St John absent – as
far as I know that Swiss Ferdinand Boller is the only student
who ever felt he got value for money from St John, thank
goodness he's stopped sending those postcards at last, they
made Thomas quite upset – but I wonder what it was he
enjoyed so much about St John's classes – perhaps the lack of
– of – I don't know what we're going to do about him in the
end, though, if we turned him out where would he go, who
else would have him, one does look after one's own, I
suppose, when it comes to it I agree with Thomas on that,
after all the school's our – our family, the only family
Thomas and I have between us, so one has a responsibility
for them – but a responsibility for the students too – (*There
should be a slightly rambling quality in the delivery of this speech*)
it's so difficult to get the balance right – so difficult – St John
forgetting to teach them, and now Melanie's starting up her
missionary work amongst them, – Thomas is going to have a
word with her too – the Catholic countries won't stand for it,
and why should they, and now our Meadle, taking to
slipping away before the bell now he's got his permanency,
trying to bluff his way past me in the hall as if I couldn't see
him – ha – well, at least Mark's pulling his weight now he's
got his Camelia back, I never thought for a moment there
was a writer in that lad, did you? – and Anita – really I don't
know how these modern young couples cope – but I gather
Nigel's taken to it wonderfully, Thomas and I saw the three
of them on the Backs the other day, a very pretty sight it was
too – so – so – good, good, – just the problems of a
flourishing school, eh? (*He laughs.*)

WINDSCAPE: Yes. Yes indeed, Eddie.

LOOMIS: Well, I'd best get back up to bed, or Thomas will have a fit, goodnight Henry, see you Monday, bless you, bless you.

WINDSCAPE: Yes, see you Monday Eddie.

LOOMIS: (*Goes off, stops*) Oh, I haven't asked for a while – how's our Susan?

WINDSCAPE: Oh I think responding – slowly – slowly responding.

LOOMIS: Good, good. (*The sound of the door closing.*)

(*During this, the sound of students' voices, young, distant, in the garden. They get closer as the scene concludes.* WINDSCAPE *stands for a moment, touches his forehead, then goes to his locker, puts away his books, gets his briefcase. The sound of students' voices, probably two girls, two boys, now laughing, calling out to each other in some sort of game.* WINDSCAPE *gets out his bicycle clips, bends to put them on. As he does so he looks towards the french windows, smiles slightly, continues putting on the clips, as the sound of voices, still raised in laughter, continues.*)

(*Curtain.*)

SCENE 3

Eighteen months later. It is around Christmas. Not yet dark, but darkening slightly. The french windows are closed, but the curtains are open. There is an atmosphere of chill. One table-light is on.
SACKLING, QUARTERMAINE, MELANIE, ANITA, WINDSCAPE *and* MEADLE *are variously sitting and standing.* SACKLING *is smoking a pipe. He has a beard.* WINDSCAPE *is also smoking a pipe.* ANITA *is pregnant.* MEADLE *has a plaster neck-brace.* QUARTERMAINE *is wearing a dinner-jacket.* MELANIE *is sitting, rather hunched, nervously smoking a cigarette. It is the first time in the play that she has smoked. She smokes throughout the scene, lighting one after another. After a pause:*

SACKLING: It's always at Christmas, somehow, isn't it?

WINDSCAPE: Yes.

SACKLING: Oh Henry, I'm sorry –

WINDSCAPE: No. You're right. I was thinking much the same

thing. Both my parents too, but – but of course in Susan's case I don't think the season was – was relevant. At least to her. The blinds were always down, you see. Because any brightness hurt her mind. Natural brightness, that is. She could tolerate artificial light. Until the last – last bit.

ANITA: (*There is a faint touch of querulousness in her voice*) Look. I'm sorry, but I'll have to go soon, I'm afraid. I promised the *au pair* she could have the night off, and Nigel's probably not coming back from London until tomorrow –

MEADLE: Yes, I've got to get back pretty soon. Daphne's not too grand, what with her morning sickness and all the redecorating – she's been over-doing it and I promised – I don't want to leave her alone too long.

WINDSCAPE: Of course – of course – there's really no need for all of us when it comes to it – it's just that – that – as soon as I heard I had some idea that you would want – well – without perhaps enough consideration – it was a bad idea, perhaps –

QUARTERMAINE: Oh, I say Henry – well, I'm jolly glad you got in touch with me – though of course I wasn't doing anything in particular –

SACKLING: Well, I must say, St John (*smiling*) you do look as if you might have been about to be up to something –

QUARTERMAINE: What? Oh – (*laughs*) well, no, no, not really – it was just – just –

(*During this, the sound of the door opening. They all look towards it: the sound of footsteps, dragging feet, a stick.*)

LOOMIS: (*In an overcoat, with a stick, and with a deaf-aid attached to his glasses*) I saw the lights on so I guessed that some of you – one or two perhaps – had come. But I didn't expect all of you. Not at this time of year, with your families and responsibilities. Thomas would have been so touched. So touched. My thanks on his behalf. My thanks. (*A little pause.*) He died an hour ago. They did everything they could, right to the end, but of course, as we've all known for some time, there was nothing to be done. (*A little pause.*) You know how much you all meant to him. He talked of every one of you, every evening, until – (*He gestures.*) But you'll also want to know what its future is to be, this school that he loved so much. I know what his wishes are, we discussed them quite openly once we both knew that he was bound to leave us. I've also talked to Henry. I'm sure it will be no surprise to all of you that I asked Henry some time ago to take over the school as its sole Principal. I've no desire to take an active part in it, now that Thomas is no longer here. I loved it for his sake, you see. I'll make no secret of that. Not this evening. (*A pause, nearly breaks down, pulls himself together*.) Not this evening. I shall be leaving the flat as soon as possible – it has too many memories – and settle somewhere by the sea. As we'd always hoped to do. I hope that some of you will come and see me – (*A little pause*.) Bless you. Bless you. (*He turns and goes. The sound of his feet dragging slowly. The sound of the door shutting*.)

(*There is a pause*.)

WINDSCAPE: I – I really don't want to speak at such a moment about plans or changes. We'll have a meeting at the beginning of term to go into those, but I should just say that I've already talked to Mark, – at Eddie's suggestion and with Thomas's approval – a few weeks ago, when it became clear that Thomas was more than seriously ill – about his following me as the academic tutor. I am happy to say that he has accepted.

(*There are murmurs*.)

So until next term – which has a very reasonable enrolment, I am glad to report, let me merely assure you that I intend to do my best, as I know you will, to maintain our reputation as a – a flourishing school. I know – I know – Thomas and Eddie wouldn't want me to let you part without wishing you all a Happy Christmas.

(*Murmurs of 'Happy Christmas'*.)

Well, see you all next term!

(*They rise to go, putting on coats, etc*.)

QUARTERMAINE: (*Comes over to* WINDSCAPE) Henry – I say, well you and Mark – that's quite a team, you know.

WINDSCAPE: Thank you, St John – I wonder if you could hang on a minute or so.

QUARTERMAINE: Absolutely. Oh absolutely, Henry.

SACKLING: (*Coated*) Well, night Henry – we'll speak. And St John – over the Christmas, eh? You must come round. (*Gesturing with his pipe.*)

WINDSCAPE: Yes, we'll speak, Mark.

QUARTERMAINE: Oh, I'd love that – thanks Mark. See you then. Love to Camelia and Tom and little Mark too.

ANITA: (*Also coated*) Sorry if I was a little edgy earlier Henry. Put it down to my current condition and Yugoslav au pairs! (*She laughs.*)

WINDSCAPE: You get home to your Ophelia, my dear, and make Nigel look after you.

ANITA: Oh, I will, Henry – see you over Christmas, St John, I hope.

QUARTERMAINE: Oh Lord yes – lovely – lovely – 'night, Anita.

MEADLE: (*Coated*) Sorry Daphne couldn't make it, Henry. She wanted to, of course. But I'll fill her in, don't worry, she's very much looking forward to her courses next term –

WINDSCAPE: And I'm looking forward to having her join us. Goodnight, Derek.

MEADLE: Drop around when you feel in the mood, St John. Lots of paint-brushes for you to wield – (*He laughs.*)

QUARTERMAINE: Terrific! I love the smell of paint – love to Daphne –

MELANIE: (*Comes up, hunched, smoking*) 'Night Henry. 'Night.

WINDSCAPE: Night Melanie my dear. And perhaps we can all get together after Christmas – Fanny was saying how much she'd like to see you, after all this time.

MELANIE: Love to, love to, and St John, if you're free pop around and have a drink. (*She laughs.*)

QUARTERMAINE: Oh yes please Melanie – I'd like that – (*As* SACKLING, ANITA, MEADLE, *and* MELANIE *leave, one after the other, the sound of their feet, and of the door opening and closing.* QUARTERMAINE *and* WINDSCAPE *are left alone on stage.*)

WINDSCAPE: Well, St John – (*He hesitates.*) Where were you off to, tonight, by the way?

QUARTERMAINE: Oh Lord, nowhere Henry. (*He laughs.*) You see, there was a suitcase I still hadn't unpacked – it's been down in Mrs Harris's cellar all these years. But suddenly she wanted the space, so she made me take it up, and of course I opened it and there was this, (*indicating the dinner-jacket*.) So I decided to try it on, to see if it still fits. And then you phoned, and Mrs Harris was doing her usual thing right beside me, glowering away (*laughs*) so – so I came straight on out here, forgetting I had it on. Stinks of moth-balls, I'm afraid, but not a bad fit, eh? Might come in useful sometime. But I say, poor old Eddie, poor old Eddie. Wasn't he – wasn't he terrific!

WINDSCAPE: Yes. Indeed. (*A slight pause*.) St John. St John. I've been worrying about this for – oh, ever since I realized I was to take over from Eddie and Thomas. If I'm to be principal, I have to run the school in my own way, you see.

QUARTERMAINE: Oh, I know that, Henry. We all do.

WINDSCAPE: And – and – I don't see, you see – however fond of you I happen to be – we all happen to be – that there's – there's any room for you anymore. You see?

(QUARTERMAINE *nods*.)

I thought it only right to tell you at the first – the very first possible moment. So that you can – well, look around –

QUARTERMAINE: No, that's – right, thank you Henry. I – oh Lord, I know that I haven't got much to offer – never had, I suppose – and recently it's got even worse – it's a wonder – a wonder people have put up with me so long, eh? (*He attempts a laugh*.)

WINDSCAPE: If I could see any way –

QUARTERMAINE: No, no – I mean, it's no good being all right in the staff-room if you're no good in the classroom, is it? They're different things.

WINDSCAPE: I can't tell you how much I'll miss you. We all will.

QUARTERMAINE: And I – I'll miss it. All of you.

WINDSCAPE: Yes, I know. Would you like a quick drink – or – or – come back and see Fanny.

QUARTERMAINE: Oh, no – no thank you Henry, I'll stay here for a while – you know – and get myself used to – used to – and – I'll go in a minute.

WINDSCAPE: (*Hesitates, looks at* QUARTERMAINE) Well, goodnight, St John.

73

QUARTERMAINE: Goodnight, Henry, see you next – (*He gestures.*)
(WINDSCAPE *goes off. The sound of feet and the door opening
and closing.*)
Oh Lord! (*He walks a few steps, stops, shakes his head, sits
down.*) Well – oh Lord! I say – (*He sits in silence, shaking his
head, gradually stops shaking his head, sits in stillness.*) Oh
Lord!
(*Lights. Curtain.*)

The Rear Column

To the memory of Clive Goodwin,
to whom I owe more than I can say

The Rear Column was presented by Michael Codron on
22 February 1978 at the Globe Theatre, London. The cast was as
follows:

BONNY	Donald Gee
JAMESON	Jeremy Irons
WARD	Simon Ward
TROUP	Clive Francis
BARTTELOT	Barry Foster
STANLEY	Michael Forrest
JOHN HENRY	Riba Akabusi
NATIVE WOMAN	Dorrett Thompson
Director	Harold Pinter
Designer	Eileen Diss
Lighting	Nick Chelton
Costumes	Elizabeth Walker

ACT ONE

SCENE I

A large store-room in the Yambuya Camp, on the banks of the
Arruwimi River, the Congo. It is June, 1887. Late afternoon.
There are boxes back left and back right of stage. Between them, back
stage centre, large double doors. A canvas flap, stage right. A large
table, centre stage. Some travelling chests which also serve as chairs.
Stage left, a travelling desk and a chair, a settee. The double doors are
partly open, to let in light. There are two turtles, attached by lengths of
string to the table legs.

BONNY is studying the room, clearly having just entered it for the first
time. He goes to the work desk, gives something on it a cursory, rather
contemptuous glance, goes over to the table, lets out an exclamation,
picks up a turtle, then the other one. Puts them on the table.

JAMESON: (*Enters through flap*) Oh, Mr Bonny – you've met
    Herman and King, I see.

BONNY: Oh. I was hoping I'd met some soup.

JAMESON: (*Laughs*) One evening, no doubt. But one needs time
    to prepare.

BONNY: It doesn't take long to boil up a pair of turtles, does it?

JAMESON: I meant for the loss.

BONNY: What, they're pets, are they?

JAMESON: Well, they've kept the Major and myself company
    through some pretty lonely times. When he was ill, they
    were all I had to talk to, and when I was ill I used to imagine
    the three of them passing riotous evenings together. I got
    them from one of the village chiefs on my first trip out after
    Stanley's departure. He assumed I was a slaver, come to steal
    his wife and ransom her for food. He offered me these before
    I could put him straight – I couldn't speak much of the lingo
    then.

BONNY: What was the wife like?

JAMESON: I didn't see her, but I'm sure she wouldn't have made
    into soup.

BONNY: No, but she might have done for a pet. Then when you'd

79

finished with her, you could have traded her in for the soup.

JAMESON: (*Laughs politely*) This one's Herman because he reminds me of a German Professor of Zoology under whom I once studied, and this is King because he reminded the Major of the horse on which he was taught to ride, as a child in Sussex. Two patient, comforting, slow-witted fellows from our past, whose own pasts go far further back than ours. If you look at Herman's markings, you'll see he must be nearly a hundred.

BONNY: Oh. (*He looks quickly, without interest.*)

JAMESON: While King is a mere stripling of some six decades. I'm sorry to ramble on. One's got out of the habit of succinctness these last two months. Where are your two companions, by the way?

BONNY: Troup's dealing with his Soudanese, and Ward with his Zanzibaris.

JAMESON: You've got your men down already have you, good.

BONNY: Oh, I didn't have charge of any men – as I'm the one with medical training Mr Stanley made me responsible for the mules.

JAMESON: Did they give you a bad time?

BONNY: Let's say we only understood each other when I was having them fed.

JAMESON: In that respect, they don't seem too unlike the men.

BONNY: A bit unlike your men, in that they were at least fed. I took a stroll around the compound after I'd done with the brutes. You're in a bad way here, aren't you? A very bad way. (*Pause.*) How many have you lost?

JAMESON: Nineteen Zanzibaris, twelve Soudanese.

BONNY: Well, you'll lose a few more tonight. Fever, ulcers on the back and legs – malnutrition, in other words. What have the poor devils been eating?

JAMESON: Much the same as the Major and myself. The odd fish they buy from the natives, or a goat, sometimes a fowl. But the staple diet is the manioc root. For the Soudanese, that is. The Zanzibaris won't eat meat, so for them it's manioc and more manioc. Of course they won't cook it properly. The manioc has to be boiled slowly and then drained. They toss it

into the pot then swallow it straight down. It frequently
swells in their stomachs . . .

(WARD *enters*.)

The Major and I have given at least twenty cooking
demonstrations between us. But they pay no attention.

BONNY: Was it like this when Mr Stanley was here?

JAMESON: Perhaps the Soudanese had a little more meat, and the
Zanzibaris a little more fish, as Mr Stanley is famously clever
at trading with the natives. But some of the Zanzibaris had
begun to die before he left.

WARD: In other words, you've been having a rather grim time.

JAMESON: It's not particularly pleasant to watch men dying. They
seem, the Zanzibaris especially, to settle into death before
they become properly ill – as if death itself were the disease.
They lie in their own dung waiting – the flies come up – well,
you've seen and smelt for yourselves. At first we tried to keep
them on the move, our policy was work and more work, but
once we'd built the palisades and fenced ourselves in there
was no work, to speak of. We can't let them out except in
small details to gather wood, and even then they try to
quarrel with the natives or what's worse trade them their
guns for food. And as we'd rather be surrounded by natives
who are reasonably friendly and unarmed . . . So we're left
with the camp routine, and that's not adequate. These men
are porters by nature, used to marching for long periods and
to camping for short ones.

WARD: So the fact of it is, they're dying of hunger and boredom.

JAMESON: In a sense, Mr Ward. Though it doesn't quite catch the
feeling of the two months they've spent doing it in.

WARD: And how many have died of a flogging?

JAMESON: (*After a pause*) One.

WARD: But there's been more than one flogging, I take it? I saw a
creature out there whose back was in ribbons.

JAMESON: There have been several floggings, Mr Ward. Once
they'd realized they could get a chicken or some fish or even
a goat for their rifles, and once they'd started thieving – the
Major began by issuing warnings, and when they didn't take
was forced to back them up with floggings.

WARD: Which doubtless haven't taken either.

JAMESON: An old debate, Mr Ward. We have no way of knowing, have we? how many we've deterred. We only know how many haven't been. You blame us for it, then?

WARD: Good God, no. Once you start, you have to go on, and nobody's yet discovered an alternative to starting. I can't really see that there's anything here to surprise. Constant sickness punctuated by regular floggings – the inevitable conditions of a large, stationary camp in the Congo. The only solution is to get moving as quickly as possible.

JAMESON: Amen to that!

TROUP: (*Enters*) It appears I'm not to get one after all, can you believe it? It's not enough that we find Stanley gone in spite of his reassurances that he'd wait on us, it's not enough that we were misled on that, but it turns out that after weeks of hard travelling by day and the utmost misery and discomfort at night, I'm still to be deprived – what the devil am I to do?

WARD: Mr Troup is talking of a bed, Mr Jameson.

JAMESON: A bed? But weren't you issued with a bed in London?

TROUP: Oh yes, Mr Jameson, I was issued with one, and here's my chit to prove it – you see, it entitles me to one bed at the expedition's expense. When I met with Mr Stanley at the Falls, I presented him with this chit, signed by Mr MacKinnon of the Committee, and he said that as all the beds were packed in the steamer, I'd have to wait until we met up here. Well, here I am, and here's my chit, but as there's no Stanley, there's no bed. (*He laughs bitterly*.) Anyway, that'll teach me a little savvy. I saw a bed lying free on the wharf at the Falls, but I refrained from taking it. And what happened? Old Ward here took it instead. He was quite right, by God, if I'd known the plight my scruples were to land me in, I'd have fought him for it, I would you know, Ward!

WARD: Yes, old chap, I know, but look, there must be a spare bed somewhere in the Camp, there always is.

TROUP: Oh yes, three. Three spare beds. But according to the Major, they belong to Mr Stanley, and are on no account to be touched. According to the Major. Though why the devil he thinks Stanley would object –

JAMESON: Mr Troup, I think I can help you. Mr Parke brought up an extra bed for Jephson, who fortunately brought his own. Parke asked me to add it to the loads for him, but he and I are good friends, I'm sure he wouldn't mind my letting you have the use of it.

TROUP: What? You mean there is a bed – I shall have a bed – tonight, you mean?

JAMESON: This very minute, if you like.

TROUP: No, no, it's just that – (*laughs*) after sleeping on wet grass between damp blankets – or propped against trees – I can hardly grasp – it's uncommonly kind of you, Mr Jameson, thank you.

BARTTELOT: (*Enters, through the flap, carrying a wooden stick with a metal tip.*) Ah, Mr Troup, Mr Ward, here you are, I've been looking for you, and Mr Bonny. We must be careful that your Soudanese, Mr Troup, and your Zanzibaris, Mr Ward, are kept separate from those already in the camp. We've had a bout of sickness, as you've probably noticed, and there's no point the fresh men being contaminated. We'll have to put guards on them or they'll drift – they'll drift – and Mr Bonny, your mules, a guard on those too, if you please. Mule meat is something of a delicacy with the Soudanese – with Mr Jameson and myself, come to think of it, eh Jamie? (*He laughs.*) Well, gentlemen, by this time you'll have some idea of our situation. I've no doubt you're as disappointed to find Mr Stanley gone as Mr Jameson and I were when we were left behind to wait for you. But he was anxious to make all possible speed to Emin Pasha, and pull him out before the Mahdi gets to him and with luck we'll either catch him up or not be too far behind him.

BONNY: As I understand it, we have to wait on for more porters.

BARTTELOT: Yes, Mr Bonny, another six hundred. We have nine hundred loads, each one of which Mr Stanley believes essential – food, quinine, rifles – and including the ones you've brought up just over three hundred porters. So we can't move until we have the other six hundred.

TROUP: Where are they going to come from? As Bonny, Ward and I were the only officers left behind –

BARTTELOT: They're being brought up by Tippu-Tib.

WARD: Tippu-Tib!

BARTTELOT: That's right, Mr Ward. Tippu-Tib. He and Mr Stanley came to an arrangement here before Stanley set out.

BONNY: Who is Tippu-Tib?

WARD: He's an Arab slave trader. Half Arab that is, and half Manyema. Which makes him wholly abominable.

BARTTELOT: But a particular friend of Mr Stanley's. You know him then?

WARD: By reputation, of course. No one who's spent any time in this part of the Congo could fail to. And I've come across his auxiliaries, who usually turn out to be his relatives as well. I've also come across his victims. I met poor Deane at Stanley Falls a year ago, just after the Arabs had burnt him out.

JAMESON: But on that occasion Tippu-Tib wasn't the Arab responsible.

WARD: Oh, Tippu is always the Arab responsible. This country is really his bazaar, you see, and the people in it his merchandise, and every Arab a relative, and every relative an agent.

BARTTELOT: Nevertheless, as I said, he and Mr Stanley are the greatest of friends.

WARD: They both choose their friends wisely.

JAMESON: And they have an agreement for the porters.

BONNY: When is he expected then, Major, with the porters?

BARTTELOT: Mr Stanley couldn't be precise. But he was hoping they'd arrive shortly after you.

BONNY: Any day now then.

WARD: Did you yourselves take part in these arrangements with Tippu-Tib?

BARTTELOT: No, Mr Stanley and Tippu-Tib kept themselves to themselves during the time the Arabs were in the Camp. None of the other officers had the pleasure of being introduced to him either, he has an aversion to any shows of white strength, apparently, we scarcely got a glimpse of him.

TROUP: And this is the man we're to wait for! An Arab slaver who distrusts white men –

84

JAMESON: He doesn't distrust Mr Stanley.

BONNY: Have you heard anything of him since he left?

JAMESON: Oh, just rumours. A few weeks ago the natives were full of talk of Arabs, I went over to explore but couldn't find any trace – the natives have a particular interest in Arabs, of course, they fear them as slavers but desire them as food.

TROUP: Food!

JAMESON: They believe they can take their cunning into their own systems, by eating them.

TROUP: But look here – do you mean to say – I thought cannibalism had been wiped out in these parts, by Stanley himself when he was here before. There was a long report in *The Times*, only last year –

WARD: The local chiefs probably haven't received their copies yet.

JAMESON: (*Laughs*) The problem is, Mr Troup, that it's hard to wipe out an appetite. Mr Stanley made the chiefs promise to stop gobbling each other up –

WARD: As he made the slavers promise to give up slaving. A promise in the jungle may become a fact in London, but you don't believe that Tippu-Tib is going to hire our six hundred men, do you? Or that Stanley believes he is.

TROUP: But good God – good God – Stanley told us nothing of this sort of thing in London. We signed on to march direct to the relief of Emin Pasha – and instead here we are hanging about waiting for some brigand of an Arab to enslave some porters –

BARTTELOT: While outside there are cannibals and inside three hundred hungry and contagious niggers. Exactly, Mr Troup. That is our situation, and will remain our situation until Tippu-Tib arrives to release us from it.

WARD: What is Mr Stanley's alternative proposal?

BARTTELOT: Alternative to what?

WARD: In the event of Tippu's not turning up shortly. He's notorious for a number of things, but not for his punctuality. At least I've never heard of it.

BARTTELOT: There is no alternative.

WARD: But in the event of his not turning up at all.

BARTTELOT: There is still no alternative. Mr Stanley will accept
no alternative to the safety of his loads. He is clear that he
expects them and must have them. There is no alternative,
Mr Ward. Tippu-Tib must turn up. And until he does we
shall have to make the best of it.

WARD: But surely – (*He stops.*)

JAMESON: You'll be wanting to settle into your quarters – there's
a shower behind my tent. The water comes up from the
Arruwimi, it's dirty, warm and it smells, I'm afraid, but it's
wet.

BARTTELOT: We've been in the habit of eating at sun-down, if
that suits you. We've kept a goat specially for this occasion –
though we've been tempted by it often enough, haven't we,
Jamie? – so at least this first night you'll have meat rather
than manioc. By the way, an unnecessary warning, I'm sure,
but anything you have in the way of provisions should be
kept locked in your trunks – they're not above trying to slip
into the tents, we caught one just the other day – and your
rifles, goes without saying.

WARD: Actually, Major, I've no provisions whatsoever. So I'd be
very glad to have what's coming to me as soon as you can
manage it.

BONNY: Yes, I'm right out of tea.

BARTTELOT: I'm sorry, Mr Ward. There's nothing coming to you
that I know of.

TROUP: Six months' provisions, guaranteed by the Committee.

WARD: To be provided when we got our men up here.

BARTTELOT: I know nothing about it.

TROUP: But they must surely have been left behind by
Mr Stanley.

BARTTELOT: Very possibly. But as Mr Stanley left no instructions
on the matter, there's no way of knowing.

TROUP: But what about you and Jameson? Have you had yours?

BARTTELOT: Mr Stanley did give some out before he left, yes.
But he left me no authorization to give you any.

TROUP: My authorization comes from the Committee in London.

BARTTELOT: Then perhaps you should take it up with the
Committee in London.

WARD: Personally I shan't be needing jungle provisions in London, at least as long as there are still shops and restaurants there. Anyway, my chit is signed personally by Mr Stanley.

BARTTELOT: Then it's to Mr Stanley you must apply, when we catch up with him.

TROUP: We need our provisions now, sir.

BARTTELOT: I can't help you, sir.

TROUP: But you can, sir. They must be here, among the loads Mr Stanley left behind.

BARTTELOT: As Mr Stanley didn't say, how can you know that?

WARD: Ratiocination, possibly. In that if Mr Stanley owes us some provisions, which he does; and has left behind a large number of loads, which he has; and arranged for us to wait here with you, to help bring up those loads, which he did; then he's scarcely likely to have taken our provisions on with him; which one can therefore conclude he hasn't.

BARTTELOT: Are you making fun of me, sir!

WARD: No, Major. I was simply helping you to a conclusion.

BARTTELOT: Well, one may conclude anything with Mr Stanley, as a sure way of ending up in the wrong for it. But one thing one can be sure about, in the matter of Mr Stanley's intentions, is that his instructions are to be carried out to the very letter, and only to the very letter, however inconvenient that may be to the rest of the world. Mr Jameson will confirm that as Commanding Officer of this Rear Column, I must do as Mr Stanley said, but I may on no account do what I think he might have said, had he been here to say it. Isn't that so, Mr Jameson? I sympathize with you, of course, and if my Commanding Officer weren't Mr Stanley, you'd find your Commanding Officer a very much more obliging fellow, believe me.

TROUP: Do you mean to say that we're not to have our provisions simply because Stanley forgot to include them in his instructions.

BARTTELOT: But we cannot say that he forgot. He may well have remembered not to include them.

TROUP: And why should he do that?

BARTTELOT: Because – because – I don't know, how should I?

TROUP: This is nonsense, nonsense! You tell us we're not to have provisions which we were guaranteed as members of this expedition, provisions that do not belong personally to Mr Stanley, because in your view Mr Stanley is some sort of – some sort of – punctilious lunatic. Well sir, let me remind you that I have had dealings with Mr Stanley, and a saner and more practical man I've never met. Sir, I believe you're making us the victims of some private misunderstanding between Mr Stanley and yourself.

BARTTELOT: Have no fear of that, sir, there's no misunderstanding at all between Mr Stanley and myself. I understand him only too well. Certainly too well to allow myself to be the victim of your misfortune. He wouldn't hesitate to use this opportunity to ruin my career, my reputation at home –

WARD: (*After a pause*) Stanley will ruin your career and your reputation if you furnish us with provisions that are rightly ours?

BARTTELOT: Ask Mr Jameson if I'm overstating the case?

JAMESON: The Major has reason to be careful, where Mr Stanley's orders are in question. Mr Stanley on an expedition is a very different man from Mr Stanley on the Falls or sitting with Mr MacKinnon on the Committee in London. Jephson, Parke, Stairs – all the officers who've gone on with him would concur.

BARTTELOT: And it is through his orders, some of them impossible to perform, that he gets at us. He's as savage with initiative as he is with inefficiency. Well, he'll not get at me, sir, not any more. And I'm sorry if others must suffer for it.

TROUP: Can we see these orders, Major? As we're to be so strictly governed by them?

BARTTELOT: (*After a pause, during which he stares at* TROUP) You would have seen them in due course, Mr Troup, whether you'd requested to or not.

TROUP: (*Reads them through quickly*) There's very little to them, and what there is can scarcely be said to have been written in a spirit of animosity. (*Passing them to* WARD) Rather the reverse.

BARTTELOT: He knew that I would not be the only one to read them.

TROUP: I see he expressly requests you to take Mr Ward's, Mr
Bonny's and my advice – along with Mr Jameson's.

BARTTELOT: No, Mr Troup, he tells me to ask you for your
advice, not take it. The responsibility remains entirely mine.
It's in the same sentence – heed their advice while being
solely answerable for the decisions. At a first reading you will
fail to detect, as Mr Jameson and I failed to detect, the real
subtlety of what he's written. Or notice a major anomaly.

WARD: I certainly can't find an anomaly – or even much in the
way of subtlety. It's all most emphatic, down to the number
of brass-rods we're to pay to the porters per day.

BARTTELOT: The brass-rods – oh yes – he'd be emphatic about
the brass-rods. He knows the value of a brass-rod in the
Congo as a Jew knows a sovereign in Kensington.

JAMESON: But apart from the brass-rods he is emphatic. But
without being precise.

BARTTELOT: Exactly. Exactly. And look – see what he says about
the palisade.

WARD: (*Looks*) Merely that you're to build one. Which you have –
an admirable one. What could be more sensible?

BARTTELOT: Ah, but what follows the order – (*He recites.*) For
remember, it is not the natives alone who may wish to assail
you, but the Arabs and their followers may, through some
cause or other, quarrel with you and assail the camp.

WARD: Well?

BARTTELOT: Well, Mr Ward, you yourself have confirmed our
worst suspicion. By Arabs whom can he mean but Tippu-
Tib. So Stanley has gone out of his way to warn us against a
man he claims as his friend, on whom he has made us
depend, without whose arrival we cannot move!

WARD: But good God, of course he'd warn you! He knows better
than anyone – friend or not, Tippu-Tib is a very dangerous
man. But he also knows that Tippu is the only man in the
Congo who could raise six hundred porters, by whatever
means. Tippu is both totally indispensable and completely
untrustworthy. That is the nature of the beast!

JAMESON: But as you've pointed out, he leaves us with no
alternative.

WARD: And as Major Barttelot pointed out – with considerable force – there is no alternative. If the loads are essential, then the porters are essential. If the porters are essential –

TROUP: So is this Tippu-Tib. Exactly! I must say (*laughs*) if this is all!

BARTTELOT: It isn't all! Or rather it is all – and that's the damned subtlety of it. Not what he's put in, but what he's left out!

TROUP: Oh this is the sheerest – the sheerest – how could he cover every contingency – look, you tell us that Stanley always gets at you through his orders – well, surely you examined him on every sentence when he took you through them.

BARTTELOT: I did not.

TROUP: Why not?

BARTTELOT: Perhaps, Mr Troup, because he didn't take me through them.

TROUP: That's irregular, I admit – but then he's not a military man – but you could have gone to him yourself, I suppose you read them before he left?

BARTTELOT: You suppose incorrectly. Mr Stanley made it impossible – quite impossible – for me to read them until he'd marched out of the Camp.

TROUP: But the fact remains there is nothing there to prevent you giving us our provisions. Good God, man, can you not see – I have two ounces of sugar, an ounce of tea – Mr Ward tells you he has nothing – Mr Bonny is out of –

BONNY: Tea.

TROUP: And the only reason you offer for denying us is that Stanley hasn't actually written it down that you should give us them. As if he didn't have enough on his mind –

BARTTELOT: Mr Stanley's last verbal orders to me, delivered before Jephson and Stairs as witnesses, was that I was on no account to exceed his written orders. On no account!

TROUP: You were on no account to exceed written orders that he prevented you from reading until he'd gone?

BARTTELOT: This is a trivial subject, trivial! There are more important matters – look outside, sir, at the state of the niggers Stanley's left us with – he made sure to take only the

healthy with him – don't doubt that – there's sickness,
pilfering – and you fret at me with your tea and sugar – by
God, I've said my last word on the subject. The subject is
closed! (*He exits through the flap.*)

TROUP: Well, it's not clos⌐d as far as I'm concerned – I've no
intention –

JAMESON: Mr Troup, your bed. Shall we go and find it?

TROUP: What? Yes, yes, the bed! At least I have a bed! (*He laughs
bitterly.*) I'm much obliged to you, Mr Jameson. (*He follows
JAMESON through the flap.*)

WARD: I remember a governess rather similar to the Major. Her
most infuriating prohibitions always depended upon some
illogically spiteful but unuttered edict of my father's. It's no
good blaming me, it's your papa says no. But he hasn't said
no. But he would if you asked him. In fact our papa hadn't
the slightest interest in us, and would have said yes to
anything. Did you have a governess like that, Bonny?

BONNY: No. But this governess'll say yes, don't you worry.

WARD: What makes you think that?

BONNY: Mr Jameson's face.

WARD: Ah, I see. That's why you kept the peace, was it? Because
you'd read Mr Jameson's face?

BONNY: Well, there was no good going on at him, was there, it
just made him more determined.

WARD: And did you like him for that?

BONNY: I didn't like him or dislike him. I recognized him for
what he is.

WARD: And what's that?

BONNY: Our Commanding Officer. (*He exits.*)
(WARD *stares after him, then walks around the store-room, stops
to look at the turtles, then walks casually on to Jameson's desk,
picks up a sketch, studies it.* JAMESON *enters, as if expecting to
find the room empty. Stops on seeing* WARD.)

WARD: You've bedded old Troup, then?

JAMESON: He couldn't get off with it fast enough. He was
probably afraid I'd change my mind and wrestle it back from
him.

WARD: I was just admiring your work – it is yours, I take it?

JAMESON: Yes. A plover, he rested ten minutes on a branch right outside my tent this morning. I shall have to wait until I get home to do full justice to his colouring – the forehead's light brown – reddish brown, really – and the crest here (*coming over, pointing*) is blacker than I've managed with charcoal – so is the top of the head. And the cheeks are a delicate grey, as is the lower half of the throat. The whiteness of the paper is about right for the whiteness of the rest of the throat, but the wing crests are a wonderful ash-green – and no paper would serve for the white bar across the centre of the wing – and the eye – imagine an ochre iris around the black pupil.

WARD: That collection in one of the small huts – it's entirely yours then?

JAMESON: Why yes. Yes it is.

WARD: Good God, I thought it had been done by four men at least. A lepidopterist, an ornithologist, an entymologist and an ethnologist. What unified them must be the artist.

JAMESON: Or perhaps a dilettante, who separates them. Do you sketch, Mr Ward?

WARD: A little. Which is how I do most things. So I'm the dilettante, Mr Jameson, and now you've come face to face with the real article, you'll have to drop your pose. Unless, of course, it's assumed for the Major's sake.

JAMESON: Major Barttelot and I have been together in rather difficult circumstances recently. We've had to depend on each other too much, in sickness, and in health, to assume poses with each other.

WARD: Good Heavens, that sounds rather like a marriage!

JAMESON: I already have a marriage.

WARD: Really? And children?

JAMESON: (*After a pause*) Two. At least I trust and pray two. The second was due last month.

WARD: May I congratulate you. Not least on your wife, who must be very understanding.

JAMESON: She is, Mr Ward. Thank you.

WARD: Did Mr Stanley choose you to stay behind with the Major, or did the Major choose you, or did you choose yourself?

JAMESON: It was understood that Stairs was to be left behind, but

at the last moment Mr Stanley changed his mind, and
appointed me. Mr Stanley being Mr Stanley, he offered no
explanation. Have you any further questions?

WARD: I'm sorry, I've been impertinent. It's just that – look – I
know from my own experience of this continent how quickly
one can come to brood on a subject when cut off – isn't it
possible that you and the Major –

JAMESON: Went a trifle mad together? Yes, quite possible.
Nevertheless Stanley did threaten to destroy the Major's
reputation.

WARD: Why?

JAMESON: Perhaps the Major wasn't used to being spoken to as
Mr Stanley is used to speaking to gentlemen who accompany
him on his expeditions. And Mr Stanley was even less used
to being answered as the Major answered him.

WARD: And because of this – this clash of temperaments, Stanley
would go to the lengths of ruining a man –

JAMESON: At the moment, Stanley is almost as powerful in
London as he is in Africa. He'd only have to speak a few
words – and Stanley is too jealous of his own fame to care
much about another man's honour. The Major is a military
man from a military family. His honour means a great deal to
him.

WARD: Yet Stanley did make him Commanding Officer of his
Rear Column. That could be construed as an honour.

JAMESON: It could also be construed as one of his insults. The
Major was appointed Senior Officer to the Relief of Emin
Pasha, and has been left behind to guard the supplies. He is a
brave and active man, rendered temporarily inactive.

WARD: A sort of Samson, blinded and chained. And yet you were
left with him – so Stanley showed some compassion to the
Major. And to the rest of us, I suspect. Bonny has already
singled you out as the peacemaker.

JAMESON: We had all of us better keep the peace, Mr Ward.

WARD: Oh, I shan't give you any more trouble, my word on it.
And old Troup is really a decent enough fellow who's never
been to the Congo before and has been out of bed too long –
one good night'll probably settle him.

JAMESON: (*Laughs*) Well, you've only to settle Mr Bonny, and we shall be all right.

WARD: Mr Bonny has already informed me that he's quite settled. It seems that he likes his Commanding Officers to be commanding, which the Major evidently is. Did you know, by the way, that he's the only white man on the whole expedition who's being paid for his services. Can that be because he's the only one among us whose services are worth hiring? Whatever you say about Stanley, his recruitment drive in London was a spectacular success – why, they said at the Falls he'd actually got some rich nincompoop to pay for the privilege of marching with him, God knows how much! (*He laughs.*)

JAMESON: One thousand pounds, Mr Ward, and in view of what I've learnt so far, I count it a bargain as well as a privilege. So the Major is for honour, and Troup, I presume, is for honour, and Bonny for money, and I for study – what about you, Mr Ward, what are you here for?

WARD: I'm a patriotic Englishman, Mr Jameson.

JAMESON: I see.

WARD: And as Emin Pasha is an eccentric German employed by the Egyptians to maintain their interest in South Equatorial Africa, it is surely the duty of all patriotic Englishmen to sign up with a Welsh adoptive American to rescue him from a rampaging Muslim. While at the same time helping the Welsh adoptive American to extend a little more Belgian influence along the Arruwimi River. Isn't it?

JAMESON: You believe the rumours then? That Stanley is really doing all this for Leopold of Brussels?

WARD: Certainly not. He's using Leopold of Brussels so that he can do it all for Stanley.

JAMESON: But if you don't believe the cause is noble –

WARD: Noble! (*He laughs.*) There are no noble causes in the Congo, and never have been. In the Congo there are only cannibals and other natives, Arab slavers, European interests and magnificent opportunists. Along with birds, butterflies and snakes, of course, for artists and naturalists like yourself.

JAMESON: Then what are you doing here?

WARD: I haven't the slightest idea. All I know is that after three years travelling around the continent, I was suddenly desperate for the sight of England. Nothing could have persuaded me to stay on another month except, it seems, the very first opportunity to do so. Stanley's expedition was the first opportunity. Perhaps it's simply the fickleness of the dilettante who decides to put up with something he's tired of, for a change, eh?

JAMESON: Or the impulse of a serious man who's not yet discovered what it is he came here to find out.

WARD: Unless, finally, I'm an unwitting agent of one of history's more grandiose schemes.

JAMESON: What would that be?

WARD: Why, to ruin the reputation of a certain Major – from Norfolk, is it?

JAMESON: Sussex, it is.

WARD: In his Sussex family, with his Sussex hunt, and in his London clubs. Think, if only Gordon hadn't fallen at Khartoum the Mahdi wouldn't be driving on to destroy Emin Pasha, Stanley wouldn't be in the Congo, and ergo: I wouldn't be quarrelling with the Sussex Major for my flour, coffee, sugar, tea and gentleman's relish, at Yambuya, on the banks of the Arruwimi River, in June, this year of Grace, 1887.

JAMESON: (*Laughs*) Well, whatever the whirligigs of history or fate, Mr Ward, I believe I'm glad they've brought you to us.

BARTTELOT: (*Enters through the flap*) Ah, you're still here then. (*To* JAMESON) I was looking for Bonny, as a matter of fact. Thought I'd better find out whether he brought up any quinine. He's not in his tent.

JAMESON: Well, he hasn't come in. He went off some time ago.

BARTTELOT: Oh.

JAMESON: He may be having a shower.

BARTTELOT: Looked there. No one in the shower.
(*Pause.*)

WARD: In that case, I'll be able to have one. (*He goes towards the flap.*)

BARTTELOT: Don't forget, Mr Ward. Roast goat. Roast goat and palm wine at sun-down, eh?

95

(WARD *exits*.)

BARTTELOT: You've been having a chat with him, then?

JAMESON: Yes.

BARTTELOT: Ah. And what's he like – when he's not drawling out his sarcasms.

JAMESON: Oh, rather sympathetic. Certainly intelligent.

BARTTELOT: You like him, then?

JAMESON: I found him rather a relief. (*Hurriedly*.) I mean, from what I'd feared earlier.

BARTTELOT: God, Jamie, I wish I had your knack – but by God, what a business, eh! Hardly arrived and they're set against me. Even Stanley couldn't have hoped for such a swift success – grown men at each other's throats – over what! Fortnum and Mason's! That's the joke of it! And that Troup – (*pacing about*) dead set, dead set against me –

JAMESON: Ward assures me that now he's got a bed he'll calm down.

BARTTELOT: What, a bed, how?

JAMESON: I remembered Parke's – the one for Jephson –

BARTTELOT: There you are, you see! And I didn't think of it – not at all, all I could think was that he was after me for one of Stanley's beds – and now the bad feeling's there!

JAMESON: We'll find a way to win them around.

BARTTELOT: Hah! You'd find a way all right, Jamie. (*Pause*.) If I weren't here.

JAMESON: Oh now come, old man, you mustn't give in –
(BONNY *enters through the flap*.)

BARTTELOT: Ah, Bonny! Here you are – I've been looking for you.

BONNY: One of the nigger boys only just told me, sir. I was talking to Troup in his tent.

BARTTELOT: What? Talking to Troup?

BONNY: Yes, sir.

BARTTELOT: Well Bonny, we'd better have a think about our medical supplies, eh?

JAMESON: I'll see you at mess. (*He exits*.)

BARTTELOT: Right, Jamie, at mess. Yes, first thing is to make sure we keep our supplies separate from Stanley's – Oh, that reminds me – here's a (*takes a little package from his pocket*) as you're desperate, not much I'm afraid, almost at the end myself, but enough to make you a pot at least.

BONNY: That's – that's very kind of you, sir.

BARTTELOT: Not at all. Not at all. (*Pause.*) Now there's one other matter I need your advice on. I've been ill.

BONNY: Yes. Mr Jameson mentioned that you and he –

BARTTELOT: This is something different. Something a medic can't detect – (*Pause.*) I don't sleep at nights, not for months, not since Stanley left, get the shakes, the fever, nightmares, that sort of thing and I can't – I find my temper, well, scarcely seems to be mine any more as if – how to explain it – as if I were being – being poisoned, do you see?

BONNY: Well, you probably are, Major, from what Mr Jameson was telling me of your diet here.

BARTTELOT: No it's not the diet, Jameson sleeps like a top most nights. He has the same diet. These nightmares, I tell you – and headaches – I can't go on with them. (*Pause.*) Well? What do you – ?

BONNY: Morphine, sir.

BARTTELOT: Morphine! Certainly not. Morphine's not the answer. (*He looks at him.*)

BONNY: No, Major, it isn't. The answer is obvious enough. A return to a different life, different food, a different country. In other words, the answer for you is England.
(BARTTELOT *looks at him, waits.*)
But as the answer's out of the question –

BARTTELOT: Why?

BONNY: I beg your pardon, sir?

BARTTELOT: Why is it out of the question?

BONNY: Well – because you're in command here, sir.

BARTTELOT: It might be better for everybody if I weren't.
(*Pause.*) Jameson – is more – more fit.

BONNY: Mr Jameson isn't an army man, though, is he, sir? He's a gentleman of leisure, from what I can make out.

BARTTELOT: Mr Jameson happens to be the finest man I've ever met.

BONNY: But Mr Stanley appointed you the Commanding Officer.

BARTTELOT: But between you, you and Troup and Ward and Mr Jameson – you could – (*pause*) do you understand what I'm asking?

BONNY: Yes, I do.

BARTTELOT: Well then, man!

BONNY: I'm not sure my recommendation would carry much weight.

BARTTELOT: But you would write one for me?

BONNY: Naturally, sir. If you ordered me to.

BARTTELOT: Ordered you to?

BONNY: I could hardly write a letter recommending that you be invalided home, without your asking me to, first. Which you have done. And I agree.

BARTTELOT: With the recommendation?

BONNY: To write the letter. It is an order, isn't it?

BARTTELOT: Of course it isn't an order! What value would a letter have that I'd ordered you to write – good God man, you have qualifications, you can judge a situation and act accordingly. Nobody would challenge a doctor's findings.

BONNY: That's true, sir, yes. But then I'm not a doctor.

BARTTELOT: Not a doctor?

BONNY: I'm a medical orderly. And that's less than third class in the medical profession. Did you take me for a doctor?

BARTTELOT: I didn't think about it one way or another. I assumed you had medical experience, I assumed – as they signed you up – you'd be, yes, properly qualified –

BONNY: I'm properly qualified as a medical orderly. And a medical orderly's services come considerably cheaper than a properly qualified doctor's. I expect Mr Stanley took that into account when he appointed me.

BARTTELOT: In that case, we've been at cross-purposes, haven't we?

BONNY: No, sir. (*Little pause.*) Well, at least I understood.

BARTTELOT: What? What did you understand? (*He moves towards him threateningly.*)

BONNY: Well, that you wanted my assurance, in as much as I could give it, that you're fit to carry on.

BARTTELOT: You want me to stay, do you?

BONNY: Yes, I do.

BARTTELOT: Why?

BONNY: Because you're the Commanding Officer. And if we're to
be here a while yet, then Mr Stanley will be getting further and
further away from us. The country is dangerous, there are
cannibals around, there could be fighting. And this Tippu-
Tib, who sounds as likely to attack us as give us our nigger
porters. We'd need you then, very badly, however nicely Mr
Jameson were to run things in the meanwhile.

BARTTELOT: You'll do for me, Bonny. You'll do for me very well.

BONNY: Thank you, Major. (*Little pause.*) You'll do for me too, if I
may say so. (*He turns, makes to go out, stops.*) Oh sir, I shan't –

BARTTELOT: What?

BONNY: Needless to say, it shall never be mentioned by me that
this conversation took place. The others might misconstrue –
(BARTTELOT *stares at him.*)
And thank you again for the tea, sir. Much appreciated. (*He
goes out.*)

BARTTELOT: (*Stands, for a moment, then lets out an exclamation,
loud, of despair. He begins to stride up and down.*) Damn – damn
– damned insolence! (*He drives the point of his stick into the
ground, plucks it out, strides up and down. Bellowing*) John
Henry! John Henry! (*He continues to stride and as lights fade to
black, still striding and jabbing his stick into the ground, at the
very top of his lungs.*) John Henry!

SCENE 2

About an hour later. The stage is in darkness. JAMESON *enters through
the flap. He strikes a match, puts it to the lamp.* BARTTELOT *is sitting at
the table, his hands to his face.* JOHN HENRY *is sitting at the end of the
table staring straight ahead.* JAMESON *takes in the scene, quickly lights
the other two lamps, goes over to* BARTTELOT, *puts a hand on his
shoulder.*

BARTTELOT: (*Jumps, removes his hands*) Oh – oh Jamie – there you
are! Well, supper, eh? Manioc soup, prime cuts of manioc,
pudding of manioc –

JAMESON: Not tonight, old man. Can't you smell the goat?

BARTTELOT: What, by God, yes – goat, eh, how did you – oh, oh yes, those others, they've arrived, it's for them. (*He looks, sees* JOHN HENRY.) What? (*Stares at him.*) Ah, that's right, there's a good boy, John Henry, told him to sit down, not on the floor like a monkey, but at the table, like a human being, eh John Henry – and then when I – I – you just sat on, eh? Yes, that's a good lad, now go and get the palm wine, John Henry. Palm wine. Fancy that. (*He gets up.*) Falling asleep – and a nice sleep, a dream not a nightmare, I've got a feeling the old pater was in it, we were walking across the paddocks, a spring morning – smelt something good – perhaps it was the goat, eh? Well, now I'm back, they'll be here in a minute –

JAMESON: Look, something's occurred to me that may help – What do you say to giving them half their six months' provision now, and leave it to Stanley to give them their other half when we get up with him. That way, you'll be recognizing their claim, while still respecting Stanley's ultimate authority. Do you see?

BARTTELOT: But it would still be a breach.

JAMESON: Yes, but if you don't give them anything then they could complain to Stanley and it might suit him to take their side. There was nothing in my orders, he could say, and no reason that you shouldn't have obliged these men.

BARTTELOT: And so he gets me either way! For being in breach of his orders if I do, or failing to exercise my command if I don't!

JAMESON: Ah, but if he says you shouldn't have given them even half their provisions, then Ward, Troup and Bonny would have to come to your defence, you see. And Stanley wouldn't like that.

BARTTELOT: I don't know, Jamie. I don't know. All I know is that I'm well and truly in Stanley's web and whatever I do – I'll have to think – make a decision – but you believe that would be all right, do you?

(*There is a pause.*)

Look, old man, I must tell you. I – the fact is, I've just done something rather shameful. I asked Bonny if he could have me invalided home. (*He looks at* JAMESON, *distressed.*) It suddenly seemed a solution, you see, that as a medical man he could get me out of all this – a letter would do it, that was my thought. Then you and the others could do as you like, wouldn't have me to contend with. I'd be out of his trap honourably and the rest of you'd be out of his trap too, d'you see? But it's not to be. He's not a doctor, it turns out. Just a medical orderly. I'd have to order him to recommend me to leave – you can imagine what Stanley would have made of that – how he could get at me as far worse than a coward – a cunning coward. Eh? (*He laughs.*)

JAMESON: Poor old boy. I don't blame you, not at all, I'm only sorry –

BARTTELOT: No, don't go soft on me. I did wrong. I shouldn't have tried. But you know, there's something I want you to understand. I couldn't have done it. Couldn't have left, I'm sure of that. All I wanted was the letter in my pocket, that meant I could if I wanted to, you see? Something I could – could touch as – to confirm I'd made a choice – a choice not to go back even though I'd been let off. I'd never desert. Not desert you, old man, after the two months we've been through. I count you my closest – my closest –

(TROUP *comes through the flap.*)

Ah, Mr Troup – well, I hear you have a bed, thank God for that, eh?

(JOHN HENRY *enters with a jug.*)

And here's the palm wine – on the table – there's a boy – now the glasses –

(WARD *enters.*)

BARTTELOT: Ah, here you are then, Ward – showered and – and – and one for Mr Ward too, John Henry – now the jug – be careful not to spill, we've only about a quart of the stuff left, old Jameson bought it from the cannibals, so you see they have their uses, Troup, eh? (*He laughs.*) Not brandy, I know, but not as fierce as you'd expect from a cannibal brew –

(As JOHN HENRY, *having filled* WARD's *and* TROUP's *and*

JAMESON's *glass comes to fill his,* BONNY *enters.*)
Ah, Bonny – Mr Bonny first, John Henry – that's right,
there's a boy, and now mine – John Henry's quite a little find
of mine, used to be one of Mr Stanley's boys, eh, John Henry?
He was in the tent the morning Stanley was leaving – Stanley's
tent – all the hullabaloo and John Henry crying, weren't you,
John Henry, because Stanley had chosen to take one of his
other boys instead, heartbroken because of it, eh, John
Henry? And when Stanley marched out – by God, what a
business he makes of it, struts yards ahead of his officers –
poor old Jephson in a terrible state of indecision, whether to
keep him company or maintain a respectful ten yards behind,
Parke and Stairs trying to look unconcerned, at the back, but
getting caught up in the Zanzibaris who wouldn't move fast
enough for all the damned fuss, drums rolling, pipes blowing,
and all the time Stanley not seeing the farce of it all, strutting
along eyes focussed on posterity by way of the London *Times*
and his publishers, old Jameson did a marvellous sketch, one
of the Soudanese he left for us to bury managed to die just as
Stanley passed him, old Jameson got him in the sketch, eyes
rolling, what was it you called it, A Faithful Zanzibari says his
Farewell to H. M. Stanley, Esq. H. M. standing for His
Majesty, hah, hah, not Henry Morton by God, and above it
Jameson's put, what was it, homage to a great man. (*He
laughs.*) And there was little John Henry trailing behind,
blubbering away, right out of the Camp, hoping right to the
end His Majesty would pardon him and take him along after
all, but I knew he wouldn't, knew he'd send him back and
next morning – next morning I kept a look out for him, found
him skulking with the Soudanese, and took him on. After a
shower, of course. Now John Henry showers once a day, don't
you, John Henry, and is my personal boy, sleeps outside my
tent – tell them how Mr Stanley came by you, John Henry.
JOHN HENRY: Tippu-Tib, he give me Mr Stanley.
BARTTELOT: That's right, our old friend Tippu-Tib. He captured
John Henry from one of the villages, and made a present of
him to Stanley the last time Stanley was in these parts. Stanley
made him his chief boy, then when he went back to England,

stuck him in a missionary school at the Pool. Collected him when he got back three months ago. And leaves him behind all over again. Jameson and I've spent hours grilling him about Tippu-Tib, haven't we, Jamie, but he only knows three things about him. Tell us, John Henry, is Tippu-Tib a good man, good man?

JOHN HENRY: Tippu-Tib good man.

BARTTELOT: And is Tippu-Tib a bad man.

JOHN HENRY: Bad man, bad man.

BARTTELOT: Now tell us why he's called Tippu-Tib? Why name Tippu-Tib?

JOHN HENRY: (*Lifts his arm, points it about*) Tippu-tippu-tippu, tib, tib, tippu tib, tippu tib.

JAMESON: Onomatopoeic, you see.

BONNY: What?

JAMESON: The noise of the rifle, when Tippu and his men come firing on the villages. Far more exact than bang, really.

WARD: Tippu's real name is Hamed bin Mahamed el Marjebi. But I never thought to ask why he was known as Tippu-Tib –

BARTTELOT: No, but Jameson did, eh Jamie? Anyway, those are the three things that John Henry knows about Tippu-Tib, that he's good, that he's bad, and how he got his name.

WARD: Which is one thing more than we know about most people.

BARTTELOT: (*Laughs with false enthusiasm*) Very neat, Mr Ward. Very neat.

JAMESON: Gentlemen, before you finish your glasses, may I propose a toast. To the Rear Column.

BARTTELOT: To the Rear Column.

TROUP:
WARD: } To the Rear Column!
BONNY:

BARTTELOT: (*Catches* JAMESON's *eye*) I've been thinking – rather Jameson and I've been putting our heads together – and what do you say to this? Three months' provision now, three months' when we catch up with Stanley. Eh? What do you say? Troup?

TROUP: Well, sir, given your – your uneasiness with Mr Stanley's
orders, that seems fair enough.

WARD: I think it's a marvellously sensible compromise. (*Glancing
at* JAMESON.)

BONNY: Certainly do for me.

BARTTELOT: Very well, gentlemen. Now I've something to show
you.
(*He looks to* JAMESON, *winks, goes to a crate, brings it over,
swings it up, jabs the point of his stick in, prises up the lid, and
begins to plonk down items.*)
One and a half pounds of coffee. One pound of tea. One and
a half tins of salt. One and a half tins of jam and of chocolate
milk. One tin of cocoa and milk. One tin of sardines. One of
sausages. One pound of fancy biscuits. One third of a tin of
red herring. Half a pound of flour. One pot of Liebig. One
quarter of a pound of tapioca. Times three, of course.
(*During this drums have begun to pound.*)

TROUP: Oh, I see. This is a *month's* rations.

BARTTELOT: No, this is three months'.

WARD: Three months' – that!

BARTTELOT: It is.

TROUP: But good God, who made up these provisions?

JAMESON: Fortnum and Mason's. They'd have done us quite
nicely for an afternoon at Lord's Cricket Ground, don't you
think?

TROUP: Good God, good God!

BARTTELOT: So there you are, gentlemen! One half of what we
were quarrelling about. And now perhaps you'll understand
something about Mr Stanley, the greatest African explorer of
our age! He has his expedition provisions made up by
Fortnum and Mason's. (*He laughs.*)
(*The drums increase in volume.*)
Now if you excuse me while I put a stop to the
accompaniment – (*He goes to the doors, unlatches them, throws
them open.*)
(*From outside, fires flaming; low keening sounds; the drums
louder; dim shapes everywhere.* BARTTELOT *strides into their
midst, with his stick.*)

JAMESON: The Zanzibaris – the Major has a running battle with them every night –

BARTTELOT: (*Off*) That's enough of the drums – damn you, enough I say –

(*The drums diminish, without stopping.*)

JAMESON: There's a particular couple I call the Minchips because it's a Dickens-sounding name, and they're both out of Dickens – he'd have set them in the Mile End Road. The husband's as lazy a vagabond as you could expect to meet – lies on his side all day while the wife collects wood, bargains for food, gathers manioc – then at night after he's eaten he retires to his tent and cleans his rifle while the wife plays for him on the drums, I think she starts all the others off, and she's always the last to stop –

BARTTELOT: (*Still shouting, off*) Quiet I say – quiet –

(WARD *goes towards the door, watches.* TROUP *joins him.* BONNY *pours himself some more palm-wine. There is now only one drum beating.* JAMESON *goes over to his desk, picks up the picture, looks at it. Drum plays a few seconds longer, then stops. On this tableau: Lights. Curtain.*)

ACT TWO

SCENE I

The same. Six months later. Morning.
The doors are open. Outside, blazing sunlight and intense heat. Off,
the sound of a voice, faint and unidentifiable, although it is WARD's.
A thudding sound, also faint, follows each count.

WARD: Forty-five, forty-six, forty-seven, forty-eight, forty-nine,
    fifty, fifty-one, fifty-two, fifty-three, fifty-four, fifty-five, fifty
    – (*Stops, pause.*) Take him down, will you? Down! Take him
    down!
    (*Movements, voices off. There is a pause.* TROUP *enters through*
    the main doors, goes to the water bucket, pours himself a mug of
    water, sits down, wipes his forehead, drinks. BONNY *enters. He*
    is carrying salt and bandages. He puts them in a box. Goes to the
    water bucket, pours himself a mug of water.)

BONNY: Jameson's due back this morning, isn't he?

TROUP: Is he? (*Pause, sips. Laughs.*)

BONNY: (*Looks at him*) What?

TROUP: Well, you're not setting any store by that, are you?

BONNY: Not setting store by it, no. Just wanting to find out.

TROUP: Well, you don't have to wait for him – I can tell you.
    They're rumours. As he knew before he left.

BONNY: They're rumours in the villages here. They may turn out
    to be facts further down.

TROUP: They're always rumours, never facts.

BONNY: But he thought these were worth following up.

TROUP: Of course he did. As they coincided with a distasteful
    duty.

BONNY: Oh well, can't say I blame him. He's a gentleman, after
    all.

TROUP: And the rest of us aren't?

BONNY: Oh, I only meant he's not an officer.

TROUP: Some of us try to be both. Not that I blame him either, if
    he can get away with it. But I wonder that Barttelot lets him,
    he wouldn't let me, or Ward, it's a collective responsibility,

we take votes on it, we should all stand by the decision.

BONNY: But Jameson voted against, didn't he? This time.

TROUP: This time, last time and the time before.

BONNY: Still, what would be the point of a vote, if we all had to vote one way.

TROUP: That's not my complaint.

BONNY: But what is your complaint?

TROUP: Only that Jameson doesn't take any of the –

BARTTELOT: (*Off*) Here you nigger – move that nigger out of the way –

BONNY: What?

TROUP: It doesn't matter.

BARTTELOT: (*Enters, followed by* JOHN HENRY) Water.

(JOHN HENRY *goes to the cask, pours a mug of water*.)

Ward went over. Over by five. We entered fifty on the log, damn nuisance!

(JOHN HENRY *brings the mug over to* BARTTELOT, *who swills it down, hands the mug to* JOHN HENRY, *who goes over, pours more*.)

Jameson should be back by now, he likes to get in before the heat – God what a business, Ward going on, thought he'd never stop. (*He takes the mug from* JOHN HENRY *again, drinks*.)

BONNY: No, but I don't understand what your complaint is.

TROUP: It doesn't matter.

BARTTELOT: What complaint?

(*There is a pause*.)

BONNY: About Mr Jameson's absence, wasn't it?

BARTTELOT: What about his absence?

TROUP: I was just saying that it was unfortunate that Jameson missed the flogging.

BARTTELOT: Why? Do you think he would have enjoyed it?

TROUP: They're meant to be a joint responsibility. We're all supposed to stand by the majority decision.

BARTTELOT: And when has Jameson rejected the majority decision?

TROUP: My point is simply that he should see it through with the rest of us.

BARTTELOT: He's seen enough of them to know how they go.

TROUP: But he voted against, and then stayed away.

BARTTELOT: And so?

TROUP: It's a way of keeping in the clear, isn't it?

BARTTELOT: Clear of what?

TROUP: The responsibility, of course.

BARTTELOT: Oh, what are you talking about, Troup? Somebody had to go up river to check the rumours –

TROUP: And does that someone always have to be Jameson? And always when there's a flogging?

BARTTELOT: Jameson goes because he's learned the lingo and is good with the natives. All right. (*Pause.*) All right?

TROUP: (*Grunts*) He'll bring back some sketches.

BARTTELOT: What?

TROUP: I said he'll bring back some nice sketches, of birds and leaves and toads and butterflies, and whatnot, I expect.

BARTTELOT: Let's hope he brings back some news of Tippu-Tib, eh?

TROUP: Whether he does or not, he'll bring back some sketches.

BARTTELOT: (*After a pause*) Well?

TROUP: Well, he's down in the log as dissenting, *and* down in the log as absent from proceedings. In the six months I've been here he's not supervised the floggings once.

BARTTELOT: And in the six months you've been here you haven't stopped complaining, to one of us about the rest of us, to the rest of us about one of us, if it's not the flogging it's wood patrol, if it's not wood patrol it's – it's something else.

BONNY: I'm sorry if I've given you cause for complaint.

TROUP: You still haven't answered the facts, have you?

BARTTELOT: What facts?

TROUP: I've done my turn on the floggings, Bonny's done his, you've done yours and so's Ward.

WARD: (*Entering wearily*) Done what?

TROUP: Your turn on the floggings.

WARD: Overdone it, I think, didn't I? This time.

BARTTELOT: By five strokes, what came over you, anyway?

WARD: Sorry. I didn't keep count of my counting. Let's just hope he didn't either.

BONNY: He couldn't. Anyway not after the first twenty. He wasn't conscious.

WARD: How very fortunate. After all, what would one do if he asked for the last five strokes to be taken back. (*He laughs weakly*.) Anyway, I gave orders for two days remission in chains, hope that's all right?

BARTTELOT: What! No, it's not all right! You should have spoken to me first.

WARD: Yes, well, sorry again. I felt as it was my mistake I must make up in some way –

BARTTELOT: You made the mistake, it wasn't for you to make it up.

WARD: Well, what do you suggest we do? Eh? Eh? (*Fiercely*.) Anyway, what difference does it make whether it's three or five, he won't last the night, will he, Bonny?

BONNY: I shouldn't think so.

WARD: There! You see! (*Puts his face in his arms*.)

TROUP: You all right, old man?

WARD: Yes, yes, thank you.

TROUP: (*To* BONNY) You'd better give him some quinine.

BONNY: Is that all right, Major?

BARTTELOT: How are the stocks?

BONNY: Beginning to run low.

TROUP: Still, if a man's ill, he must have medicine.

BARTTELOT: He can only have medicine if there's medicine to give him.

TROUP: But it's no good making sure there's medicine to give him by not giving him any.

WARD: (*Laughs*) Very neat, Troup, very neat.

TROUP: It wasn't meant to be. Because it's not funny when you think about it. If Barttelot starts refusing us medicine –

BARTTELOT: I've never refused when Bonny's said it's absolutely necessary. Nevertheless the fact remains there soon won't be any medicine.

WARD: Oh, don't squabble over my health, I'm all right, I tell you, short on sleep, that's all, my tent isn't conducive to it, the glow of their fires throws up peculiar images and their voices go on very shrill and the whole effect – you know it occurs to me, at least it did occur to me, when I'd counted to twenty-three strokes or twenty-four, somewhere in that passage anyway, the twenties it did occur to me that old Jameson was quite right, he usually is, you know, when he put forward the argument that we should abandon flogging for a while, we really are losing them fast enough at what's the current rate, one and an eighth a day Bonny worked it out at, from starvation, sickness etc., for us not to need to flog them to death too.

BARTTELOT: It's the one matter on which Jameson is not right. We have no choice. If a nigger thieves or deserts or trades his rifle for food or sleeps on sentry duty, he is to be flogged.

TROUP: But we do have a choice, that's what I was saying. If Jameson votes against, and now Ward votes against, it only needs one more vote – then what would you do?

BARTTELOT: I see. You intend to vote against, do you, in future.

TROUP: Or Bonny might.

(BARTTELOT *turns, looks at* BONNY.)

BONNY: What, me? Of course I wouldn't.

BARTTELOT: (*To* TROUP) Well?

WARD: If Troup votes against, I shall have to vote for. I agree with the Major. But I'll tell you what, Troup, shall we make a deal, take it in turns, that way we honour the law and satisfy conscience, how many judges manage that? With the Major's permission, of course.

BARTTELOT: I don't give a damn what you do between you as long as discipline is maintained. If you all voted against I'd enter it in the log and still have them flogged. And by God! order whichever of you I wanted to supervise it. And now that we've cleared that up, I've work to do – (*He exits.*)

WARD: Work, what work?

BONNY: He's counting the brass-rods. He started last night, in here. I was just going to bed, he came bursting in, didn't even notice me, started pulling the cases out – then at dawn he was into the tents –

WARD: Well, it put him in a good humour for the flogging, didn't it? I saw him joking with a couple of Zanzibaris just before I began the count, you were at his side, Bonny, as you usually are, was it a good joke?

BONNY: It wasn't a joke. He was grinning at them.

WARD: Grinning at them?

BONNY: He's discovered that they're more frightened of him when he grins at them.

WARD: Really? Well he's got an excellent set of teeth. Why, that might solve our problem, instead of lashing a man to the post and having him flogged, we can lash him to a post and have Barttelot grin at him. Fifty, fifty-five times, it wouldn't make any difference . . .

BONNY: Yes, it would. They'd go off from fright even quicker.

TROUP: They hate him.

WARD: They hate us all.

TROUP: But they hate him most. He goes out amongst them looking for trouble, poking at them with his damned stick, as if trying to stir them up.

BONNY: Perhaps that's what he's trying to do. Stir them up to life. Hate might sustain them a day or two longer –

TROUP: That's not why he does it. He does it because he hates them back.

WARD: So do I.

TROUP: What?

WARD: When I see them lying about in the compound, in their sickness, as if they were the image of sickness itself. Or while they stand there, heads lolling, while I supervise one of them flogging another of them to death. That makes me hate them.

TROUP: We can't go on week after week – something must be done, and soon.

BONNY: But what do you propose, Troup?

TROUP: Simply that we do something, anything, to get on the move. Look here, Bonny, this is confidential.

WARD: (*Laughs*) Yes, do be discreet, old man. By the way, that woman I saw you with last night –

BONNY: What? What woman?

WARD: I saw you in silhouette, tip-toeing past my tent –

BONNY: Then you were seeing things.

WARD: Yes, lots of things, you and the woman among them. But you've got a way with the ladies, haven't you? Old Troup here was telling me the other day how you managed coming out on the boat, you had to travel tourist as you were on the expedition's expense, isn't that right, old man, but before you were three days out – you did say three days, didn't you, Troup? You'd insinuated yourself among the ladies in First Class, by making free with little remedies for *mal de mer*, and ended up dining between two absolute beauties, Troup called them, didn't you, Troup, at the Captain's table. Two absolute beauties?

TROUP: Look here, Ward, I didn't mean – I didn't intend any slight –

WARD: Of course you didn't, he was most complimentary about your gifts, Bonny, he didn't end up at the Captain's table between two absolute beauties, did you, Troup, even though you went first at your own expense, he was envious, you see, so there's nothing to be ashamed of in taking a Zanzibari or Soudanese or native lady by the neck, eh, as long as there's no outraged husband –

BONNY: (*Gets up, comes over*) Lift your arms.

WARD: What?

BONNY: Lift your arms.

(WARD *does so.*)

(*Feels in* WARD's *arm pits.*) Swollen. (*He puts his hand to* WARD's *brow.*) You'd do better lying down.

WARD: No, I wouldn't.

BONNY: Well, if you don't lie down soon, you'll fall down later.

WARD: Right. I'll wait until then.

BONNY: Then you're a fool. And that wasn't me or a woman you saw last night, it was your delirium.

TROUP: Look here, let's get back to what's important. Can I speak plainly?

WARD: (*Laughs*) Plainly, Troup. Good God! You certainly can.

TROUP: What, look, I'm not advocating going behind Barttelot's back, but simply that we all have a reasoned and proper discussion –

WARD: (*Gets to his feet, as sudden noises off*) He's here!

TROUP: What?

(JAMESON *enters through the flap. He is carrying a shoulder-bag.*)

WARD: Welcome back, old man. (*He shakes his hand.*)

JAMESON: Thank you. Troup – Bonny – how are you –

TROUP: Any news?

JAMESON: Oh, nothing very definite, I'm afraid, although –

BARTTELOT: (*Comes striding in*) Ah, here you are then, Jamie, thank God, I was getting worried, well, what news, what news?

JAMESON: None really, I'm afraid. Lots of rumours, but I didn't actually find a native who'd seen an Arab. Mark you, there was a great deal of excitement, more than usual, but the only significant thing was that in the village by the second river-bend – where the Chief wears those boots Stanley gave him – a more preposterous figure – (*He laughs.*)

BARTTELOT: Well, what about him?

JAMESON: I know it doesn't sound much, but you see, he claimed he hadn't heard anything at all, not even a rumour.

TROUP: It certainly doesn't sound much, other than that there might be one honest nigger in the Congo after all.

JAMESON: No, my impression was the opposite. I couldn't be sure the other chiefs were telling the truth, but I was quite sure he wasn't. He knew something –

BARTTELOT: By God, you mean you believe he's seen Tippu-Tib?

JAMESON: Not quite that. But perhaps an Arab or two.

BARTTELOT: But by God, that's something. That's something more than we've had this last six months!

TROUP: But you're only guessing. It doesn't seem much to me, to go on.

JAMESON: There was one small piece of evidence. Just outside his village I came across the remains of a feast, a few bones –

BARTTELOT: An Arab feast?

JAMESON: Oh no, quite distinctly a native feast. But an exceptional one. An Arab might have furnished it.

TROUP: Furnished what? A goat?

JAMESON: No, no. Himself. He might have been caught and eaten. But really there was no way of knowing, because if it was an Arab, he was presumably in the belly of the Chief who said there wasn't.

WARD: That's what's called digesting the evidence.

JAMESON: There were only a few digitals sucked clean and a couple of shin bones to go on. It could equally well have been a nigger from one of the other villages who'd come up too far, and the chief might well have been emphatic about there being no Arabs because he didn't want a fuss over his meal. I can't say.

BARTTELOT: And nothing else?

JAMESON: No.

BARTTELOT: (*After a pause.*) So we're no further ahead?

JAMESON: Not really. I'm sorry.

BARTTELOT: Not your fault, old man.

JAMESON: Still, the bearer of no news – I say, (*to* WARD) you don't look at all well, your fever still running?

WARD: (*Gestures*) Oh, I'm much better. Much.

JAMESON: That's good. By the way, I caught the most beautiful parakeet, I shall have to stuff him this evening – and look – (*He takes a sketch out, shows it to* WARD.)

BARTTELOT: (*To* BONNY) You'd better come and have a look at a Soudanese lying on the bank, some sort of green bile coming out of his mouth –

WARD: Ah, and here's our Stanley-booted Chief. Yes, I see what you mean, embarrassed but replete – certainly a large, illicit meal not far from his memory –

TROUP: No! no! (*Suddenly loud.*) What are we going to do? Are we going to look at Jameson's sketches, or study sick Soudanese we can't do anything for anyway, or are we going to talk, to talk for once about what we're going to do? This situation can't go on, don't you see, Barttelot, you Jameson, surely you see – all we have to show for six months' waiting, for some sixty dead men, is a loathsome story of shin bones and cannibalism. It's the last straw. (*Pause.*) Don't you see! We must act! We must act!

BARTTELOT: And what action do you suggest we take?

TROUP: Stanley can't possibly want us to linger on here –

BARTTELOT: I assure you he does.

TROUP: Well, for how long? Another month? Another two months? What use will we be to him then? He might already have reached Emin Pasha, for all we know. He might even be

dead, they might all of them have been massacred by the
Mahdi –

BARTTELOT: Yes.

TROUP: And meanwhile we're to go on waiting?

BARTTELOT: Yes.

TROUP: Rot among rotting niggers for no reason? Or wait for
them to turn on us when we're in the middle of one of our
floggings and tear us to pieces, do you really think that's
what Stanley would want? Tippu-Tib's not coming. We all
know it. There will be no six hundred porters. There's
nothing to wait here for –

BARTTELOT: Except one's honour.

TROUP: Your honour, you mean, with Stanley. Oh, come man,
your silly feud with Stanley is eight months past, he's long
forgotten it, if he's even alive. Don't you see –

BARTTELOT: I see what you're proposing. It's desertion.

TROUP: I'm proposing that we act with common sense. I tell you,
Barttelot, whatever you may claim, Stanley is not a
murdering maniac.

BARTTELOT: I never said he was.

TROUP: The other night you accused him of attempting to
poison –

WARD: A figure of speech, old chap. A figure of –

TROUP: Well, his attitude to Stanley is poisoning us, that's the
point. Good God man, those orders of his you're so
frightened of contravening, they were written on the
supposition that Tippu would be here months ago – Stanley
didn't even deal with the contingency that's arisen, he never
expected it.

BARTTELOT: You've forgotten the brass-rods.

TROUP: What? You mean we're running out of those, too? Then
we'll certainly have a rebellion to deal with, the only thing
the niggers look forward to is their brass-rods –

BARTTELOT: We're not running out. Stanley's left us enough to
pay the men for another six months. Another six months,
Troup.

(*There is a pause.*)

JAMESON: (*Suddenly laughs*) No, just a minute old man, you've forgotten that we also have to pay Tippu's men on the march. He'd take that into account.

BARTTELOT: I did. If Tippu's men had been paid from the day Stanley left, we'd still have enough for another six months. As Tippu's men haven't arrived we've enough for another year and a half. This from Mr Stanley, who knows the value of a brass-rod in the Congo as a – a Jew does of a sovereign in Kensington. So there you are, Troup, there's your evidence, Stanley acknowledges through the brass-rods that we might have to wait, and wait, and wait.

(*There is silence.*)

TROUP: Then what about the quinine, how do you explain that?

WARD: Perhaps he got Fortnum and Mason's to package the quinine.

BONNY: In my experience of medical supplies, there are never enough of them. Specially quinine.

TROUP: (*Goes to sit down*) Oh this is all – all speculation. The fact of the matter is, we don't know what Stanley intended – if only you'd found some way of getting him to take you through those damned orders. I still don't understand how it is you didn't get the chance, did he refuse to let you read them before he left, what?

JAMESON: I really don't see the value of going back –

BARTTELOT: No, I'll tell you what happened, Troup. I wasn't going to give him the satisfaction. That's what happened.

TROUP: What satisfaction?

BARTTELOT: Of watching me read them. When I went to his tent to get them he wasn't even dressed, that's how much – how much – he was just getting into those damned ridiculous togs he puts on specially for his marches, I had to stand there, to stand there while he crammed himself into those knickerbockers he wears for showing off his calves and then his Norfolk jacket, which he thinks turns him into an English gentleman, and his German officer's cap, which he thinks turns him into a – a – German officer, and all the time strutting about gobble-de-gooking John Henry here who was blubbering away, and gobble-de-gooking the Soudanese in Soudanese and Zanzibaris in Zanzibari or the other way around for all I knew, to let me see the niggers were more important than his own senior officers, and sending messages to Jephson and Parke and Stairs – and in the middle of it all he shoved the orders into my hands and went on gobble-de-gooking, and when he saw I'd just shoved them into my pocket, that I was just going to go on standing there watching him with a smile he was forced to come back to me, and by God how he hates that, standing eye to eye with another white man. Well, Major (*he does a poor imitation of a high voice with a nasal twang*) not interested in your orders? I take it, I said, I take it they don't apply until you've left the camp, Mr Stanley. Besides there's really no need, sir, as they shall be carried out to the letter, whatever they are. But not beyond the letter . . . or to your own letter . . . something like that, because I turned on my heel, and walked over here, leaving him to get on with his circus – so Troup, now you know why it was impossible, and why I wasn't going to give him the satisfaction, I hope it's given you some, eh?

TROUP: I can't believe it! You mean he actually invited you, – I can't believe it!

WARD: If you'll excuse the observation, old chap, one of your small weaknesses is that you can't believe what you clearly know to be true, it's far too human to be anything else, surely. You can believe it, can't you? If you try?

TROUP: Do you really find all this *amusing*, Ward?

WARD: Well yes, it's odd, I admit, but I put it down to my temperature or temperament –

TROUP: Well, because you didn't want Stanley to have the satisfaction, what it comes to is this. We have no idea what to do next –

BARTTELOT: We wait.

TROUP: For death?

JAMESON: Oh, I don't really think it'll come to that –

BARTTELOT: In view of the brass-rods anything else would be desertion. And that's what Stanley hopes for.

WARD: Well, actually Major, the brass-rods have nothing to do with anything at all. The perfectly simple and reasonable explanation for them came to me while you were describing –

with great vivacity may I say – your last meeting with Stanley
and then I became so engrossed with the – sorry – sorry – the
delightful interchanges between yourself and our good
Troup that I forgot to mention – and then you've such an
assertive manner, do you see?

BARTTELOT: What are you talking about?

WARD: What?

JAMESON: It's his fever – (*goes to him*) old man, do lie down.

BONNY: I warned him.

WARD: Nonsense, no old boy, I'm quite – if you don't mind – the
brass-rods, yes, the reason Stanley left them behind, yes,
well it's because they're damned heavy, you see. Took as
many as he calculated he'd need, and left us to bring up the
rest with the porters, which porters and what porters being
an entirely different question, but what would be the use of
them if they weren't to bring up the brass-rods among the
other things, eh?
(*There is a pause.*)

JAMESON: He's perfectly right, of course.

TROUP: Of course! My dear old Ward – well – so there we are, the
rods mean nothing. Surely you agree?

BARTTELOT: It's a – possible – explanation.

TROUP: Well now can we – can we discuss it in a different
atmosphere, I've been partly to blame, I admit, we bring out
the worst in each other at times, eh, Major?

BARTTELOT: We wait. That's what we must do. For Tippu-Tib,
or for a message from Stanley, or for news that Stanley is
dead. We wait.

TROUP: No. No, I'm not going to wait. I'm going home. Who's
coming with me? Ward, Jameson – you must see this is
madness – come with me –

JAMESON: Excuse me, may I? (*Gently, takes* BARTTELOT's *stick.*)
Stanley appointed me to stay with the Major, my place has
been with him from the beginning – (*Moving gently towards*
TROUP.)

WARD: There's no doubt honour's involved somewhere, you
know, Troup, even if one can't – can't quite –

BONNY: I'm staying too. If you're interested, that is.

TROUP: Honour, there's no honour –
(JAMESON *springs forward, with stick upraised, as if to strike* TROUP, *knocks him out of the way, and brings it down again and again, violently.* TROUP *has lurched back with a cry of terror.*)

JAMESON: (*Fishes up a dead snake with the tip of the stick*) Probably the mate of that one I got a few days ago – or were you simply after a spot of shade and a drop of water, can't blame you for that. (*He loops it over the rafters.*) You all right?

TROUP: What? All right? Yes, yes – what does another snake or two matter in all this madness.

BARTTELOT: When will you be leaving, Mr Troup?

TROUP: I can't go on my own, you know that.

BARTTELOT: One of us would accompany you, with the soundest of the Soudanese. We won't let you end up in the belly of an Arruwimi, don't worry.

TROUP: That's not what I meant. I stand by the majority decision.

BARTTELOT: We've each decided for ourselves, what our duty is. If you think yours is to leave –

TROUP: I'm staying.

BARTTELOT: In that case, Mr Troup, perhaps you will allow me to get on with my duties. Mr Bonny, shall we go and look at the Soudanese – (*He goes towards the flap. Turns, looks at* TROUP) But by God, Troup, by God I shall put it in the log! (*He goes out.*)

TROUP: The log? What does he mean? We had a discussion, I stand by the majority decision – does he mean I was proposing to desert, to abandon you and Stanley – he can't put that in the log! I shall – I shall write a letter to the Committee in London, to Mr William MacKinnon himself, stating my position. I shall get it on record that there was never any question – never – (*He goes out.*)

WARD: I wonder who he thinks is going to deliver his letter, or perhaps he'll ask for a majority decision to pop over with it himself to, what's the address, somewhere in Cutter's Lane, Holborn, isn't it? I say, Jameson, that's a fine specimen you slaughtered there, much better than its wife or husband, was

it? Are you going to add it to your collection or have you got
one already, how you sense these things! The way you moved
I thought – I thought you were going to strike down old
Troup or even the rest of us, all of us, a single blow, while
you were away I've taken up sculpting again, but fretfully,
fretfully, tried to model Herman and King, but they would
keep their heads in, because of Bonny's remarks about
cooking them, you know, I was looking forward to showing
you, but it's rotten work, rotten work I'm afraid, I –
(*Swaying as he speaks, and collapses just as:*)

JAMESON: (*Gets to him quickly, to support him.*) My poor old fellow
– here – let me – better get you to bed –

WARD: No, not to my tent. Not to my tent, if you please.

JAMESON: Well then, come – (*He helps* WARD *over to settee.*)
There, lie down.

WARD: Sorry, sorry, Jameson – did you know I went on to fifty
(*very brightly*) five and a fraction, didn't matter though,
Bonny says he'll die anyway, it became a bit hypnotic, you
see, telling off the strokes, and he got into a rhythm you
know, his arm sweeping back and then forward, and then the
scream, and then my voice, and his arm sweeping back and
the screams stopped, and my voice, and his arm, and my
voice –

JAMESON: It must have been quite horrible for you.

WARD: No, no, it was quite pleasant, (*fretfully*) quite pleasant,
don't you see, could really have gone on and on, why don't
you do it, Jameson, don't you enjoy it, Troup says Barttelot
lets you off, is that true?

JAMESON: I supervised it once or twice, before you other chaps
came up.

WARD: And didn't you find it pleasant?

JAMESON: No. But I didn't have a fever when I did it, perhaps
that helps.

WARD: (*Sitting up, very brightly*) What about your wife and child,
children you pray and trust, it must be awful for them having
you away, when people count on you so much, if we need
you here she must need you there, do you ever think about
them, do you, Jameson, do you worry if they're all right?

JAMESON: Yes.

WARD: And I worry about you, you know, when you're away, so
    does Barttelot tramping about at top speed ordering
    floggings and kicking niggers and grinning, have you heard
    about his grinning? And worrying about you, he misses you,
    doesn't he?

JAMESON: You're really rather ill, you know. You must try and
    sleep.

WARD: No, but Jameson –

JAMESON: You must sleep. You must.

WARD: But you'll look in on me later, won't you?

JAMESON: Of course. (*He goes to the doors, makes to shut them.*)

WARD: Oh, don't shut them, if you please.

JAMESON: Oh, I think so. They'll light their fires, and the din –

WARD: Oh, I don't mind, truly I want the light please.

JAMESON: (*Hesitates*) All right, I'll leave them half and half – (*He
    half closes the doors, then turns, looks at* WARD, *goes out through
    the flap.*)
    (*The stage dims slowly to night.* WARD *is tossing and turning on
    his bed, in a troubled and feverish sleep. Suddenly a blaze off,
    and cries. The light of a large bonfire getting brighter and
    brighter. Voices chattering. The drums begin, as at the end of Act
    One.* WARD *lets out a cry. Sits upright. The drums continue.*
    WARD *stares wildly about, then fixes his gaze on the snake which
    appears, in the changing light from the blaze, to be writhing.*
    WARD *stares transfixed, then begins to babble, shaking his head
    and clasping himself tightly. He is shivering. He moans, lets out
    shrill cries.* TROUP *enters, through the flap, carrying a lamp. He
    goes to* WARD's *bed.*)

WARD: The worm, the worm – (*Pointing.*)

TROUP: What worm? (*He turns.*) Good God! (*Laughs.*) It's only
    Jameson's snake – (*He goes to the rafter, pulls it down.*)

WARD: Be careful – be careful – Jameson will want it.
    (TROUP *puts the snake on the table, then goes to the doors.*)

BARTTELOT: (*Off*) Stop it, damn you! Stop it, I say!

TROUP: There's old Barttelot on his rounds again, eh? Having a
    go at Mrs What-d'you call her, Minchip –

BARTTELOT: (*Off*) Damn you, will you stop it!

(*The drums begin to quiet, as at the end of the previous scene.*)

TROUP: (*Closes the doors, comes over*) I say, old boy, you've got it badly, eh?

WARD: (*Is sitting up, shaking hideously*) You mustn't go away again, you mustn't leave me again.

TROUP: No, no, of course not, old man, I'll sit by you. (*He gently pushes* WARD *back.*) There now, old man, that's better, isn't it? I'll be here, you'll be all right, eh?

(JAMESON *enters through the flap, also carrying a lamp and some blankets, comes over, looks down at* WARD.)

Not too good, eh?

JAMESON: No.

(*He begins to put blankets over* WARD, *assisted by* TROUP.)

WARD: Jameson, Jameson – you there? (*Teeth chattering.*)

JAMESON: Yes. Right here.

WARD: You will stay, won't you?

JAMESON: Yes. Yes, I'll stay.

BONNY: (*Enters through flap*) Here we are, some quinine, compliments of the Major.

TROUP: Thank God for that.

BONNY: (*Goes to* WARD, *lifts his head*) Now get this down you – (*He administers it.*) There we are.

WARD: Thank you, Jameson.

BONNY: He's very bad. Very bad. If he'd lain down at the beginning – somebody'd better stay with him.

JAMESON: Yes, I'm going to.

BONNY: Then the rest of us better leave him in peace.

TROUP: Right. If you're sure –

JAMESON: Quite sure.

TROUP: Well then – (*He puts his hand on* WARD's *shoulder.*) Good-night, old man.

BONNY: Good-night.

JAMESON: Good-night.

(TROUP *and* BONNY *go towards the flap.*)

BARTTELOT: Ah, you're all here are you, how is he?

BONNY: At the crisis. Jameson's going to sit with him.

BARTTELOT: Ah. (*He comes over to the bed.*)

(TROUP *and* BONNY *exit.*)

BONNY: Good-night, Major. (*As he goes.*)
    (*There is a pause.*)
BARTTELOT: He's had the quinine then?
JAMESON: Yes.
BARTTELOT: Ah. Well, be careful, Jamie, don't want you going
    out on us, we can take turns.
JAMESON: No, I'll be all right.
BARTTELOT: Ah. (*Pause.*) Well – (*He puts his hand on* JAMESON's
    shoulder.) Good-night, old Jamie.
JAMESON: Good-night.
    (BARTTELOT *hesitates, turns, goes out through the flap. There is*
    a silence.)
WARD: Jameson!
JAMESON: Yes.
WARD: Jameson, are you there?
JAMESON: Yes, I'm here.
    (*There is a silence.* JAMESON *sees the snake, goes over, picks it*
    up, then draws a chair to the bed, arranges the lamp so that the
    light falls on him. He takes a knife from his pocket, and begins to
    skin the snake. On this, lights.)

SCENE 2

Some days later. Night.
A brazier is the first glow, followed by the other lights. WARD's
make-shift bed has been disestablished. JOHN HENRY *is moving*
around the table, clearing away the remnants of a meal. BARTTELOT,
BONNY *and* TROUP *are seated around the brazier.* BARTTELOT *is*
smoking a pipe. After a pause, JAMESON *gets up, goes to the brazier,*
stokes it up.
Off, a single drum starts, very low, almost a murmur.
BARTTELOT: There she goes.
TROUP: I can't hear her. Oh yes. Still, they're very quiet tonight.
    Do you think they know? I mean, they might have felt
    something today. From us. The way we've behaved.
    (BONNY *laughs.*)
    Well, she's beating very soft, and the others haven't joined

in. How do you explain that?

BONNY: Not by sentiment, anyway. The wonder is she can play at all, after what the Major did to her last night, eh Major?

BARTTELOT: (*As if not listening*) Mmmmm?

TROUP: Why does she do it anyway, what do you think, Jameson?

JAMESON: What? Oh – (*coming from the brazier to sit down*) for the magic, I should think. As long as Mrs Minchip plays, the sickness will stay off Mr Minchip.

BONNY: Seems to work. They die around him, but every morning he's as fresh as black paint, except for a few patches of red and blue from the Major's stick or boot, eh Major?

JAMESON: Yes, well it's really very reasonable. Mr and Mrs Minchip are evidently genuinely attached to each other. Her continuing to play the drums for him in spite of the Major's attempts to stop her, only proves it to both of them. And so provides them both with a reason for living.

BONNY: There you are, Major, you're part of her magic too.

BARTTELOT: Mmmmm? What do you mean?

BONNY: Well, you're helping to keep their marriage together and that always takes magic. Are you going to go out to them?

BARTTELOT: No, no. Not tonight. It would be wrong tonight.

TROUP: And they *are* very low. I tell you they feel something of what we're feeling. (*Pause.*) There! She's stopped altogether! (WARD *enters through the flap. He is carrying a large tray, on which is an object covered with a handkerchief. Under his arm, a bottle of brandy.*)

BARTTELOT: Ah, there you are at last. What have you been up to?

WARD: Gentlemen, my apologies for the delay. There's a little something I gave myself to, in an idle kind of way, during my convalescence that I hesitate to present to public view (*putting the tray on the table*) but I hope that my main contribution (*holds up the brandy bottle*)
(*laughs and cheers*)
will help to render the other more tolerable. And his own to the evening has been so extreme that, however inadequately, he must be honoured. So gentlemen, Troup old man, if you would – (*hands him the brandy bottle*)

(TROUP *pours into glasses.*)

While I propose, thank you old man, a toast –

OTHERS: (*Standing*) A toast!

WARD: To our tender and succulent benefactor! (*He removes the handkerchief, to reveal the head of a goat, modelled in clay.*) (*Exclamations and applause.*)

To dear old Nanny!

OTHERS: (*Laughing*) Dear old Nanny!

JAMESON: (*Studying it*) But look here, old man, it's a real piece of work, something really done – the mouth is wonderful, quite wonderful – the sardonic grin, the twist there of the lips, the very essence of goatiness –

TROUP: (*Belches*) The substance being somewhere else.

WARD: (*To* JAMESON) I'm not thoroughly shamed by it, I admit.

BONNY: The funny thing is, I shall miss him.

TROUP: That's charitable, Bonny, considering the devil never stopped trying to kick you.

BONNY: The devil's always trying to kick me, in some manifestation or another.

JAMESON: Now the brandy's arrived – (*taking a newspaper packet out of his pocket*) may I present my little – (*Holding it out. They take from it a cigar each, with little exclamations.*)

BARTTELOT: (*Pocketing his cigar*) I'll hang on to this a little longer, by God, it's good, Troup, damned good! Thank you for it.

BONNY: We all owe Troup thanks for it. He's sweetened the atmosphere around you.

BARTTELOT: What? (*He looks at* BONNY.) Oh. (*He laughs.*) Neat, Bonny, very neat.

JAMESON: (*Who has been about to thrust the cigar newspaper into the brazier, checks himself*) Good Heavens, here's something – the personal column. If the gentleman who waited outside the Savoy on Friday of last week at the appointed hour should care to do so again this week, he will receive a full explanation, and an assurance of –

TROUP: Assurance of what?

JAMESON: It stops there.

BONNY: An assurance of nothing, then.

TROUP: Or of everything.

JAMESON: (*Looks at date*) Fourteen months ago. Well, let's trust the matter's been settled between them, whatever it was.

TROUP: Oh, it's obvious what it was. The writer is a lady and her message is addressed to a – well, gentleman.

JAMESON: Well, go on, old man. Give us the whole scene.

TROUP: Well, well it's a sacred tryst, what? They meet, let's see, they meet every Friday, for a few precious moments. They don't touch, scarcely speak, look into each other's eyes –

JAMESON: And what happened on that last Friday?

BARTTELOT: I'll tell you what, she has a fierce pater who locked her in, and the gentleman in question's an officer – penniless but true, they're planning something dashing – an elopement – eh?

BONNY: Mark my words, it's either money or – the other thing. If it's the other thing he didn't turn up because he's tired of waiting for it, if it's money she's not giving the other thing until she's got her hands on it.

JAMESON: How does that end?

BONNY: Oh, in the usual way. With an arrangement. The question is how *that* ends?

WARD: How does it usually end?

BONNY: Why, if it's bad, in the law courts. And if it's worse – in church.

BARTTELOT: Careful, Bonny, careful.

TROUP: Oh, I say, why is that worse?

BONNY: Because then it never ends.

JAMESON: Ah, but that song, Bonny – the one you were humming in the shower – I believe you're a sentimentalist at heart, like all cynics.

BARTTELOT: What song?

BONNY: Oh, just a song –

BARTTELOT: Sing it for us.

BONNY: What?

BARTTELOT: Sing it for us. (*Little pause.*) Come on, Bonny!
(BONNY, *after a moment, stands, sings a Victorian love song, delicately and with feeling.*)

TROUP: (*Rises, emotionally*) Gentlemen, to a young lady – a young lady in Highgate!

REST: A young lady in Highgate!

BARTTELOT: And a young lady in Sussex!

BONNY: To a young lady in Pimlico. Another in Maidenhead. A
third in Greenwhich!

BARTTELOT: No, no, only allowed one, Bonny.

BONNY: Ah, then I choose – a young lady in Clapham!

REST: (*Laughing*) A young lady in Clapham!

WARD: To them, all plain and pretty, amiable and otherwise the
true, the false, the young, the old – so long as they be ladies!

TROUP: You're worse than old Bonny – you've taken them all!

BONNY: No, he hasn't. Just one. Pretty, amiable, young and true
on the way to the altar! Plain, false, old and otherwise from
there to the grave!

BARTTELOT: You go too far, Bonny! Too far! Remember Mrs
Jameson!

BONNY: Oh, I'm sorry, I didn't mean to give –

JAMESON: Oh good Heavens, I can easily refute our Bonny – by
inviting you all to take dinner in my home this day a year
hence. Mrs Jameson and I and our (*hesitates*) children will be
grateful for the chance to prove that what begins in church
can continue ever more happily, please God! Will you come,
all of you? Mrs Jameson would be so pleased.

BARTTELOT: (*Solemnly*) Mrs Jameson!

REST: Mrs Jameson.

(*A respectful silence.*)

JAMESON: Or of course, *two* years hence, depending on
circumstances known to us all –

(*Laughter.*)

WARD: And that's the real interpretation to put on the message in
the Personal Column – it's not written by a lady at all, but by
some desperate fellow trying to do business with Mr Tippu-
Tib. Who is now outside the Savoy –

JAMESON: Or indeed inside it, with his six hundred porters
turned waiters.

(*Laughter.*)

BARTTELOT: You know what my pater says, he says 'It's a funny
old world.' And he's right. Here we all are, we've had our
quarrels and our worries, God knows – old Troup and I are a

pretty peppery couple of fellows from time to time, eh? But here we are – and somewhere out there, Stanley, please God, as Jamie said – and tonight – well tonight, my spirit's at peace with him. I'll never like him, I can't promise to like him but by God I can't help wishing him safety, and an evening of fellowship like this one. Eh?

REST: Hear, hear!

TROUP: And I'll wager he's wished us the same, eh? And look, I want to endorse everything the Major's said – whatever – whatever the hazards – we are – we remain
(BONNY *is quietly pouring himself more brandy*)
united, I mean we've forged a bond – between us – that – that – speaking for myself I know will last to the end of my life. I shall look back on this Christmas together to the – to the end of my life.
(*There is a pause.*)

JAMESON: Amen to that.

BARTTELOT: Bonny, give us a carol, there's a chap. My heart yearns for one.
(BONNY *begins to sing 'The Twelve Days of Christmas'.*
OTHERS *join in. Half-way through the drums begin, very low, scarcely noticeable.* BARTTELOT *has put his hand on*
JOHN HENRY's *shoulder. As they sing, lights and curtain.*)

ACT THREE

SCENE I

The same. Six months later. It is morning.
The doors are open. Around the room are various pieces of sculpture, in clay, heads of natives, animals, etc.; and some sketches, stuffed birds, stuffed snakes.
A NATIVE WOMAN, *naked, her arms tied behind her, a halter around her neck and attached to a rafter, is squatting on the floor, right.* WARD *is seated on a packing case, modelling her head in clay.* BONNY *enters, drifts over, watches* WARD, *then sits down at the table, close to the woman. There is a silence. He stares at the woman, suddenly smiles at her. The* WOMAN *smiles back.* BONNY *laughs. The* WOMAN *laughs back.* BONNY *laughs again. The* WOMAN *laughs again.*

BONNY: Funny, they squat for hours without an expression until you laugh at them. And they always laugh back.

WARD: Yes, they have very pleasant dispositions. Unless of course she was laughing at you for laughing at her – who can say whether the man is playing with the cat or the cat with the man . . .

BONNY: More like cattle than cats. Although she might have a game or two in her . . . eh, my darling? (*He laughs.*)
(*The* WOMAN *laughs.*)

WARD: Could you, do you think, hold back on your wooing a while – I'd prefer her to keep her head still. Besides, the days when you were the Lothario of Yambuya are over by some months, aren't they – ever since our Commanding Officer delivered his *en passant* homily on what he'd do, by God, to any white man he caught, by God! etc., etc.
(BONNY *yawns, puts his feet on the table, his head back. Begins to hum.*)
(*Glances at him with irritation*) Why don't you join our Commanding Officer, he'd be glad of your company, I'm sure.

BONNY: Where is he?

WARD: Having a word.

BONNY: Who with?

WARD: A couple of Soudanese who fell asleep on watch last night. The second provisions tent, I believe it was. Some of Stanley's medical supplies are in there, so he should be lathering up nicely, you'll catch him at his climax if you run.

BONNY: (*After a slight pause*) Anything missing?

WARD: Mmmmm?

BONNY: Anything missing?

WARD: Why don't you scamper over and see for yourself, there's a good man.

(BONNY *gets up, goes over to the water bucket, tries to pour himself some. It is empty.*)

BONNY: John Henry! John Henry!

WARD: Oh for – do stop shouting, Bonny! He won't come. At least, not for you.

BONNY: Well, he'd better, for his sake. If the Major finds out he's forgotten the water – John Henry!

WARD: (*Throws down the clay in disgust*) He's probably unconscious, you fool.

BONNY: What? (*Little pause.*) Oh.

WARD: Didn't you hear his screams?

BONNY: No.

WARD: Really not? About midnight, from his master's tent?

BONNY: No.

WARD: Nor his master's bellow, stick and boot?

BONNY: No.

WARD: How do you manage those slumbers of yours? You seem to have found the secret that eludes everyone but the niggers on watch and the dying, of course.

BONNY: Perhaps I've given up worrying.

WARD: But what have you taken up to give up worrying? (*He looks at him.*) Eh, Bonny?

BONNY: The thing about you, Ward, is you can't let up, can you? You set out to make him worse, the way you went on at him in mess, counting off the niggers who'd died or escaped this last month –

WARD: I was merely trying to engage his attention, with a little mental arithmetic.

BONNY: Yes, well you left him in a proper state, then banging
   your hand up and down to the drums – that's probably why
   he went off and battered John Henry.
WARD: Ah, I see. And that's why you needn't concern yourself
   with his health. Don't types of your rank have to take the
   Hippocratic oath, Bonny?
BONNY: (*After a pause*) Oh, shut up, Ward.
WARD: You feel no professional obligation, to minister to him,
   eh?
BONNY: What am I meant to do? He hasn't consulted me, has he?
WARD: And he won't. He's far too frightened.
BONNY: What of?
WARD: You.
BONNY: Oh very funny, Ward.
WARD: You can have my next year's ration of goat if he isn't.
BONNY: You honestly mean to tell me that Barttelot's frightened
   of *me* –
WARD: Barttelot? Good God, Bonny, you'd better not go about
   confusing our Commanding Major Barttelot with his
   battered little nigger of a serving boy. No, no, get it clear in
   your head, they're fearfully distinct, you know. The battered
   little nigger of a serving boy is the one who's frightened of
   you, even though he needs your skill and bandages. The
   Commanding Major Barttelot is the one you're frightened of,
   and with good reason, as he's quite clearly mad. And now
   you've got something to report to the Major, you'll hurry
   along, won't you, please, and report it?
BONNY: You want me to tell him that you say he's mad, do you?
WARD: Yes please.
BONNY: Why?
WARD: So that I can tell him what it is you've started taking to
   give up worrying. Then he'll have you flogged, I should
   think, and I'd quite enjoy that. Wouldn't you?
BONNY: I warn you, Ward, if you make any trouble for me with
   Barttelot, I'll make a damned sight more back.
   (TROUP *enters. He looks very ill, thin and yellow complexioned.*)
   Oh hello, old man, how are you?
   (TROUP *pays no attention, goes on to the water bucket.*)

You really shouldn't be up, you know.

WARD: There you are, old man, Bonny's just made out his favourite prescription. That should make you feel better. (TROUP *drops the cup, comes back to the table, sits down.*)

BONNY: I'll get you some water – (*He rises.*)

TROUP: No, you won't.

BONNY: You're thirsty, aren't you?

TROUP: Yes, but you won't get any water. You'll go out for it, but you won't come back with it.

BONNY: What do you mean?

WARD: You know what he means. He means that you'll go out for it but you won't come back with it.

TROUP: Because you haven't asked him, have you?

BONNY: I haven't even seen him to speak to this morning.

TROUP: But you're not going to ask him, are you?

BONNY: Of course I am. I said I would. But I also said I didn't see the point because we all know what the answer's going to be.

TROUP: What about you, Ward, will you speak up for me?

WARD: Of course. But I won't do any good, old chap. Quite the reverse, I'm afraid.

TROUP: I see. So I'm to die then? Is that it? To die without making a fuss.

BONNY: Look, I don't think it's quite that bad –

TROUP: Oh yes it is. Oh yes it is. I'm weaker every time I come out of it. I shall die all right, I've known it for days now. I shall die. Die here in this place because a lunatic, a lunatic – (*He stops, trembling.*)

WARD: I say, old man, be careful. The faithful Bonny, you know, is at your side.

TROUP: I don't care. I'm past caring. You tell him I saw him, Bonny. He didn't know I was watching, but I saw him, from my tent flap. I saw the lunatic go out and –

BARTTELOT: (*Enters, carrying his stick and a basket*) Two rotting fish! Two rotting fish!

WARD: Three dying niggers, four flogging gentlemen –

BARTTELOT: What?

WARD: Oh nothing, just what promised to be an amusing

anecdote of old Troup's you've interrupted, what were you saying about two rotting fish –

BARTTELOT: That's all her husband thinks she's worth, smirking outside as if he were redeeming from a pawn shop – (*going over to the woman, untying the rope from the rafter*) come on, get up, get up, he's bought you back with two rotting fish – go on, get along with you – and take these with you – (*he hooks basket around her neck*) tell him to choke on them himself – (*he grins at her, she cowers away from him*) go, get along with you – (*he propels her out through the door*) swears there isn't a goat to be had, stinks like a goat himself, a morning wasted catching her for two rotting fish – well, I got them to admit it at last, they'd been asleep all right, thank God they hadn't got into the boxes, none of them opened and they're not cunning enough to put the lids back on – by God if any of the medicine had been touched Stanley'd never have believed it was the niggers – not with a chance like that – Troup, you're closest to the tent, did you hear anything last night?

TROUP: I'm still ill, thank you for asking. Worse, as a matter of fact.

BARTTELOT: What?

WARD: Still ill, thank you for asking. Worse as a matter of fact.

BARTTELOT: I'm talking to Troup, Ward.

TROUP: I said I'm worse.

BARTTELOT: But you're up, aren't you?

TROUP: Oh yes. Yes, I'm up, Barttelot.

BARTTELOT: Slept through the night, did you?

TROUP: No, Barttelot. No sleep. None at all.

WARD: Loyal Bonny did, though, didn't you, Bonny? Slept like a top.

BARTTELOT: Well then, did you hear anything, see anything?

TROUP: Oh yes. I saw and heard quite a lot.

BARTTELOT: What?

WARD: He saw and heard –

BARTTELOT: From the provisions tent?

TROUP: No. Not from there.

BARTTELOT: Well, Ward, what about you?

WARD: Screams, oaths and blows from your tent. From the provisions tent, nothing. So I'm afraid I can't help you either, sir.

BARTTELOT: (*Goes over to the water*) Well, we've got to find out who's responsible, there's a clutch of Soudanese scum who're up to some mischief – (*Tries to pour water.*)

WARD: How remarkable.

BARTTELOT: What?

WARD: (*After a little pause*) Why, that anyone in the compound, apart from your energetic self, of course, could be up to anything as taxing as mischief.

BARTTELOT: Well, you're damned well not are you, been idling in here all day – John Henry, John Henry! Where is the little –

BONNY: Haven't seen hide nor hair of him, Major.

WARD: From which we can conclude, sir, that he must still be out.

BARTTELOT: Out where?

WARD: Of his senses. And after the kind of night you had together, it's not to be wondered at, is it?

BARTTELOT: You drank the last drop of water, I suppose, Ward, but damn you if you were going to get some more for the rest of us, eh?

WARD: Damn me, sir, if I was.

BONNY: I'll go, Major, I was just about to fetch some for Troup anyway – (*Getting up.*)

BARTTELOT: Thank you, Bonny.

WARD: Before you go, Bonny, would you kindly ask the Major what you promised old Troup here you'd ask him.

BONNY: What?

WARD: Before you go, Bonny, would you kindly ask etc.

BONNY: It's only what I've already mentioned, Major. I explained that the situation being what it is –

BARTTELOT: You know the situation, Troup. You've known it for months. There isn't any.

TROUP: Yes, there is. There is!

BARTTELOT: But it's not ours, Troup. It's Stanley's. We've used up ours.

TROUP: So. So I'm to die –

BARTTELOT: You're not going to die.

TROUP: – because the rest of you used up our stock before I could
  get ill, is that what it comes to?

WARD: Yes, even you must find that a trifle bizarre, sir. That poor
  old Troup's superior robustness has had such an unhappy
  effect on his health. (*He laughs.*)

BARTTELOT: What?

WARD: Yes, even you must find that a trifle –

BARTTELOT: By God, Ward, how sick I am of your jokes.

WARD: Ah, but fortunately – for you – you don't need quinine to
  recover from them.

BARTTELOT: But I know how to stop you making them.

WARD: So do I, sir. Some humanity, or failing that, a dash of
  intelligence, in the running of this camp. Or did you mean
  bellow, boot and stick, as usual.

TROUP: You're just going to stand by, then, and see me die, are
  you, Barttelot? My death shall be on your head. I've written
  to MacKinnon, my letter to be conveyed to him with the rest
  of my effects, Ward, if you'll be so good.

WARD: Of course, my dear chap. Though I should point out that
  having over a hundred dead blacks on his head already –

BARTTELOT: That's right, Troup. You can die if you want to. I've
  long wanted you gone, you've never had anything to give to
  the Rear Column but bluster when you're well and snivelling
  now you're sick. It's not medicine you lack, Troup, but
  fortitude.

TROUP: (*After a pause*) You refuse me, then.

BARTTELOT: Of course I refuse you.

TROUP: And that's your last word?

BARTTELOT: I hope so. Though knowing you –

TROUP: Very well. I give you warning, Barttelot. I shall help
  myself from Stanley's supplies.

BARTTELOT: What? (*Pause.*) What did you say?

TROUP: I shall help myself –

BARTTELOT: By God – by God, you already have, haven't you? It
  was you, wasn't it, in the provisions tent last night! It was
  you! I'm going to open every load, every one, and if there's a

drop of quinine missing, I'll – by God, Troup, I'll have you flogged for the thieving nigger you are.

TROUP: (*Runs over to him*) You're mad, Barttelot, a lunatic, a lunatic! I saw you last night, I watched you, I wrote it down. It's in my letter to MacKinnon, don't forget the letter, Ward –

WARD: Certainly not, old man.

TROUP: Everybody'll know you for what you are – do you know what he did last night?

BARTTELOT: (*Advances on* TROUP, *grinning*) Hah, hah, hah, hah! Hah hah hah hah!

(JAMESON *appears at the door. He is carrying equipment, as in Act Two, Scene One. He is not, at first, noticed.*)

Hah hah hah hah!

TROUP: You, you –

WARD: Ah, welcome home, old man – oh, the Major and Troup are just sharing a joke on the subject of the Major's sanity.

BARTTELOT: Hah hah hah hah!

(TROUP *draws back a fist, to strike* BARTTELOT. BARTTELOT *thrusts his face closer to* TROUP.)

Hah hah hah hah!

(JAMESON *moves very swiftly, catches* TROUP's *arm, pulls him away. He stands between* BARTTELOT *and* TROUP, *facing* BARTTELOT.)

Ah – ah, there you are, Jamie, you're back then are you?

TROUP: He's trying to murder me, murder me, Jameson – well – (*trying to pull* JAMESON *away*) let him do it so everybody can see – go on, Barttelot, kill me, kill me now, in front of everybody –

BARTTELOT: By God I will, Troup, if you don't get out of the Camp and back to England. I'm sending you home, now, this minute.

TROUP: See, see, he's frightened of me because I saw him – Oh, I saw him –

JAMESON: Please. Please, listen to me. (*Little pause.*) I've news. I've seen Tippu-Tib.

BARTTELOT: What? (*As if dazed.*) Seen him?

JAMESON: Yes. He sends his greetings and his apologies for the delay.

BARTTELOT: The delay! For the delay – after a year!

JAMESON: But he solemnly undertakes to be with us shortly, with the porters. He swore it to Allah, and in friendship to Stanley. Apparently he lost his first catch through a series of monstrous misfortunes – escape, sickness, capsizing boats, but he sent messengers to let us know – presumably they were the cannibal victims. But his second lot, with a large guard of his Arabs, are on their way. He's just had word. He's going back to the Falls to bring them up himself.

BARTTELOT: About – about three weeks then! A month at the most!

JAMESON: His own calculation was a month.

BARTTELOT: By God – by God – of all the wonderful – but what was he doing in these parts, if his slaves are at the Falls?

JAMESON: Coming to see you. But I told him that as he'd seen me, you'd prefer him to get back to the porters –

BARTTELOT: By God yes – and Stanley – any news of Stanley?

JAMESON: He must be alive as he'd have heard if he were dead. He's a rather extraordinary chap, our Tippu, by the way, you'll enjoy –

BARTTELOT: (*Is pacing about, talking almost as if to himself*) So Stanley's still alive, the porters coming up – can't be more than a month away – we'll meet him on the march, by God – with the loads – with the loads – how d'you do, Mr Stanley, here are your supplies, sir – by God we've beaten you, Stanley – beaten you, sir – (*He goes on out through the doors, and his voice, off.*) Up on your feet, scum, up on your feet, you're going to learn how to walk again – up I say – up with you – by God I've beaten him – march – march along I say – I've beaten the devil – (*His voice fading, but sounding now and then.*)

TROUP: So we'll be moving from this place after all, is that what you mean, Jameson? Is that it?

JAMESON: Yes, old man. That's it.

TROUP: But what about me, what's he going to do about me? I told him, you see, I let him know that I'd seen him – oh why did I, why did I? Now he'll send me home to die in the jungle, or leave me here to perish by myself while you march on –

JAMESON: My dear old chap, there's no question of your being left,

or of your being sent home, and certainly not of your dying. I
do assure you.

TROUP: Oh, I shall die, Jameson, one way or the other. He'll see
to that. Anyway I won't live without quinine, and he won't
let me have any of Stanley's, that's how he'll do it –

JAMESON: But there's no need of Stanley's. I've got some. Here.
(*He takes a phial out of his equipment.*) I've always kept some
of my personal stock in reserve for my expeditions, in case
I'm taken with a fever away from base – but I shan't need it
now, shall I? Besides, I've never felt so well in my life.

TROUP: Oh, thank you, Jameson. Thank you. God bless you.
God bless you. (*He bursts into tears.*) I'm sorry, I'm sorry –
(*He sinks to his knees.*) Oh Jameson –
(JAMESON *lifts* TROUP *up, holds him.*)

BONNY: He should be in bed.

WARD: Well, why don't you put him there.

JAMESON: Yes, I'm sure you're the chap he needs –

BONNY: Yes, come along, old man, let's get you down. (*He puts
his arm around* TROUP, *who is in a state of semi-collapse, and
leads him off.*)
(*There is a pause.*)

WARD: Well. (*Smiling.*) You got back in the nick of time.

JAMESON: I've never moved so fast in my life. (*Little pause.*) How
are you?

WARD: I'm anxious to hear about your adventures, what sort of
chap is Tippu after all?

JAMESON: Oh very amusing. I kept storing away all sorts of
things to tell you, (*going to the water bucket*) he goes in for a
grand, not to say flamboyant style of hospitality, I've done
one or two sketches of him in characteristic postures, I must
show you later, by the way, oh, and I picked up a spectacular
lizard and a butterfly I've never seen before, he fluttered over
Tippu's head on my second morning and settled in a branch
– (*Makes to pour himself water.*)

WARD: I'm afraid it's empty. John Henry being hors de combat,
let me get you some.

JAMESON: No, no, I'm not really thirsty, I stopped for a drink
when I came in. I wasn't thirsty then either, but one gets into

the habit of taking a drink where one can as if it'll make up for the times one can't, which of course it doesn't. (*He laughs*.) But you haven't told me how you are?

WARD: All I can really say is that I'm no worse.

JAMESON: No worse?

WARD: Than the rest of us. I haven't been beating children senseless, for instance. But then that's the Major's way, not mine. Nor have I been stealing morphine from Stanley's supplies. But then that's Bonny's way, as it turns out.

JAMESON: Ah, I did wonder, before I left –

WARD: Troup's way you know about, as you caught the climax of his performance.

JAMESON: Yes, poor old Troup.

WARD: For my part, I've mainly lolled.

JAMESON: Lolled?

WARD: Yes, about and about, you know. Inflaming the inflammable, goading the goadable and despising the despicable. That's been my way.

JAMESON: But I see you've made an attempt – (*Indicating the head of the woman*.)

WARD: Yesterday afternoon I dragged myself over to the river-bank, where I lolled in the hope of catching you in an early return. But all I saw were the corpses of two drowned niggers, rolled along by the sluggish current, and a few minutes later one nigger drowning. He sank some yards from me but bobbed up half an hour later, his head tangled in weeds, to be rolled off in his turn. I took him to be a deserting Zanzibari.

JAMESON: I'm sure there was nothing you could have done.

WARD: No, there wasn't, really.

JAMESON: Thank God you didn't go in after him. That current – you wouldn't have had a chance.

WARD: Not much of one, certainly.

JAMESON: So you mustn't reproach yourself.

WARD: Oh, I haven't been. Nor have I reproached myself for not reproaching myself, if you see.

JAMESON: Well I don't quite –

WARD: What I'm trying to say is, well, that given our different

forms of degeneration, you were quite right to lie about
seeing Tippu-Tib. False hope is probably our only hope
now.

JAMESON: I didn't lie about seeing Tippu-Tib. I spent three days
in his camp.

WARD: I see. Then you lied about what he said.

JAMESON: I reported him absolutely faithfully.

WARD: But you can't have believed him!

JAMESON: (*After a pause*) Of course not. It was understood
between us at once that his lies were a courtesy. Kindness,
even, so that I shouldn't feel obliged to accuse him of
treachery when hopelessly outnumbered. As I said, he's an
excellent host, he really went to extravagant lengths to make
me comfortable. (*Pause.*) I hoped you wouldn't be taken in. I
shall need your support more than ever when the month is
up and the doubts return.

WARD: And the whole process starts again. Although we shan't
survive a whole year this time.

JAMESON: But if we can stretch the month into two and then
three – until Stanley comes back, or we have news of his
death. We have a chance. (*He smiles.*) At least we'll survive
until tomorrow.

WARD: Of course if we were all like you, we could survive here for
ever. And you could certainly survive without us, couldn't
you?

JAMESON: Not quite. (*Pause.*) I say, would you like to have a look
(*going to equipment*) at my rendering of Tippu, I think I've
caught something of his –

WARD: No! No I wouldn't! (*Little pause.*) I'm sorry, I know it's
infernally weak of me, I admire you more than any man I've
ever met, and I'm flattered, flattered of course, that you
should have counted on me for your support, even though I
know you could manage without it, but it's just that – at the
moment I wish – I wish you hadn't – no, that's not fair – I
hadn't insisted on the truth. I'm sorry. Infernally weak. But
then I am. I've learnt that much – (*He turns, goes towards the
flap, stops, looks at* JAMESON.)

JAMESON: I'm sorry. If I'd realized –

WARD: Don't worry. You *can* count on me. For what I'm worth.
(*He exits.*)
(JAMESON *stands for a moment. From off,* BARTTELOT'*s voice,
roaring out orders, and the sound of the Soudanese, and the
Zanzibaris, calling to each other excitedly, coming near, then
turning, going further off.* JAMESON *goes to the doors, draws
them almost closed, but allowing light to enter, comes back, stares
at his equipment, then after a moment takes out a dead parakeet,
gutted; then a small object, presumably the butterfly; looks at it;
takes out several more objects, a bowl and a wooden spoon;
finally his sketch-pad and note-book. Opens the note-book, sits
looking at it.* JOHN HENRY *enters through the flap, limping
bruised, carrying a water-bucket. He looks furtively over at*
JAMESON, *who watches him go to replace the empty water-
bucket with the full one, and then turn to go out.*)
JAMESON: John Henry. John Henry – come here.
(JOHN HENRY *comes over.*)
Are you all right?
(JOHN HENRY *nods.*)
Well, you will be from now on. I promise you. No more
bruises. No more. All right? (*He pats his head.*) Now you go
and find your master, eh?
(JOHN HENRY *nods, goes out through the flap.*)
(JAMESON *sits for a moment, looks at the sketches, then puts his
face in his hands, as if tired. The voices off become less and less
distinct. The lights fade slowly down to darkness.*)

SCENE 2

A couple of hours later.
*The set is in darkness. There comes from the darkness a low murmur,
an exclamation, silence. Then another exclamation.* BARTTELOT
enters, left, carrying a lamp. JOHN HENRY *is at his side. There is
another exclamation.* BARTTELOT *goes over to the work desk, holds
the lamp up.* JAMESON *is slumped over the desk, asleep. On the desk
his note-book. His sketch-pad has fallen to the floor.* BARTTELOT
lights the lamp near the table, gives his own lamp to JOHN HENRY,

who lights the other lamps. JAMESON *groans heavily.*

BARTTELOT: (*Stands looking down at him. Then puts a hand on* JAMESON'*s shoulder.*) All right, Jamie. All right, old boy. It's only me.

(JAMESON *lifts his head, sees* BARTTELOT, *lets out a cry of terror.*)

Only me, Jamie. Only me.

JAMESON: Oh, I'm – I'm sorry.

BARTTELOT: A bad dream, eh?

JAMESON: Yes.

BARTTELOT: And are you properly awake now?

JAMESON: I'm not sure.

BARTTELOT: Well, I'm no dream, I can tell you. (*He laughs.*) I've had them on the march, up and down and around the compound, then out into the jungle, making them walk, making them feel their legs again, you see, the halt, the maim, tomorrow I'll have the strongest moving with loads, some will have to carry double when Tippu's lot arrive, we've lost so many, but by God we won't lose another one, not another one – John Henry – go and get some manioc – manioc, John Henry – tell you the truth couldn't keep still myself, thinking of his face – the expression on the devil's face

(JOHN HENRY *has gone out for the manioc*)

– when he finds every one of them intact, eh? Well, Mr Stanley, what sort of year have you had? Let me tell you about ours – oh, and here's our Mr Jameson, Mr Bonny, Mr Ward and even Mr Troup, you do remember us, I take it, or had you thought us dead, sir. Or deserted even? By God – by God –

(JOHN HENRY *returns, pours the manioc.*)

That's the boy, John Henry, keep off that bad leg, eh? (*He drinks.*) Well, Jamie – and what about Emin Pasha, I thought of him when I was marching them, first time for nearly a year I remembered him. Make nonsense of the whole business if Stanley hasn't got him out, if the Mahdi got to him first, eh? All that we've been through because of Emin Pasha, and none of it to do with him, just a battle between Stanley and

ourselves, and ourselves and the damned niggers, and
ourselves and ourselves, eh? (*He drinks, looks at* JAMESON.)
But I'll tell you something. He nearly won, old man. He did.
If you hadn't come back God knows what – Troup called me
a lunatic and – by God he was right. Because last night I
committed the act of a lunatic and Troup saw me at it. It was
your Mrs Minchip who drove me to it, on her drums, I sent
John Henry out, and they went silent, then started again,
and – I couldn't endure it, couldn't endure it, but I did, you
see, instead of going out and giving her a cuff myself I
endured it, until the others had gone to bed, and then I went
out, walked over them, trampled on them where they lay, or
put my stick into their sides and stirred them out of the way
with the point, walking in a straight line to their tent, and
when I got there I went up to the woman squatting there,
beating away, and I grinned at her, you know how my grin
works, a grin and then a cuff, how they fold before it, but
this time not a bit of it, she kept on pounding away, not even
seeing me, and then I looked up, and there was his face in the
slit of their tent, peering out and grinning back at me, and
beneath that another slit, freshly cut, the barrel of his rifle
sticking out of it straight at me, right at my chest, you see,
and the woman pounding on, so I looked back at him,
grinning at his grin to wipe it off, and I could see him losing
his nerve, the barrel wavered, so I bent over the woman, you
see, didn't know what I was doing until my teeth were in her
neck. Sank them deep into her neck, to stop her on the
drums at last. I looked back at the slit and I thought now –
now you nigger, if you dare – with her blood still around my
mouth, and I laughed into his face. Laughed into his face
with his woman's blood around my mouth and his gun
against my chest. It was a good laugh, a good long laugh, all
the time I was waiting for the rifle to go off, thinking now,
nigger, do it now – until I turned and walked away, stepping
on them again, on their arms and legs and bellies and faces
and when I got back to my tent I remembered the blood was
still around my mouth. I licked at it with my tongue. Licked
it off with my tongue. Drank some manioc to get rid of the

taste, and more manioc to keep the dear old pater, you see, from watching his son lick up nigger blood from around his mouth – or Stanley seeing – what I had come to. And there was John Henry – and so he got the brunt of it, poor little mite. Poor little mite. You see. Had to tell you myself. Before you hear it from Troup. (*Pause.*) Well, Jamie – what do you think of me now?

JAMESON: Why, exactly as I've always thought of you, old man.

BARTTELOT: You don't despise me for it.

JAMESON: No.

BARTTELOT: That's a relief. I care what you think of me, you know. Always have. You, with your strength – well, you know that. (*Pause.*) By God, you know, I may be the wrong man for the Rear Column, that's why he chose me, but I did one good thing, right at the beginning, I had the beating of Stanley right at the beginning, when I made him give you over to me.

JAMESON: Give me over to you?

BARTTELOT: 'One of Parke, Jephson or Stair will remain behind with you, Barttelot,' he said. 'You may choose.' And I said, 'None of them, thank you, Mr Stanley, the man I want is Jameson.' 'Jameson, Jameson,' he said. 'But Jameson isn't an officer, he's a paying gentleman.' And I said, 'It's Jameson I want, Mr Stanley.' And he gave me a Stanley look, and I readied myself for a row, instead he whinnied out some laughter, 'Very well,' he said. 'Very well. But I advise you, Major Barttelot, for the sake of harmony between you, not to tell him he's staying behind at your request. Even Jameson, gentleman though he is, might come to hate you for it.' Stanley, the great judge of men! Didn't know you as I knew you, even then – and that's where I had the beating of him. And beaten him all over again by telling you. Although I've waited until today to do it, I admit, and probably wouldn't have today if – if –

JAMESON: Fate hadn't worked things otherwise.

BARTTELOT: That's it, old man! That's it!

JAMESON: But then fate, being fate, never does. At least in as much as you've been mine, and didn't.

BARTTELOT: All I can say is, in spite of everything, I wouldn't have had it different.

JAMESON: Amen to that!

(BONNY *enters through the flap*.)

Ah, Bonny, here you are then – Jameson and I were just having a glass – John Henry, a glass for Mr Bonny –

(JOHN HENRY *pours* BONNY *a glass. Off, the drums start, with a flourish*.)

BARTTELOT: There they go, eh Jamie? So that's all right then – well, they've something to celebrate tonight, John Henry, go tell them with the Major's compliments that tonight they may play their drums – but low, tell them – low.

BONNY: (*Meanwhile, spotting* JAMESON'S *fallen sketch-pad, picks it up*) Brought back some drawings too, eh?

JAMESON: Yes.

BONNY: So quite a successful trip, what with one thing and the other.

(JOHN HENRY *goes out*.)

(*Looking through the pad*) Any of Tippu-Tib?

BARTTELOT: What, Tippu, I must have a look at those, get to know the devil on different terms, eh? By God, it'll be hard to keep a check on my tongue when he comes in here – How d'you do, Mr Tib, glad to make your acquaintance at last, sir –

(WARD *enters through the flap*.)

Ah, here you are, Ward – here's a glass of Yambuya champagne for you – and *I've* got good news – fish stew tonight.

BONNY: What?

BARTTELOT: (*Laughs*) No, it's all right, Bonny, three I picked up down-river when I was marching the men, not the rotting pair this morning – Jamie, you haven't heard about that yet, Bonny and I caught ourselves a woman yesterday, hobbled her, brought her back, her man came in this morning with two stinking fish –

(*The drums have quietened*. TROUP *enters through the flap*.)

Troup, by God, you've come – here – a glass for Troup – but should you be up, even for Yambuya champagne, old man –

here – (*pouring him a glass*) should you be?

TROUP: Thank you. Jameson's quinine, you know – (*He clears his throat.*) Um Major, I want to say – say before everybody – that – I said some things this morning I – I deeply regret, accused you of all sorts of nonsense, which Bonny tells me – I realize was just – just delirium –

BARTTELOT: (*Pause.*) Well – you and I have had our – our – what's passed is passed, eh? That's the thing – let's drink instead – drink to, to –

WARD: Tippu-Tib. (*He glances at* JAMESON.)

BARTTELOT: Why, yes – Tippu-Tib, damn his soul!

REST: Tippu-Tib, damn his soul!

BONNY: I saw him a minute ago, yes, here he is – (*Flicking open the sketch-pad.*)

BARTTELOT: What, let's see, why that's as good as your famous A Faithful Zanzibari says his Farewell, Jamie – what slyness, what pomp, eh, and his rifle – the one Stanley gave him – over his chest – hah, hah, hah!

(JAMESON *puts his hand to his forehead.* BARTTELOT *goes to get the manioc jug.*)

WARD: (*To* JAMESON) Are you all right?

JAMESON: Yes, yes – just a touch tired –

(BONNY *is casually turning over pages of the pad.*)

TROUP: (*To* JAMESON) I'm very conscious of my debt to you, Jameson. For the quinine – and everything else.

JAMESON: Oh.

(JOHN HENRY *enters.*)

BARTTELOT: Ah, there's a good boy – well done John Henry, well done – (*Coming back with the jug.*)

BONNY: (*Lets out an exclamation*) What's this?

JAMESON: (*Looking up*) Mmmm?

(WARD *saunters over to look.* BARTTELOT *comes over with the jug, offers to pour for* TROUP.)

TROUP: No thank you, Major, feeling a bit – a bit – (*Goes, sits down.*)

BONNY: A little girl tied to a tree.

JAMESON: Oh. (*Little pause.*) Yes.

(BARTTELOT *comes over, looks over* BONNY'S *other shoulder.*)

146

BARTTELOT: What, what is it, Jamie?

(BONNY *turns another page, stares at it*. WARD, BARTTELOT *also stare*.)

WARD: But she's – they're –

BARTTELOT: Can't make it out, what's going on?

(*There is a pause*.)

JAMESON: It's a cannibal feast. (*Pause*.) I happened to mention to Tippu that once or twice I'd come across the remains of one, but never the beginnings or middle of one. So the next morning he invited me to accompany him and some of his chaps to a village where a couple of Tippu's men had been doing a bit of slaving. Among their merchandise was a girl of about thirteen, I suppose – that girl. I bought her from them, at Tippu's suggestion, for five brass-rods, and then we took her off to a cannibal chief Tippu knew of, who was told he could have her for lunch on the understanding that I did drawings of him while he was at it, and Tippu got a goat for our supper. (*Pause*.) To my knowledge it's the first time the whole process has been recorded. (*Pause*.) He was my host.

WARD: You bought the girl, then watched her being killed and prepared for the pot and cooked and eaten. And made sketches of it?

BONNY: And here, asleep under a tree, that's him is it, afterwards?

JAMESON: Yes.

BARTTELOT: (*Quietly*) What have you done?

JAMESON: What? (*He looks around at their faces*.) Nothing very terrible, surely. The girl had already been caught by slavers, she was bound to end up in the pot – they have no other use for them at that age. Good Heavens, we've flogged them to death, we've watched them die by the score, what does it matter, one nigger girl – (*He stops, looks at* WARD.) Yes. I see. I suppose I've slightly lost my – my – My curiosity and the uniqueness of it evidently blinded me to the – the – (*Stops*.) I'm sorry.

BONNY: Tippu-Tib doesn't have any of these, by any chance, does he?

JAMESON: Some rough versions, yes.

BONNY: Did you sign them for him?

JAMESON: Yes.

BARTTELOT: Do you know – do you know – what he'll do with them? Why, he'll head straight back to the Falls and show them – show them around to everyone, everyone. The story will be all over the Congo, in England, in London, on the first steamer – that we participated – participated in a cannibal – cannibal –

BONNY: They'll say you ate your share of her, too.

BARTTELOT: All these months – this year – of waiting and hoping – and then just as the end is in sight you – you – with your damned – your damned – collection – you bring us down! (*The drums increase, and increase, through* BARTTELOT's *next speech, almost drowning it towards its end.*) Why, it's all been for nothing, nothing! Worse than nothing, to dishonour, to disgrace – by God man, after all this you've destroyed us, worse than death, worse than desertion, in England, with Stanley, here, destroyed – destroyed – is that why Stanley gave you to me, because he knew, he knew you'd – you'd – (*he is shaking, as if in a fit*) do his work for him, you and Stanley, is that what it was, – (*he holds his stick towards* JAMESON, *makes as if to thrust it into him, then wheels around, sees* JOHN HENRY) I told you – I told you to stop them, told you, (*gouges the stick into* JOHN HENRY) little black – scum – scum – (*as the pounding of the drum is at its fullest pitch.*)

(WARD *runs over to stop* BARTTELOT. BARTTELOT *shakes him off savagely, then rounds on him, raises his stick, makes to thrust it into* WARD, *then turns, flings open the doors, on the darkness, with fires burning, drums pounding, strides off.* BONNY *goes over to the door, stares out.* WARD *goes to* JOHN HENRY, *bends over him, then straightens.* TROUP *is sitting, motionless.* JAMESON *is sitting, motionless. The drums stop. There is silence.*)

BARTTELOT: (*Off*) Hah, hah, hah, hah! Hah, hah, hah – (*There is a shot. Silence.* WARD *moves towards the doors. There are sudden cries, shouts, off.* BONNY *pushes the doors closed before* WARD *reaches them, locks them. Turns his back to them.*)

BONNY: If you go out there they'll do the same to you. And then come on in and do the same to us. (*Pause.*) We'll get him in the morning.

(WARD *hesitates, then turns away. Looks at* JAMESON. *He goes over to him, looks at him.* JAMESON *looks slowly up at* WARD. *There is a pause.*)

TROUP: (*In a dull voice*) Now perhaps you'll listen to me. Now perhaps we can go home.

(BONNY *goes over, helps himself to manioc from the jug.* WARD *puts his hand on* JAMESON'*s shoulder.*)

Go home at last, eh?

(BONNY *drinks.*)

(*Lights fade slowly on this tableau, to darkness, as the drums start up again excitable, unrhythmic.*

The same. Some days later.

The doors are slightly open. From off, the sound of voices, Zanzibari, Soudanese. BONNY *is moving about, doing an inventory of the boxes, but slowly. The sound of* STANLEY'*s voice, off, commanding.* BONNY *straightens, listens.*

STANLEY *enters through the doors, pulling them wide.*)

STANLEY: Well Bonny, Parke is back from the Falls, with some news. He spoke to Mr Troup, who is in excellent health, and has booked his passage back to Southampton. He is also in excellent voice. His self-justifications and denials have fuelled the scandal, God knows what form the story will finally take when it appears in *The Times*, but it will certainly have precedence with the public over my own poor efforts, who will want to read of the successful relief of Emin Pasha when there are tales of Barttelot's lash and Jameson's experiments in slaughtering, cooking and consuming infant girls to wallow in, eh? Mr Jameson, by the way, is dead.

BONNY: Oh.

STANLEY: He died at a Mission House between here and the Falls. He went too fast, in no state to travel, though if he'd had quinine with him he would probably have survived, why he didn't have quinine is another of the incomprehensible – as there is quinine here – is there not? But let us be charitable and assume that his neglect of himself had something Roman in it. If not Roman, then at least English. He was buried by

Mr Ward, some nonsense about a Union Jack draped over a coffin rough-hewn from a tree – no doubt a bugle carved on the spot to sound a lament, eh? Pshaw! The good people at the Mission were much moved, being ignorant at the time that they were officiating over the remains of a celebrated cannibal, with his good friend, the opium fiend.

BONNY: I can't be sure it was Mr Ward who took the laudanum – all I know is that some is missing –

STANLEY: (*Looks at him*) Mr Ward left the Mission House, and has completely vanished. You, on the other hand, Bonny, are here, the only survivor, in the moral sense, of the Yambuya fiasco. So let us make sure that your reputation is unsullied, eh?

BONNY: Thank you, sir. I felt somebody had to stay behind until you –

STANLEY: I'm not interested in your motives, Bonny. One can't plan motives only results. But there's no way of planning for gentlemen like Jameson, or a maniac like Barttelot. I did my best. I knew him to be a danger to us all, that's why I left him behind, in this place, where he could do no harm. (*Laughs.*) With an English gentleman to keep a check on him. And a set of orders that couldn't have been simpler, clearer or more flexible. All he had to do was to follow my orders. Easy enough, easy enough, even for a maniac, eh?

BONNY: At least you rescued Emin Pasha.

STANLEY: Who resents it bitterly, being comfortable and probably safe where he was. By the way, Bonny, where did you bury my John Henry?

BONNY: Outside the compound, with all the other – um –
(STANLEY *looks at him, then bends, begins to pull off one of his boots.* BONNY *waits.*)

STANLEY: Be so kind as to take those damned turtles to the kitchen, would you?
(BONNY *releases the turtles, takes them out through the flap.* STANLEY *straightens for a moment, then begins to take off the other boot.*)
(*Curtain.*)

Close of Play

For Piers

Close of Play was first performed on 24 May 1979 in the Lyttleton auditorium of the National Theatre, London. The cast was as follows:

JASPER	Sir Michael Redgrave
DAISY	Annie Leon
HENRY	Michael Gambon
MARIANNE	Anna Massey
BENEDICT	John Standing
MARGARET	Lynn Farleigh
JENNY	Zena Walker
MATTHEW	Adam Godley or Matthew Ryan
Director	Harold Pinter
Designer	Eileen Diss

ACT ONE

The curtain rises on the stage in darkness. There is the sound of organ music, at first faint, then swelling until it fills the theatre. As it does so a faint pool of light spreads over JASPER *in his armchair. He appears to be asleep. The music stops mid-chord.* JASPER *opens his eyes, as the rest of the lights come up steadily, until the room is filled with bright summer sunshine.*

Off, left, from beyond the french windows in the garden, the sound of children playing football. HENRY's *voice sounds among theirs.*

DAISY: (*Comes through on the run, goes to the french windows, calls out*) Henry – Henry dear – will you ask them to keep it right down – right down dear – because of the windows – oh, they can't hear – and as they're going to the Piece later on surely they can wait – and Marianne's forgotten Nindy's pottie again, can you believe. I know what she says about wee-wee being perfectly hygienic and Romans brushing their teeth in it but I don't like her putting her on our soup tureen, do you – but oh Good Heavens Jasper, you've got the lights on, didn't you realize dear, you don't need the lights now it's so light – it's not going to rain for a bit yet you know – (*turning them off*) – there – there, that's better isn't it, now then, tell me, what did you think of the dumplings, nobody's mentioned them, I was afraid they hadn't thawed right through and I saw your face when you bit into one, you didn't bite into ice, did you dear, I know how you hate cold in your mouth – it goes right through your system I know, is that what happened, did you bite on ice?

(JENNY *enters, left, carrying a shopping bag.*)

Oh there you are, dear, back already, that was quick.

JENNY: Is Matthew here?

DAISY: What, Matthew, no dear, isn't he with you? He ran after you to catch you up, didn't he Jasper?

JENNY: Oh, what a nuisance. Why on earth didn't he stay here, as I told him.

DAISY: What dear, well, never mind, you got the muffins did you, that's the main thing. (*Going to take them.*)

155

JENNY: Oh yes, well I'm afraid I could only get a dozen, Nanty, so I got half a dozen rock-cakes as well, I hope that's all right.

DAISY: What, what do you mean, but I ordered a dozen and a half muffins specially, didn't I Jasper? They promised to keep them, they swore they would, did you say who they were for, did you say they were for Professor Jasper Spencer?

JENNY: Well no, I think I said they were for you, Miss Blightforth –

DAISY: Oh well that explains it, you should have said Professor Jasper Spencer, they know his name in all the shops, don't they Jasper, particularly the baker's, well never mind dear, but rock-cakes you say, I don't know who's going to eat rock-cakes –

JENNY: Matthew loves them, I know.

DAISY: What, Matthew, well of course if Matthew – anyway how much is that I owe you, dear, the muffins are three and a half p each I know, at least they were last week and they can't have gone up again in spite of the Common Market, can they Jasper?

JENNY: Oh please, let them be my contribution – as a matter of fact I –

DAISY: What, certainly not. Good Heavens, we wouldn't dream, would we, Jasper, you're our guests you know – so say three and a half p the muffins, now Matthew's rock-cakes dear, how much were they?

JENNY: Oh four p I think, but really Nanty –

DAISY: What, four p! Did you hear that, Jasper, four p Matthew's rock-cakes! So that's three and a half times twelve equals forty-two, now, where's my handbag, the muffins plus six time four equals twenty-four, the rock-cakes, it was on the table, I know! Plus forty-two the muffins comes to sixty-six p ah here it is sixty-six p I owe altogether dear. (*Rooting around in her handbag.*) Oh but it's not here, but I'm sure I put it back after the milkman, Jasper do you know what I did with it?

JENNY: Actually Nanty, I do think I'd better get back to the High, you see Matthew's only got today off from school, I

have to take him back first thing tomorrow. (*Moving off left.*)
So I'll see you later.

DAISY: What, but it was here you know, you know the one
Jasper, small, green, in velours, you gave it to me yourself,
you know how careful I am –
(MARGARET *enters through the arch*.)
Oh hello dear, we're just looking for my purse, my small
green one in velours, you haven't seen it have you?

MARGARET: No I'm sorry I haven't.

DAISY: That's strange, where on earth . . . thank you so much for
the dishes.

MARGARET: The dishes?

DAISY: Helping Marianne with them, so sweet of you.

MARGARET: Actually Nanty, I'm afraid I didn't.

DAISY: What, oh then she's had to do them all by herself, oh dear,
well – well never mind, she'll have finished them by now
almost won't she Jasper, so you come and tell us all your news
dear, it's so difficult at lunch isn't it, with all Henry's and
Marianne's little ones, and it's such a long time since we've
seen you and Benedict, we're dying to hear all about your
adventures on that TV programme, we saw you, you know,
did Jasper tell you, sitting there as cool as a cucumber with a
beret on, wasn't it, and the way you talked to that little man
with the working-class accent, where was he from, anyway?

MARGARET: Oxford.

DAISY: What, not the University, you don't mean?

JENNY: Yes. All Souls –

DAISY: Good heavens, Jasper, did you hear that, the little
working-class man who interviewed Margaret was from
Oxford, aren't you glad you didn't take that Chair after all,
well you certainly put him in his place, dear, asking you all
those questions and paying you those ridiculous
compliments, and you just saying yes and no as if you
couldn't be bothered with him to the manner born, I always
say Jasper should have been on TV, don't I Jasper, especially
now they've got colour, because of his white mane you know,
so distinguished, but I suppose they're not interested in
Latin translations and medieval what-nots dear, you should

have been a novelist like Margaret dear, and you could too, couldn't he Margaret, with his imagination, not that yours isn't very interesting too dear, oh yes I've read your novel you know, as soon as I heard you and Benedict were really coming down at last I went straight out and borrowed a copy from the library, didn't I Jasper?

(BENEDICT *enters through the french windows.*)

BENEDICT: Oh, you're in here, are you darling? I've been waiting for you in the garden for our little walk.

DAISY: Oh well, she's been talking to your father, dear, telling us all about her success and fame and what have you, you must be so proud of her, dear.

BENEDICT: What, Nanty?

DAISY: What, dear?

(*There is a pause.*)

Proud of her, I mean.

BENEDICT: Oh. Maggie you mean?

DAISY: Yes dear.

BENEDICT: Yes. Yes I am, Nanty. Very proud. (*Little pause.*) *Very* proud. Very very proud. Aren't I darling? Um – um – (*Sits down.*)

DAISY: Are you all right, dear? Is he all right?

BENEDICT: What Nanty?

DAISY: Are you all right, dear? You've been very quiet and grave, you know, all through lunch, and he hardly ate a thing Jasper, did he Margaret, you didn't touch the dumplings didn't you like them?

BENEDICT: Oh. Oh well I'm not very – very keen on food at the moment, am I darling?

DAISY: But you didn't speak either, hardly a word, and look at you now, not at all your usual self, is he Jasper – but I know – I know what you want to cheer you up, oh how silly of me to have forgotten when I went to all the trouble of remembering to get it in specially, but then it's your fault, it's been such a long time since you came to see us, now where did I put it – oh in the hall – or – anyway Jasper you tell him all our news while I go and find it – I'll be right back dear. (*Going off left.*)

(*There is a pause.*)

MARGARET: (*Goes to* BENEDICT, *sits down beside him*) You're doing marvellously darling.

BENEDICT: What, darling?

MARGARET: Marvellously.

BENEDICT: I feel – I feel –

MARGARET: I can imagine, darling. I can.

BENEDICT: (*Emotionally*) I know. I know you can. Thank you darling. (*Looks towards* JASPER) Daddy – I – um – I know I owe you an explanation for not being in touch for such a long time. The truth is I've been going – going through rather a bad time, haven't I darling? And – and I didn't want to worry you. I expect you can guess what it was. My drinking. Well, not to put too fine a point on it, I wasn't just getting drunk now and then, which is what you must have thought, Daddy, I was actually on my way to becoming an alcoholic, wasn't I darling? So Maggie finally – bless her – put it to me that I had to choose. Between her and my Scotch. And she meant it. Didn't you darling? She really meant it. So, I – I put myself in the hands of a psychiatrist who had a very good reputation – at least some friends of Maggie's thought very highly of him, didn't they darling – Roger and Liza – but he turned out to be an old-fashioned, rather hard-line Freudian. So as far as he was concerned, I was classic textbook stuff. Went into all my relationships – sibling rivalry of course – you know, that I'd always been jealous of Henry and Dick – Dick particularly, of course, said one of the reasons I drank was because I was guilty because I was glad that Dick was dead and – well, you can imagine – and you, of course, Daddy, which he got down to the old penis envy, naturally, and when I told him I'd never actually seen your penis so how could I envy it, it might be smaller than mine, after all – (*laughs*) well, that was in our first session, believe it or not – eventually he got on to Maggie, of course, said I envied *her* penis, didn't he darling, in the form of her talent, you see – and on top of all his – his clap-trap he was a pretty heavy drinker himself, I could smell alcohol on his breath and – well, by and large he was making things worse not better but

of course the trouble was – I did develop a degree of
dependence on him and – well, God knows what would have
happened to me if I hadn't finally broken free – with the help
of, well, Maggie of course, I can't tell you how wonderful –
wonderful! she's been – but also of a new chap I happened to
hear about at the BBC – Vintross. Norman Vintross. It's
because of him that I haven't touched a drop of Scotch for
what is it, darling, six, no, no, he insists on an absolutely
ruthless accounting – it's part of his therapy, five, five weeks
Daddy, isn't it darling?

MARGARET: Days, isn't it, darling?

BENEDICT: What?

MARGARET: Days, I think, darling.

BENEDICT: Yes, darling?

MARGARET: Didn't you say weeks.

BENEDICT: Oh, good God, did I really? (*Laughs.*) Days I meant of
course, Daddy, six days. But when you think what I was up
to – four bottles a day, Daddy.

MARGARET: More like three really, wasn't it darling?

BENEDICT: Oh now darling – well, between three and four – three
and a half on a good day, bad day, that's what Vintross has to
contend with, Daddy, so in my view he's a bit of a genius,
quite simply. But absolutely practical, that's his great – his
great, isn't it darling?

MARGARET: But he does fairly sophisticated things too, doesn't
he darling, hypnosis for example.

BENEDICT: God yes, and you should see his eyes when he's
putting me under, Daddy – brrr – like chips of blue ice, little
chips of blue ice, aren't they darling?

MARGARET: Well, I've never met him, don't forget, darling.

BENEDICT: Oh. No, of course you haven't – but what he goes for
above all is character, Daddy. In the traditional sense, rather
like a Scots school-teacher, eh Maggie? Says I've only one
basic problem. I'm weak. Feeble. Gutless. A moral no-
hoper. So the only possible solution for types like me is to
avoid drink altogether. To stay out of pubs and licensed
restaurants – I virtually move with the luncheon voucher set
now, Daddy, and he's even shown me a trick for dealing with

the BBC parties I can't get out of – he says most of the
newsreaders have had to come to him at one time or another
– anyway, how to stand – look, legs splayed and hands
locked behind my back – (*does it*) to make it difficult to whip
a glass from a passing tray or otherwise receive one –

MARGARET: Darling, I think I'll go for a little walk.

BENEDICT: What, on your own, you mean?

MARGARET: Well, I think you and your father should have some
time together –

BENEDICT: Oh, well that's all right, isn't it Daddy? Don't go on
our account – unless you want to do a bit of creative mulling,
of course – did you know Maggie's just begun a new novel,
Daddy – last week – isn't that marvellous! and I expect she's
frightened that I'm going to launch into one of my
panegyrics about what she's meant to me – her support and –
(*takes her hand, kisses it*) and in fact you can thank her for our
getting down to see you at last, Daddy, she absolutely
insisted we come, didn't you darling – well then, don't be too
long – I'll miss you –

(MARGARET *exits through door left.*)

Isn't she remarkable, Daddy? Oh, I don't just mean in her
talent, although that's remarkable enough God knows when
you think what the odds were against her finishing it. I mean
me, of course, I was the odds. Because you see Daddy – oh,
it sounds so bizarre now but in my worst phase – when I was
adding Scotch to my breakfast coffee, you know *that* stage, –
I got it into my head that – well, that she was having an
affair. A real love affair, you see – and what made it more
dreadful, more nightmarish, was that I thought it was with
someone I knew but I didn't know who, if you follow – I
knew I knew the chap, even though there wasn't a chap at all
– not even evidence, Daddy, which of course simply made
me more insane. It got so I started to pick quarrels with
friends, people I work with at the Beeb, interpreting their
remarks, their looks, even – eventually even their smells –
tried to sniff them, if they'd been out of their offices a
suspiciously long time – and of course trying to catch poor
Maggie in the act, taxiing home at any hour, climbing in

through the lavatory window so they wouldn't hear me in the hall, then up the stairs in my socks, flinging her study door open after crouching outside it for hours – and there she'd be, typing calmly away, with her glasses on, you know she wears glasses for her writing, and of course the inevitable cigarette hanging from her lips, and she'd give me such a distracted, absent-minded look, as if for a second she didn't know who I was, let alone why I was there – and so – more and more often I'd go well berserk – quite berserk – and oh God – well the drink, you see, and knowing she was being unfaithful and not knowing who with but knowing I knew him and then realizing it was all a delusion – but now when I think, think of the Hell I put her through, what she's suffered – endured because of me – well even Vintross, who's pretty tough about these things was appalled when I told him – he said – he said that I – I – was a lucky man to have such an unlucky wife – (*puts his hand to his eyes, in tears.*) Sorry. Sorry Daddy – but I – I've always loved her you know but now – now – sorry – I'll be – I'll be all right – (*Sits, overcome.*)

DAISY: (*Enters from left, carrying a Scotch bottle*) Upstairs – it was upstairs in my bedroom, in the carrier bag, you see, the one with the pink wool and the door knob, anyway I've found it, that's the thing – (*is pouring some into a glass*) I got it in specially for you, because I remembered how you like to settle down with a nice large one after lunch – there, dear, you keep it beside you so you know where it is – what dear?

BENEDICT: (*Is staring appalled from the Scotch to* DAISY) Nothing. (*Laughs.*) Nothing Nanty that a – a Vintrossian gesture – (*Gets up.*)

DAISY: What, dear?

BENEDICT: I've just realized that I haven't – haven't given you a proper cuddle yet Nanty – (*Goes over, puts his arms around her.*) There, now I feel safe, eh Daddy? From temptation and harm.

DAISY: Aaaah – aaaah – I always say you're the feeling one, don't I Jasper, feel things so quickly – anyway that's cheered you up, has it, I knew it would, didn't I Jasper, and it's a malt,

you know – I asked for a malt – and now you can relax and
tell us some of your funny stories about your life at the BBC
– I was just thinking the other day about my favourite,
wasn't I, Jasper, that Hugh Rhys-what's-it on the religious
talks programme of yours, the one who does the interviewing
sometimes, you used to keep us in stitches about, every time
I hear him talking things over with Bishops and atheists and
such I laugh out loud, I do, don't I Jasper, he sounds so
solemn and Welsh but there he was getting himself locked in
his office cupboard with his secretary and she thought – oh
dear, all those scratches, poor man! (*Laughing.*) – And that
quarrel with his wife over the dish-washer he insisted took
saucepans and suds all over the kitchen floor short-
whatnotting the fridge and the ice-cream gateau for his
daughter's birthday melting into the fish for the cat – oh
dear, oh dear – (*laughing*) what's he been up to recently your
Hugh Rhys-what's-it, something hilarious, do tell us?

BENEDICT: (*Who has moved away from* DAISY, *grinning fixedly, his
hands locked behind his back*) He's – um – actually he's dead,
Nanty.

DAISY: What dear?

BENEDICT: Dead.

DAISY: Good Heavens do you hear that, Jasper, Hugh Rhys-thing
– but how, how dear?

BENEDICT: Oh it was a – well as a – what happened apparently –
(*Stops.*)

DAISY: What dear?

BENEDICT: (*Looks yearningly towards the Scotch*) Well – well
actually Nanty do you mind – (*goes and sits down some
distance from the Scotch*) if we – I – I don't go into it at the
moment I'm – you see it – it upsets me to think about it
because in a way, well, in as much as I used to – to make him
a bit of a butt and forgot how fond – how fond – you know
what I mean, don't you Daddy, perhaps you could explain –
explain to Nanty? (*Sits head lowered.*)

(*There is a slight pause. Off, the sound of boys' voices, and*
HENRY'S *getting louder as they advance in a rush. A ball bounces
into the room and towards* JASPER.)

DAISY: Of all the – of all the –

HENRY: (*Bounds in through the french windows breathing hard and sweating*) Oh golly – everyone all right?

DAISY: Well dear, it nearly bounced into your father's face, didn't it, Jasper.

HENRY: Oh, sorry Daddy – (*Takes the ball from* DAISY.) All right boys (*going to the french windows*) now keep it down at the bottom – right to the bottom – (*Throws the ball out.*)

DAISY: Yes dear, but you see I can't help worrying about the windows –

HENRY: No, further down, Tom – right down – (*turns*) we're going to the Piece soon Nanty, so don't worry –

DAISY: I know dear, so couldn't they wait until then – because even at the bottom there are the outhouse windows –

HENRY: (*Has gone to the drinks table, squirted himself some soda water*) Whew! (*Draining it off.*) You were wise to stay out of that, Ben, I remind me of that chap, I told you about him, didn't I Daddy – (*Squirts some more.*)

DAISY: You do see what I mean, don't you dear?

HENRY: – did a dozen laps around the park in the sun, gulped down a jug of lemonade, dropped dead.

DAISY: I don't want to spoil their fun, you know that dear, but – what, good heavens, why?

HENRY: Bad heart, Nanty.

DAISY: Well then why did he do it, run a dozen times around in the heat, any fool knows that's madness, don't they Jasper, why did he dear?

HENRY: Well, actually, now I come to think of it, because I told him to, Nanty.

DAISY: What, oh well of course that's different dear – but why did you?

HENRY: I must have thought he needed the exercise, I suppose. Perhaps if he'd taken enough of it earlier, he wouldn't have killed himself taking it later.

DAISY: So really he only had himself to blame, you mean, dear.

HENRY: Well, no. Really he had me to blame, didn't he? Or would have, if he'd survived. But to be fair to myself I didn't tell him to do his running in the midday sun, nor to gulp

down ice-cold lemonade afterwards. At least I hope I didn't.
But on the other hand I certainly didn't warn him not to,
either. But then I didn't know at the time he had a bad heart.
And nor did he, come to that. Still, we got to the right
diagnosis between us at the end, didn't we? Poor chap. I
liked him rather a lot, he played the clarinet for the LSO, I
always try not to think of him every time I hear that Mozart
piece you're so fond of Daddy, how does it go – you
remember it Ben? (*Tries to hum a few bars.*)

DAISY: Oh, I know – (*Hums it very pleasantly.*)

(HENRY *joins in.* DAISY *and* HENRY *hum the opening section.*)

HENRY: (*Squirts more soda water*) And here I am myself, my
stomach packed with casserole, golly it was good Nanty,
wasn't it Ben, *and* jacket potatoes and those doughy things –

DAISY: Dumplings, dear, did you like them?

HENRY: Oh damn!

DAISY: What dear?

HENRY: I'm on call today and I think I forgot to leave your
number Daddy – well, I expect they'll know where I am.
And anyway the call I don't make may save a life, eh?
(*Laughs.*)

DAISY: Oh don't be silly Henry, you're a very good doctor, isn't
he Jasper, isn't he Ben, a very good doctor, Henry –

MARIANNE: (*Enters from left flourishing a child's pottie*) Dum-dee-
dee-dum-dum-dee-dee-dum – it was under my seat all the
time, Nanty. In the van.

DAISY: What, oh good dear, I'm so glad – but isn't he a very good
doctor, Henry?

MARIANNE: I should jolly well say he is, who says he isn't?

DAISY: Henry, dear.

MARIANNE: Oh ho, at it again, are we, hubby mine, I don't know
what's been getting into him recently apart from the usual
overwork, but the only thing wrong with him is that he's too
jolly good a doctor, isn't he Gramps, and cares far too much
and won't let himself let up for a minute, have you heard
about his latest acquisition, I bet he hasn't even mentioned
her, has he?

DAISY: Who, dear?

165

MARIANNE: Mrs O'Killiam, Nanty.

DAISY: Oh, is that the lady whose hair has been falling out, and wants a golden wig on the National Health –

MARIANNE: No no Nanty, that's poor old ga-ga Mrs MacDougall, no Mrs O'Killiam's a real case, in fact she's simply the most desperate case in the whole practice, Gramps, none of the others will touch her with a barge-pole.

HENRY: Now darling, that isn't quite true –

MARIANNE: Oh yes it is, darling, you know perfectly well her husband's in jail for some quite unspeakable offence against an eighty-year-old woman, Gramps –

DAISY: Why, what did he do to her?

MARIANNE: Well, for one thing he –

HENRY: Darling, I don't think – um you know –

MARIANNE: All right darling, for Nanty's sake –

DAISY: No no, I like hearing about things like that, don't I Jasper?

MARIANNE: Anyway Gramps, as if that wasn't bad enough she's got two brutes of sons of about twelve and fourteen who are always in trouble with the police themselves –

HENRY: Well, of course with their background –

MARIANNE: Oh I know darling, absolutely *no* chance, and a little girl called Carla –

HENRY: Wanda, darling.

MARIANNE: Who's hydrocephalic, Gramps.

DAISY: What, dear?

MARIANNE: Water on the brain, Nanty. (*Holding her hands away from her head.*)

DAISY: Oh, we've got one of those, haven't we Jasper, he rides past here on his bicycle looking like Humpty Dumpty poor thing –

MARIANNE: But the worst of it is she's in a hideous way herself, I shall never forget Henry's description of her the first time he saw her, Gramps, he said he said to himself as soon as he clapped eyes on her, 'Hello! Carcinoma!' didn't you darling?

DAISY: Hello who, dear?

HENRY: Although actually I was wrong, it's almost certainly a form of anorexia nervosa –

MARIANNE: Well, anyway, she's called him around every night this week, and after surgery too, he comes back looking grey with fatigue, Nanty – and this morning, Gramps, just as we were leaving one of her boys turned up and told Henry his mum wanted him straight away –

HENRY: But I really don't mind darling –

MARIANNE: Oh, I saw that look on your face before of course he said of course, Gramps, and you would have gone too, wouldn't you, if I hadn't asked him if it couldn't wait until this evening, and do you know what he said, you didn't hear, did you darling, the little squat one with the dribble and the funny lip, he said – well, he'd fucking well better come then.

DAISY: What dear?

MARIANNE: Sorry everybody, but that's what he said.

HENRY: Oh, it's his normal vocabulary, he talks to everybody like that, and I *am* on call darling.

MARIANNE: Yes darling, when aren't you on call? I'd better get this to Nindy before it's too late if it isn't already.

DAISY: Oh and thank you for doing the dishes, dear!

MARIANNE: What, oh golly, Nanty, did you mean for me to do them?

DAISY: What, you mean you haven't you mean!

MARIANNE: No Nanty, I'm sorry, I haven't.

DAISY: But I saw you at the sink, you see, so I assumed – I wish I'd known you weren't going to do them dear, because then I could have got them over and done with by now myself, you see.

MARIANNE: Well honestly Nanty, one moment we were all in the kitchen, and then Jenny'd gone –

DAISY: To get the muffins, dear.

MARIANNE: And then old Margaret had sloped off somewhere – and then you'd vanished –

DAISY: Only because I was worried about the ball and the windows –

MARIANNE: Oh golly, well let me deal with Nindy and I'll come back and do your dishes for you, all right? (*Goes out through the french windows.*)

DAISY: No no dear, I'll do them, I don't mind doing them, oh I do hope she didn't think I meant, Henry you don't think she thought I meant –

HENRY: No no Nanty, of course she didn't – but hey, I haven't asked after your headaches – Nanty's been getting some very bad headaches, Ben, hasn't she Daddy – (*Putting his arm around* DAISY.)

DAISY: Oh they've been terrible recently, haven't they Jasper? I've tried doing what you said, lying on a hard surface in a dark room with moist pads over my eyes, but it doesn't stop the throbbing or the nose-bleeds, does it Jasper?

HENRY: Nose-bleeds?

DAISY: Oh yes, terrible nose-bleeds and a humming in my ears and seeing things double –

HENRY: I see. Well, Nanty, I think we ought to have someone take a proper look at you. I can't promise he'll cure them but I won't let him make them any worse.

DAISY: Oh Henry – aaah – so kind, so thoughtful – oh and look dear, tell Marianne she's not to touch the dishes, I never meant her to, you know – they won't take a minute tell her – (*Going out through the arch.*)

HENRY: Actually daddy, I think I'd better try and fix up an appointment for Nanty as soon as possible – nothing to worry about, just a few tests, X-rays, that sort of thing – all quite routine, but to put our minds at rest, we don't want anything happening to our Nanty, do we, Ben?

BENEDICT: (*Who has been gazing at floor, hands locked*) Mmmm?

HENRY: You all right?

BENEDICT: Oh. Oh well um – yes, yes. Thanks.

HENRY: I must say it's terrific to have you here again after all this time.

BENEDICT: Oh. Yes. Thanks. Thanks Henry.

HENRY: And Maggie too.

BENEDICT: Oh she was very keen to come. Very keen. Very very keen.

HENRY: Oh. Well that's flattering, eh Daddy? Where is she, by the way, I've hardly had a chance to speak to her.

BENEDICT: No.

HENRY: What?

BENEDICT: What?

HENRY: Maggie?

BENEDICT: Oh. Oh yes.

HENRY: Has she gone out?

BENEDICT: Yes. Yes I think so, yes. For a walk, hasn't she Daddy
– something to do with her novel you see. She gets these fits.
Inspiration, I suppose. Yes.

HENRY: Are you sure you're all right, Ben?

BENEDICT: No. No I seem – something slightly wrong with my –
my stomach – perhaps those doughnuts in the casserole – but
very queasy.

HENRY: I'll get you some Alka Selzer, where is it Daddy?

BENEDICT: What – oh no, no, not Alka Selzer, never works for me
besides I don't want to make a fuss – I'll tell you – I'll tell you
what, (*getting up*) perhaps a drop – just a little drop of this
might do something for me (*picks up the glass with a trembling
hand, takes an enormous gulp*) have to be careful though, eh
Daddy, no back-sliding, eh, you see, Henry, I was telling
Daddy, I've given this stuff up virtually at last, haven't I,
Daddy? I go to a chap, you see.

HENRY: A chap?

BENEDICT: Yes. His name's Vintross. A bit of a genius in my view.
He's been treating me for – things.

HENRY: Oh. A psychiatrist.

BENEDICT: No. A paediatrician, actually. But he does things like
me on the side. Privately. God you should see his eyes when
he's doing hypnosis, I was telling Daddy about them, wasn't
I, Daddy? (*Pouring himself more Scotch.*) They're the deepest
brown eyes I've ever seen, and they burn, burn, down – he's
bloody expensive, you can imagine.

HENRY: Yes. Yes, I can.

BENEDICT: But then that's part of his treatment, you see. Charges
the equivalent of a double Scotch for every three minutes of
his time, he worked it out at. You're not cured, he said, until
you get my bill. If you can look at it without taking a drink,
there's hope, and if you pay it you won't be able to afford a drink,
apart from meths, of course, and if you don't pay it, I sue.
(*Laughs.*) Vintage Vintross, that is. Jokes are a part of his style.

HENRY: Oh – oh well he sounds just the job, doesn't he Daddy?
(MATTHEW *enters through left door, stands uncertainly.*)
Oh hello Mat, and what have you been up to?

MATTHEW: Oh – um – well um – nothing um – (*Laughs.*)

HENRY: How's the soccer coming?

MATTHEW: Oh – well I mean um – you know.

HENRY: Made a team yet?

MATTHEW: Well – just the house team.

HENRY: Oh, well that's jolly good – isn't it Ben – congratters,
Mat.

MATTHEW: Oh – well, um, thanks. (*Laughs.*)

HENRY: Oh and hey, I don't know if Marianne mentioned to you
– we're taking the boys to the Piece soon for a footer around
– why don't you come along and show them what you can do,
and then show me how to do it, eh?

MATTHEW: Oh – well – I – Mummy asked me to go for a walk
with her, you see – I – I – was meant to meet her at the
baker's but well, you haven't seen her?

HENRY: She hasn't been through here.

MATTHEW: Oh well, she's probably gone looking for – I'd better
– better go and see if – um – (*Makes towards the exit, left.*)

HENRY: Anyway we'll be on the Piece later if you *do* want a
game –

MATTHEW: Right – right – (*He goes out.*)

BENEDICT: (*Who has poured himself more Scotch*) God he's getting
like Dick isn't he – it makes the brain to reel and the heart to
lurch how like Dick he's getting, doesn't it, is he top dog at
school, the way Dick used to be?

HENRY: Well actually that reminds me – I was going to mention it
Daddy – and I'm glad you're here Ben, you can tell me what
you think – you see I had a letter from his housemaster the
other day, he seems to think of me as in sort of loco parentis
and he didn't want to worry Jenny with it – but he's a little
concerned about our Mat. Says he's been rather withdrawn
this term – well, since Dick's death – well, I suppose that's
hardly surprising, but apparently although he's dropped
every one of his old chums he's taken up with a boy – well,
quite a bit younger than himself and – in a nutshell, the

housemaster isn't too keen on it. Thinks it's all a bit too hot-housey. That's why he's wangled Mat into the football team, to make him mix more you see, although actually Mat's not too good at football, but then this friend of his doesn't play at all. He's an asthmatic.

BENEDICT: Ah-hah! One of those, eh?

HENRY: What? Well, you see what troubles me is I'm not sure he should interfere at all – I mean, the football's all right, *if* Mat comes to enjoy it – but otherwise well this relationship may be filling an important need, mayn't it, and then given how delicate – delicate these matters are, especially at that age – well, what do you think, Daddy?

BENEDICT: (*Laughs*) God, doesn't it bring it back though?

HENRY: What?

BENEDICT: All of it – the sodomy, buggery, public-school duggery – much more fun than State schools. In State schools you give them ten quid a week, kit them up with contraceptives, hand them a list of VD clinics, pack pot into their lunch-boxes, nothing furtive, nothing passionate, nothing to prepare them for life – hey, remember old Prothero, Hen, old Prothero, did we ever tell you about old Prothero, Daddy, used to come and sit on the edge of the bed after lights, tucking in the middle-school chappies, and if there'd been a caning he'd want to inspect the stripes, put on ointment –

HENRY: Golly yes, old Cheeks! (*Laughs.*)

BENEDICT: That's it! Cheeks – Cheeks Prothero! Had a crush on Dick, didn't he Hen – and old Coote – Coote Wilson – and – all of them come to think of it, didn't they Hen? Had crushes on Dick, fighting over him they were! Like bloody monkeys! God, I'm glad you sent us to one of the best schools in the country, Daddy, aren't you Hen?

HENRY: I certainly don't think it did us any harm.

BENEDICT: (*Pouring himself another drink*) Vintross is queer. Gay, I mean. Did I tell you?

HENRY: Is he? No, you didn't.

BENEDICT: He's got this Filipino house-boy. Opens the door, takes your coat. Got a pretty beaten look to him, so I expect there's a cupboard full of things, eh, handcuffs, leg-irons, whips, masks, SS uniforms, that sort of gay, you see. Ballsy-gay. Sometimes his eyes go just like a cat's – a vicious green. You know?

HENRY: The house-boy's?

BENEDICT: Vintross's. Vintross's eyes.

HENRY: I thought you said they were brown –

BENEDICT: No, no. Green, eh Daddy? Vicious green. Like a cat's.

HENRY: How's the stomach?

BENEDICT: Flat as a board. Keeps himself in top nick, you see. Probably with the Filipino, eh? (*Laughs.*)

HENRY: No, I meant yours. Is it settling down?

BENEDICT: Oh. Well still a bit – hey Hen I must show Hen, eh Daddy – Vintross's party posture – look – hands so – feet thus – (*tries to adopt it, still holding his glass, stumbles backwards*). Oooooooops!
(HENRY *catches him.*)
Thanks. See what I mean, bloody difficult.

HENRY: Yes. (*Watches him, looks anxiously towards* JASPER.) Oh – that reminds me – that little Welsh friend of yours, the one that got his finger stuck in his flies at the Israeli Embassy – we were having a good laugh about him just the other week, weren't we Daddy? What's he been – (*Laughing.*)

BENEDICT: (*Laughing*) Old Hugh Rhys – um –

HENRY: Yes –

BENEDICT: (*Stops laughing.*) Oh. Dead, Henry.

HENRY: What?

BENEDICT: Dead. Yes. Dead.

HENRY: That little Welsh – good God, good God, but – but well how, Ben, what happened?

BENEDICT: Killed himself. Didn't he Daddy? Telling Daddy and Nanty earlier –

HENRY: But why?

BENEDICT: Don't know Henry. Don't know. All I know is that one night last week he got out of bed, told his wife he wanted some air, walked up to Hampstead Heath, took off his trousers, hanged himself.

HENRY: With his own trousers?

BENEDICT: They found a washing-line too, but it had got tangled in the tree.

HENRY: And he didn't leave a note – nothing to explain –

BENEDICT: Oh yes. He left a note. Pages and pages in fact. Must have spent the day writing it – alone in his office – pages and pages – pinned them to his shirt.

HENRY: Well, what did it say?

BENEDICT: Don't know. It rained during the night. Illegible. Every word. Pathetic, eh Daddy? Poor little Hugh Rhys – um –

(*There is a pause.* HENRY *releases a sudden wild laugh.*)

BENEDICT: What?

HENRY: Oh I'm sorry – so sorry – don't know where that came from – I certainly didn't mean any disrespect to Hugh – Hugh Rhys um –

BENEDICT: That's all right, Hen, we know why you laughed, don't we Daddy, matter of fact I laughed myself when I heard – I mean trousers, tangled washing-line, unreadable suicide note – like all the other stories I used to tell about him. Right?

HENRY: Well yes, I suppose –

BENEDICT: Except this time he's dead, of course. That's the difference. But a big one. Crucial, in fact.

HENRY: Yes. Yes indeed.

BENEDICT: Isn't that right, Daddy? (*Pours himself more Scotch.*) And of course appropriate. Hugh Rhys – um's death. An appropriate death. Like Dick's, in a sense. Eh? (*There is a pause.*) I mean, you think of Dick, the brightest and the best of us, eh, we know that, Daddy, don't we Henry, well of course he was, because he was just like you, Daddy, wasn't he, fellowships just like you, lectureships just like you, a readership just like you, would have ended up with a professorship just like you. Maybe even an OBE, Daddy, just like you, and then a wife he loved, just like you, Daddy, I mean you loved Mummy didn't you, the tragedy of your life her death, wasn't it, if you see, and a son he adored, just as you adored him, and is turning out just like him as he

went on turning out just like you. Apart from being dead.
Just like Mummy. See Daddy.

HENRY: No. No. I don't think we do see, quite, Ben. But perhaps
we shouldn't discuss –

BENEDICT: No no, look at it this way. Where was Dick different
from Daddy? Where? A bit raffish, right? Bit of an
adventurer, right? (*Laughs.*) Reckless. Reckless and raffish –
not like Daddy, eh, nobody's ever called you reckless and
raffish, have they, Daddy? And so his motorbike. See. See
how it fits?

(HENRY *looks towards* JASPER.)

Roars over here, has one of his intimate chats with Daddy,
and then later, far too late, when he was tired, his head
spinning with Daddy's ideas and jokes and anecdotes and
gossip, eh Daddy? What does he do? Does he stay the night?
Upstairs in bed in his old room? Does he stay the night? No.
Not old Dick. Back, back on his motorbike, roaring off again
– past Newmarket, past Baldock, Royston, Hitchin – faster
and faster, and then off – off the road – hurtling right off the
road and over the bank and into the tree into the dark! And
we say – *we* say – if it hadn't been for his motorbike Dick'd
still be alive. True. But – but if it hadn't been for Daddy,
then he wouldn't be dead. Vintross says. (*Pours himself more
Scotch.*) Now do you see?

HENRY: Well – um, Ben – look, what would Vintross say if he
could see the amount of Scotch you're knocking back, old
chap?

BENEDICT: Say it was quite all right. As long as I can cope with it
in a situation I can't cope with without it. That's what he'd
say.

JENNY: (*Enters left*) Oh sorry – but has he come back, Matthew?

HENRY: Yes. But he went out again – I think he was looking for
you –

BENEDICT: Hey Jen, we were just saying about Matthew – so like
Dick, isn't he? So like him?

JENNY: Yes – yes I suppose he is –

BENEDICT: Henry was telling us about that letter he got from his
housemaster – on his little sexual problems – don't you pay

any attention, Jen, Dick had the same, used to steal too, didn't he, Hen, has Matthew started stealing yet? Well, don't worry, if he turns out like Dick he'll be all right, eh? Apart from being dead, I mean.

JENNY: Matthew's housemaster wrote to you?

HENRY: Yes, well it was just a – nothing to – didn't want to bother you –

JENNY: I see. Which way did he go, Matthew?

HENRY: Out the front way I think – but Jenny really –
(JENNY *goes out left*.)
Golly Ben, I do wish you hadn't mentioned that to Jenny.

BENEDICT: What? (*Pouring himself more Scotch.*)

HENRY: About Matthew. I did say it was confidential, didn't I, Daddy?

BENEDICT: Oh. Right. But there's another thing. The funeral. We've never talked about the funeral, have we, remember it, Daddy? Our standing there in the Chapel and they brought him in and put him down on that conveyor belt and that lady started on her organ, that old lady with the deaf-aid. And then the door in the wall, the trapdoor in the wall slid open, and he began to slide towards it and then through it, remember Hen? You don't do you?

HENRY: Of course I do, it's just that – well I don't think we should –

BENEDICT: Well, what happened? What happened as he slid through?
(*There is a pause.*)
You don't want to say, do you? Well, I don't mind saying. I'll say it, Daddy. What happened as he slid through is – I threw up. That's what happened. Isn't it? Because I was drunk. (*Pause.*) You know, I used to be pretty ashamed about that. Thought I'd disgraced the whole proceedings. That's what I thought. (*Drinks.*) Until Vintross put me right. Know what he said, Vintross? He said it doesn't matter whether you're drunk or sober, sober or drunk, the coffin slides through just the same, the door in the wall slides open just the same, same old lady plays an organ just the same – and then, next please! Next please! You can't disgrace it

because you can't even interrupt it. Unless there's a resurrection of course! (*Laughs.*) Just a business, disposing of the dead. That's how he cuts through things, old Vintross. Right to the heart. (*Pours himself more Scotch.*)

HENRY: (*Goes to him*) Ben that's enough. Quite enough. (*Tries to take the bottle away.*) Think of Daddy –

BENEDICT: What?

HENRY: Think of Daddy! (*Low and intense.*)

BENEDICT: Think of – oh oh shit-eating time come round again, eh Henry. Shit-eating time. Well let me tell you something else Vintross says.

HENRY: I don't think we want to hear anything else Vintross –

BENEDICT: He says – he says the trouble with me – he says the reason I was nearly an alcoholic virtually until he got his hands on me – was that all my life I've been made to eat shit, I've been the family shit-eater – apologize, explain, grovel – and he said – when I told him Maggie wanted me to come up he said – go – he said go – but on no account – never – never – again – for any reason – was I to eat shit. Never again, not for you, not for Daddy even. No more shit-eating. See! Never! (*There is a pause.*)

MARIANNE: (*Enters through the french windows laughing*) Darling I must show you – (*Shows Henry contents of pot.*)

HENRY: Golly, yes!

MARIANNE: It was Gramps' magic, honestly Gramps! She sat there straining and straining until I said do it for Gramps! And out it came. Gushing!

HENRY: Golly!

MARIANNE: What she must have gone through holding it back, poor darling – anyway, thank you Gramps – and darling, they really are a bit desperate about going to the Piece, they're loading themselves into the van, so if you'd just give this a sluice – (*Hands HENRY the pot.*)
(*There is a long honk from off, left.*)
Oh oh – I told Tom not to – anyway I'll see you out there – (*Sees BENEDICT*) Is everything all right?

HENRY: Oh yes, fine, fine, just having a jaw!

MARIANNE: The three chaps together, eh, jolly good for Gramps.

(*Goes out left to another long honk.*)

(*There is a pause.* HENRY *looks at* BENEDICT, *looks at* JASPER, *looks at* BENEDICT *again, puts down the pot, goes over. Puts a hand on* BENEDICT's *shoulder.*)

HENRY: We never knew you felt like that, did we, Daddy? But Ben I promise you I've never wanted you to eat – and nor has Daddy, I know – but perhaps it was important for you to say it, eh Daddy, and get it out of your system once and for all.

BENEDICT: Old Hen. (*Puts a hand on* HENRY's *hand on his shoulder.*)

HENRY: Old Ben.

BENEDICT: Old Hen.

HENRY: You don't think you ought to lie down now? You look – um –

BENEDICT: No – no – I'm all right now. Purged, you see. Purged. Just as Vintross said.

HENRY: Well that's – that's –

(*Low honk, off.*)

Oh I'd better – (*Looks towards* JASPER, *smiles reassuringly.*) You um – well, you won't have any more of that though, will you?

BENEDICT: What? Oh no – no – don't need it now – just want a nice calm chat with Daddy now. That's all. Eh Daddy? Talk over old times. Without – without any – eh Daddy?

HENRY: Good. That's the job, eh Daddy? Well then, see you both later. (*Goes out left.*)

BENEDICT: God, I love Henry, don't you, Daddy? Oh I know Dick was always his favourite brother and he was always Dick's favourite brother and I was the one left out from their favouritism, but God how I loved them both. I suppose that's what I was, am, Daddy, when you think about it a – a sort of only son with two favourite brothers and a dead mother and a – a father who – who – well, why should you? Nobody has to. (*Gets up, pours himself more Scotch.*) Nobody. Vintross says – (*Gulps down Scotch.*) My Maggie's frightened of the dark. Did you know that? My Maggie? I hold her against it very tight, tight against it, and I say don't be afraid Maggie, don't be afraid my Maggie, I'm here – Ben's here,

Ben's here – and when I painted her study up for her I did it
in light colours, pastel colours Daddy, and I bought her a
typewriter, and I change her ribbons you know, all she has to
do is the writing you see, clackety-clackety, clackety-
clackety – pages on pages, chapters on chapters, clackety-
clackety-clackety, and then when I come back, grey with
fatigue, back from the BBC, and loving her and holding her
and changing her ribbons – up I go to see her, longing to see
her – and looks at me – she looks at me as if I wasn't there,
Daddy, and never had been. Never had been. But *he'd* been
all right, *he'd* been – I catch the whiff of him now and then,
smell the smell of his spoor on her, smell it all over her, on
my Maggie, and I know who it is, I know who it is, and one
day I'll get him by his whiff, the whiff of his spoor, or catch
them at it, the two of them. Whoever he is. At their fuckity-
fuckity, clackity-fuckity, fuckity-clackity! (*Lurches
sideways.*)

DAISY: (*Enters through the arch*) What dear? Having a nice chat the
two of you that's nice dears, I've done the dishes, just as well
as Marianne's gone off to the Piece, I heard the honking, I do
wish he wouldn't, Jasper, it's little Tom you know, sets my
head off, and now the mat – the mat's gone from the back-
kitchen, would you believe Jasper, after I put it down
specially, so I've got to get the one from the front – and how
are you feeling now, dear, you look much more relaxed,
doesn't he Jasper, much more yourself dear, that's good –
(*Goes out left.*)

BENEDICT: What? (*Stumbles after her. Stops.*) And do you know
what Vintross says about her, Daddy, says she made me eat
shit too, when I was little, because she wanted to be our
Mummy, and when she couldn't be our Mummy made me
eat shit to make up –

DAISY: (*Returns carrying a large doormat*) For the mud you see.

BENEDICT: – when I was little –

DAISY: What dear?

BENEDICT: Saying Vintross says – Vintross –

DAISY: Who dear? Oh, that little Welsh friend of yours, so sad, so
sad –

BENEDICT: When I was little, Nanty, you made me eat and eat and eat.

DAISY: What, oh well dear, I did my best to keep your tummy full, of course I did, didn't I Jasper, but then you were such a greedy mite, you know, wasn't he Jasper, like Oliver Twist dear, always asking for more. (*Laughs*.)

BENEDICT: Wanted to be our Mummy, didn't you Nanty? Take the place of my Mummy?

DAISY: What – oh oh – oh no – I knew I could never take *her* place, didn't I Jasper, even though people said we were almost look-alikes – didn't they, Jasper – not usual you know in second cousins once removed except she had golden hair that came right down her back to sit on, sit on her own hair, she could, couldn't she Jasper, oh really very glamorous your mother dear, aaah, such a pity she didn't live to see what you've become! – Isn't it, Jasper?

BENEDICT: What?

DAISY: She adored you all, didn't she Jasper?

BENEDICT: Me? Adored me? Me too?

DAISY: Well dear, it was different with you, you were just an insignificant scrap at the time, and always crying for a feed, you know, while Henry was bigger and she could talk to him and Dick – well Dick, she idolized, Dick – but then we all did, didn't we Jasper? Because he was so pretty and clever. (BENEDICT *laughs*.)
What dear?

BENEDICT: Dead, Nanty. Gone. Pretty Dick. Clever Dick. Through the door in the wall. On his motorbike.

DAISY: Yes, dear, I know dear. So sad.

BENEDICT: Why didn't you stop him?

DAISY: What dear?

BENEDICT: Why didn't you stop him, Nanty. Killing himself. Why?

DAISY: Oh really Benedict, oh really dear, I've told you before, haven't I Jasper, every time you come down dear I've told you, you can't have forgotten, can he Jasper, I've told you and told you dear I told him not to, didn't I Jasper, and if he'd listened to me it wouldn't have happened, would it

Jasper, it's late I said, you're tired I said, stay the night, make him stay the night, Jasper, didn't I Jasper, and he said, what was it he said, or was it you Jasper, one of you said, oh nobody can stay the night Daisy or Nanty whichever of you it was said it, and they both laughed, the pair of them, and off he roared, off he roared, poor silly boy, in that helmet pulled down and those great gauntlets, and his head so low over the handle-bars, roaring off, and I knew, I knew, if he'd listened to me it wouldn't have happened, would it Jasper, but then nobody listens to me, it was just the same with your mother you know, when I told her to go straight to the doctor with that lump, I knew that lump as soon as I saw it, didn't I Jasper, Rose, I said, Rose, Rose –
(BENEDICT *stumbles towards the door, left.*)
What, where are you going, dear?

BENEDICT: (*In a child's voice*) Old room, Nanty, lie down in my old room when I was little Nanty –

DAISY: There's a good boy, aaah, but oh, not your old room dear, Matthew's in there, and all his things and Jenny's using Dick's of course, they're staying the night you see, so you use Henry's dear – Henry's old room –
(BENEDICT *goes out.*)
(*As she speaks the stage begins to darken.*) Did he hear, oh I hope he heard, he always makes such a mess when he comes down, not that it isn't lovely to see him, for your sake. I know dear, but sometimes I think he tipples (*lifts her hand to her mouth in a drinking movement*) a little too much, it's all very well to say he needs relaxing but not when he turns things upside down, and he takes after Rose that way, she liked her glass too, but of course she didn't let it go to her head like that, and oh why did he have to upset me with remembering Rose and Dick poor dears, and now my head, pounding because of the honking, pounding you know – and all the times I've asked them not to let Tom – but then it's true, true nobody listens to me, they go in and out and don't do the dishes and make fusses but not one of them says about tea, what am I meant to do about tea, Jasper, do I lay for everybody on the assumption or what, do I, do I lay on the

assumption, that's what I want to know Jasper, well, that's what comes of letting them treat me as housekeeper, that's what they think I am, well it won't do, it's not good enough, it's time they were told what I really am, and you should tell them dear, yes, it's up to you to tell them, Jasper, now we've got them all together and – oh, good Heavens, oh no (*seeing the pot*) what's this doing – but it's half full, you see, you see what I mean – left for me to – sometimes I think Marianne – no wonder my head – my poor head – (*begins to go out under the arch*) and oh, the windows, I'm locking the windows so they can't come in this way (*shuts them*) and tramping mud (*locks them*) there, there, at least I won't have mud this time – (*Going out through arch.*)
(*The stage continues to darken to half-light.* JASPER *lets out a sudden, terrible groan. Puts his head back. Curtain.*)

ACT TWO

The same. About an hour later. JASPER *as before. The stage is in semi-darkness. It is raining heavily. There is a sudden rattling at the windows.* MARIANNE's *voice,* HENRY's *urgently, with the cries of children.*

MARIANNE: (*Off*) Gramps – Gramps –

HENRY: (*Off*) Daddy – Daddy – can you hear me!

DAISY: (*Enters on the run through the arch*) No, no, not there – not that way – oh it's so dark – (*turns on the lights*) I've opened the back-kitchen door – I've put a mat down in the back-kitchen – the back-kitchen dears please –

HENRY: For heaven's sakes Nanty, we're getting – all right, but you go in that way, darling. I'm not having you get any wetter – Nanty – Nanty – open the door for Marianne!

DAISY: What, oh – (*opens the french windows*) oh, there you are dear, are you all right? I didn't mean you of course, just the children – I wanted to make sure they'd go around by the back-kitchen where I've put another mat especially you see –

MARIANNE: (*During this enters, with a man's raincoat over her head, in Wellington boots.*) I must say Nanty, I didn't expect you'd actually lock the door on us – but golly, what a business – (*Taking off her raincoat.*)

DAISY: Here dear – let me – (*Taking the coat.*)

MARIANNE: One minute thumping the ball about, the next absolute buckets, like the Old Testament, Gramps – (*Lifts a leg.*) I say Nanty, do you mind –

DAISY: What, oh. (*Pulls at the boot.*) And the one in the back-kitchen had gone, I think the boys must have – (*Pulls the boot off.*)

MARIANNE: (*Staggering back*) Whhoops!

DAISY: All right dear? You know for football posts, I know they do sometimes.

(MARIANNE *lifts the other leg.*)

(*Pulls it off*) So I had to put the one from the front door down – there, there we are –

MARIANNE: Thank goodness we had our bad weather gear in the

van – we had to sprint like billy-oh to get it and then we
thought Nindy had dropped her pot –

DAISY: What, oh no dear, her pot was here, where you left it.
Half full and more.

MARIANNE: (*Laughing*) Yes, Henry remembered after we'd sent
poor old Nigel haring back for it with my plastic bonnet over
his head –

DAISY: I suppose I'd better go and put these –

HENRY: (*Enters under the arch, towelling his head*) Phew, what a
soaking –

DAISY: Oh Henry, you saw the mat, did you?

HENRY: What, Nanty?

DAISY: The mat. I put down the mat.

HENRY: Oh.

DAISY: Well, they did use it, dear, didn't they, I had to get it
round from the front, you know, because the one at the back
– I think the boys – must have taken it for their football –

MARIANNE: No, they didn't Nanty. They haven't touched it, not
after all the business last time when they were using it as a
sleigh and you were jolly sharp with them.

DAISY: Oh, well as long as they've used the one I've just put
down, they did didn't they, Henry?

HENRY: Well, actually Nanty, there wasn't a mat there.

DAISY: What, what do you mean. I've only just put it there,
haven't I, Jasper? It can't have gone too.

HENRY: Well, Nanty, I can assure you, there's no mat there.

DAISY: Where?

HENRY: The kitchen.

DAISY: The kitchen! But I told you to go by the back-kitchen – I
opened the back-kitchen door especially – I told you –

HENRY: Oh sorry, I just heard kitchen –

DAISY: Oh good heavens – and after all the trouble I went to –
well where are they now, what are they doing, and there'll be
mud on their boots – where are they?

HENRY: Now now, Nanty, don't panic, I've told them to take off
their shoes and dry and wash themselves and to sit quietly
down at the table.

DAISY: The table, which table?

HENRY: Well, the kitchen table.

DAISY: Why?

HENRY: Well, for their tea.

DAISY: Their tea! But they can't have digested their lunches yet!

MARIANNE: Well, you know the boys, they can be digesting their
    lunches while they're eating their tea – (*laughs*.)

DAISY: But I've laid for everybody, haven't I Jasper, I've laid for
    everybody, a proper family tea – muffins and – rock-cakes even –

MARIANNE: Oh, they don't need muffins and rock-cakes, just
    some bread and butter and marmite and milk –

HENRY: We'll do it, Nanty, no need for you to bother yourself.

DAISY: Oh, it's not bothering myself I mind, I'm used to that,
    aren't I, Jasper, the point is I laid tea for everybody, as nobody
    told me any differently, can't they wait?

HENRY: They can't really, Nanty, no. I know it's unreasonable of
    them, to be at the age when they're permanently hungry –

MARIANNE: And anyway Nanty, as you won't allow them
    anywhere *but* the kitchen – and what can they do there *but* eat
    – at least that's the way they see it –

DAISY: I've never said they can't go into the spare rooms upstairs,
    I've never said that, although now you mention it they
    couldn't because of course Jenny's in Dick's and now
    Matthew wants one to himself he's in Benedict's and
    Benedict's lying down in Henry's and they'd wake him,
    wouldn't they Jasper?

MARIANNE: Well, of course, if Benedict needs to lie down –
    Anyway, they've got to have it now because poor old Henry's
    got to go and see Mrs O'Killiam –

DAISY: Who?

MARIANNE: – and it's all getting a bit – so, for goodness' sake
    darling, let's give them their tea at home –

DAISY: What, take them home, you can't take them home, I've
    sliced three loaves and buttered the slices, no no, you can't take
    them home you know, not without their tea, can they Jasper?

HENRY: But Nanty, if it's asking too much of you –

DAISY: If they need their tea now, let them have it now, by all
    means, I'll go and see to it straight away – here, Henry,
    you'd better give me that – (*takes the towel away from him*)

and I'll put these in the back-kitchen – (*as she goes*) and oh, by the way, if Nindy wants her pot you'll find it sluiced in the down-lavatory.

(*There is a pause.*)

MARIANNE: Golly, well we seem to have put our foot in it again, don't we darling?

HENRY: I think she's got one of her headaches, darling, and a bit tired with it. You know.

MARIANNE: Oh. Oh well, poor old Nanty – I'd better go and keep the peace.

HENRY: No, I'll go darling, you relax and have a jaw with Daddy, you haven't had a proper one yet.

MARIANNE: Well, you *are* marvellous at dealing with her, I'll take over later, when you've got her back under your thumb.

HENRY: Righto, darling. (*Goes out through the arch.*)

MARIANNE: I don't know what it is about Nindy's pottie that brings out the worst in Nanty, do you Gramps, all that fuss over the soup tureen last week and then hiding it in the kitchen cupboard did Henry tell you about that Gramps, before lunch when she thought I'd forgotten it again, not that I hadn't learnt my lesson though what could be less offensive than a toddler's wee, I mean I wasn't going to dish it out as soup or anything – Oh I'm not getting at Nanty, Gramps – Gosh I'm just as bad as she is sometimes. I know I am, why just the other afternoon I had quite a funny moment, well it wasn't funny at the time, oh it was the usual sort of thing Gramps, Nigel and Simon were quarrelling in the cubby-room over whose turn on the skate-board I think it was while I was dishing up their six o'clocks, Horlicks for Nigel and Tom and Piers, Ovaltine for Simon and Nindy and me, and I was stirring away as usual, out of the corner of my eye I caught myself watching them at it, Simon had the skate-board hugged to his chest and Nigel trying to struggle it out of his arms, and on their faces there were such expressions, but oh, perfectly normal, Gramps, golly! (*Laughs.*) They were just being children, humans, that's all, but still I caught myself, I was the horrible one, caught myself wishing they were, all of them, Tom and Piers and

Nindy too, though Piers and Tom were upstairs quite
innocent in front of childrens' television for all I knew and
Nindy was sitting in her highchair humming bubbles out
quite nicely and for all I knew feeling quite nice, but all of
them, I wished all of them, this one too, isn't it a horrible
Mums? (*To her belly*.) Oh, it was just a flash, Gramps, just an
out of the corner of my eye thing, deep and midnight stuff,
but it had never happened before, you see Gramps, so of
course now I keep remembering it, it pops in and out when I
least expect it, that I actually wished – oh, I know I'm not
like that really, or the house would be full of corpses, (*laughs*)
all I mean is that it's a jolly funny business, life and
parenthood and all that – and if my Henry weren't around
now that this thought's taken to popping in and out more
and more and sometimes all the time even – I might be in
danger of going – well, a bit potty. (*Laughs*.) What do you
think, Gramps?

(MARIANNE *enters. She is smoking*.)

MARIANNE: Oh hello Maggie!

(MARGARET *smiles*.)

But I say, you haven't been out in this have you?

MARGARET: Yes.

MARIANNE: Golly, why?

MARGARET: Oh – for a walk.

MARIANNE: Gosh, didn't you get wet?

MARGARET: I took shelter in a phone box.

MARIANNE: Oh. How did you get back?

MARGARET: In a taxi.

MARIANNE: Gosh, that was lucky, how did you get hold of one?

MARGARET: I telephoned for it.

MARIANNE: Oh, of course. Not lucky then, just jolly sensible.
(*Laughs*.)

MARGARET: Do you know where Ben is?

MARIANNE: No – oh, yes – upstairs, didn't Nanty say Gramps,
having a snooze.

MARGARET: Oh (*makes to go off*).

MARIANNE: Why don't you let him get on with it, as he probably
needs it from what Henry says – I mean, it's such a long time

186

since we've seen each other and I'm longing to hear all about
your success, aren't we Gramps?
(MARGARET *hesitates*.)
Come on then!
(MARGARET *sits down*.)
Jolly good! Now – now then tell us all about your – whoops!
(*Little pause*.) Whoops! (*Little pause*.) And again! He still
thinks we're footering about on the Piece with Henry and the
boys – and a hefty kick – and a hefty kick – he's developing
too, aren't you? (*Looks down, pats her stomach*.) I just realized
the other day that that's why I always assume my babies are
he's, even Nindy, they've all had such hefty kicks, even
Nindy (*laughs*) although Tom was the worst, I honestly think
he decided to boot his way out, while Nigel was a bit more
like a clog-dancer Henry used to say (*laughs*).
(*There is a pause*.)

MARGARET: (*As if making an effort*) And which would you prefer
this time?

MARIANNE: What?

MARGARET: Boy or girl?

MARIANNE: Do you know, I really don't mind, Maggie. I mean, I
suppose a sister for Nindy would be convenient. At least for
Nindy. But then so would another brother for Nigel, Simon
Tom and Piers. Or a sister for Nigel, Simon, Tom and Piers,
come to think of it. Or a brother for Nindy. Not that *they've*
given it a thought one way or another, and Henry says he'll
take what comes as usual, and Gramps hasn't expressed any
views either way, have you Gramps, so I'll settle for my
routine, run-of-the-mill eight pounder thank you very much
God, if you know what I mean (*laughs*).

MARGARET: I think so. You incline towards a baby, and you have
a strong preference for either sex.

MARIANNE: Yes. (*Little pause*.) I really shouldn't make such a
display, should I?

MARGARET: I don't see how you could help it.

MARIANNE: (*Laughs*) No, that's true enough. Anyway, enough of
babies! I was saying to Henry on our way here this morning
that the few times you and I have had a proper natter it's

really only me nattering away about the one I'm in the process of having or the ones I've already had and you have to go through the same old motions and ask the same old boring questions, and this time I wasn't going to let you, especially with so much to talk about yourself, I mean blossoming virtually overnight into a famous writer and tele-person even, golly, you must be jolly chuffed!

MARGARET: Well, um –

MARIANNE: No honestly, I'd be swollen with pride, wouldn't I Gramps! And what have the reviews been like, I've scarcely seen any.

MARGARET: Oh. What are called mixed.

MARIANNE: Jolly good, eh Gramps? One of the ones I read was very nice. It said you were like a scalpel, gosh (*laughs*) I think it was meant to be nice, anyway.

MARGARET: That was *The Times*.

MARIANNE: Was it, you read them all then, do you, I don't know how you could bear to. I mean the bad ones. If there were any.

MARGARET: I'd rather read them myself than have them read out to me by friends.

MARIANNE: You're absolutely right, anyway what does it matter what they say, it's been a great success, hasn't it, and I'll bet that infuriates them.

MARGARET: Who?

MARIANNE: The ones who were snide and snarky, there was one I came across made me absolutely livid!

MARGARET: Oh. The *Guardian*.

MARIANNE: No, it wasn't the *Guardian*. Could it have been the *Telegraph*?

MARGARET: No.

MARIANNE: Oh, that was a good one, then?

MARGARET: They didn't review it.
(*There is a pause.*)

MARIANNE: Anyway, as long as *you* think it's good, that's what counts, isn't it Gramps?

MARGARET: Thank you. (*Lights another cigarette.*) And have you read it yet?

MARIANNE: Oh gosh, yes, haven't I said?

MARGARET: I had the impression you called out something at
lunch. As you passed the dumplings.

MARIANNE: I know, it's such a shambles, isn't it, I was just saying
to Henry that our lot must do a marvellous job of putting you
and Ben off family life (*laughs*).
(*There is a pause.*)

MARGARET: And what did you say?

MARIANNE: What?

MARGARET: As you passed the dumplings.

MARIANNE: Oh – oh golly, nothing profound, knowing me. Just
the usual congratters, I expect.
(*There is a pause.*)

MARGARET: Did you enjoy it?

MARIANNE: Oh – oh, now I've got to be careful not to plonk my
great foot in it, but to be honest I can't say I actually *enjoyed* it,
Maggie, I didn't know you wanted me to, I mean let's face it, it
isn't just a jolly good snorter of a read, like the usual stuff I get
my nose into, for one thing you have to be on your toes all the
time, but I admit I've done my share of boasting about our
being fellow-sisters-in-law, especially after that TV thing.

MARGARET: I'm glad you got something out of it.

MARIANNE: Of course we always knew you were brainy, but not so
devastatingly brainy, eh, Gramps? The way you conjured up
all those weird people and being so – so ruthless and – and
devastating about the whole bunch of them. Am I being very
feeble?

MARGARET: You found them weird, did you?

MARIANNE: You and old Ben don't actually *know* types like that,
do you?

MARGARET: Yes, actually.

MARIANNE: Then no wonder you put them in a book, that's where
they belong, isn't it Gramps? Whoops – he's at it again!
(*Laughs.*)
(*There is a pause.*)
But tell me, how long did it take you to write, I can never
remember when you started, but you seem to have been at it
for years.

MARGARET: Two.

MARIANNE: Years?

MARGARET: Yes.

MARIANNE: Golly!

MARGARET: From conception to delivery.

MARIANNE: Gosh!

MARGARET: I know. Especially when you think what can be turned out in nine months.

MARIANNE: What do you – oh, I see! (*Laughs.*) Oh, but anyone can produce one of these, can't they – or is that what you meant?

MARGARET: No, I think I meant – (*Stops.*)

MARIANNE: What, Maggie?

MARGARET: Oh – merely that we're very different people.

MARIANNE: Who, you and I, you mean? Well, I'll say we are! (*Little pause.*) Although when you think about it we're only different because you're brainy and I'm not, otherwise we're at least women, after all, aren't we?

MARGARET: Which amounts to what? That we've both got wombs for breeding and breasts for feeding but we're under no obligation to use what brains we've got for thinking.

MARIANNE: Yes, I know, but isn't it awful how they rust over if we don't.

MARGARET: Which?

MARIANNE: What?

MARGARET: Which rust over, our wombs, our tits or our brains?

MARIANNE: Oh, I was thinking of myself, so I meant brains of course. But perhaps all three when you put it like that. (*There is a pause.*)

MARGARET: (*Lights another cigarette, puffs at it, looks at* MARIANNE) Actually, my reproductive organs work with regulation efficiency.

MARIANNE: Oh. Oh, well jolly good, eh Gramps?

MARGARET: Otherwise I wouldn't have needed two abortions.

MARIANNE: Oh. Oh, I didn't know.

MARGARET: I know.

MARIANNE: I'm sorry.

MARGARET: What for?

MARIANNE: Well, if I've been clumsy.

MARGARET: I don't think you've been at all clumsy. I had the first when I was nineteen, to prevent an unwanted baby – by an unwanted middle-aged schoolteacher.

MARIANNE: I suppose somebody might have wanted him though, mightn't they?

MARGARET: His wife didn't, when he tried to go back to her.

MARIANNE: I meant the baby. Because of all the people desperate to adopt, you know.

MARGARET: Yes, I do know. But I wasn't prepared to be their beast of burden. The second was Benedict's, two years ago.

MARIANNE: You really don't have to tell us about it, does she Gramps?

MARGARET: Oh, I don't mind.

MARIANNE: But I do rather, I'm afraid.

MARGARET: Really, what of? You've always been so open and free about that aspect of your life. Not that the Ben abortion's particularly interesting, I admit. But it happened to coincide with my beginning my novel, and as I didn't want a baby anyway, I wasn't going to let it muck up my creative processes, if you follow. Fortunately there's a bright lady gynaecologist in Hampstead –

MARIANNE: (*Rising, takes a few steps*) Oooh-oooh –

MARGARET: What, what is it? (*Going to her.*)

MARIANNE: Sofa – sofa – Henry – quickly – ooooh – (*Collapses awkwardly on it.*)

MARGARET: Oh my God, oh my God, I'll get him – (*Goes towards the arch.*)

(MATTHEW *has appeared at the french windows. He stands uncertainly watching. He enters hesitant.*)

MARIANNE: (*Holding* MARGARET's *arm*). No no – my leg – please rub it – quickly.

(MARGARET *seizes her leg, begins to rub.*)

MATTHEW: Um, if – if you see Mummy – um –

MARIANNE: No, no, the other one, the other one (*irritably*) quick – quick – rub!

MATTHEW: I'll be – um – I'll be up in my room – (*Goes out left quickly.*)

MARIANNE: Oh God! God! Rub – rub!

HENRY: (*Runs easily through the arch*) Ah, the old crampers, eh darling – here, let me, Maggie, I've got the trick of it – (*Takes* MARIANNE's *leg, begins to massage it expertly.*)

MARIANNE: Aaah, aaah – (*with increasing relief*) that's it, aaah, clever old stick – there now – Golly, poor old Maggie, she thought I was going to litter right at her feet, didn't you Maggie?

HENRY: (*Laughs, turns, sees* MARGARET's *face*) Are you all right?

MARGARET: Yes thank you. As everything seems to be under control I think I'll go and look at my husband.

MARIANNE: Jolly good! (*And as* MARGARET *goes out*) Not that I'd have dared, would I Gramps? Litter I mean, she'd probably have trampled on him, well, at least now we know, don't we Gramps, she's not infertile or frigid, darling, she has them killed, she sat there boasting about it, didn't she Gramps, she was horrible, quite horrible, wasn't she Gramps, so you come here for a minute, come on.

(HENRY *hesitates, sits beside her.* MARIANNE *takes his arm, wraps it around her, leans into him.*)

There, now I feel safe, no one can harm us now, can they, we won't let her get you – aah – squeeze me, a little pressure, *you* know – that's right – aaah – aaah –

HENRY: Well, don't get too comfy darling, or you'll go into one of your snoozes.

MARIANNE: No, no, course I won't – course I won't – (*In a little girl's voice.*)

(HENRY *strokes* MARIANNE's *hair, pushes a lock back, looks into her face. After a moment an expression of enormous sadness comes over his face. Then he looks at* JASPER, *smiles.* DAISY *enters under the arch.*)

DAISY: Oh, oh you're *both* in here now are you, no, no, it's all right, it's just that Henry suddenly vanished and there's a terrible squabble over those blasted rock-cakes.

(HENRY *makes to get up.*)

MARIANNE: No, you don't, you've done your stint with Nanty and you've still got Mrs O'Killiam to come –

(DAISY *goes out under the arch.*)

HENRY: (*Lets out his sudden strange laugh*) Golly, sorry, sorry
   Daddy. (*Does it again.*) – Must be – must be what they mean
   by *fou rire* – because actually she's not really quite as – as
   grotesque – Mrs O'Killiam – as somehow I'd led Marianne to
   believe, I mean it's true that she's thin, she was certainly off
   her food, from depression, really terrible depression, but her
   face – her face is – rather touching, delicate and there's
   something in her eyes, behind the fatigue and giving up –
   rather – well, rather lovely, haunting – she touches one, you
   see, in her despair. I don't know why I led Marianne to
   believe, even right at the beginning that she was – of course
   it's true her boys are brutes, that's certainly true and – they
   like to catch cats you know and tie plastic bags around their
   heads – and the little girl, well she's not a hydrocephalic but
   she does have adenoids that give her face a swollen – from
   time to time – and her husband, well it's nothing to do with
   an eighty-year-old woman, I don't know why I – I – you
   know how truthful I've always been, perhaps it was simply
   lack of practice that led me to – to – (*laughs*) he's certainly
   been in trouble with the police, of course, for something to
   do with cars, I think it was, and he's abandoned her and as I
   say she is – quite naturally – given the way life's treated her –
   and – and – but please don't believe I ever, I ever intended,
   planned, or wanted to – actively wanted to – make love to
   her. I didn't Daddy, I didn't. Even though she is now my
   mistress. (*Pause.*) You see, what happened was well about a
   month ago I went around to see her, and the door was open,
   on the latch, so I knew she was expecting me, and so I went
   in. And there she was. On the sofa. And a strange noise
   coming from upstairs. Rather alarming, actually, until I
   realized it was just the little girl asleep, snoring – and the
   boys were out, doing something hideous I suppose, anyway
   they weren't doing it inside – So. So it was just her. On the
   sofa. Looking so defeated and – and hopeless – and the
   snoring from above. And me. And she said, oh doctor, oh
   doctor. She's – she's Irish you know. And started to cry. So I
   went over to her and put my arms around her, to comfort
   her. And she seemed to want, to expect – to *need* me to – and

– well – anyway – I did. You see, it was something I could
do, something I could give her, there being so little one can
give even those who love one, isn't that true, Daddy, and
here was something so simple, I've always found it easy to,
well – and there's always been something about her that
touched me you see – and – and afterwards she clung to me
as if – and I cuddled her and everything was – I like to think
it was peaceful for a little time, it wasn't sex, you see, not for
her either. (*Pause.*) I prescribed myself, if you like. On the
National Health. Anyhow that's how I tried to look at it.
(*Laughs.*) As I say holding her. (*Little pause.*) I didn't feel
guilty or ashamed, or embarrassed. Not at all. And I
massaged the back of her neck, where she gets pain, and
looked in on Carla, and discussed an operation on her
adenoids and then went home as if I – as if for once I'd been
an effective doctor. (*Smiles. Pause.*) But of course nothing
ends – nothing like that ends with the act, does it? Why
should it? Give someone valium for much needed calm and
in no time they're desperate for their calming valium, and it's
no good explaining to them – Anyway. (*Laughs.*) Now she
looks upon me as her lover. Her man. She's as possessive of
me as – well, she feels she has a right to me, as she's given me
her body, as she puts it. She is Irish, after all. And so in
return she thinks she's entitled to something from me – oh,
not just money, other than the odd pound here and there,
and who can blame her for that? But well, more of *me*. My
time. My attention. My love. And now she's taken, poor
soul, to threatening me. (*Pause.*) I have a feeling she's told
her brutes of boys. Or perhaps they've watched. Or she's
allowed them to watch – no, no, I'm sure that's unfair,
unworthy – it's just that there's a window and once I thought
I – oh, I don't know. It doesn't really matter does it? But if I
don't go around then they come around, to the surgery – and
this morning, of course, to the house – so – so – it'll get
worse. I've tried to think it through – right to the worst end –
the scandal, and I'll be struck off, I suppose, and then what
it'll mean for old Marianne and the children – one day – and
– and – then I've tried to put it in the larger scheme, *sub*

specie aeternitas, no *aeternitatis* sorry Daddy. (*A little laugh.*)
And then it struck me, you see. The real thing. That I didn't
care. I'd even quite welcome it. Because once you do begin to
look at it *sub specie* it's really all such a pitiful charade, isn't
it, or perhaps not even pitiful, merely a charade, with none
of it mattering at all in view of what happens all over the
world, every minute of the day, and when one thinks it
through that far – no, no, when *I'd* thought it through that
far I felt a tremendous relief, you see, because then I could
face the fact – the fact that I've never cared, never, I've
always really known that nothing matters, and I remembered
the night Dick was killed – when I left you that night and
went home and sat in the kitchen, the house was breathing
you know, with life. Marianne upstairs waiting for me,
children in all the rooms, another in Marianne's womb – and
Mrs O'Killiam in her loneliness also, as it's turned out,
waiting for me – and some poor devil who'd lost his eye and
his daughter in a car crash I'd been to see – and Dick dead,
Dick, and I didn't care, not about any of us, not about
Marianne or Tom or Piers or Nigel or Simon or Nindy or the
unborn or any of the Mrs O'Killiams anywhere or you here
mourning the only one of us you loved – and so I gave myself
a couple of jolly hard punches, Daddy, right in the face, to
make myself care about something – and then old Marianne
came down, poor old Marianne, and I looked at her and
thought, no, no, I don't care about you either, poor old girl,
and now there's Nanty with a brain tumour more than likely
so you see, Daddy, so you see, what is the point, the point of
caring for each other and loving each other when the end is
always and always the same, *sub specie* or any way you look at
it, Daddy, do *you* know by any chance, God given chance?
(*Pause.*) Do you? And if you don't why did you bring us into
the world, how did you dare – how did you – I'm sorry. I'm
sorry to be so childish. I should probably have asked that
years ago, but if you can answer now I'd be jolly grateful. So
I'll know what to say to my lot when the time comes. Can
you, Daddy? (*Laughs, stares desperately at* JASPER.)
(MARGARET *enters from left. There is a pause.*)

MARGARET: Sorry. Am I interrupting?

HENRY: What? Oh good Heavens no, Daddy and I were just having one of our jaws, weren't we Daddy?

(MARGARET *lights a cigarette. Her hand is trembling.*)

HENRY: I gather you and Marianne had a bit of a ding-dong, I hope you didn't take it too – too – I know she didn't.

MARGARET: Look, the thing is, I've got to get back to London soon.

HENRY: Oh. What a pity.

MARGARET: And I've just looked in on Ben.

HENRY: Ah. Yes. How is he? I'm afraid he might have had a spot too much, we were reminiscing, you know what it's like when we haven't seen each other for a bit, eh Daddy? (*Laughs.*)

MARGARET: He's sprawled across the bed of his childhood, with his thumb in his mouth. He's making little mewling sounds at the back of his throat. He's dribbling. And he stinks of Scotch.

HENRY: Oh. Well um –

MARGARET: So I gather he's been through his fit and frenzy stage, has he?

HENRY: Well. Well, perhaps he did become a little – I'm sorry, Maggie.

MARGARET: I'm not, I'm afraid. He was due for another bout, and I wanted him to have it here. I'm returning him, you see. Giving him back. Sorry. That's unnecessarily brutal. But I've had quite enough of him, and I need you to keep him here, please, until I've moved myself out of the flat and found a place where I'll be safe. Actually, my publishers have already set that side of things in motion. (*Pause.*) No doubt you think I'm being very hard. Yes. Besides, I'm not Ben's wife anymore. Let alone his nurse, surrogate mother, victim and tart on demand. I'm a writer. My first book taught me that much. Whatever you think of it. And now that I've begun a new one, I'm going to need all my wits and as much peace as I can manage. Along with the usual ration of luck and inspiration. You see. I'm sorry. I *am* sorry to take advantage. But then Henry is a doctor, so he'll know what to do. And as you're also a decent man and a loving brother I'm fairly sure you'll do it. Oh, and there's something I should tell you. As far as I can establish, his Vintross doesn't exist. At least the only Vintross I can trace is a car-park attendant at the BBC. And I don't know if he got on to Hugh Rhys Jones, but if he did, Hugh Rhys Jones didn't stab himself to death in a Chinese restaurant or whatever. He's merely been transferred to Cardiff. Which may amount to the same thing of course. (*Gets up*.) I've heard there's a good clinic outside Staines. I'll get my publisher to send you its address. And of course any committal papers you want me to sign. Oh – and my apologies to Marianne – explain that I was a trifle on edge. And now I'd better get away before he makes one of his spectral recoveries. They can be rather unnerving. (*Turns left to go out*.)

(BENEDICT *enters from left. He is trembling. His colour is ghastly. He walks slowly to* MARGARET. *Stands in front of her.* HENRY *gets up*.)

BENEDICT: It was Dick, of course. Wasn't it? Yes, it was Dick. He's just come back you see and told me so. Back, Henry, Daddy. Old Dick. Just as he used to be, twenty-five years ago. And he was wearing that smile, you'd know the smile, Henry, when we'd caught him out in one of his little meannesses, his stealings, and he'd decided to make it up. And then – then Daddy – he put his hand out towards me, as if he was going to touch me. And I said, 'Dick, Dick –' and he turned and went. Went away from me.

HENRY: Ben – old Ben – it wasn't Dick –

BENEDICT: Yes, it was, Hen. It was, Daddy. And I understood what it was old Dick, our old Dick, Henry, had come back to tell me, Daddy. What was it like to have Dick's willy inside you, darling? Did he hold you against the dark, as I did. Did he? (*Smiles pathetically*.)

(JENNY *enters through the french windows*.)

JENNY: I take it he's not come back, then?

HENRY: Oh. Well actually I think Ben saw him a short while ago. Didn't you Ben?

BENEDICT: What?'

HENRY: He came into your room for a moment, you were just telling us. Because that's where he's staying the night, you see. Matthew.

BENEDICT: Matthew?

HENRY: Yes, Ben. Matthew, old chap. (*Goes to him gently, takes his arm.*) Matthew, you see.

BENEDICT: Oh. Oh yes Matthew – so alike, so alike it makes the heart – heart – sorry Hen, sorry – sorry – darling. Sorry Jen. Sorry Daddy.

JENNY: Did he say anything?

HENRY: No, apparently he came in and saw – well, old Ben was having a nap, weren't you Ben, so he went away again, apparently, from what Ben was saying, didn't he, eh Ben?

JENNY: Well, that's our day together. He has to be back first thing tomorrow. Our only day together in a month and then another month until half-term, and I can't go on looking for him any more, I'm soaked through, my feet are wet and I'm worn out, he's quite worn me out with his – of course you realize it's deliberate, don't you, I expect you've all noticed how he avoids me, when I so much as put my hand on his arm he flinches, draws away from me – he loathes my touch, you see, his mother's touch. Oh yes – yes – I'm sure you've noticed – perhaps you want it even, do you? So that you can see he's still Dick's son, not mine, I expect that's why you wanted him to stay on at the school – isn't it – well, I'll tell you one thing, he's not going back, no, he's not going back there, with that housemaster – I hate that housemaster – writing to you, how dare he write to you! How dare you let him! (*To* HENRY) Well he won't any more, you won't any more, he's coming back home with me to live with me where I can watch him and guard him and look after him, I've a right to that, if I'm going to die for him a thousand times a day I've a right to that, I'm not going to let him end up like Dick, no I'm not, we're never going to set foot in this house again – neither of us! Neither of us! He's *my* son. Not *yours*! (*Looks around at them.*) Yes, this is Dick's frump speaking. Dick's frump! That's what you all thought of me as, you couldn't understand how your brilliant Dick could come to

marry me, could you – but then you didn't know him, didn't
see him as I saw him, night after night, crying, or curled up –
so pathetic – but I knew it was hopeless, hopeless, nobody
could have saved him, nobody, every time he went off on
that motorbike I knew – knew what he wanted and at the end
I almost wanted it too, yes I did, because if he couldn't find
anything in me or our Matthew to keep him then he might as
well – well I'm not letting him go like that, not letting my
Matthew go like that. I'm not. I'm not.

MARGARET: (*Goes to her*) Jenny – Jenny – I know what you're
feeling –

JENNY: (*Slaps her*) Do you? (*Laughs.*) Do you? With your nasty
mean little novel, do you think – do you think he cared for
you either, why, why you were one of hundreds, hundreds,
there was an Australian sociologist at the same time as you,
the very same time, she was called Dick's Kangaroo because
she'd hop into bed with him anywhere, even places where
there wasn't one, that was the joke about her, and his
students, Dick's lucky dips, and that furry little woman in
the bursar's office, all going on at the same time –
(MATTHEW *enters through the french windows. There is a
pause.*)

MATTHEW: Um – (*clears his throat*) – Hello Mummy.

MARIANNE: (*Enters through the arch*) Ah, all here, jolly good –
Nanty's seeing them around to the van, darling, and I've just
potted Nindy but no luck this time, even Gramp's magic
didn't work, you must have spent her last penny after lunch,
eh Gramps, anyway we're all set darling, sorry we've got to
leave so early, old Henry's fault for being needed as usual,
but golly it was lovely seeing us all together again, eh
Gramps?

DAISY: (*Enters from left*) I've got them all in dears, now Nindy's
got the pottie and Nigel's looking after the boots and Simon
and Nigel are in charge of the coats and Tom's promised not
to toot the horn, but before you go dears there's something
you want to tell them, isn't there Jasper, I've been thinking
dear, and they have a right to know who I am, haven't they
dear. We're married, you see. Jasper and I. (*Pause.*) Aren't

we Jasper. There! (*Laughs.*) We knew that would surprise
you. Didn't we Jasper?
(*There is a pause.*)
Oh, it wasn't a proper ceremony, in church and in white,
with bridesmaids and bouquets or anything like that, no no,
it was just a thing in an office, the most ordinary thing in the
world except for a sweet old lady who played the organ,
didn't she Jasper, but it was all a bit of a rush, you know,
people waiting in the waiting room, and leaving as we
entered, weren't there Jasper, but they have to keep at it all
the time, you know – quite a little business in its way but
Jasper was, well you know how he feels things, always so
quick, isn't he dear? His shoulders shook and his mouth
trembled, it did you know! And so distinguished with his
white mane and a carnation in his button and he even cried,
didn't you Jasper, and he was so ashamed because he
thought he was holding them up you see – with so many to
come, and probably queues forming – but I said, I told him,
they're used to it you know, people crying and overcome and
behaving strangely, they allow for it dear, they take it into
account, they'll fit everybody in so don't you worry, and sure
enough it just swung open, the door on the other side you
see, not where we'd come in, but on the other side – oh so
well organized – and out we went, didn't we Jasper, out we
went! And the people who'd been before us were still on the
pavement, laughing and chattering weren't they dear and
clambering into their cars, and another car arrived, didn't it
Jasper, with a new lot you see just as I said, and then our car
came up, we'd hired it especially, oh so grand it was, shiny
and black to take us home, and home we came, didn't we
Jasper, and I said as we went, there there my love, my sweet,
my darling – it's all over, it's finished, wasn't it easy and
quick, all finished at last and he said 'Rose, Rose – ' aaah! –
and I said 'No no Jasper, I'm not your Rose my dear, I'm
your Daisy dear', and 'Oh my dear Daisy' he said, so sweet
he was – 'Oh my dear Daisy, not over, my Daisy, but
beginning my love', he was tired you see, weren't you Jasper,
quite dead you were, weren't you my dear, we'll have

children he said, to keep us going, send them forth in life, didn't you Jasper, think of them waiting, waiting to enter, we'll bring them forth, for life awaits them, the door will open, we'll send them towards it – didn't you love, aaah aaaah my darling – the door will open, we'll send them towards it –

(*During this speech and the following speeches the room is brightening – through natural sunlight after the rain to an unnatural brightness.*)

The door will open, we'll send them towards it – the door is open –

THE REST (*except* JASPER): We'll send them towards it.

(JASPER *is struggling, as if to rise. His eyes fixed in wonder.*)

HENRY: The door will open –

BENEDICT: We'll send them towards it.

DAISY: The door is open –

ALL: We'll send them towards it!

JENNY: The door is open.

ALL: We'll send them towards it, the door is open, the door is open, we'll send them towards it.

(JASPER *has almost made it to his feet.*)

ALL: The door is open, the door is open, the door is open!

(*Stillness.*)

(*A prolonged honking of the horn.* JASPER *subsides into his chair.*)

DAISY: Oh really – I did tell him not to!

HENRY: Sorry Nanty, but it's hard to resist –

MARIANNE: – Anyway Nanty, we are just off, this second, don't worry – well Jenny – (*kisses her*) and Margaret (*coolly*) and Ben (*kissing them both*) I hope it won't be so long next time because Gramps does love it when you – and old Mat – see you next hols, eh –

HENRY: (*Meanwhile*) Ben, you um, well we'll be in touch and – and Maggie – um, um, take care the two of you um (*putting a hand on* BENEDICT's *shoulder, kissing* MARGARET) and Jenny my dear, now you're not to worry, everything'll be – and Mat – keep up the good work!

DAISY: (*Throughout this*) – aaah, what a shame you couldn't stay

for tea, it was all laid you know, especially, but everything's
in, don't worry, Nindy, the pottie, Nigel and Tom the boots
and coats – so that's all right – nothing forgotten this time –

HENRY: And Nanty – (*kisses her*) I shan't forget about the
headaches, I'll see to that straight away –

DAISY: Oh thank you dear, so sweet, and I'll keep on with the
moist pads, shan't I Jasper?

MARIANNE: (*Kissing her*) I hope we weren't too much for you this
time –

DAISY: What, no no, of course not dear – they were no trouble,
the boys and little Nindy – aaah! – You're never any trouble,
are they Jasper?
(*Honking off.*)

MARIANNE: Well darling, mustn't keep Mrs O'Killiam waiting!

HENRY: Golly no, well God bless, God bless – and see you
Daddy, as usual.

MARIANNE: Yes God bless Gramps – see you as usual.
(HENRY *and* MARIANNE *go out left to the accompaniment of
honking. The honking stops.*)

DAISY: Oooh – you see how it starts my head off – well, there we
are, at least we can have a proper grown-up tea, we adore the
little ones, don't we Jasper – but I must say they make it
difficult to have a proper grown-up – but I've kept most of
the rock-cakes for you, Matthew, I know Jenny got them for
you specially so I only allowed them half each so you can
have a good tuck-in dear, but oh that reminds me I still
haven't settled – now how much did we say it was Jenny,
sixty-six p but of course my purse, I still haven't found – did
I ask you if you'd seen it Matthew, have you seen it dear, my
purse, small, green, in velours –

MATTHEW: (*With sudden fluency*) Your purse, gosh no Nanty, I
haven't seen any purse at all, a small green one did you say in
– well I'll certainly keep an eye out for it, it's terrible when
one loses things, I do it all the time don't I Mummy, I hope
there wasn't any money or anything valuable in it.

DAISY: Well about four pounds eighty-five p but it must be here
somewhere, you see it's the purse, that's what I care about, it
was a present from Jasper, years ago, wasn't it Jasper?

JENNY: (*Who was watching* MATTHEW *during his speech*) Ready for our walk, darling?

MATTHEW: Oh but –

DAISY: What, walk, but what about your tea, aren't you going to have our tea first?

JENNY: No, I'd like to go now. And straight away darling and together if you please – (*goes over, takes him by the hand, tightly*) so that we can't lose each other.

DAISY: Oh well I must say – you'd have thought they'd have waited, wouldn't you Jasper, they could have had tea first as they're always so hungry –

BENEDICT: (*During this, has gone over to* MARGARET, *has stood staring directly into her eyes*) Ready, darling? I'm rather anxious to get back. To give Vintross a ring. He'll want to know how things are. And you must want to get back, too. I know what it's like now – when you start a new one. (*Little pause.*) Coming? (*Little pause.*) Coming darling?

DAISY: What, what do you mean – you're not going too – but the tea's out you know – or Benedict a drink, dear – you always like a drink before you go.

BENEDICT: Oh no, Nanty – (*Leading* MARGARET *towards the french windows.*) I've given that stuff up now virtually for good, haven't I Daddy – but we'll be back soon – We won't leave it so long before the next time, Daddy, that's a promise. (*They go.*)

DAISY: What, well that's all very well but after all the trouble I went to – and the muffins – all those muffins – and what for? What for? Lay it down on the assumption and then just clear it all away again – you see – like a housekeeper – but what about you, Jasper, how do you feel, are you all right dear, you've gone very quiet all of a sudden.

(JASPER *makes a slight noise.*)

What, dear?

JASPER: The door is open!

DAISY: Dear?

JASPER: The door is open!

DAISY: Oh, you're feeling the chill again, and such a warm sunny evening now that it's rained, but of course if you're feeling

the chill, I know how it goes right through you, right
through your whole system – (*going to the french windows,
shutting them, locking them*) there – is that better – and oh the
light – we don't need the light any more now that it's light
(*turns off lights*) – and my headache you know, much better
now that everybody's – (*collecting the Scotch bottle and glass*)
not that we don't like having them of course – though they
might have stayed for tea – (*as she goes out through the arch*)
don't we, dear?
(*Pause. The lights continue to go down steadily, until only*
JASPER *in his chair is lit. That light remains for a few seconds
and then as it goes down, the sound of organ music, distantly,
then swelling to fill the theatre as: curtain.*)

Stage Struck

Stage Struck was first presented by Michael Codron on 21 November 1979 at the Vaudeville Theatre, London. The cast was as follows:

ROBERT	Alan Bates
HERMAN	Andrew Sharp
ANNE	Sheila Ballantine
WIDDECOMBE	Nigel Stock
Director	Stephen Hollis
Designer	Carl Toms

ACT ONE

SCENE I

*The living-room of a large house in the country, not far from London.
Say, between London and Brighton. It is an old farmhouse,
modernized but not too radically converted. Stage right there are french
windows. Stage left a door that leads to the hall, front door, and stairs
to the upstairs part of the house. Stage back, an arch that leads to the
kitchen. The walls of the room are panelled, rectangularly from
three-quarters of the way up, down to the floor; and in large squares
above. One of these squares, in the middle, is in fact a concealed
opening to a large cupboard or hidey-hole – originally, perhaps, the
entrance to a loft. There is another one directly opposite, but not of
course visible to the audience.*

*The furnishing in the room consists of a desk near the french windows
(stage right), several armchairs and a sofa, a small table, a drinks
sideboard, etc.; There are books in bookshelves, some to do with the
theatre and its history, others complicated do-it-yourself books. There
is also the odd poster for plays, featuring* ANNE ROBERTS *from under
to above the title. There is a telephone on the desk. There is a ladder
against the wall, built so that it blends against it, which leads to the
cubby-hole panel. A rope pulls the panel open.*

*When the curtain goes up it is late evening, in summer. The french
windows are open. The cubby-hole panel is open. There is a pile of
magazines,* Stage, Plays and Players, *etc.: at the foot of the ladder.*
ROBERT *appears from the loft, scales nimbly down the ladder,
humming. Picks up the pile, goes on up the ladder. Goes into the
cubby-hole.* HERMAN *appears through the french windows. He is
carrying a gun, looking thoughtful. He looks around, makes to go
towards the kitchen.* ROBERT *reappears at the top of the ladder, begins
to come down.* HERMAN *sees him. He hesitates, then slips the gun
back into his pocket.*

ROBERT: (*Pushing the ladder against the wall*) Oh, hello Herman.
  How are you.
  (HERMAN *shrugs.*)
  Working hard?

HERMAN: Well, I haven't done much recently.

ROBERT: Why not?

HERMAN: For one thing I can't get to the library.

ROBERT: Why not?

HERMAN: On Monday there was a tube strike. Then on Tuesday the library porters were on strike so they wouldn't fetch any books up, then on Wednesday the librarians came out – and then yesterday when I telephoned to find out what was going on nobody answered, so I suppose the telephonists were out to show solidarity with the librarians who've probably gone back.

ROBERT: What I'm looking forward to is a tourists' strike, a day when they'll all refuse to come out of their hotels and spend their money looking at our pageantry and picket-lines, so I can go into town and do some exotic shopping without being treated as an undesirable resident. Drink?

HERMAN: No thanks.

ROBERT: Oh. Are you all right. You look a bit low.

HERMAN: Do I? Perhaps because it all seems so bloody pointless.

ROBERT: Oh it is, from what I can make out. Because apparently the money they finally get is worth less than the money they were getting when they went on strike for it by the time they actually succeed in getting it which is why they have to come out again immediately they've got it to get some more of it and so forth, don't worry about it and do have a drink.

HERMAN: No, I was talking about my research into Henry James. It doesn't matter to me whether I get on with my thesis or not. (*He sits down.*)

ROBERT: Poor old Henry James, oh that reminds me, I've forgotten to let the wine breathe. (*Taking a bottle out of the cupboard, checking the label, replacing it with another of something different*) I've got a little pheasant in the oven, a very little one, sadly won't go around for three, or I'd ask you to stay on to dinner.

HERMAN: You mean you want me to go?

ROBERT: No no, of course not, I say aren't you a mite touchy for you, at least wait and say hello to Anne, she shouldn't be too long now they've persuaded her leading man to cut down on his curtain calls, and then push off when we make you feel *de trop*. (*As he puts out knives and forks rapidly on the table*) But excuse me if I just – so we can start as soon as Anne gets back, she's always peckish – there – (*Turns, looks at* HERMAN.) I say, you really do look subdued, what have you been up to?

HERMAN: Tell me something, Robert.

ROBERT: Yes?

HERMAN: What do you think of me?

ROBERT: What?

HERMAN: What do you really think of me. Straight out.

ROBERT: Straight out?

HERMAN: Yes.

ROBERT: Well, I don't know, Herman, I haven't thought too much about you. But we're both delighted you've taken over the cottage, and not simply because you're a guaranteed short-term tenant, and I do enjoy your little droppings-in and just-passings-by when I'm on my own, if that means anything.

HERMAN: But you do think there's something odd about me, don't you? I've noticed the smiles you give Anne sometimes when I say something.

ROBERT: I'm sorry. I never meant you to notice them.

HERMAN: But what do you say about me when my back is turned?

ROBERT: Well, nothing really cruel Herman, I promise, none of the current round of anti-Australian jokes, it's all very affectionate. And some of your little gestures have touched Anne quite deeply, you know. The note and flowers you sent her for getting you a ticket to her play, for instance. Although while we're on the subject I should perhaps take the opportunity of warning you against lilies for actresses, even famous and successful ones like Anne are superstitious.

HERMAN: What, do they mean bad luck?

ROBERT: Well, death, usually. I must tell you all about actors' superstitions, whistling, Macbeth, green, there was an old ham I used to know in Worthing who'd worked with Wolfitt –

HERMAN: In other words, I'm what you'd call gauche, right?

ROBERT: Naïve, I'd call it. Refreshingly naïve.

HERMAN: Let's face it, Robert, I'm a hick.

ROBERT: Herman, I believe you're suffering from delayed culture shock.

HERMAN: Right. I am. Because I'm in love, you see.

ROBERT: Ah. Ah-hah. Who with?

HERMAN: Her name's Griselda.

ROBERT: Griselda, eh? Well – well, that's a very nice name. And with a built-in defence against diminutives. Well, that's good news, Herman.

HERMAN: Is it? She's married.

ROBERT: Oh. Who to?

HERMAN: Some man or other.

ROBERT: Well, that certainly narrows the field.

HERMAN: Grisle won't talk about him. Except to say she doesn't love him any longer, and she hasn't for years but he doesn't know it.

ROBERT: Still, she's already told you more about him than he knows himself.

HERMAN: The poor bastard thinks he's blissfully married. And he thinks she is too. Even though he's been unfaithful to her right from the beginning almost. So really he's got it coming to him, hasn't he? I can see that. But then why do I feel such a – a shit.

ROBERT: It does you credit. No pommy of your age would feel a shit in those circumstances, I can tell you.

HERMAN: That's what Grisle keeps saying. She thinks I'm being naïve too, at least until last night she did.

ROBERT: Why, what did you do last night?

HERMAN: Well, she came around to the cottage – hey, I hope you don't mind my having her in the cottage.

ROBERT: Good God, Herman, you have her where you can.

HERMAN: Thanks Robert. And afterwards I tried to make her understand what I felt about what we were doing, and suddenly she turned really nasty. She said I was like a convict.

ROBERT: Oh good Heavens, that's a simple matter of changing

your clothes and letting your hair grow –

HERMAN: She was talking about my post-coital guilt. She said I looked so guilty and beaten and ashamed, and I said, I can't help it, that's how I do feel, and I can't see how you don't feel the same way. And she said, the trouble is, I'm not good enough for a hick like you, and she walked out.

ROBERT: Oh dear.

HERMAN: It'd be all right if she married me. I know it would.

ROBERT: Married you?

HERMAN: Right.

ROBERT: Well – look, have she and – some man – any children?

HERMAN: Two little boys.

ROBERT: Well, that does complicate things. They can be a dreadful nuisance, especially in divorce proceedings. I remember one of Anne's friends, she played Laerta to Anne's Hamlet in the all-female a few years back, by the way, had a nightmare time of it over the custody of their twins. Her husband fought her at every turn.

HERMAN: But she won in the end, I hope!

ROBERT: Oh yes. He had to keep them. But she has to do a few weeks every Christmas and Easter and Summer.

HERMAN: But I wouldn't mind her having them, I love kiddies.

ROBERT: Do you really? Well, what about her, does she want to marry you?

HERMAN: She's said so, once or twice. Until last night.

ROBERT: Oh, last night was just a lovers' tiff, really Herman, I can't see your problem.

HERMAN: The husband, of course. What about him, the poor bastard!

ROBERT: Oh, good God Herman, you really are being a little over-scrupulous there, you know. I mean, (a) he's not a friend of yours , (b) she doesn't love him, (c) he's been consistently unfaithful to her

HERMAN: What's that got to do with it? What about you and Anne?

ROBERT: Mmmm?

HERMAN: Well, you and Anne lead pretty free sexual lives, don't you?

ROBERT: Anne's reputation is absolutely spotless. Even in the Green Room almost. Really Herman, I don't want to come the heavy hubby, but I'd really rather you kept Anne out of this.

HERMAN: What about you then?

ROBERT: What about me?

HERMAN: Well, a couple of nights ago when I dropped in you told me a story about a girl you had a fling with you called it when you were stage-managing somewhere in Worthing and then from something Anne said over supper I worked out afterwards you and Anne must actually have been married at the time.

ROBERT: Whatever you do, Herman, you mustn't abandon research, you've got a nose for it. (*Little pause.*) Well. So what?

HERMAN: So. Suppose I came along to you and said too bad, old son, I'm taking your Anne away from you.

(ROBERT *laughs.*)

What would you do?

ROBERT: I hope – (*recovering himself*) – I'd have the grace to accept it.

HERMAN: Would you really? So you're telling me to go ahead then, Robert, and to Hell with the consequences.

ROBERT: Under the circumstances, I can't think of a better place for them.

(HERMAN *takes the gun out of his pocket, very slowly. Points it at* ROBERT. *There is a pause.*)

Is that loaded?

HERMAN: Right.

ROBERT: With live bullets?

HERMAN: Right.

ROBERT: Well Herman – (*laughs nervously*) – I'm sorry if my – my – my advice hasn't been on the right moral lines but – but we're probably confronted here with a classic case of culture gap, aren't we. In the old country we don't pull guns on people whose advice we disagree with, especially when it's offered in the best of faith. (*Pause.*) If I've once or twice seemed to be frivolous about your problem please forgive

me, I picked up some rather unattractive habits during my
years in – in rep. (*Pause.*) Sorry.

HERMAN: What?

ROBERT: I'm apologizing.

HERMAN: What for, Robert?

ROBERT: Whatever you're pointing that thing at me for.

HERMAN: What, oh sorry, Jesus, did you think I was going to
shoot you? No. It's from her, from Grisle. You see, this
afternoon I went out for a walk, to try and get things clear in
my mind about her walking out last night, and to keep away
from the telephone, because I promised her I'd never phone
her at home in case he was there, and when I got back this
was on my pillow, no, on her side of our pillow, no message
with it, I haven't done a year's post-graduate on Henry
James without being able to interpret a symbol when I see
one! But what does it mean, Robert? What does it mean?

ROBERT: Are you sure Griselda is English, this has more than a
touch of the Teutonics or Scandinavians about it, can I see
it? (*He takes it from* HERMAN, *hand trembling, opens it, looks in
it.*) Yes, live all right, like old times, the number of Agatha
Christies and so forth I've had to handle these in, or had
them pointed at me and been shot at and killed by with
blanks of course. (*Laughs.*) Or keep them loaded up for the
last scene of *Hedda Gabler*, three different productions and
in two of them I longed for live ammunition, given the ladies
in question, Anne was a superb Hedda by the way, even
though not quite ready for it, the truth is Herman, the truth
is that the old cliché holds true, never, never, never point
these things at people, particularly when loaded –
(*There is the sound of a car, off, left.*)
Oh, there's Anne, put it away, she hates the things, even on
stage. (*He gives it to* HERMAN.)

HERMAN: Don't tell her, will you. About Grisle and me.

ROBERT: Really? Why not?

HERMAN: I just don't want her to know. I respect her too much,
and I'd feel treacherous to Grisle too, letting another woman
in on it. So please –

ROBERT: All right.

HERMAN: Promise.

ROBERT: (*Laughing*) I promise.

(ANNE *enters, carrying carrier bags etc.*)

Hello darling, you've timed it bang on for the pheasant, how did it go?

ANNE: Bloody quickly, that's how it went. That bugger Tom cut into every single one of my lines, even when I was announcing the suicide, he rattled straight in as if I'd said she's put the chicken in the oven and not her head, so it went for nothing, my only real moment in the play, and when I asked him afterwards what the hell he thought he was up to, he said, well darling, if we're all so desperate for our din-dins we're not allowed a decent curtain, and I said it wasn't din-dins it was just that the rest of us didn't particularly enjoy going on bowing after the audience had stopped clapping.

ROBERT: What sort of house? Full?

ANNE: Only seventy-five per cent.

ROBERT: Well darling, that's really not bad for a Tuesday night considering it's not a comedy or a musical or a thriller or even much of a play, so it must be you, darling, packing them in.

ANNE: From the response at the end what we're mainly packing in is the Japs and the raincoats because of poor little Alice's two-minute nude scene. Her tits looked really weird tonight. I think she's been oiling them, every time her nipples caught the light they sort of winked at me – oh, and there was my usual couple in the front row, 'she's not as pretty as her picture, is she' 'no, and why that dreadful wig!'

HERMAN: Well, you know what I think, Anne, I think you're just great in it. Just great!

ANNE: Oh hello Herman, who is she?

HERMAN: Who?

ANNE: The lady who was letting herself into the cottage just now as I passed.

HERMAN: Oh – oh yes, I'd forgotten she was coming over, just a friend, Anne, a musician, well I'd better get down there – well thanks, Robert, thanks for everything, good-night both.

(*He goes out through the french windows.*)

ROBERT: What did she look like?

ANNE: Blonde and dumpy, as far as I could make out. Who is she?

ROBERT: (*Who has been mixing a drink*) Ah, well, I'm afraid I promised Herman I wouldn't tell you that her name's Grisle, for Griselda, he wants to marry her, she might want to marry him, but he's conscience-stricken about her husband and two children, so she sent him a loaded gun symbolically which he then drew on me. I think that's everything I promised not to tell you, sorry darling.

ANNE: A loaded gun?

ROBERT: With real bullets.

ANNE: And Herman pointed it at you?

ROBERT: Indeed.

ANNE: Why?

ROBERT: Ah. Well let me break his confidence properly while we're noshing. It deserves a bit of scene-laying and tension-building. I'll be putting it on the table in (*looks at his watch*) five minutes, I promise – so, in the mean time you settle yourself with this – (*hands her the drink*) – and I'll dispose of the day's little businesses. (*He goes to the desk, picks up a sheet of paper.*) Phone calls. Paddy, just after you'd left, to ask whether you'd read it yet. I said no, but I'd had a little dip myself and had to say I couldn't imagine you wanting to do a musical. Even of the life of George Eliot. He's going to phone again over the weekend. Then Janie phoned, wanting to know when you're going to pick up those three scripts or should she send them, there's one she thinks you might find quite exciting, I couldn't get much out of her except that as it stands you'd be playing an eighteen-year-old. (*He looks at her.*)

ANNE: (*Abstracted*) Mmmm?

ROBERT: You'd be playing an eighteen-year-old.

ANNE: Oh. (*Little pause.*) What at?

ROBERT: (*Laughs*) But if the author knows you're interested he'd rewrite it for a twenty-eightish to thirty-sevenish-year-old – anyway, she wants you to read it quickly, so we finally worked out that she'll drop it at the stage door tomorrow, and post the other two – now – oh Patty yes – (*He looks at her*.) Head, neck, or shoulders?

ANNE: What? Oh – a – a slight headache –

ROBERT: And on an empty stomach. Quick. (*Comes around the back of her, and puts his thumbs on the back of her neck*.)

ANNE: No – it's not that sort of ache.

ROBERT: Still, a few minutes of thumb-work never does you any harm – (*He begins to knead, glancing down at the note as he does so*.) Yes, Patty, *three* calls from Patty, about that interview you gave to that bloody woman's magazine. I finally succeeded in even explaining to her why she had to explain to them why we objected to our house being described as rural-bijou and our life-style as humdrum – I also got her to get them to get my name right, they still had me in as Robert O'Neill – but that's all sorted out now, subject to a final check on the proofs and – your approval of the photograph, they want to use that one taken in Antibes last year, only with me cut out, which I don't at all mind, especially as they're titling the piece 'The Lonely Queen of the London Stage', and I wouldn't want people to think they meant me, especially as I'm leering over your shoulder like a drunken lesbian, bad for both our images, as Patty pointed out, although of course there are some perfectly decent photographs of the two of us somewhere about, I suppose. Mmmm? Ah, there's a knot – (*Working hard with his thumbs*) – what do you think?

ANNE: Mmmmm?

ROBERT: About their using the Antibes photograph? (*Stopping the massage*.)

ANNE: Oh. Fine. Fine.

ROBERT: It wouldn't be a sympathetic twosome, just of you. As they've cut me out.

ANNE: Oh. Well, you're not really in it, anyway.

ROBERT: No. Right, well, we've cleared that up, then. Though after dinner we might have a little riffle through the photo files to see what else we do have. Now let's see – what's this – how's that?

ANNE: Oh. Better. Much better. Thanks.

ROBERT: (*Smiles at her*) Good. (*He looks at the list.*) Old Harriet
phoned, could we have dinner after the show next week, I
said conditional on your being up to it, we'd absolutely love
to on the further condition that it wasn't at a restaurant with
an Irish owner who (a) insists on joining us at the table and
then (b) falls asleep at it with (c) his hand in your lap and his
hair in my duck, and she said, well, at least he'd torn up the
bill and I *didn't* say, knowing how fond of her you sometimes
are, that that was no consolation to *us* as *we* hadn't been
expecting to pay it anyway, she's going to phone on Monday
to confirm, and in the meanwhile I hope is working on my
hint about her recently revived taste for Chinese food with
the opening of that new place behind Covent Garden, and
then lastly – what, oh yes, well I won't bore you with an
account of my twenty-five minute altercation over the Stilton
I sent back, or with my various other altercations with
electricity people over the two plugs they failed to put in last
week, etc.; – so that's the lot, oh, except for the post, which
came at one-thirty today, can you believe, and which divides
itself into the two usual piles –

(*A bell rings in the kitchen.*)

Ah, ready! – fan letters and bills. So why don't you look
through the fans while I toss the salad – oh, oh sorry darling,
wrong way around, those are the bills – these are the fans –
not the usual proportions I know, a lot of things have come
in together, but we'll go through them on Sunday, shall we,
there are one or two items that might seem a little bizarre at
first glance – these are the fans oh, but not that one, or that
one, both written by the same person, I suspect, and drunk
at the time, anyway if he's so keen to get his money back he
should have applied to the box-office – but the other two are
very charming, in their simple-minded way. Now for the
salad. (*He bustles off to the kitchen.*) Oh, perfect!

(ANNE *tosses the letters down. Sits for a moment, then takes out a
cigarette. Her hand trembles slightly. Lights cigarette, hand
steady.*)

ROBERT: (*Re-enters, carrying a salad bowl, condiments*) Perfect. As

soon as you've finished your one fag – oh, by the way, no
fresh vegetables because of the trucker's strike, or seed
strike, or sun strike, whichever, but I've had a lettuce
thawing out of the freezer, we must remember to stock up,
we're running low, I'm doing Italian for a change, OK.

ANNE: Actually, I'm not very hungry.

ROBERT: You didn't have a sandwich – or one of those sodding
yoghurts?

ANNE: No. I'm just not up to one of your elaborate meals.

ROBERT: (*Looks at her, makes as if to say something, checks himself*)
Look darling, I can see you're tired and past it (*takes her
hands*) and that swine Tom cutting your lines, we'll find a
lovely way to strike back, and there's nothing wrong with
your wig –

ANNE: Yes, there is.

ROBERT: Well, a bit rat-tailey perhaps, the last time I saw it,
tomorrow morning we'll make smashing fusses on the
telephone and screw another one out of Michael but what
you need now my love is a proper meal and bed, eh?

ANNE: Oh, for God's sakes, don't baby-talk me.

ROBERT: Baby-talk you!

ANNE: You were almost lisping, it was revolting.

ROBERT: Sorry. I was merely trying to get you to the table and
some food down you – and perhaps I'm a bit peckish myself,
you know, I did spend the afternoon moving all your
unwanted magazines into the loft and the evening doing my
best to get a meal you'd enjoy – and I asked you if you'd like
pheasant –
(ANNE *groans*.)
What?

ANNE: Now it's the put-upon housewife.
(*There is a pause.*)
I'm sorry. That's not how I meant to start. We've got to talk
darling.

ROBERT: What about?

ANNE: You mainly. And me. Our marriage.

ROBERT: But – but what about the – the pheasant.

ANNE: (*Looks at him*) Oh God, Robert.

ROBERT: All right. Where do we begin – with me mainly or you or our marriage. I mean, we've been perfectly happily married for seven years without having to talk about it, which is perhaps why it's been a perfectly happy marriage, while all our friends have been analysing and fretting their way to divorce courts and shrinks and so forth.

ANNE: It's never been a perfect marriage. From the beginning. Or why have you had to have all those affairs?

ROBERT: What affairs?

ANNE: Oh Robert, I've always known – right from the days in rep with those little scrubbers in jeans and vests and Caroline Wycherley and Hazel Montague and on and on – you're a lousy adulterer. An insultingly lousy adulterer, you must be the only man in the western world, darling, who lays girls with smeary lipstick, on your handkerchiefs and your shirt-fronts and even on your Y-fronts, once, just like a husband in an old Susan Hayward movie – and your habit of coming to bed without taking a bath, smelling as if you had, which means you must have without my knowing, and perfumes and hairs on your jackets and – oh good God, darling, all those wrong-number phone calls or stilted conversations with your new agent or somebody you said wanted to be your agent, which were totally meaningless from what you let me hear of them from your end, but always involved lunch arrangements which weren't. Meaningless, I mean, as that's what the calls were about. I can always tell when you're lying, you see, darling, you do it in such a reppy style, and look so pleased with yourself for having got away with them – why, you even phone them up when I'm in the room, don't you, I expect it gives you quite a thrill, nodding and smiling at me as you pretend to be taking a strong line with some script-editor while you're actually sorting out a screw with his weak little secretary or whoever, how she must have admired your nerve, eh, and laughed at me, and brought back your great days in Worthing, and that's the only thing I've really had against it recently, in the end, your taste. (*Pause.*) So you see darling, I do know, really.

ROBERT: And yet you let me go on and on – without saying a

thing, without even hinting or looking upset –

ANNE: I put up with them because I thought you must need them – because I was making a career and you weren't, and if it hadn't been for me and the money I was beginning to make you'd never have given up stage managing, which you were so good at, and concentrated on your acting –

ROBERT: Which I wasn't.

ANNE: You were all right.

ROBERT: I was bloody better than all right, and you know it! I was offered lots of things, they simply weren't worth my while.

ANNE: I know. And I blamed myself for that. If it hadn't been for me you'd have had to take them. And one thing might have led to another –

ROBERT: Yes, one sten-gun carrier to another in those Shakespeares at the RSC, or one PC at Brighton to another at Croydon – I gave them a chance, I was killed seven times on television in my last year of work – seven times killed for one and a half minutes' exposure. And four of those times my face wasn't visible. I wore a beard, a stocking-mask, heavy scar-tissues.

ANNE: I know, I know. I'm not blaming you.

ROBERT: You're accusing me of living off your money.

ANNE: Well, you are.

ROBERT: But you've always insisted on calling it our money. Whenever I've objected to your paying some of the bills –

ANNE: All the bills darling. These last few years. And you didn't object to my paying them, simply at your not being able to pay them.

ROBERT: Yes, well you're one of those people whose talent is recognized and who get rewarded for it too. I'm not. And if it hadn't been for me, supporting you, running our lives – who chose this house, who furnished it, keeps it going, cooks the meals – how would you have managed without any of that, eh?

ANNE: Oh yes. I know all that you've done. And why. I was just explaining to you why I let your affairs go on and on. It was because I thought you needed them when you were just a stage-manager to make up for not being an actor, and that you needed them when you tried to make a go of it as an actor to make up for not making a go of it, and that you've gone on having them to make up for not making a go of it as a writer since you gave up acting, not that you've made much effort to write since your first two plays were turned down.

ROBERT: I see. So really you're only using your knowledge of my little peccadilloes as a way of threading together my life as a failure.

ANNE: You are a failure. You're not even what you used to call yourself, a success manqué. You're a failure.

ROBERT: Thank you. Thank you, darling.

ANNE: I'm sorry. But he said that when I was ready to tell you, I mustn't try to spare your feelings.

ROBERT: He did, did he? I see.

ANNE: Haven't you wondered what I was really doing, all those afternoons these last six months.

ROBERT: You said you had director's notes, publicity, interviews, lunches with – no, I haven't. I haven't wondered. Who is it? What's his name?

ANNE: Widdecombe.

ROBERT: Widdecombe? I don't know any Widdecombe, he's not an actor.

ANNE: He's an analyst.

ROBERT: An analyst? An analyst of what?

ANNE: People. People like me. And you.

ROBERT: You mean he's a shrink! You've been having an affair with a shrink!

ANNE: I haven't been having an affair with him. I've been seeing him professionally. I was desperate, you see, quite desperate without knowing why, all I knew was that I didn't want to talk to you about it, which was significant in itself, and all the good things that had happened, my third West End success in a row, the Evening Standard Best Actress, the Plays and Players Best Actress – didn't seem to matter a damn, and then I remembered that supper we had with Humphry Ditch last year, and he told us about the

analyst who'd sorted him out when he'd had a near
breakdown over that revolting little Tunisian boy –

ROBERT: May I remind you that Glycerine Ditch committed
suicide two months ago. Or is that your Widdecombe's idea
of sorting people out.

ANNE: That was over the antiques swindle he got caught out in –
he was going to go to jail –

ROBERT: Anne – Anne darling – for God's sakes – look, all right,
I admit, I admit perhaps I've been a bit naughty over those
girls – and perhaps I haven't tried enough to – get my own
career going again – but you didn't need to go to a shrink to
find that out –

ANNE: That's not what I found out. I knew all that. What I
needed was Widdecombe to help me get a perspective –

ROBERT: Just a minute – I'm just beginning to realize – you lay
there on his couch and told him – told him all about us,
about me and – and you talk of *my* infidelities – oh, I bet he
had a wonderful time nodding and clucking the famous Anne
O'Neill through her marital problems –

ANNE: As a matter of fact he doesn't know who I am. I gave him
an assumed name.

ROBERT: What?

ANNE: Ellen Winterspot.

ROBERT: Ellen Winterspot.

ANNE: I made it up, because that's what I felt like. Hell in Winter
spot. And I wore one of my wigs and dark glasses – he knew I
was in disguise, and he approved – he says that people in
masks are more likely to tell the truth. Especially women.
Actually I doubt if he'd know who I was anyway, he seems to
have no interest in the theatre or television or anything like
that, he's mostly interested in money. In fact he's a bit like a
bookie. But I'm deeply grateful to him. I've come to think of
him as the sanest and wisest man I've ever met. Here's his
card.

ROBERT: Thank you. Are you doing some part time as his sales
rep?

ANNE: I think you should see him. He says from what he's heard
about you you need help far more than I do. He says my only

real problem was you – not recognizing what a sterile
marriage of accommodation and sexless comfort I'd betrayed
myself into.

ROBERT: Sexless! What does he mean, sexless!

ANNE: Last night when you came to bed, all buttoned up in your
nice new silk pyjamas, grumbling because the battery had
run out on your toothbrush, and in those floppy carpet-
slippers – all on my account from Harrods – and climbed
between the sheets with a little noise somewhere between a
grunt and a purr, you reminded me of that theatre critic, the
one you called the Spayed Cat. I described that to
Widdecombe this afternoon. He said actually your self-
pampering, your domesticity, your perpetual promiscuity
and the insult all these things are to me, in my womanhood,
aren't just symptoms of your failure, but of something
deeper wrong with you. He thinks you're probably a
repressed homosexual. And then I remembered that when I
first met you I thought you were gay. Widdecombe says first
sexual impressions are usually right.

ROBERT: I can't believe – I don't believe – that you can believe –

ANNE: Widdecombe says you've got to go.

ROBERT: Widdecombe – *Widdecombe* says – (*Laughs.*)

ANNE: He's right. I want you gone, Robert, and I won't have you
making any trouble or fuss about it. I'm far more ruthless
than you, we've both always known that, and I'll do
anything, however cruel, to get you out of my life.

ROBERT: This isn't true – this isn't happening – I'm not some
bloody servant or gigolo –

ANNE: Yes you are. That's exactly what you are. Widdecombe
used both those words of you. But I don't need a servant or
gigolo anymore, I didn't make you one in the first place. You
did it yourself. You're going, Robert.

ROBERT: Oh no I'm not, Anne. Oh no I'm not. I'm not going.
Not anywhere. This is my home. I love it. I've spent years –
seven years – nursing you and your monstrous ego from one
crisis to another, one triumph to another, I've listened to you
night after night after night whine and snivel and bitch, I've
fed you, I've comforted you, I've kept you calm when you

were frightened and together when you were going to pieces,
that's seven years *hard*, Anne, seven years hard with a vain,
boring not particularly talented and totally selfish woman,
i.e. an actress, and all I've got to show for it are a few badly
needed luxuries and hard-earned comforts, and this home,
which is mine, not yours, mine, because I've loved it and
looked after it and appointed it and put up with you in it for
its sake, and I'm not leaving it, Christ I'm not leaving it, on
the say-so of your Widdecombe. I'll kill him first.

ANNE: Widdecombe suggests that a five thousand pound cash
settlement for the work you've done to the house, and for
your sexual, emotional and domestic services over the years,
would be quite adequate. He's had a great deal of experience
in these matters. Anyway, it should tide you over and into
your new life. If I were you, I'd think about going back into
stage-management, it really is your forte, and I've kept up
payments on your Equity card, haven't I? You can take all
personal gifts from me, and all the gifts you've given yourself
from me, including the portable but not the electric
typewriter. No furniture and only your own books.

ROBERT: There aren't any books here, except the ones I've
bought. You don't read anything unless it's got your
photograph in the middle of it – Anne O'Neill, a very private
person, and her husband Robert what's-his-name, out of
camera –

ANNE: You have until the day after tomorrow to clear out. I shall
come back promptly at four, with your cheque in my hand,
and if you're still here at five minutes past I shall tear it up
and call the police to have you removed. Until then I'm
staying in London. Don't attempt to see me, and don't you
come anywhere near the theatre and ruin my performance.
Or no cheque and I'll fight you for every stitch of clothing
you haven't paid for, which means everything including the
knickers you're standing up in. (*She goes to the door, left.*) If I
were you, I'd spend some of the five thousand on
Widdecombe. If he'll accept you. He's very choosey as well
as expensive.

ROBERT: Have you any idea what you've just done?

ANNE: I've tossed you out. And it's been just what Widdecombe
said it would be. The most exhilarating act of my life. If you
do decide to see him, you can tell him who Ellen Winterspot
was and that he was right, I'm cured, and give him my
greetings and my thanks. Now I'll just go and get some
clothes and night things, and I'll leave. (*Exits upstairs.*)
(ROBERT *stands, stunned. He goes to the sideboard, pours
himself a glass of Scotch. Begins to walk up and down, drinking.
Suddenly stops, looks at the card in his hand.*)

ROBERT: Ha! (*He walks.*) Ha! (*Makes as if to hurl his glass through
the french windows.*)

HERMAN: (*Enters through them*) Oh, you've finished your supper
then?

(ROBERT *lowers the glass.*)

How was the pheasant, nice?

ROBERT: Ashes, ashes, as ashes.

HERMAN: Oh, yes. I can smell burning.

ROBERT: My soul.

HERMAN: What?

ROBERT: What do you want, Herman?

HERMAN: Is Anne safely out of the way?

ROBERT: Quite safely.

HERMAN: Then here. Take this. (*He hands him the gun, from his
pocket.*)

And this. (*He takes out of his pocket an extremely large flick-
knife, the blade in. He presses it out as he shows it to* ROBERT.)

(ROBERT *starts back, reflexively.*)

Another symbol! See. (*He flicks it back in.*) She was gone by
the time I got there, but this was lying on my pillow. Take it!
Go on! (*He presses it into* ROBERT's *hand.*) I don't know what
she means, whether to kill her, or to kill her husband or to
kill myself even, but I can't keep my eyes off them, Robert,
or my hands, I've been sitting in the cottage with one in one
hand and one in the other and they frighten me, what I could
do with them, I'm beginning to think I'm in the middle of a
nightmare, so if you'd keep them here somewhere out of my
way I'd be ever so grateful. And somewhere where Anne
won't see them, of course. The truth is, I've even imagined

myself using them on him. (*Pause.*) See what I mean,
Robert?

ROBERT: Yes.

HERMAN: Right. Thanks Robert. Thanks. Now I'm going to go
and write her a letter care of the London Symphony
Orchestra.

ROBERT: Will it get to her there?

HERMAN: Oh yes. It'll get to her all right. She plays the violin for
them, you see. She fiddles. She fiddles while I burn, eh?
'Night Robert. And give my good-nights to Anne. (*He goes
out through the french windows.*)

(ROBERT *stands holding the knife closed in one hand, the pistol
in the other.*)

ANNE: (*Enters from stairs*) Four o'clock. (*Makes towards the door,
left.*) The day after tomorrow. Right?

ROBERT: Just a minute darling. (*Fires the gun into the floor.*) I've
got some goodnights to give you. (*Releases the flick-knife, rises
and advances on* ANNE.)

(ANNE *screams. On her scream: lights.*)

SCENE 2

Lights up. It is about three thirty – 'the day after tomorrow'.
ROBERT *is standing down stage centre, having removed the coffee
table and reset the sofa, a table and lamp – as a psychoanalyst's couch.
He goes to the kitchen door, closes it and locks it. Removes the key.
Closes the curtains at the up-stage window. Closes the curtains at the
down-stage window. He goes to the stool, picks up the gun, sits on the
stool, and checks the gun is loaded. Sound of a car arriving off left.*
ROBERT *puts the gun in his pocket, rises and goes to the hall door and
checks the lock, then looks round. There is a ring at the door bell left.*
ROBERT *goes off left. Sound of a door opening, off left.*

ROBERT: (*Off stage*) Mr Widdecombe?

WIDDECOMBE: (*Off stage*) Mr Simon?

ROBERT: (*Off stage*) Yes.

WIDDECOMBE: (*Off stage*) Could you take this please.

ROBERT: (*Off stage*) Certainly.

WIDDECOMBE: (*Off stage*) Is it through here?

ROBERT: (*Off stage*) Yes it's through here.

>WIDDECOMBE *enters.* ROBERT *follows, closes the door, locks it deftly, slides the key into his pocket, as* WIDDECOMBE *turns.*) Well, here you are then, Mr Widdecombe.

WIDDECOMBE: Yes.

ROBERT: And on time, too. So no mishaps. I mean, you weren't mugged by West Indians, or bombed by Irishmen, or ganged up on by squads of Japanese in dark suits or sang at by Welshmen or bought up by an Arab. Oh, I must be careful, or you'll think I'm xenophobic too, and that's really not one of my problems. A xenophobe in England today would be in an even worse pickle than I am, I should think? (*Laughs.*) I'm trying to make chit-chat, probably not the right thing to do, as it seems to be coming out all wrong. Look, you say something.

WIDDECOMBE: It's rather dark in here, isn't it?

ROBERT: Yes I know, but so cosy and snug. Do you mind? I thought you chaps were used to working in it. Burrowing down and down so to speak, through the layers of phoney brightness.

WIDDECOMBE: But we like to see the people we're dealing with, if we can.

ROBERT: Right. Right. Well – um, well, I'll tell you what, I'll put them on, but I won't open the curtains if you don't mind – I don't like glimpses into the wings, if you see, it always looks so unreal out there – (*turning on the lights*) – there – there – there – there – (*The room is now hideously over-lit.*) How's that?

WIDDECOMBE: (*Blinking*) Well, a trifle bright perhaps.

ROBERT: Still, I'm glad you suggested it. Now I can see you in detail, you look jolly comforting.

WIDDECOMBE: Good. But will you allow me – (*He turns off a couple of lights.*)

ROBERT: How's that?

WIDDECOMBE: Just right.

ROBERT: I'm so glad. Can I get you anything else before we begin?

WIDDECOMBE: No thank you.

ROBERT: Well – perhaps later you'll think of something?

WIDDECOMBE: Yes, perhaps later.

ROBERT: If you do, you will mention it?

WIDDECOMBE: I will.

ROBERT: Right. What sort of thing do you think it's likely to be?

WIDDECOMBE: Well, I won't know that until I've thought of it.

ROBERT: No, of course you won't. Just like God himself, eh?

WIDDECOMBE: Like God?

ROBERT: Well, nothing exists unless he thinks of it. Which is why he has to keep thinking about himself. To go on existing. Which doesn't give him much time to think properly about the rest of us. Which is why we all lead such half and half and finally temporary existences. What do you think of that?

WIDDECOMBE: It's a bit theoretical for me, I'm afraid.

ROBERT: Oh, I'm glad you're going to take a practical and down-to-earth tone – I can't tell you how grateful I am to you. For coming here like this. The way you responded to my midnight SOS was very moving.

WIDDECOMBE: You're obviously in great trouble.

ROBERT: I am, I am, but I've made lots of troubled phone calls over the years, to plumbers and gas-men when our boiler's gone and so forth, they could take a leaf out of your book, I can tell you – not that they'd make much of it, they can scarcely understand the instructions in their own manuals, – oh, I'm so anxious to get started, shall I just take the plunge, I've got a couch ready, go to it and lie on it and surrender myself to you. Like they do in all those cartoons and films and plays – shall I? (*Going to the couch.*)

WIDDECOMBE: Well, first there are a couple of little matters I'd like to get straightened out. I would have explained on the phone but you hung up so quickly –

ROBERT: I know, I'm so sorry. But I was frightened you'd change your mind, and I've heard such things about you – the effect you have on people, how you go to the very heart with your capacious and incisive intelligence – a force, a force for life as it were – and I didn't want to lose you by chatter-boxing on as I am now. And give myself away with some significant slip

– I mean I didn't want you pegging me as a ghastly little pansy before you'd even clapped eyes on me. Oh – (*Claps his hand to his mouth.*) Oh that's all right, isn't it, they won't get me for that will they.

WIDDECOMBE: Who?

ROBERT: Those language purists we hear so much about these days.

WIDDECOMBE: Yes, that's very interesting. Perhaps we can follow that up in a minute. But – now can we just –

ROBERT: What? Oh yes. I'm sorry. So sorry. Those things I didn't give you the chance – what are they?

WIDDECOMBE: Well firstly, this can only be an exploratory session. I can't commit myself further at this stage.

ROBERT: Commit yourself?

WIDDECOMBE: To accepting you as a patient.

ROBERT: Accepting me? I see. So really you're the sort of Garrick Club of the mentally distressed? Well I hope I get in.

WIDDECOMBE: Secondly, if I do decide that we should go further, you should realize that it's likely to be a long-term business.

ROBERT: How long?

WIDDECOMBE: I've had some people on my books for ten years.

ROBERT: Ten years – well, that only proves how much they must like you. I switch dentists all the time, I can never find one to suit. No no – you haven't said anything to put me off. I'm going to do my best to qualify.

WIDDECOMBE: There's a third thing.

ROBERT: Yes.

WIDDECOMBE: I'm very expensive.

ROBERT: Well, of course you are. You *must* be. I mean you can't just dispense your diagnoses as if they were horoscopes in the evening papers!

WIDDECOMBE: I charge thirty pounds a session.

ROBERT: Oh. (*Little pause.*) Well –

WIDDECOMBE: For a preliminary consultation, which this is, I charge fifty pounds. Plus expenses. The petrol, and a cancelled session with another patient. Would be seventy pounds in all. And I have to ask for it in advance.

ROBERT: (*After a pause*) Perfectly fair! because if you don't get it in advance, you might never get it at all. Right? (*He goes to the desk*.) Seventy pounds did you say? (*He takes a cheque out of the drawer, writes*.) What initial?

WIDDECOMBE: F.

ROBERT: F for?

WIDDECOMBE: Just F will do.

ROBERT: (*Writes, brings the cheque around, hands it to him*.) This is therapy isn't it?

WIDDECOMBE: What? (*Taking the cheque*.)

ROBERT: Well, I feel better already. This simple transaction means that I've got you all to myself, doesn't it? And the feeling of confidence that gives me – I have got you all to myself, haven't I? I mean nobody from your office is going to disturb us, nobody knows you're here, do they?

WIDDECOMBE: Only my secretary.

ROBERT: Do you sleep with her?

WIDDECOMBE: It's a him, actually.

ROBERT: Is it? Well, do you sleep with it, then? (*Laughs*.) See. I feel I can take risks with you now. Tease you a little. That must be good, mustn't it? But look, I've just thought of something – Supposing I fall in love with you, that's quite usual isn't it, and then you reject me? Or I fall in love with you and you accept me but I need to see so much of you at thirty pounds a session that I'm impoverished and *then* you reject me – what would become of me then, Widdecombe?

WIDDECOMBE: Let's not worry about that right now. Let's see if we can find out what's the matter with you. Why did you phone me?

ROBERT: Well, the worst thing is this room. You've already noticed – I can't bring myself to leave it – except to perform my natural bodily functions and gulp down a glass of milk and a crust. It's as if it were a – a stage, do you see, and I was going to be forced to play out some hideous drama of murder. Suicide. Revenge.

WIDDECOMBE: So you're suffering from acute agoraphobia.

ROBERT: Is that what it's called. Oh good!

WIDDECOMBE: With the usual traces of psychosis and persecution mania.

ROBERT: Oh good.

WIDDECOMBE: You can get on the sofa now.

ROBERT: (*Goes over to the sofa, sits on the edge then lies down.*) The funny thing is – (*lying down*) – that now I'm here, prone, my whole body at your mercy –

(WIDDECOMBE *draws up a chair and puts his hand inside his jacket, fiddles briefly.*)

I feel a little frightened of you suddenly.

WIDDECOMBE: That's because I'm an authority figure. You need my help, but you resent and fear me. Right, tell me about your father.

ROBERT: Daddy?

WIDDECOMBE: Yes. Daddy.

ROBERT: Well what?

WIDDECOMBE: Begin with your last memory of him.

ROBERT: Well – he was lying on the bed – his and Mummy's – and she was bent over him, doing something to his trousers. Buttoning them up, I suppose. She always tended to him on special occasions.

WIDDECOMBE: (*Suppressing a yawn*) What was the special occasion?

ROBERT: I think it was his funeral. Shouldn't you be taking this down – they always do in plays –

WIDDECOMBE: I know how to do my job. What was she like, your mother?

ROBERT: Oh, very much in the usual run of mothers, really. She was – well tall, voluptuous, with warm, inviting eyes.

WIDDECOMBE: Dead too, is she?

ROBERT: Oh no – don't say that – Widdecombe (*rearing up*) – please!

WIDDECOMBE: You said was. She was.

ROBERT: Yes, *was* tall, voluptuous, so forth, but now she *is* a bit shrunken, her hair's white, what there is of it, and her eyes run. She's in her eighties, we were very close to begin with, but then we grew apart. I was a forceps delivery, do you think that's significant, and another thing, once she caught me playing with myself in my bath, I was only thirteen –

WIDDECOMBE: And now your wife.

231

ROBERT: What?

WIDDECOMBE: You're married, aren't you?

ROBERT: How did you know?

WIDDECOMBE: Because you've been *acting* queer.

ROBERT: How did you know?

WIDDECOMBE: Because you've been acting it badly.

ROBERT: (*Coldly*) I see.

WIDDECOMBE: You're married aren't you?

ROBERT: Yes.

WIDDECOMBE: Something's gone wrong with the marriage, has it?

ROBERT: Can we talk about it later, please?

WIDDECOMBE: I'd rather talk about it now. Don't worry, nothing you say will shock me.

ROBERT: Still, later please.

WIDDECOMBE: How often have you been unfaithful to her?

ROBERT: What?

WIDDECOMBE: How often have you been unfaithful to your wife?

ROBERT: Well – (*little pause*) – three hundred and fifty-seven times, at the last count. But that includes one nights and uprights in cupboards and on the stairs, some of them were really more like sneezes – even so you don't seem very impressed.

WIDDECOMBE: Has she been unfaithful to you?

ROBERT: No. But there's a man in her life, Widdecombe, what you call an authority figure, who's poisoned her against me.

WIDDECOMBE: And do you hate him?

ROBERT: Oh yes. I intend to ruin him.

WIDDECOMBE: And her?

ROBERT: Ah. Ah – hah. (*Little pause.*)

WIDDECOMBE: What do you mean, ah – hah? Have you harboured any desires to kill her? Have you behaved violently towards her?

ROBERT: Yes.

WIDDECOMBE: So to sum up. You've committed three hundred and fifty-seven acts of infidelity. As far as you know, your wife isn't sexually unfaithful to you. She's turned for help and advice to an older man. This has made you jealous, you want to hurt her because of it, is that right?

ROBERT: A rather bald outline, surely Widdecombe –

WIDDECOMBE: We won't get anywhere unless you're honest. Is it right?

ROBERT: Yes. You've got an alarming amount of the policeman in you – I feel less inclined to fall in love with you – are you going?

WIDDECOMBE: (*Has risen*) I've got enough.

ROBERT: Rather a short session, for seventy pounds.

WIDDECOMBE: It's not the length, it's the depth.

ROBERT: And when will I see you again.

WIDDECOMBE: You won't be seeing me again, Mr Simon. If you're sensible.

ROBERT: You don't want my money, then?

WIDDECOMBE: You haven't got enough, is my impression. Whatever money there is, isn't yours, it's your wife's, is my impression.

ROBERT: Indeed. And what gives you that impression?

WIDDECOMBE: The way you throw it around. She's either left you or leaving you, isn't she?

ROBERT: No, she's not. You can see her for yourself. In fact, she's coming straight down to give you her greeting and her thanks. (*He strides to the rope, pulls it.*) Darling – you're on! (*The trap door to the loft opens.* ANNE's *body, with a rope around its neck, arms and feet tied, tongue protruding, eyes bulging, comes plummeting down.* HERMAN's *knife is plunged into her chest. There are blood-stains around it.* ROBERT *laughs insanely.*)

(*Lights. Curtain.*)

ACT TWO

As before. Two seconds later. The body is still twitching.

ROBERT: All right, I concede it's not one of the great coups, but in Worthing it made a small boy actually throw up with terror. Right over the hat of the woman in front of him. Of course they tried to take that away from me too by claiming it was the hat that did it. (*He takes the knife out as he talks.*)

WIDDECOMBE: (*Is studying the mask*) Is this thing meant to be your wife?

ROBERT: Well, of course I've never seen her with quite that expression. Except when reading some of her reviews. You're a coolish customer, Widdecombe, I'll give you that, it took me two days to work this out. I've been responsible for some flops in my time –

WIDDECOMBE: But her hair's like this, is it?

ROBERT: Isn't it? (*Stands, facing* WIDDECOMBE, *knife pointing towards him.*)

WIDDECOMBE: (*After a pause*) Will you put that down, please.

ROBERT: Why?

WIDDECOMBE: I don't like knives.

ROBERT: Oh. (*Little pause.*) Sorry. (*He puts the knife down.*) Well, I still haven't aroused your interest in my situation?

WIDDECOMBE: What's interesting about a trick like that?

ROBERT: Well, what about my agoraphobia, my being imprisoned in this room?

WIDDECOMBE: There's the door. Go through it.

ROBERT: But how?

WIDDECOMBE: That's your problem, old man. (*He turns, goes to the door left.*)

(ROBERT *watches him, smiling.* WIDDECOMBE *tries the door, several times.*)

ROBERT: It seems to be your problem, too.

WIDDECOMBE: (*Comes back.*) Key please.

(ROBERT *smiles.*)

I don't like being locked in rooms I want to get out of.

ROBERT: You like your freedom, do you?

WIDDECOMBE: Give me the key.

ROBERT: But a very limited freedom, if it means you have to exit through the door you entered by. There are doors behind the curtains, you know. They're open.

(WIDDECOMBE *looks towards the french windows. Goes to them.*)

(ROBERT *takes the pistol out of his pocket*) Oh Widde-combe – (*In a singing voice. Points the gun at him.*) Moment please. Old cheese. Something you haven't realized.

(WIDDECOMBE *stops, turns, stares at* ROBERT.)

Of course, freedom is also a matter of having the nerve to exit through doors you haven't entered by, when doing so may bring a bullet in the back. Or gut. On the other hand it may bring fresh air, the scent of roses, a sunny path to a gate in an ivied wall, a stroll around the house to your car – freedom, in other words, is an indifference to consequences. That was rehearsed, I'm afraid. This moment means too much to me to be improvised. Which do you choose, Widdecombe? (*Little pause.*) Do you need a prompt? (*Turns, fires into the dummy, which jumps.*) See. It is.

WIDDECOMBE: I'll stay.

ROBERT: Thank you. Come right back then, if you please.

WIDDECOMBE: (*Comes back into the room*) If you want your money back, I'll be only too happy –

ROBERT: No no. I'm sure you'll earn it in the end. Would you strike that prop though, please.

WIDDECOMBE: What?

ROBERT: Sorry. The jargon of my ex-trade. As 'authority figure' is of yours. So 'strike the prop authority figure' translates as 'get rid of the dummy, shrink'. (*Little pause.*) Just pull on the rope by the fire place.

(WIDDECOMBE *pulls on the rope. The dummy goes back into the loft.*)

Thank you. Anything like this ever happened to you before, Widders?

WIDDECOMBE: No.

ROBERT: What, no violent patients, ever?

WIDDECOMBE: Well, not with me.

ROBERT: (*With concern*) But you're trembling.

WIDDECOMBE: Yes. I don't like guns you see.

ROBERT: I say, you are a chap with pronounced dislikes. You don't like knives, don't like being locked in rooms, don't like discarded gigolos, don't like guns – and yet here you are, locked in a room by a discarded gigolo who's got a gun and a knife and doesn't like you. And I'm afraid the fact that you've chosen to exercise your freedom by coming back into the room because I threatened to shoot you, doesn't mean I can't exercise mine by shooting you anyway, does it? (*He points the gun into* WIDDECOMBE's *face*.)
(WIDDECOMBE *says something*.)
Now Widdecombe. No asides, please.

WIDDECOMBE: I said don't. Please.

ROBERT: Well, I've certainly bouleversé'd you a little this time, eh? I'm sure you're going to be worth my seventy quid. Let's start a new session. But this time you do the work. Sit down.
(WIDDECOMBE *goes to sit down*.)
No, not there. The sight-lines are terrible. Nor there – (*As* WIDDECOMBE *moves to another chair*) – you'd be up-staging me. Now bring that chair over – that's right! And put it there. I could make a good props man out of you, Widdecombe, if I didn't need you for a leading part. Right. Off you go.

WIDDECOMBE: (*After a pause*) What do you want?

ROBERT: A bit of rapid depth analysis. Tell me about yourself.

WIDDECOMBE: Well – um – what?

ROBERT: F. What does it stand for?

WIDDECOMBE: Ferdinand.

ROBERT: I prefer you as Widdecombe. I've got used to you as Widdecombe. Widdecombe calm, Widdecombe threatening, Widdecombe greedy – above all Widdecombe greedy – and now Widdecombe cowed. But all of them Widdecombe. Well, Ferdinand, let's begin with Daddy, your last memory of him.

WIDDECOMBE: I haven't got one. He died before I was born.

ROBERT: Oh well then, your mother. What was she like?

WIDDECOMBE: Well, I don't know really. She died while I was

being born. I was brought up by my aunts in Godalming, you
see.

ROBERT: Well then, and now your wife. You're married aren't
you?

WIDDECOMBE: Yes.

ROBERT: Your wife, what's she like?

WIDDECOMBE: Well – her name's Rosalind.

ROBERT: Oh come, you can do better than that? Is she an anal
retentive, a womb hysteric, – give us depth, Widdecombe,
depth.

WIDDECOMBE: She's – she's very nice. I mean, she's small and –
and a bit plump and – and looks after me and the two boys.
And – and really – there's nothing wrong with her, you see.
She's just – normal. Really.

ROBERT: Do you love her?

WIDDECOMBE: Yes.

ROBERT: Is she good in bed?

WIDDECOMBE: (*After a little pause*) Yes.

ROBERT: Details.

WIDDECOMBE: Well I – she – we have just an ordinary sex life.

ROBERT: You don't want to talk about it?

WIDDECOMBE: No – well, it's difficult –

ROBERT: Right. We'll come back to her in a minute. I expect it's
the phallic symbol I'm pointing at your head, distracting, eh?

WIDDECOMBE: Yes.

ROBERT: Now the two boys.

WIDDECOMBE: Well, Piers is ten and Nigel's twelve. Piers is good
at football and Nigel – well, he stammers. Piers is well-built
and Nigel's a bit on the plump side.

ROBERT: What about sibling rivalry, masturbation problems,
penis envy?

WIDDECOMBE: No, just the normal amount. No problems really.

ROBERT: Tell me about your vices. Be frank but not fearless.

WIDDECOMBE: Well I – I eat too much, and sometimes I have a
spot too much to drink.

ROBERT: Go on.

WIDDECOMBE: Well – I go after money a bit too much –

ROBERT: That's a symptom of anal retentiveness, isn't it?

WIDDECOMBE: I suppose so.

ROBERT: Give me a brief résumé of your qualifications.

WIDDECOMBE: I – I haven't got any.

ROBERT: None at all?

WIDDECOMBE: No, I'm what's called a lay analyst. I don't need any qualifications. It's perfectly legal.

ROBERT: Is it? Good God! So, to sum up you're a family-loving orphan with swinish appetites and unusual acquisitiveness in a fraudulent profession. But what's beginning to worry me, old bean, is whether you're up to the role I've cast you in. You're such a coarse and palpable fraud, even by the standards of your profession. How do you get away with it? How do you take them in?

WIDDECOMBE: I think it's my manner. They – they like it. They find it very reassuring – I mean, most of the people I get don't know what to do so I tell them.

ROBERT: And they're mostly women, are they?

WIDDECOMBE: Yes. And artists and actors and university teachers. That type. But I've done good – honest.

ROBERT: Guv.

WIDDECOMBE: Pardon?

ROBERT: Shouldn't it be 'honest Guv'. What about your accent? Just ten minutes ago it had a certain plummy confidence, now it's slipping past the suburbs.

WIDDECOMBE: Because – because I'm frightened, I expect.

ROBERT: So it's returning to base, is it?

WIDDECOMBE: Yes but I have done good.

ROBERT: All right. Persuade me. One case. Choose carefully. Think quickly. (*Looking at his watch.*) Time is running out.

WIDDECOMBE: Well, one that comes to mind, an opera singer. She was – she was terrified her voice was going. And it was. From what the papers said. She refused to go on stage three times running, she'd been to all sorts before she came to me – Freudians, Laingians, Jungians – on drugs, drink, I got her functioning again.

ROBERT: Kept her singing?

WIDDECOMBE: Yes – yes, she's still performing, I think. I don't go to the opera myself –

ROBERT: And that's one of your triumphs?

WIDDECOMBE: Yes. Well –

ROBERT: Not good enough, Widdecombe. You've forgotten Bernard Levin.

WIDDECOMBE: Who?

ROBERT: Our most famous living opera goer. He expects the best and he's entitled to the best. Not only does he pay through the nose for his ticket, but his opera-going kit must cost him a fortune – his cloaks and waistcoats and shiny little pumps, all his fol-de-rol and furbelow? You have no right to ruin his evening by putting on to the stage a clapped-out singer who's lost her voice – I take a very serious view of that, Widdecombe. (*Putting the pistol close to* WIDDECOMBE's *head*.)

WIDDECOMBE: Wait, wait, wait, – (*Desperately*.)

ROBERT: What, what, what, – ?

WIDDECOMBE: Well, there was this – there was this – (*desperately*) there was a lad who came to me because one night he'd blinded some horses, though he loved them, and I made him relive it all again, you see, and I taught him to realize that these horses were really just naked men prancing about in his head –

ROBERT: Widdecombe, Widdecombe, they asked me if I'd be interested in stage-managing that one.

WIDDECOMBE: I'm sorry – I can't think – I can't think, not like this – all I know is – that I've done some people a lot of good, helped them out in their marriages, particularly, got to the bottom of things, worked them through their divorces –

ROBERT: Like a private detective.

WIDDECOMBE: Yes. No – I've *helped* people –

ROBERT: Like Ellen Winterspot.

WIDDECOMBE: Who?

ROBERT: You don't remember her?

WIDDECOMBE: Well, I get so many – I can't remember every one – not without going through my books.

ROBERT: You know I've been looking forward to this particular moment, it was one of the climaxes you see – and I'd worked on the speech a little – and now I see what you are, you really are – (*shakes his head*) – still, perhaps I'll get myself going eh?

WIDDECOMBE: What?

ROBERT: Ellen Winterspot came to you in a state of stress, of
course she did, she's always in a state of stress, being highly
ambitious, extremely vain and hopelessly insecure in a
business run on ambition, vanity and insecurity, there was
nothing out of the normally horrendous wrong with her at
all, but you didn't bother to find that out, did you, you
couldn't even be bothered to penetrate a simple disguise to
find out who she really was and what business she was in,
you simply gave her some of your off-the-cuff advice in your
usual brutal style for your usual brutal fees, no doubt,
months on months of sessions and sessions of thirty-guinea
fees, and her marriage, my marriage, her happiness, *my home*
meant nothing to you at all – you didn't give any of it as
much as a thought, how could you, clearly incapable as you
are of giving a thought to anything but the profits from your
sordid swindles – even with a gun pointing at your head – but
there were lives at stake, Widdecombe, yours among them as
it's turned out, because Widdecombe, the truth about you is
– (*All this with mounting fury.*)

WIDDECOMBE: No!

ROBERT: It's no good. Nothing there. Nothing there at all. You
really are a dreadful disappointment, you know. I'd really
imagined – ah well, the only thing is to plough on. Get up
Widdecome, the spayed cat is about to strike back.

WIDDECOMBE: What?

ROBERT: Get up. It's all built around my shooting you, you see.
I'll tell you what, I'll give you a last chance – see if you can
come up with something – but no clichés or whinings or
bang!

WIDDECOMBE: Look, please, please –

ROBERT: That's a whine, Widdecombe.

WIDDECOMBE: I've got a wife. A wife and two kids –

ROBERT: That's a cliché *and* a whine. I can't waste any further
time giving you chances. If you can't take the centre, even at
a moment like this, you can't. One –

WIDDECOMBE: No – no no –

ROBERT: Two.

WIDDECOMBE: No no no no no –

ROBERT: Three.

WIDDECOMBE: Oh God!

(They stare at each other for a second. ROBERT *shoots him in the stomach.* WIDDECOMBE *screams, lurches back, clutching at stomach, stops.)*

ROBERT: That last bit was rather good. No notes at all there. You're still grasping the first stage of my plan, are you? It's to give you, you see, a vivid taste of death. A glimpse over the abyss. A spasm of eternity. And so forth. So that you'd learn something about the irrationality of the human psyche, those you tamper with so callously – as well as your own. But now please pull yourself together, your next scene is far bigger. Not a simple matter of dying, you know. *(He turns irritably to the telephone.)* Oh, where are they – come *on* – *(He looks at his watch.)* Do you think they're on strike again? Hello, Kent Television? News Desk please. What? Yes, I'll hang on.

WIDDECOMBE:* *(Stands up, still trembling, clearly not aware of what he is saying)* Think you had to teach me – think I don't know – don't see things before I go to sleep just like everybody else, myself laid flat on a board, eyes closed or open staring, and the cheeks funny, and my feet sometimes crossed and sometimes pointed sideways and my arms down along my sides or hands folded across my chest, I got a wife, a wife and two kids, a home in Cricklewood, a small garden, one of my kids has got a stammer and the other's good at football, he despises me, I see it in his eyes when we knock it about in the garden and the old ticker goes tick-tock tick-tock and my head swimming and I stumble about chortling like I was one of them, and when I tell Rosie, I say I've seen it, Rosie, how he despises me, she does her best to comfort and control me, she says of course he doesn't he loves you Fred, we all do, and there I am, I love him and I can't stand

---

*This speech is optional, and the play can be performed either with it, or not, at the Producer's discretion.

Nigel, I want to take him by the throat every time he tries to
say butter, *he* loves me all right, but Piers – and Rosie says I
smell and sweat and snore at night, and I think yes, well,
that's what I am, that's my being to this one and the other
one, and what am I doing here, how did it happen, I had a
life to lead too, once, what's gone wrong, *what's gone wrong*,
it's not fair Fred, this isn't what you had twenty years ago
when you were free in Cyprus, a seedy man in a seedy job,
and boards and crossed hands and my cheeks, these cheeks
funny, why that's not what my mum meant when she started
me out, is it, was it in my dad's mind when he took her and
fired me up her, this is no life for you old man. See. There's
nothing you can teach me about anything of that, see, I have
the experience all the time, every night, but what you did
just now when you fired that at me and made me think and
feel is you've made me hate you as I've never hated anyone
before, there was a boy called Roger used to wait for me
when I went to school, mornings when I went there,
evenings coming back, and the things he'd do to me, I
thought I'd never hate again as I hated him, but I hate you
more, more than Roger Speke, for the way you treated me a
minute ago, I wouldn't have done that, never have done that,
to any living person, and let them live through it. (*He stands,
still shaking.*)

ROBERT: There, you see. The same thing happened to
Dostoevsky, and it had the same sort of effect – perhaps
you'll start turning out novels too – oh, hello Kent
Television, News Desk, I expect you'd like to hear of the
murder of Mr Robert Simon, *homme de théâtre* – man of the
theatre! – of Globe House, Maddingley, Kent. The two
parties responsible for his death are Mr Ferdinand, alias
Fred Widdecombe, the distinguished psychoanalyst, and Mr
Simon's wife, Anne O'Neill, that's right, *the* Anne O'Neill,
alias Ellen Winterspot – have you got that? So you just toddle
along with your cameras and catch Robert Simon's last death
appearance – and try to get his face, this time, eh? (*Hangs
up.*)

WIDDECOMBE: What? (*He makes towards the french windows.*)

ROBERT: (*Dials again.*) Of course as far as your professional association goes, murdering one of your patients may simply be the ultimate therapy, but the news media will take a vivid interest I assure you – Hello, police? I want to report a murder, the murder of Mr Robert Simon of Globe House, Maddingley, Kent, by Mr Ferdinand Widdecombe, Widdecombe and Mrs Anne Simon, the deceased's wife. (*Little pause.*) This is the deceased speaking, but it's not a joke, try and make it by a few minutes past four, won't you, the TV boys are already on their way, it would look better from your point of view if you managed to get here a few seconds before them. (*He bangs up.*) There! See!

WIDDECOMBE: You know what your trouble is. You're mad! (*He makes another attempt to leave.*)

ROBERT: Oh, you're not leaving the stage yet, Widdecombe. *En garde!* (*He flashes the knife about, stops.*) Oh, I forgot to tell you – (*as* WIDDECOMBE *cowers back*) – the next bullet in that gun is live. The question is whether you've got the nerve to fire it – I don't think you have, in which case it'll be *your* body that will get the coverage – *en garde!* (*Stops.*) Pick it up, I should.

WIDDECOMBE: (*Runs to the pistol, picks it up.*) Live!

ROBERT: That's right, but you'll never squeeze the trigger – *en garde!* (*Comes flashing towards* WIDDECOMBE.)

WIDDECOMBE: Won't I, oh won't I? (*Stands pointing the gun at* ROBERT.) Well, don't try me. After what you did, you're just a walking shit-house, a piss-pot on legs as far as I'm concerned I'll kill, don't you worry.

ROBERT: No, you won't.

WIDDECOMBE: Listen matey, I was in the army out in Cyprus. I did things then would give you nightmares to hear about –

ROBERT: (*Slashes forward*) You're lying, Widdecombe.

WIDDECOMBE: Oh, am I? Once we caught them in their truck, made them kneel with their hands on their knees, put a bullet in the back of their heads, then put bullets in them everywhere, the front, their legs, their arms, their bums, then blew the truck up with their own bomb, made a mistake there, it was a big bomb, Sergeant Winters lost a foot, Hadley had his teeth scattered – I'm telling you this so you'll know. I've had a

gun in my hand before, I've killed, I've seen friends die –
(ROBERT *jumps forward with the knife*.)
(*Shrilly, jumping back*) Don't! It's my death I'm afraid of
matey, not yours.

ROBERT: (*Glances at his watch*) Four o'clock. Come on then,
Widdecombe – let's see you do it! (*He leaps after him, flashing
the knife*.)

WIDDECOMBE: (*Backing faster and faster*) Don't – don't I tell you
– please –
(ROBERT *stops, stares at* WIDDECOMBE. WIDDECOMBE *stares
back, as if hypnotized*. ROBERT *makes a little jump*.
WIDDECOMBE *fires*. ROBERT *stops*.)
You bastard!

ROBERT: Must be the next one. Try again. (*Pause, then jumps
screaming at* WIDDECOMBE.)
(WIDDECOMBE *fires*. ROBERT *jerks to a stop, his hand pressed to
his stomach. Then he lurches towards* WIDDECOMBE, *the knife
raised*.)

WIDDECOMBE: (*Retreats behind the sofa*) Don't!

ROBERT: (*Lurches after him*) Now your turn, WIDDECOMBE!
(*He raises the knife*.)
(WIDDECOMBE *trapped behind the sofa, shoots again*. ROBERT
*spins around, drops the knife, clutches the back of the sofa with
one hand*. WIDDECOMBE *squeezes out, steps away*.)
(*Facing the stage, smiles*) Bravo – bravo Widdecombe! (*Blinks
for a second, takes his hand away from his shirt. Blood seeps
down from his stomach*.)
(WIDDECOMBE *stands, horrified, drops the gun. There is the
sound of* ANNE's *car arriving, off, left*.)
(*Looks at his watch*) Just – perfect – timing. For – her –
entrance. But – for – me – bring – bring down – the curtain!
Bring down the tabs! (*He collapses slowly behind the sofa*.)
(*There is a pause*.)

HERMAN: (*Off, left*) No you stay there until I see –
(WIDDECOMBE *looks towards the french windows, then runs
towards the door, stage left, tries to open it, remembers, lets out a
groan*.)
(*Inside the french windows behind the curtain*) Hey, Robert,

you in there, what's going on? (*Pause.*) Mind if I come in.
(*Pause. Pulls back the curtains, enters.*) Oh – hi.

WIDDECOMBE: Hello.

(*There is a pause.*)

HERMAN: What's going on?

WIDDECOMBE: Pardon?

HERMAN: I heard shots. I heard one earlier, when I was in the
cottage.

WIDDECOMBE: Gun back-firing.

HERMAN: A gun?

WIDDECOMBE: Car. I mean. Car back-firing?

HERMAN: That's what I thought the first time, but we were just
coming up the road and heard them again. We both did.

WIDDECOMBE: Oh.

HERMAN: It *was* a gun. Where *is* Robert?

WIDDECOMBE: Ah. Not back yet. Waiting for him myself.
Actually can't hold on any longer. Tell him I waited, would
you. (*He turns to the door, left, stops, when he remembers.*)

HERMAN: Well, who are you?

WIDDECOMBE: Mmmm.

HERMAN: Who *are* you?

WIDDECOMBE: Oh just a chap. (*Pause.*) Looking in. Personal
matter. But really can't wait any longer. (*He looks at his
watch.*) Good God, nearly four, I'll miss my lunch if I don't
hurry. That way's quicker for me. (*He points towards the french
windows, then takes a step towards them.*)

HERMAN: (*Who has been looking around the room*) Christ! The gun!

WIDDECOMBE: Indeed! (*He makes to pass.*)

HERMAN: (*Picks the gun up*) You'd better wait a minute, man. Sit
down.

(WIDDECOMBE *sits down on the sofa.*)

Robert! (HERMAN *takes a few steps towards the kitchen, sees
behind the sofa. Goes to it, looks down.*)

HERMAN: Je-sus! Jee-sus! He's – he's dead!

WIDDECOMBE: Yes.

(HERMAN *steps away, faces* WIDDECOMBE, *holding the gun.*)
Look – look you see it – it was an accident – he made me do it –
he wanted me to do it –

HERMAN: Wanted you to kill him?

WIDDECOMBE: Yes, but it was all a – he thought I was a – because of my being a psychoanalyst.

HERMAN: He wanted you to kill him because he thought you were a psychoanalyst?

WIDDECOMBE: Yes, but I'm not, you see, that's the point. I'm a Private Detective.

HERMAN: You're a Private Detective, is that what you're saying?

WIDDECOMBE: Yes – (*He puts his hand in his pocket.*)
(HERMAN *checks him with the gun.*)
If you'll just – please – it's my tape-recorder – Just a minute – (*He takes out the tape-recorder carefully.*) You just listen to this. (*He presses a switch.*)
(*Voice over, tape*) How often have you been unfaithful to your wife?

ROBERT: (*Voice over, tape*) Well, three hundred and fifty-seven times at the last count. But that includes one-nights, uprights in cupboards and on the stairs, some of them were really more like sneezes.

WIDDECOMBE: (*Turning it off*) See. I've got masses of stuff. For the divorce, you see. The settlement, all the usual – look, it was his wife's idea – she came to me with a proposition – she wanted shot of him, and she had all the money and he was broke, he's been living off her for years, see, but she said he was the sort to make trouble and screw her for all he could get and she wasn't having it, but she could persuade him to see a shrink, see, she'd set it up that she'd recommend me, and she even had a card printed with my name on it – I've still got them, look – Consultant and all those letters, F. Widdecombe – but here's my real card, see – Private Enquiries, Complete Discretion – Pre-Marital Investigations Our Speciality, Mediterranean Clients Especially Welcome – that's me, what I really am. See.
(HERMAN *takes the tape-recorder from him and pockets it.*)

HERMAN: And you say his wife – his wife – Anne was behind this.

WIDDECOMBE: Well, Mrs Robert Simon she said her name was – yes, it was all her plan, to get me close, ask questions, she told me how to behave and a few words to use, she said he was so obsessed with himself he wouldn't notice me anyway, thing was to get him chattering ask a few questions about his girls, his wife, that, and get down anything useful, she didn't tell me what he was really like, that he was a real nutter and that he had it in for shrinks, the things he did, a dummy and then shooting me with a blank and then coming at me with a knife and making me kill him all because he hated shrinks, see.

HERMAN: Then why didn't you tell him you were a private detective?

WIDDECOMBE: I thought about it, but then I thought that'd make him even worse – I mean the way I'd tricked him and – and look, I've *got* it, if you don't believe me – phone the police, that's right, *he* phoned them, see, told them I'd killed him before I had, now I haven't phoned, you know that, and you haven't, have you, that'll help me, that'll prove it, you'll be able to tell them it must have been him, go on – go on, phone them now and ask them.

HERMAN: You want me to phone the police, is that right?

WIDDECOMBE: Yes – yes – please – it's my only chance. Please.

HERMAN: (*Goes to the telephone, dials*) Has anyone phoned in to report the murder of Mr Robert Simon. That's right, Robert Simon. (*Little pause.*) Oh, well in that case, I'm reporting it now – yes, he's been murdered, shot – by F. Widdecombe, Private Investigator of – hang on – (*Searches his pocket for card.*)

WIDDECOMBE: Then he pretended.

HERMAN: He's of 16A Old Compton Street, London, W1. Yes, he's here now. He admits he did it. Yes, it's Globe House, Maddingly, Kent. Yes, right.
(*Puts the telephone down, stares at* WIDDECOMBE.)

WIDDECOMBE: – I don't understand – but it's all true – true I tell you.

HERMAN: You can't tell me that a lady like Anne would have anything to do with something like this, what a story!

ANNE: (*Appears nervously at the french windows*) Robert – Herman – what *is* going on.
(*As she enters, she sees the gun. There is a pause.*)

247

HERMAN: You'd better wait outside, Anne.

ANNE: No, I want to know what's going on, where's Robert? (*After a pause*.) Who is this man!

HERMAN: The thing is Anne – look – there's been a – it seems as if – as if – there's been an accident.

ANNE: Robert?

HERMAN: He's dead, Anne. Behind the sofa. But don't look. Don't look Anne.

(ANNE *goes to sofa*. ANNE *looks, turns quickly, in horror, and collapses into the chair by the fireplace*.)

And this bloke did it. I've sent for the police, but – well I don't know if you can follow this, but perhaps I'd better warn you. This bloke says Robert made him, and Anne, that *you'd* put him up to it.

ANNE: (*Looks at* WIDDECOMBE) He says I put him up to it?

WIDDECOMBE: That's not her. I've never seen her before – yes, I have, on television, advertising something, baked beans. Anyway you're not the one. She had long ginger hair and dumpy and funny teeth. He set me up. He set me up. I don't understand the rest of it, but I know that much. (*Gets up*.) Well, I'm going. You won't shoot me – it's hard to pull a trigger on somebody – and even if you do I don't care. I'm going.

HERMAN: They'll catch you. I've got your card.

WIDDECOMBE: Oh, I know that. It happened just as I said, but they won't believe me. Not a chance. I've got a record. Breaking and entering, a bit of receiving, forging official documents to get my licence – they'll think I shot him when he caught me trying to steal – he can't tell them any different even if he wanted to, can he, and that woman's not going to come forward now and say she had anything to do with it, is she, whoever she is, so I'm going home, I've got to explain to Rosie and speak to the kids. Prepare them. They've a right – I've got a right – to that. Tell them they can find me at home. Unless you're going to shoot me. Are you?

HERMAN: I can't Anne.

(WIDDECOMBE *goes out. There is a pause*.)

Jesus Annie! Jesus Christ! It worked.

ANNE: Yes darling, you're even more brilliant than you thought. I feel rather cold.

HERMAN: Now come on Annie, you know me, I'm not some creepy wizard, I'm your simple-minded outgoing Okker boy, don't go getting frightened of me – look, it was just an instinct with someone like Robert, that's all.

ANNE: We got him killed, darling.

HERMAN: No, we didn't Annie. He got *himself* killed. All we did was create a highly charged situation, in which he felt humiliated, rejected and deprived, and then provided him with someone to blame it on, and then gave him a loaded gun and a knife and kept out of the way while he got on with it. That's all we did. Now that may be a bit of a sin, but it's no crime, as my old English teacher used to say – I mean, old Robert could have done any number of things Anne, he could have given me back the gun and knife and left quietly, with his little tail between his legs, the way you asked him to, or he could have played out some fool charade with old Widdecombe, which is what I expected, and left us with the goods on him – or he could have killed old Widdecombe and not got killed himself – it was a multi-option situation, Annie, and the options were all his. (*He puts the tape-recorder into his pocket.*)

ANNE: Well, one of the options he nearly took, darling, was to put a bullet in me and carve me up with that ghastly knife!

HERMAN: (*Violently*) Look, we've been over this a hundred times. I thought you'd gone when I gave him the gun and the knife. Anyway, I knew he wouldn't harm you. Now is there anything else besides the tape-recorder – no, there can't be, can there – (*striding about, looking*) – that's the beauty of it, nothing to do with us – just like Brucie, all over again.

ANNE: Brucie.

HERMAN: Didn't I tell you about Brucie, my kid brother, that's where I got the idea from – when he was six and I was eight he used to give me a real wanker's time of it, always telling tales and pinching my cricket pads, so one day I heard Mum telling Dad that she'd caught him playing with the matches again, and that if we didn't look out little Brucie would set

249

himself on fire, so I took the matches down from the mantel shelf in the kitchen and stuck them where he'd find them in the toilet after breakfast along with the morning papers and Dad's lighter fluid, and sure enough up he toddled to relieve himself and in no time smoke was pouring out of the toilet window, he's still got the scar-tissue on his bum.

ANNE: Oh.

HERMAN: I know just what you want Annie, you want a Herman special to set you on your feet – eh? And I want an Annie special – (*kissing her*) – and Annie, the way you looked at Widdecombe. Straight in the eye. That was great acting. Hours in his office fixing it up with him to get himself killed or convicted, and he thought he might have seen you selling baked beans!

ANNE: It must have been my Portia, that was my last telly. But I knew he wouldn't recognize me – all he could see was long red hair, funny teeth and those obscene falsies.

HERMAN: I'll bet you were a great Portia.

ANNE: I didn't wear a blonde wig, funny teeth or falsies for Portia.

HERMAN: Well, I'll still bet you were a great Portia. (*He looks at her.*)

ANNE: (*Suddenly laughs*) You're a swine.

HERMAN: There, that's better – Oh, I want you – I really could go one right now – to celebrate – tell you the truth, I'm high on it, Annie, but I'd better control myself, don't want the police turning up while we're having it away on the sofa, with hubby lying dead behind it. Eh?

ANNE: (*Laughs again*) Oh, I mustn't – it's just the thought of him – the only part he could *ever* play – lying dead behind sofas waiting for the police – do you think they'll let me go on tonight, that's what I want to do, that's what I need to do, I'd give the performance of my life –

HERMAN: No Annie, that's out of the question.

ANNE: Yes, they'd say I was hard, wouldn't they – but it is really rather a beautiful part, so fragile, so wistful.

HERMAN: *You* make it fragile and wistful, Annie. (*Going to the telephone.*)

ANNE: I know.

HERMAN: (*Dialling*) When are we going to get married, Annie, how long will we have to wait?

ANNE: (*Little pause.*) I don't know darling.

HERMAN: Of course I can't move in straight away, but then on the other hand I could, as a friend to keep an eye on you after the tragedy – oh hello, is that the police, what's going on in the matter of Mr Robert Simon's murder, the man who did it's on the run, Mrs Simon has arrived on the scene and she's a very upset lady – are you on strike, or what? (*Little pause.*) Jesus, well how long then? (*Listens, puts the phone down.*) They're working to rule, Jesus, what a country. But they've left, they'll be here in a few minutes – now how are you going to receive them, Annie, tears or the shakes or should I tuck you up in bed, with a nice cup of tea and do all the talking –

ANNE: Don't worry, darling, I'll improvise quite naturally – one always does find the appropriate response, somehow.

(ROBERT *rises up from behind the sofa, shaking, pointing a finger. His eyes upwards, as in death, his mouth open, a great spurt of fresh blood pours from his mouth. He picks up gun and aims at* ANNE. ANNE *screams and screams and screams.*)

HERMAN: (*Gapes*) Jee-sus! (*Terrified.*)

ROBERT: Yours – from – the – ranks – of – death! (*He takes a few steps around the sofa.*)

(HERMAN *steps back.* ANNE *screams again.* ROBERT *dashes over, picks up the gun. There is a pause.*)

Sorry. (*He wipes away the blood.*) Couldn't resist using the extra blood capsule. Still, it's what I always say. Certain moments when you *can't* go over the top. (*Little pause.*) You bitch! (*He points the gun at them.*) And as for you, Herman young cheddar, well what a turn-up, eh, thinking you can walk straight out of the bush into the home of an English chappie like me, and take over all his comforts not to mention his wife and her money and their water-bed, beats hell out of Earls Court, eh? (*To* ANNE) Did you really think I'd die for you? All I had in mind was a little game, to teach you and Widdecombe a lesson, the pleasure of seeing and hearing you recriminating over my corpse, and a little publicity – I did phone the TV people by the way, I was going to rise up before them and announce our divorce, how typical of them to pass me over yet again – and then I was going to walk with dignity out of your life, perhaps even into a bit of real telly work on the strength of my little self-promotion – but real killing – real death –

ANNE: (*To* HERMAN) You fool! Didn't you look properly! Don't you know the only thing he can do is blood and falling about and pretending to be dead. I told you often enough.

ROBERT: Do you really prefer Brucie's homicidal brother to me! How you've hated me then.

ANNE: From the first time you betrayed me. Everything I said Widdecombe said about our marriage was true. And I knew you'd make a misery of my life once the time was come to throw you out – and I was right, you have. You would! And now you're standing there looking self-righteous – you who screwed all the girls –

HERMAN: Three hundred and fifty-seven, Robert. Widdecombe's got it on tape see. (*He shows him the tape-recorder.*) So nothing's really changed, apart from your being alive that is. You're still through.

ROBERT: I never betrayed you. Not once. A dab of lipstick on an item of laundry, an occasional bath, telephone conversations which were what I didn't want them to seem – to you – and what was worst of all you never bothered even to notice. As far as I could tell. This is very humiliating, in front of Brucie's homicidal brother but I loved her, yes and was happy looking after her and her monstrous ego and her merely average talent, yes I was, but I did now and then want you to care, you see, to show a little courteous jealousy – I knew perfectly well that my only real gifts were a stage-manager's gifts, and how could I spend the rest of my life being a stage-manager when the woman I adored made us so rich that *my* pay was simply a tax burden, what was the point? So if I was happy enough running the house while you were out rehearsing, and cooking you special little meals at night when you came back exhausted from your triumphs, I still wanted you to believe that I had some value to others –

three hundred and fifty-seven others, which were my three
hundred and fifty-seven failed attempts to get you to see it –
(*Goes to the phone and dials.*) – oh, and what about your
Grisle. What had you planned for her.

HERMAN: There wasn't any Grisle. Apart from Annie.

ROBERT: Ah, just a way of handing over gun and knife, eh?

HERMAN: That's right, Robert. But it was quite instructive,
listening to your advice to go ahead and take her from her
husband, remember?

ROBERT: (*Is now dialling on the telephone*) Hello, can I speak to
Fred Widdecombe, please. Oh, is that Rosie, hello Rosie,
this is a colleague – of your husband's. Would you please tell
him that Robert Simon phoned, as right as rain, that it was
all a joke and that he's absolutely in the clear whatever he
hears, he's not involved. OK? And give him my – my
regards. And to Nigel and Piers – oh, by the way, try one of
the elocution classes in the acting schools for Nigel's
stammer, they're quite good at that, goodbye.
(*Hangs up. He goes to the sofa, sits and does something to the
gun, very deftly, but looking at them when he speaks.*)

HERMAN: The police will be here any moment, they'll give you a
bollocking –

ROBERT: I didn't call them, Herman. You did.

HERMAN: (*Goes to* ROBERT) Anyway, you can piss off now, man.
And you won't be getting any five thousand, even. Will he,
Annie?

ANNE: (*Rises and goes to the desk, collects some scripts, etc.*) Oh, you
two can sort it out between you, I've got my half to make,
you know, and you've put me in a dreadful state, damn you,
all for nothing.

HERMAN: What do you mean, Annie, half? Half of what?

ROBERT: She's got to be in the theatre half an hour before the
curtain goes up. She's not with you or me, you know, she's
already in the theatre. You wouldn't have lasted with her
seven days – let alone seven years. Not once you'd done her
job for her.

HERMAN: (*Goes to* ANNE) I'll come with you Annie – and you'd
better be gone when we get back.

ROBERT: (*Rises and stands centre stage*) Just a minute. (*He points the gun at them.*)

HERMAN: Oh come on, man, they're blanks. Annie – (*Tries to open hall door – it is locked.*)

ROBERT: *Don't* call her Annie, if you please. Especially in that accent. They're not blanks. I've just put one of your bullets back in.

HERMAN: Oh, ha, ha.

ROBERT: (*Fires at plate on wall which shatters.*) This time I'm going to do it right – come here, darling.

(ANNE *doesn't move.*)

HERMAN: Better do what he says, Annie.

ROBERT: Get the knife, Herman.

(ANNE *goes to* ROBERT)

HERMAN: What?

ROBERT: Get the knife.

(HERMAN *gets the knife.*)

Back to the beginning. A knife and a loaded gun in a multi-potential situation. It could come out anyway. You've got ten seconds, darling, (*moving himself to stand with his back to* HERMAN) and then I fire. Last words, please? One – two – three –

(ANNE's *lips move desperately.*)

ANNE: Herman –

ROBERT: Quote then. You've done Cleopatra, Hedda – just a few lines to exit on. Don't worry about context. Four – five – six –

(HERMAN *creeps across the room.*)

– seven eight nine –

ANNE: Herman!

HERMAN: Don't!

(ANNE *screams.* HERMAN *plunges the knife into* ROBERT's *back.* ROBERT *stumbles, points the gun at* ANNE *again, struggles towards her.* ANNE *grabs the gun, shoots, as* HERMAN *pulls* ROBERT *back. There is a pause.* ROBERT *reels away, sits down on the floor.*)

ROBERT: Now – now we'll see – how the real process is when – when there's a knife in my back, Herman, from you and a bullet in my gut darling from you? – we've got what you wanted in the end, eh? This is the first death speech I've ever been allowed to make, and look, I can taste it – real blood – and when they come tell them – of carnal bloody and unnatural acts – accidental judgements – casual slaughters, of deaths put on by cunning and forc'd cause, and in the upshot, purposes mistook fall'n on the inventor's head – and that none of it – would have – happened – if it hadn't been – stage-managed by – by – a – poet – (*He reaches out a hand to* ANNE, *dies.*)

HERMAN: Jesus. (*Little pause.*) He made us do it – (*Anne drops the gun.*)

ANNE: What – what will we do, darling?

HERMAN: The thing is not to panic, Annie. Let's look at it rationally. Rationally. I've already reported the murder to the police – and here's the body, right, murdered. So we're all right on that one. Now what's our problem? Our problem is that he was murdered twice, once from the back, once from the front. Bit difficult to explain. We can still finger Widdecombe for the shooting. But it would help if we had someone else – an accomplice for the stabbing. Still, we haven't got one, have we, Annie, so – oh hell, we'll just have to make it look as if your Widdecombe was so determined to do the job properly that he stabbed him and shot him himself. No problem really.

(*Distant sound of police siren.*)

Oh, here they come. Your English bobbies moving smartly for once, eh? And who's that coming down the drive? (*Goes to window and looks.*) It's Kent Television. Well, we'll give them a story, won't we, Annie? (*Laughs.*)

ANNE: Yes, we will, darling. A wonderful story of how I shot the man who murdered my wonderful Robert.

HERMAN: What, Annie?

ANNE: So much neater this way, darling. Even though I've missed my half. It's hard to forgive you for that.

HERMAN: Oh come on, Annie, you haven't got the balls to pull that – and anyway you'll miss –

(ANNE *shoots him.*)

Jeez, Annie – (*Dies.*)

(Sound of vehicles, etc. now in the drive, voices off. ANNE *adopts a posture of frozen tragedy.* ROBERT *jerks into hideous half-life, drags himself as if toward* ANNE. ANNE *whimpers with terror, pulls trigger again and again. The gun clicks empty again and again.* ROBERT *sways, releasing dummy as he does so. Dummy plummets down.* ROBERT *clutches at it, dies.* ANNE *screaming hysterically, as all around sound of sirens, voices shouting, doorbell ringing, etc.)*
(Curtain.)

Tartuffe

An Adaptation

Tartuffe: An Adaptation was first performed at the Kennedy Center, Washington DC, in May 1982. The cast included:

TARTUFFE	Brian Bedford
ORGON	Barnard Hughes
ELMIRE, Orgon's wife	Carole Shelley
CLEANTE, her brother	Fritz Weaver
MARIANE, Orgon's daughter	Christine Andreas
MME PERNELLE, his mother	Margaret Barker
DAMIS, his son	Boyd Gaines
DORINE, THE MAID	Barbara Bryne
PHILPOTE, Mme Pernelle's servant	Marlene Bryan
VALÈRE, Mariane's suitor	Jeff Hayenga

ACT ONE

ELMIRE *and* CLEANTE *are sitting talking.* DORINE *and* MARIANE
are sorting through a box of jewellery. MME PERNELLE *and*
PHILPOTE *are sitting on hard-backed chairs, each reading the Bible,*
PHILPOTE *with difficulty, lips moving. A sudden burst of laughter*
from ELMIRE, CLEANTE. MME PERNELLE *shoots them an angry*
glance, goes on reading. PHILPOTE *looks towards them, grinning.*

MARIANE: (*Meanwhile, shakes her head, laughing, at a ring that*
　　　　DORINE *has put on her finger*) Oh, Dorine, I can't, can I,
　　　　Mama? Look (*Goes to show* ELMIRE) – Dorine insists, but it's
　　　　far too big and – glittery. Don't you think, Uncle? (*Showing*
　　　　it to CLEANTE.)

DORINE: Glittery! If anything, it's too dull. At least for Miss
　　　　Mariane's complexion – these were your mother's, child. If it
　　　　becomes you, you should be pleased, not ashamed.

MARIANE: I'm not ashamed, Dorine, it's just – well, the way it
　　　　catches the light.

DORINE: Won't stop Valère looking into your eyes, I promise.
　　　　(*Laughter, in which* PHILPOTE *joins.*)

MME PERNELLE: (*To* PHILPOTE) Back! Get back to your reading!
　　　　How dare you blaspheme. (*She begins to read in a low,*
　　　　emphatic voice, out loud.)

ELMIRE: I agree with Dorine, my dear, it looks ravishing.

CLEANTE: And as Valère's already asked for your hand, he won't
　　　　spurn it, now one of its fingers is sporting a fortune.

MARIANE: Oh, Uncle –

ELMIRE: But, my dear, if it makes you feel uncomfortable – is
　　　　there something of your mother's that *you* feel she'd have
　　　　wanted you to wear? What about this? Or the pendant?

DORINE: We've been through them all, madame. And each
　　　　insists on being noticeable. I tell you, madame, this ring is
　　　　the shyest thing in the collection, and she's already –

DAMIS: (*Enters*) That's it! I've had enough! I wait all morning –
　　　　all morning for Alphonse and Mélian to come by, and when I
　　　　hear them at the door at last, and rush down – they're gone.
　　　　And do you know why? Because Laurent has sent them

away. Told them I wasn't at home. Told them none of us was at home! And when I ask him what the Devil – what the Devil he means by it, he says his master has forbidden visitors. Tartuffe has forbidden visitors. Tartuffe! Can you believe it! First he worms his way into our home, now he's actually running our lives. Well, that's it! It's time I had a few – words – with that – that –

MME PERNELLE: Oh, I wouldn't advise that, Damis, no, no, I think you'd do far better to control yourself. For one thing, your father left Monsieur Tartuffe in charge while he's away, and for another, Monsieur Tartuffe is quite right, as always. I don't approve of all these nonsensical comings and goings either, people dropping by as if we were a café or a hotel or – or worse; the carriages on the streets, the servants hanging about the hall, the buffoonery and noise and loutish laughter – a bedlam, that's what this place is, a bedlam. And what about the neighbours, do you ever think of them? Well, I can tell you, people are talking. Yes, talking.

DAMIS: Talking! What on earth about, Grandmother?

MME PERNELLE: About the sort of thing you get up to. All of you.

ELMIRE: But what sort of thing *do* we get up to, Mother?

MME PERNELLE: It doesn't matter what you get up to, it's what you let them *think* you get up to that they talk about. And that's what matters!

CLEANTE: Well, madame, in my experience people would talk just as much if we lived like monks and nuns. More, I expect, if even half of what's said to go on in some monasteries and convents –

(MME PERNELLE *lets out a cry*.)

Exactly, madame, my point exactly. Not even our holiest brothers and sisters are immune from gossip. And yet they proceed with their – um, devotions, I trust. Don't you?

(MME PERNELLE *is clearly suspicious and makes no reply*.)

DORINE: If there's any gossip going on about us, I know who'll be at the bottom of it. Daphne, and her poodle of a husband. They're always spreading gossip about others so nobody will notice what they get up to themselves. But I could tell you a thing or two about Daphne, madame –

MME PERNELLE: I'm not interested, not the slightest bit
interested in Daphne or her husband of a poodle, I assure
you! I was thinking of Madame Orante. Yes, Madame
Orante disapproves of your household, child (*To* ELMIRE),
its frivolity and – and lack of propriety. She told me so
herself. And even you will agree, I think, that Madame
Orante is a very model of correct behaviour.

DORINE: Oh, she is now, yes. (*Laughing*) She certainly is now,
these days. But the stories about her in her saucy prime,
madame, gadding about to all the balls and soirées, people
used to say she could roll her eyes at two men at once, one for
each eye, that's why she's got that squint. (*Laughs*) And, of
course, now all her old beaux are dead, or too crippled and
ancient to crawl to her door, she sits at her window squinting
down at all the young people, hating them for having the fun
she'll never have again, this side of heaven. Oh, madame,
Madame Orante's not good from choice, madame, but from
envy, poor old prune. But I'll tell you why Tartuffe doesn't
like people calling on us, especially young chaps like
Alphonse and Mélian: if you ask my opinion, it's because of
you, madame; (*To* ELMIRE) he's jealous, you see, he's
afraid –

MME PERNELLE: Stop, stop, will nobody stop this creature! Oh,
oh – the smutty, vicious talk you encourage in my son's
house, child! (*To* ELMIRE) Well, I've heard enough of it.
(*Turning to* DORINE) You impertinent, interfering, vulgar
little chit – (*To* ELMIRE) How could you permit her to wait
on my son's daughter, she would be a disgrace in a – a –
(DAMIS *lets out a snort of laughter.*)

MME PERNELLE: (*Glares at him*) And as for you, my lad, you're
nothing but a fop and a fool. I'm ashamed, yes *ashamed* to be
your grandmother, I've told my poor son so a hundred times,
you'll drive him to his grave –

MARIANE: Please, Grandma –

MME PERNELLE: – and you're no better, with your pretty little
ways and your shy little smiles, and this is too big and that's
too gorgeous and, oh, I couldn't wear that, no, no, no – but

you'll end up wearing them all, looking like a – a – oh, still waters run rancid in your case, my dear, but you don't deceive me – (*Turning sorrowfully to* ELMIRE.) Oh, my child, my child, when my son bestowed on you the honour of becoming his wife he also bestowed on you the honour of becoming the mother of his children. But what would she say, the poor dear woman, if she could see from her grave the extravagance, the vanity of the woman who has replaced her? If you spent as much time on your prayers as on your dress, oh, how healthy your soul would be! You do realize, don't you, child, that an immodestly dressed wife is already an unfaithful wife. And you, sir (*Turning to* CLEANTE), you who might be expected to guide your sister in her duties to my son and her God, well, all I can say is that if I were you (*To* ELMIRE) I'd go down on my bended knees to him, madame, and beg you to stay away from my home, sir, with your cynical talk and – and blasphemous attitudes. There! No doubt you're very shocked – but I owed it to my heart and to my son and to my God to speak out! And that's why you all hate Monsieur Tartuffe, isn't it? Because he speaks out too. He not only knows you for what you are but tries to make you into what you should be. How wise my son was to bring him here. How wise he was to beg him to instruct you. Monsieur Tartuffe sees the paths of righteousness, as he sees the ways of the Devil. Heed him, heed him, and you may yet save yourselves from damnation, shame and scandal!

CLEANTE: (*After a little pause*) In that order, madame?

(*Suppressed laughter, perhaps, from* DAMIS, MARIANE, DORINE.)

MME PERNELLE: What, oh snigger away, monsieur, snigger away to your doom's content. I'm leaving this house, child, the house of my own son. And I shan't set foot in it again until Monsieur Tartuffe has cleansed it into a fit place for people to visit. As he will, in spite of you! Come along, Philpote, come along – not another *second* of contamination!

ELMIRE: Oh, Mother, please don't leave. Especially like this. I'm sorry if we've given you cause – we're all sorry – aren't we?

MME PERNELLE: (*Goes to* PHILPOTE, *who hasn't moved*) I told you to come along – (*Slaps* PHILPOTE) Gawking and gaping like an imbecile – move, move! (*Turns and goes out.* PHILPOTE *runs after her.*)

ELMIRE: At least let us see you out. (*Going after her*) We must try and persuade her –

MME PERNELLE: (*Exiting*) Oh, there's no need, I know my way to the door, and I don't need you bowing and curtsying me on to the street just so you can show off your manners and costumes.

(*Exit* DAMIS *and* MARIANE.)

CLEANTE: (*Who has been about to go out, stops, comes back*) No, on second thoughts I think I'm safer here. Well, Dorine, further evidence of the power of love, eh?

DORINE: Sir?

CLEANTE: She's evidently infatuated with him. Her Tartuffe.

DORINE: Oh, nothing like as much as her son is, sir. You should see *him* at it. He talks to Tartuffe as if he were – were one of the sacred martyrs, sir, begs for his advice on this, for his permission to do that, hands him huge sums of money as soon as he as much as hints – for *religious* purposes of course, sir – and thanks him for taking the trouble to order the rest of us about and give us lectures. And it's not just Tartuffe himself, sir, but his odious little puppy of a servant: Laurent's taken it up, too – he comes yelping into our rooms, frothing and moaning about our Lord in heaven. The other day he tore one of Miss Mariane's handkerchiefs into shreds because she left it between the pages of some holy book or other, he said we were committing a hideous sacrilege. And then he went and told Tartuffe what he'd done, and Tartuffe blessed and thanked him and went and told the master, who blessed and thanked *him*. And master gives him such doting looks, sir, as if – as if – as if he were his – his mistress, sir, he actually cuddles and caresses, and fondles and pampers him, sir – puts him at the head of the table at meals, sir, picks the daintiest pieces of meat off our plates, all our plates, including madame's, and pops them on to Tartuffe's, sits admiring him as he washes them down with pints of wine, and when he sags back into his chair, belching and burping, coos out, 'Oh, are you all right, Tartuffe, oh, God preserve you, brother, you dear old chap, oh, you poor dear man, are you sure you're all right?' It's – it's disgusting, sir, that's what it is! And to think that just a short time ago, when there were all troubles and rebellions and politics, the master was famous everywhere for his good sense and manliness and courage, the king himself said how *grateful* he was to him for his loyalty, we were all so proud of him.

DAMIS: (*Enters with* MARIANE) What a pity you missed her farewell. She drew quite a handsome crowd on the street. Some of them applauding her, the rest laughing at us –

MARIANE: Father's here!

ELMIRE: Oh. (*Hesitates*) Well, I'll wait for him upstairs. Or somewhere. (*To* CLEANTE) You'll stay and welcome him back for me, won't you, my dear?

CLEANTE: Well, as a matter of fact I was just off myself, I only looked in to see how things were –

ELMIRE: Please.

(CLEANTE *nods.* ELMIRE *exits.*)

MARIANE: I'll come with you, Mama. Oh, Uncle, would you mention Valère to him?

CLEANTE: Valère?

MARIANE: Yes, our getting married. Father's stopped talking about it and – and I'm getting a little worried, will you, Uncle?

CLEANTE: Well – (*Nods*) I'll try.

MARIANE: Thank you. (*She exits.*)

DAMIS: Yes, please sound him out. I've got a feeling that – that – Tartuffe! has turned him against Valère. Poor Mariane. And you see where that leaves me.

CLEANTE: No.

DAMIS: Well, I'm in love with Mélanie, Valère's sister. So if he stops Mariane from marrying Valère – you see –

CLEANTE: Yes.

DAMIS: Thank you, Uncle. (*He exits.*)

CLEANTE: Well, Dorine, have you any emotional attachment you'd like me to discuss with him?

DORINE: I'll show you what I mean, sir. You just listen.

ORGON: (*Enters carrying a box*) Ah, Cleante. You're here then, are you?

CLEANTE: Yes, just looked in to – to see how things were. I gather you've been in the country.

ORGON: Yes.

CLEANTE: Not too much in the way of flora and – and verdure, though, at this time of year, I shouldn't think, eh?

ORGON: What?

CLEANTE: Grass and flowers.

ORGON: Grass and flowers?

CLEANTE: Yes.

ORGON: What about them?

CLEANTE: Oh, nothing. I just meant – did you go away on business or pleasure?

ORGON: To see an old friend.

CLEANTE: Ah, pleasure then.

ORGON: Pleasure! Certainly not! Do you think I'd leave my house for pleasure, when my Lord above –

CLEANTE: You went on business then?

ORGON: Yes. To see an old friend, Argaz. He wanted me to – to do something for him. Look after a few – um – papers.

CLEANTE: Ah. Well, good to see you back.

ORGON: What's been going on?

CLEANTE: Going on?

ORGON: Yes. These last few days. While I've been away. How is – everyone? Where is – everyone?

CLEANTE: Oh, I think – around the house, you know. In fact, they've just been seeing your mother off – rather emotional occasion actually – as your mother seemed to feel she might not be back for some time. So they're probably all feeling a – a trifle (*Laughs*) – you know how it is – low, you know.

ORGON: And, um – Tartuffe?

CLEANTE: Oh. *He*'s still here, I believe.

ORGON: Ah.

DORINE: Madame your wife had a fever the day before yesterday. And a dreadful headache.

ORGON: Ah, but he's all right, is he, Tartuffe?

DORINE: Oh, yes, sir. In the pink and the plump. She felt very sick in the evening, couldn't touch her supper. Her headache was worse –

ORGON: (*Little pause*) So poor Tartuffe was left on his own, you mean?

DORINE: No, he allowed himself to sit with her while he polished off a couple of partridges and a leg of mutton, hashed. She spent a completely sleepless night. We sat by her and tried to keep her fever down.

ORGON: So poor Tartuffe got no sleep either, then?

DORINE: By 'we' I meant your son and daughter and myself. Tartuffe went straight from his mutton hash to his bed. We persuaded her to be bled, sir, madame your wife. She began to feel better in the morning.

(ORGON *makes to speak*.)

Rallied wonderfully, too, sir. He made up for the blood your wife lost by putting away four carafes of port before breakfasting on goose liver, sausage and cheese. May I go now, sir, (*Curtsying*) and tell madame how delighted you are at her recovery?

ORGON: Yes, well, everything seems to be in order, then. (*Little pause*) But perhaps I should just go and see if I can find him – hear from him himself how he is and whether there's anything he needs –

CLEANTE: Let's consider the facts!

ORGON: Mmmm?

CLEANTE: Excuse my abruptness. There's a conversation we have to have, that I had to find a way of forcing myself into. Can we look at the facts, dear, together, calmly and with dispassion?

ORGON: Certainly. (*Little pause*) What facts?

CLEANTE: About you and your Tartuffe. As far as I understand them, you rescued him from destitution when he was little better – sorry, *more* – sorry, *other* – than a tramp. Barefooted and tattered robe and – and the rest of it. You took him – no doubt from the best of motives, they do you honour, no doubt – into your home. Which he now appears – after you've fed him and clothed him, and his servant, I take it? – to run. Along with your son's and daughter's social and

266

TARTUFFE

emotional lives. You appear to be positively proud that this
quondam tramp, who many would be inclined to describe as
an unscrupulous parasite, has allowed you to put yourself at
his service, in a role that you yourself seem to see as
somewhere between a religious valet and a moral butler.
(*Little pause*) I refrain from discussing my own sister's
situation, in consequence. (*Little pause*) Those are the facts,
as far as I understand them.

ORGON: From what you say it's evident – sadly evident – that you
don't know the facts at all. Oh, Cleante, my brother, my
brother-in-law but still my brother, I beg you to try and
understand. Once you know him properly – you see, he's a
man – a man – a man who – (*Gestures.*)

CLEANTE: Ah huh!

ORGON: He looks at the world and says: 'This is a cesspool.'
D'you see?

CLEANTE: Mmmm?

ORGON: A complete cesspool! That's what he's made me – made
me – (*Gestures.*)

CLEANTE: A complete cesspool?

ORGON: Exactly! Yes! Absolutely! And so leads me to a perfect
detachment. From all those bonds that drag one down. From
my children, my mother, my wife – all of you together, come
to that, I could see you all die – there! There! (*Pointing in
front of him*) At my feet, without caring so much as a – a –
(CLEANTE *snaps his fingers.*)
Yes!
(ORGON *snaps his fingers.* CLEANTE *snaps his fingers.* ORGON
snaps his fingers.)

CLEANTE: All of them dead! (*Snaps his fingers.*)

ORGON: Every one of them! (*Snaps his fingers.*)

CLEANTE: Every one of them! (*Snaps.*)

ORGON: All of them! (*Snaps*) Oh, if only you'd seen him as I first
saw him! In church! I couldn't take my eyes off him! One
moment raising his arms to heaven, just like an innocent
babe, the next prostrate on the ground, kissing the very
flagstones in self-anger and humility! He made me feel so –
so inhibited and ashamed, offering up my own awkward shy

little prayers – When I left he was waiting at the doors, with a cup of holy water. He held it out to me. I took it from him. I sipped. As I lowered the cup our eyes met. And he gazed through mine eyes straight into my heart, into the very depths of my heart. I stood there pierced. I knew – even in my ignorance I knew – that a great change had come into my life. I swooned, Cleante. Swooned from revelations. (*Little pause*) When I came back to myself he'd gone. I felt such a loss, such a trembling of loss. But by the Grace of God his servant and disciple, my friend for life, Laurent, was still at prayer.

CLEANTE: How fortunate!

ORGON: I waited for him, I quizzed him about his master, I learnt that his master was poor and hungry, a holy vagabond in the service of the Lord. So I sent his master food and I sent him gifts of clothes and money, which he brought me back from his master. 'Too much, my master says, oh, far too much for minion of the Lord. We love your love. We don't desire your compassions.' And when I refused to take them back, his master sent for me to watch him distribute my gifts to the needy, the oppressed, the (*Gestures*) – and permitted me to accompany him as he spoke and blessed all those who (*Gestures*) – and so to learn charity from him, and at least he consented – His will be done, His will be done! – to come into my home!

CLEANTE: Ah, um – whose will, exactly, is that?

ORGON: (*With sudden anger*) His! His!

CLEANTE: Ah!

ORGON: And now my house is his house and mine father's house, touched with divine favour! His influence is everywhere, in every nook and cranny of my life, instructing me by example. Have you heard – have you heard – about the flea?

CLEANTE: The flea? No, no, I don't think –

ORGON: He killed it. In anger. At his prayers. But, oh, Cleante, the agony of Tartuffe afterwards, the tears of Tartuffe, Tartuffe's despair. I wish you'd heard him, wished you'd seen him – foaming and weeping. He, Tartuffe. For a flea. Oh, oh, Cleante, if only I could reach into your soul, as he has reached into mine. Then you'd know, as I know.

CLEANTE: Well, I do know – something of what's happened to you, anyway. Because it happens all the time to men of a – a certain age. Look, you and I, we're more than halfway through life, we live in doubt, don't we, terror, even, of – well, you know. And we long for – for certainties. At least I do. (*Laughs*) Something to make sense of all the years we can't call back. I – well, I remain a bachelor – because it's too late for me to set forth on the main adventure – a bit of a coward, you see. While you, having bravely done it once, and then again – marriage, I mean – and what greater compliment could you pay your first beloved wife than to replace her immediately, eh?

ORGON: Replace her?

CLEANTE: Well, yes.

ORGON: With what?

CLEANTE: Well, um, a second beloved wife. My – sister, old chap.

ORGON: Oh. Oh, yes.

CLEANTE: Um – um, I've lost the – oh, oh, yes. And there, suddenly you see in front of you, not a new life, through a second marriage, but doubts, fears – (*Gestures.*)

ORGON: Ha!

CLEANTE: You've no idea what you've lived for all these years, what to go on living for. And so – and so – Tartuffe! Like a gift from heaven! And suddenly it's all quite simple, just as in childhood or at school, eh? (*Laughs.*)

(ORGON *stares at him unnervingly.*)

You know what I mean – this is good, that is bad, do this, don't do that, here heaven, there hell, etc. – and – and suddenly – no more confusion, no more terrors, eh? Your love for – for Damis, for Mariane, for my sister, previously complicated and full of bewilderment – a family being a family, eh? From what I can make out of that sort of thing (*Laughs*) – um, you know, 'How do I look after them? What do they expect from me?' is reduced to a magnificent – magnificently simple. (*Snaps his fingers*) What are *they* compared to the great truth that your Tartuffe has delivered to you?

ORGON: (*Snaps his fingers*) Exactly!

CLEANTE: I think you've missed my point – I suppose I've misjudged my – my – lost, what I mean is – look, there's no clarity like blindness, don't you see? Blindness to life and all you love – that's what Tartuffe's done to you, made you blind, d'you see?

ORGON: I see. Blind.

CLEANTE: Well, yes, in a manner of –

ORGON: (*Laughs contemptuously*) Your servant, sir. (*Bows, makes to go.*)

CLEANTE: (*Hesitates*) But – one more word, though, if you please. Just on the – the question of Mariane and her Valère. You have fixed the happy day, I suppose.

ORGON: Yes.

CLEANTE: Oh, good. When is it to be?

ORGON: Don't know.

CLEANTE: Don't know?

ORGON: Decided to postpone.

CLEANTE: Any particular reason?

ORGON: Don't know if it's particular. But it'll do for me. (*Laughs.*)

CLEANTE: But you haven't changed your mind?

ORGON: Possibly.

CLEANTE: You mean you intend to break your word?

ORGON: What word?

CLEANTE: Didn't you give your word to Valère?

ORGON: Did I?

CLEANTE: Do you intend to break it?

ORGON: Do I?

CLEANTE: Well, do you? Your daughter would like to know. And so would Valère. Her fiancé. (*Little pause*) I think they both have the right –

ORGON: Indeed?

CLEANTE: What do I say to them?

ORGON: You? Why, whatever you like.

CLEANTE: Whatever I like may not be true. What are *your* plans?

ORGON: To do the will of heaven.

CLEANTE: The will of heaven must be that you honour your word, mustn't it?

(ORGON *smiles*.)

Well, do you intend or don't you, sir, to honour your word?

ORGON: Good day to you, sir.

(CLEANTE *stands for a moment, makes an angry gesture, exits*.)

Tartuffe! Tartuffe! Come down! Where are you? Where is he, why hasn't he come –

(MARIANE *appears at the door*.)

Ah – (*Peers at her*) Mariane?

(DORINE *is briefly visible. It is evident that she listens to the ensuing exchange*.)

MARIANE: Father?

ORGON: Tartuffe not with you, then?

MARIANE: No, Father.

ORGON: Ah. Where is he then?

MARIANE: I don't know, Father. I thought you called me.

ORGON: What for?

MARIANE: I don't know. (*Hesitates*) Well –

(*During this* DORINE *has closed her door. Now opens it again, so that she can see in, and listens*.)

ORGON: Mariane, my dear, you're very dear to me, very dear my – um – dear.

MARIANE: Thank you, Father.

ORGON: With your exceptionally sweet nature and – (*Gestures*.)

MARIANE: Thank you, Father.

ORGON: Now, tell me – tell me, what do you think of our guest?

MARIANE: Our guest?

ORGON: Tartuffe, child. (*Little pause*) Well, what do you think of him?

MARIANE: I – I – what do you think I should think of him, Father? I think what – what you think. Of course I do.

ORGON: Ah! A most loving reply. Well, that's settled then. You shall have him for your husband.

(MARIANE *cries out, recoiling*.)

What's the matter, child?

MARIANE: I – I must have misunderstood.

ORGON: You said you thought of Tartuffe as I think of him. And I think of him as your husband. What misunderstanding can there be?

MARIANE: But –

ORGON: In joining you to him I join him to us – to all my family, in a sacred union. As you love me, so you love him. In making him my son, you remain my daughter, daughter. If I were to give you to any other man, I would lose you. For ever. Consider that!

DORINE: (*Enters, pretending to laugh*) Oh, master –

ORGON: What do you want?

DORINE: I had to come and tell you! I've just heard the most ridiculous nonsense, some – some malicious idiot is putting it about that (*Laughs*) – Tartuffe's going to marry Miss Mariane, not that anyone would believe it, even if you went around saying it yourself, would they, sir?

ORGON: It's true.

DORINE: (*Laughing*) Oh, sir –

ORGON: I tell you, it's true!
    (DORINE *laughs again.*)

ORGON: It's true, true, true! I tell you it's true. It's true!

DORINE: (*Laughing*) Oh, sir, do stop – poor Miss believes you – he's only joking, Miss –

ORGON: Are you trying to drive me mad?

DORINE: No, to drive you sane, sir!

ORGON: What? You take too many liberties in this house, girl –

DORINE: Oh, please, sir, don't be angry, I only meant – well, for one thing are you sure Monsieur Tartuffe needs a wife? With so many saintly matters to worry about, and so busy guiding people to heaven and keeping them out of hell, wouldn't a silly little wife just get in the way?

ORGON: He would soon make her serious, and a help to him. Through prayer and instruction, my child. Rejoice.

DORINE: Well, but, sir, from the business point of view, have you given that enough thought? An appetite like that in the family – just consider how much he eats and drinks, sir, and not a penny to his name, not a very practical – (*Calms down.*)

ORGON: (*Bellowing*) Now try – try to understand. His poverty is a dowry. His hatred of wordly goods raises him above the world, to far, far greater riches. Those riches he brings to you, my child. Rejoice.

TARTUFFE

DORINE: Oh. Well, in that case he won't want what she brings him, will he, sir? *Her* dowry, I mean –

ORGON: What he wants and what I want have nothing to do with you!

DORINE: What about what Miss Mariane wants, sir? And that's Monsieur Valère. (*To* MARIANE) Isn't it?

ORGON: Kindly do not try to drag my daughter into this. Although, as you've mentioned Valère – I regret to inform you, my dear, that I've unmasked a number of weaknesses in our young Valère that would make him an unsuitable husband, even if you were free, which, of course, you no longer are. For one thing he's an inveterate gambler –

DORINE: For a few shillings. At cards. With his friends –

ORGON: – and for another he's not serious. You've noticed yourself, I'm sure, his tendency to laugh and make jokes all the time. And finally and most importantly, I have grounds for believing that – he's a free thinker! I have never once seen him at church. Not once!

DORINE: Perhaps he goes at different times, in which case he could say he'd never seen you at church either, sir, couldn't he? Does that make you a free thinker?

ORGON: (*Confused*) What?

DORINE: I was just wondering –

ORGON: Then wonder to yourself. I am talking to my daughter. Now, my dear, try to think of the pleasure, the joy, you'll share with Tartuffe. I warrant you that once you're used to him the two of you will be like, why, turtle-doves, billing and cooing away at each other all day, all (*Checks himself*) – and how good you'll be for each other, he with his strength and passion – religious passion – and you – oh, I can see what you'll be able to make of him, my dear, with your enchanting little ways, eh? (*Chuckles.*)

DORINE: A cuckold.

ORGON: What? What did you say?

DORINE: A cuckold, sir, that's what I said. Because that's what she'll make of him, well, it stands to reason, master – how can you expect her to be a faithful wife when you hand her over to a man she loathes, and even if she is, nobody will believe it, will they, sir, everyone will take it for granted that she'll have somebody else, quite a few somebody elses to make up, won't they, sir, so in the end she might as well anyway. I mean, why expect her to have the bad reputation without the pleasure of earning it, poor lamb, and she can always tell herself it's not her fault either way, it'll be yours, master, for leading her directly into temptation –

ORGON: One more word – one more word out of you – and you'll get the back of this! Understood?

DORINE: Yes, master.

(ORGON *turns back to* MARIANE.)

I was only trying to warn you, sir, so that I couldn't say 'I told you so' afterwards, and I don't want people going around laughing at you for marrying your daughter off to a fraud and a bigot, that's all, sir, and it's not as if he'll be happy either, women have ways of making life miserable for men the –

ORGON: (*Advancing on* DORINE) I warn you! I warn you!

(DORINE *nods. They stand staring at each other*.)

Your last chance!

(DORINE *nods*.)

(*Turns back to* MARIANE) Now, my child, I hope you understand (*Glances at* DORINE) – that what I propose for you (*Glances at* DORINE) – is – is – um (*Glances at* DORINE) – and that you believe the husband I selected is (*Glances at* DORINE) – is – (*In a roar*) Well!

(DORINE *shakes her head*. ORGON *turns back to* MARIANE, *makes to speak, turns back to* DORINE, *his hand raised*.)

Go on. One word. Say one word!

(DORINE *stares at him*. ORGON *turns, looks at* MARIANE. *Opens his mouth*.)

DORINE: Never. That's the word. Never, never, never. I'd never, never, never let myself be forced into marriage with that brute –

(ORGON *rushes to her*. DORINE *skips out of the way*.)

Never, never.

(DORINE *runs out of the room*. ORGON *makes to run after her. Stops himself, stares around as if in momentary bewilderment*.

Then, as if seeing MARIANE, *goes to her. Stands for a moment, as if about to speak.*)

ORGON: That – that girl has made me – I – I – I – where is he? I must go and find him. I – I – (*Turns, goes to the door. Stops. Turns*) So what it comes to is this. I've decided. You'll obey. Nothing more to be said. Nothing. (*He goes out.*)

DORINE: (*Has been watching from behind the other door, enters*) What's the matter with you? Have you lost your tongue? You should have been saying those things to him, not me.

MARIANE: I couldn't.

DORINE: Why not?

MARIANE: He's my father. I'm not brave enough to defy him, Dorine.

DORINE: I see. You don't love Valère then?

MARIANE: Of course I do. You know I do.

DORINE: Well then? What are you going to do about Tartuffe? Have you got a plan?

MARIANE: (*After a little pause*) Yes.

DORINE: What?

MARIANE: I shall kill myself.

DORINE: (*Claps her hands*) How clever! I'd never have thought of that! And it would solve all your other problems as well. Idiot!

MARIANE: Oh, Dorine – have pity –

DORINE: I'm not wasting my pity on a weakling.

MARIANE: But what can I do? Anyway, why should I have to do anything? Valère should do it – if he loves me as I love him.

DORINE: But if your father's gone mad, and fallen in love with a fraud of a bigot, and won't let you marry Valère, what *can* he do about it? Or do you think it's his fault? The only person who can do anything is you, and you know it, and what you have to do is tell your father you won't be ordered into a marriage you don't want, and you know that too. Don't you?

MARIANE: But I've told you – I can't – I don't know my father any more. And he doesn't seem to know me – or want to know me.

DORINE: You don't have to know each other particularly well to say no to him. He'll understand what it means. No. (*Little pause*) No, love, you must. You must find the courage.

MARIANE: (*After a small pause, in a low voice*) And my modesty?

DORINE: Your modesty?

MARIANE: If I – if I defy my father, everyone will know it's because of Valère.

DORINE: Yes. (*Looks at her*) Oh, I see! That's not your modesty, it's your pride. Well, of course, if you're ashamed of having people know you love the man you want to marry – then that settles it, my dear, naturally. And anyway, what's so dreadful about Tartuffe? He's a man of substance and weight, a man not to be trifled with. I wouldn't want to trifle with him, certainly not, and with those fine red ears and magnificent whiskers and those jowls, and those eyes that burn with passion when they look at pork and port and cheese – think of them turned on you!

MARIANE: Oh, God.

DORINE: And those arms around you – those lips pressing against yours – that stomach –

MARIANE: Oh, God!

DORINE: Night after night. And what a wedding it'll be! You and Tartuffe kneeling together, perhaps you can persuade him to say the prayers himself, *and* deliver the sermon, and then turning to face the congregation – how they'll admire your modesty and your pride then – as you walk arm in arm down the aisle – oh, I shouldn't think Valère will dare to show his face, presumptuous young popinjay for thinking he meant anything to you at all – and then your wedding night, the lips – the whiskers, the jowls. The eyes. The stomach – your first taste of your husband, your lord, your master. For night after night. For year on year –

MARIANE: You're killing me, Dorine!

DORINE: Your servant, mademoiselle.

MARIANE: Please – Dorine, please help me!

DORINE: To do what? It's all arranged. You're to be – Tartuffed. And Tartuffed *and* Tartuffed. Night after night. Year on year.

MARIANE: I shan't have to kill myself. I'll die anyway. (*Pause*) Oh, Dorine – (*Throws herself into* DORINE's *arms*.)

DORINE: (*Stroking her hair*) There, there, child.
There, there – we'll find a way. We'll find a way – ah, Valère.
(*Curtsies*) Your servant, sir.

VALÈRE: (*As he enters*) I've just heard – I've just heard the most
amusing piece of news. From one of your footmen. Who got
it from Tartuffe's servant. Who, I suppose, got it from
Tartuffe himself. Who, I suppose, got it from you,
mademoiselle.

MARIANE: Indeed? What, monsieur?

VALÈRE: That you're going to marry him. Or is that as much of a
surprise to you as it was to me?

MARIANE: He's only just told me.

VALÈRE: Who? Tartuffe? So that's how one gets one's way in
these matters, eh? One informs the lady she's to be one's
bride –

MARIANE: My father told me –

VALÈRE: Oh, excuse me, your father. Your father has just told
you you're going to marry Tartuffe? Excuse me while I sort it
out, it's really all a little confusing for a chap who thought he
was the fiancé. Has he told my replacement yet? Does he
have any views, I wonder? (*Little pause*) And do you?

MARIANE: I don't know.

VALÈRE: You don't know?

MARIANE: No.

VALÈRE: No?

MARIANE: What do *you* think I should do?

VALÈRE: Why, accept the situation, of course.

MARIANE: Are you being serious?

VALÈRE: Absolutely. Marriage only requires two consenting
parties. And if Tartuffe and your father have consented,
there's nothing left for you to do, or for me to say, is there?
I'm sure they'll both be very happy with their choice. And
you, too, no doubt.

MARIANE: I'm grateful for your advice, sir. And thank you.

VALÈRE: You won't have any trouble following it, then?

MARIANE: No more than you in giving it.

VALÈRE: I gave it to please mademoiselle. Isn't it what you
wanted to hear?

MARIANE: I shall follow it to please monsieur. Isn't it what you wanted to give?

(*There is a pause.*)

DORINE: This is all going swimmingly.

VALÈRE: So this is your idea of love, is it?

MARIANE: And is this yours? Besides, what has love got to do with it? You didn't mention it when you gave me your advice. Which was that I should accept the husband that's been selected for me. I intend to follow that advice.

VALÈRE: I'm flattered. You never really loved me.

MARIANE: (*Hesitates, then tremulously*) If it pleases you to think so.

VALÈRE: Yes, yes, if it pleases me! Hah! Well, mademoiselle, shall I race you to the altar? A lady I know might be quite pleased to sprint up the aisle with me.

MARIANE: I'm sure she will. After all, the love *you* can command –

VALÈRE: Let's just say she won't mind consoling me for what I've lost.

MARIANE: Which is nothing much, if you can find consolation so easily.

VALÈRE: I have a right to it, I think. A man has his pride. It would be something of a weakness to go on loving where there's no hope, wouldn't it?

MARIANE: How noble!

VALÈRE: Well, what would you have me do? Stand nobly by while you throw yourself into Tartuffe's arms, and then mope about to the end of my days? Refusing to look at any other woman because of my undying passion, my unquenchable love – hah – yes, I can see that might suit you. It doesn't suit me.

MARIANE: Then, monsieur, do, by all means, what does suit you. I wish you both every happiness. (*Curtsies*)

VALÈRE: Thank you. (*Bows*) I'll take my leave –

MARIANE: Yes, you'd better. With a marriage to arrange.

VALÈRE: (*Bows*) And yours already arranged.

(MARIANE *curtsies.* VALÈRE *bows, turns to go, comes back.*)
You've driven me to this. Please remember.

MARIANE: I shall.

VALÈRE: I'm merely following your example.

MARIANE: I'm flattered.

VALÈRE: And doing your bidding.

MARIANE: I'm grateful.

VALÈRE: So, mademoiselle, so. (*Hesitates*) We say goodbye.

MARIANE: Indeed.

VALÈRE: For ever.

MARIANE: For ever.

VALÈRE: (*Goes to the door, returns*) Mademoiselle?

MARIANE: Monsieur?

VALÈRE: You called, mademoiselle?

MARIANE: You dream, monsieur.

> (*They stand looking at each other.* VALÈRE *turns to go.*)

DORINE: (*Claps*) Thank you, thank you, most enjoyable, most –
but you can stop now. Monsieur Valère (*Taking hold of his
arm*) –

VALÈRE: (*Resisting*) What do you want, Dorine?

DORINE: Come here.

VALÈRE: No – no – there's something I promised mademoiselle
there I'd do.

MARIANE: And he's in a hurry to do it. So let him go, Dorine.
(*Turns to go.*)

DORINE: No, you don't – (*Running after her, catching her arm.*)

MARIANE: What do you want, Dorine?

DORINE: Come here. And you (*Grabbing hold of* VALÈRE) – and
you (*Grabbing hold of* MARIANE) –

MARIANE: What do you want? You saw how he treated me.

VALÈRE: You heard what she said to me.

DORINE: Yes, yes, I saw, I heard, idiots, both of you. She wants
to be yours, I can vouch for it. He loves only you, I swear on
my life.

MARIANE: Then why did he tell me to marry Tartuffe?

VALÈRE: Why did she ask me whether she should?

DORINE: Yes, yes, now give me your hands. (*To* MARIANE)
Yours. Please.

MARIANE: (*Gives it*) What for?

DORINE: (*To* VALÈRE) And now yours.

VALÈRE: Why?

> (DORINE *puts their hands together. They clasp hands, as if unwillingly. There is a pause.* VALÈRE *looks at* MARIANE. MARIANE *looks down.*)

Not so much as a look!

> (MARIANE, *after a slight pause, looks at him.* VALÈRE *smiles.* MARIANE *smiles.* ELMIRE *enters, stands watching as* MARIANE *curtsies to* VALÈRE, *slowly, smiling at him.* VALÈRE *holds her hand still, bows to* MARIANE. *They rise, stand looking at each other.*)

ELMIRE: Valère.

VALÈRE: Oh – madame, excuse me, I didn't see – (*Performs a hurried bow*) Your servant –

ELMIRE: Monsieur, you must leave this house immediately.

VALÈRE: Madame?

ELMIRE: And not return to it until you can come with honour, as my step-daughter's intended husband. And you, my child, will obey your father and agree to accept Tartuffe.

MARIANE: But, Mama —

ELMIRE: Meanwhile we'll find reasons for putting the wedding off.

DORINE: Yes – yes, madame is right, it's the only way. You can be ill sometimes, and superstitious sometimes. Bashful brides are always superstitious – you can say you broke a mirror or dreamt of muddy water or saw a corpse when you were out walking –

ELMIRE: Sooner or later my husband – your father – will recover from his – his indisposition, I know he will. Just as we all know that he is a good man, and wouldn't willingly allow harm to any of us. But you must go now –

DORINE: No – not together! Don't you understand what madame's just said – you go that way and you that –

VALÈRE: (*Goes to the door, turns to* ELMIRE) Thank you, madame. (*Bows, then looks at* MARIANE) But my best hope is (*To* MARIANE) – you, mademoiselle.

MARIANE: I promise I shall belong to no man but Valère, monsieur.

> (*They look at each other.*)

DORINE: Go!

(MARIANE *and* VALÈRE *exit*.)

And how is the master now, madame?

ELMIRE: In despair. He came looking for his Tartuffe, and found only his wife. His consolation was to tell me of the marriage he had arranged. It seemed to bring him closer to Tartuffe, to imagine him in his daughter's arms. Then he went looking for him again – he thinks he might be at church, at prayer.

DORINE: Has he tried the kitchens? Or the wine cellar?

ELMIRE: I want to speak to him.

DORINE: To Tartuffe?

ELMIRE: Before my husband finds him, if possible. To dissuade him from going through with this marriage.

DORINE: Well, if anyone can, it's you, madame. I'm sure he dotes on you –

DAMIS: (*Enters*) May – may lightning strike me dead! Here, on this very spot! (*Points to the spot*) May I be for ever branded a blackguard, villain, liar, coward! If I let anything – anyone – man or devil – get between me and that – have you heard the news, madame? That I'm to acquire a brother-in-law?

ELMIRE: Yes.

DAMIS: And who it's to be, madame, who it's to be!

ELMIRE: The same man that I'll be acquiring as a son-in-law, no doubt.

DAMIS: And so goodbye to Valère. And to Valère's sister. And to the family honour. Father gave his word to Valère, how *can* he?

ELMIRE: Damis, we must be calm –

DAMIS: Calm! Calm, madame – I heard it from Laurent. The last time he was turning away our friends. Now he's turning away our fiancés.

(*There has been a sound of wailing, off.*)

DORINE: (*Goes to the door, looks out*) Madame, he's here! Tartuffe!

DAMIS: Is he? Is he, by God! Good!

ELMIRE: Now, Damis, listen to me. I'm going to try and talk to him. To see if I can dissuade him from the marriage. Do you see? So please – for everybody's sake – your own as well – (DAMIS *hesitates*.)

TARTUFFE: (*Off*) Laurent – put away my hair shirt and lock up my scourge. Later we distribute alms to the poor wretches in prison. Pray to heaven for guidance. His will be done! (DAMIS *hesitates*.)

ELMIRE: We must be alone.

DAMIS: Very well. (*Turns to go out*.)

(ELMIRE *turns towards the table, nods to* DORINE.)

DORINE: Monsieur Tartuffe – monsieur –

(DAMIS, *having pretended to leave, slips into one of the side rooms*.)

TARTUFFE: (*Enters. Doesn't see* ELMIRE, *who is arranging herself at the table, as* DORINE *is blocking his view*) Yes, my girl. Is your master looking for me? He returned while I was at my devotions, I believe.

DORINE: Yes, sir, but –

TARTUFFE: Oh, but mine eyes – mine eyes receive offence – oh, quick, take this. (*Hands her a handkerchief*) For the love of heaven, use it!

DORINE: Yes, sir. What on?

TARTUFFE: Your bosoms, child. The sight of them sears mine soul. They give rise to evil thoughts.

DORINE: Really? Well, you must be easily tempted then, if a little patch of skin does that to you. The sight of you naked from top to toe wouldn't stir me up –

TARTUFFE: Enough, child! Enough of this – this shameful chatter. Now where is your master?

DORINE: I don't know, sir. It's Madame Elmire who wants a word – (*Stepping aside*.)

(TARTUFFE *sees* ELMIRE. *There is a pause*.)

TARTUFFE: (*Steps forward*) May a supremely bountiful heaven continue to smile upon you, madame, and bless all the days of your life with peace and joy is the desire of this its most humble servant, and yours.

ELMIRE: How kind of you, monsieur. And pious. (*Glances at* DORINE. DORINE *exits*.) But let us sit down. And make ourselves comfortable.

TARTUFFE: And have you quite recovered from your little illness?

ELMIRE: Oh, yes. Yes, the fever's quite gone. Thank you.

TARTUFFE: Can heaven have answered my prayers then? No, no – a vainglorious thought, madame. But every cry I've cried up to our Lord – and I've cried up – but again vainglorious, vainglorious to count, vainglorious to say, madame – but every cry I've cried up has been for your recovery, madame. Your recovery. And if the Lord had demanded it, I'd have sacrificed my own health for yours, madame, my own life. Like Abraham and – and David, madame.

ELMIRE: Isaac, surely, monsieur.

TARTUFFE: Yes, Isaac, too, madame, and Abraham and Esau and Rebab and Mlictan and Rebecca and (*Gestures*) – all of them, madame.

ELMIRE: Christian charity can go no further, monsieur.

TARTUFFE: Your servant, madame. Before God.

ELMIRE: And yet here we both sit, in the best of health, Monsieur Tartuffe. No sacrifices required. (*Laughs charmingly.*)

TARTUFFE: It is true that you look – you look – more than well, madame. Thanks be to – (*Lifts his eyes.*)

ELMIRE: Monsieur. (*Little pause*) I'm so glad we find ourselves alone.

TARTUFFE: For once, madame. For the first time since I came into this house. In spite of my most fervent – now at last answered me. (*Lifts his eyes.*)

ELMIRE: We can speak confidentially with each other. You will be frank with me, won't you, Monsieur Tartuffe?

TARTUFFE: Bare, madame, bare to the bottom, the very bottom, of my soul.

(ELMIRE *nods, smiles thanks.*)

I trust you understand why – during your husband's absence – I felt it necessary to put a stop to – to certain things. Your visitors, for example. It was from my concern for your religious – and moral – well-being. I wanted to – to set your soul in a cage, madame, and have it sing to God – and he would put his finger out, madame, and touch and stroke his sweet child, to make her sing so pure – so pure and clear – (*Putting his fingers out, taking hers.*)

ELMIRE: Oh! (*Smiles*) You squeeze rather – rather roughly, sir.

TARTUFFE: It is the thought of you in your (*Lifts his eyes to heaven*) – but I would never hurt you, madame. Never! How could I, when I long, so long to – do you (*Puts his hand on her knee*) – all manner of good – madame?

ELMIRE: What are you doing?

TARTUFFE: This dress, madame, made from what material – so soft – so delicate –

ELMIRE: Please. I'm – I'm rather ticklish, monsieur. (*Pushes back her chair.*)

TARTUFFE: Ticklish, ah, ticklish. (*Pushes his chair forward*) But this lace – exquisite – exquisite (*Fingering the lace at her throat*) – example of modern craftsmanship – how snugly it rests against your warm –

ELMIRE: (*Gets up*) Monsieur Tartuffe, monsieur – may I come to the point, monsieur. Can it be true that my husband is arranging a marriage between you and his daughter?

TARTUFFE: Well, madame, yes, I believe he has some such scheme, but, of course, as far as I'm concerned – (*Getting up, gesturing.*)

ELMIRE: Yes, monsieur?

TARTUFFE: My desires – my heart – my bliss – madame, lie somewhere else. I think you know where, madame.

ELMIRE: Yes, of course I do. In heaven. Your concern is for things of the spirit, not of the flesh.

TARTUFFE: Ah, madame, I am a man, with the feelings of a man. Our Lord would not have me otherwise. He who made heaven made perfections here on earth, too, through which we see his goodness shine. You are one of those, madame. Of his perfect works the most perfect. On your face he has lavished a – a beauty which dazzles mine eyes and uplifts mine soul, yea! How can I gaze on you without adoring him who made you, without mine heart contracting in love for his own divine features expressed in yours. At first I was afraid – yes, I, Tartuffe, madame, was afraid – that my growing devotion to you was a trick of the Devil. I resolved to flee from you before I was led into temptation and from temptation to destruction through and in you, but at last, madame, almost too late, ah, my most beautiful creature, I realized that I was being directed to your heart by his will, to which it is my most sacred duty to succumb. In all modesty, in humility, in the love of God – his will be done! – I offer myself to you, madame. On your reply my happiness in this world, yes, my salvation in the next, depend! In these hands (*Taking them*) – those eyes, those lips – my life and immortal soul!

ELMIRE: (*Turning away*) Should you not be more cautious, monsieur?

TARTUFFE: With what, madame? As you already have my life and soul? (*Little pause*) You'll be safe with me, madame, I'll guard your honour and your good name. I'm not like these young bucks who strut about boasting of their successes – no, no, with me, madame, you shall have love without scandal, pleasure without fear.

ELMIRE: But if I should tell my husband what you've – offered me, monsieur.

TARTUFFE: The fault is his. For taking to wife my – my little temptress! (*Kneels to* ELMIRE) Stoop down, stoop down to your unworthy slave – and with what obedience, what devotion he will live under your spell. Ah, madame – madame –

ELMIRE: You are lucky in your temptress, monsieur.

TARTUFFE: (*Lets out a cry of pleasure, looks up*) Madame!

ELMIRE: I shall not repeat a word of what you've said to me. But there is a price for my discretion. You must not only renounce any intention of marrying my step-daughter. You must also do everything in your power to influence my husband to honour his promise to Valère. On those terms I shall keep secret –

DAMIS: (*Erupts from the small room*) No, madame, no! You cannot make such a bargain! This must be made public. I overheard it all – yes, monsieur, every word – as if God himself had directed me – the will of heaven, monsieur – is there! (*Points.*) To show me how to destroy a hypocrite, a scoundrel and a traitor! Hah, you're finished, Tartuffe, finished. And out of your own mouth! Revenge is ours, madame!

ELMIRE: No, Damis, leave things as they are. I implore you.

Monsieur Tartuffe and I have reached an understanding, have
we not, monsieur? He promises to promote Mariane's
marriage to Valère, do you not, monsieur? And as I have no
inclination to be involved in a scandal – Damis, I do assure you
that we women become quite used to this sort of thing. It's
always much better not to make a fuss. Unless it's necessary,
of course. Which in this case it isn't. Is it, monsieur?

DAMIS: I'm sorry, madame. This pest has already caused too much
misery in our house. Now we have the chance to be rid of him
– it's not only a pleasure – it's a duty – to expose him! (*Turning
to* TARTUFFE.) Well, your holiness, are you going to stay
while I do it – or skulk off like the wretched cur you are? Ah!

ORGON: (*Off*) You say he's here – where – where?

DAMIS: Ah!

ELMIRE: Damis, I beg you, please – you'll regret it –

ORGON: (*Enters*) At last, at last, but where have you been, I've
looked everywhere for you – are you all right? You look –
what's the matter?

DAMIS: All, right! Hah! Father, I'll tell you all you need to know
about the condition of your Tartuffe. In fact he's just about to
leave our premises, but before he goes you might want a few
words with him, Father, on the subject of his attempt to
dishonour your wife! Yes, father, *that*'s how Monsieur
Tartuffe has seen fit to repay your kindness! I need hardly say
that Madame was a most unwilling victim of his – his – and
sweet-natured as she is, not only endured it, for my sake, and
Mariane's sake, but doesn't even want me to upset you by
revealing what I – happened to witness. But I know, Father,
that I'd be doing *you* a great wrong if I failed to speak out. I'm
sorry, madame, I have no choice. It's a matter of your honour,
as well. Tell him what happened, madame.

ELMIRE: My honour has never depended on describing the attacks
that have been made on it. But on defending it myself, with
dignity and discretion. (*To* ORGON) There was no need for you
to be distressed, sir. (*To* DAMIS) I wish you'd let yourself be
guided by me. (*To* ORGON) My – apologies, sir. (*She exits.*)

DAMIS: Well, Father, what should we do with him?

ORGON: (*Throughout has been staring at* TARTUFFE) Tartuffe – it's not true, is it? That you would – you would – (*Shakes his head*) Tartuffe? No.

TARTUFFE: Yes, brother, true, all true. (*Pause*) Look, brother, upon this wicked, miserable and guilty sinner, the saddest wretch ever to have crawled across the face of the earth. The soul of pollution, a mass of corruption, called at last to account by his God! His will be done! Oh, brother, in your righteousness – in your righteousness – drive this unclean beast from your door. I am yours! Yours – for punishment!

DAMIS: (*Laughs, applauds*) What a performance!

ORGON: (*Turning on him*) That my son – my own son!

DAMIS: What! But – but you don't believe – you can't believe this – this posturing hypocrite –

ORGON: Quiet!

TARTUFFE: No, no, brother, let him speak! Better, far better to believe him, who is your son, brother, than put your faith in me, brother . . . What am I, to have earned your faith? No, no – look first upon this, your son, whom thou lovest – and then – then look upon me and into me – and find in me what he says – your son says – is to be found, brother. Do you not see me as I am? Thief! Murderer! (*On his knees, moving from* ORGON *to* DAMIS) I bend my head! I submit unto mine enemy! (*Bends his head*) His will be done!

(DAMIS *stares down at him, lifts his fist to strike him.*)

ORGON: Noooo!

(DAMIS *lowers his fist. There is a pause.*)

DAMIS: But, Father – don't you see, can't you see, the effrontery – the sheer effrontery – (*Rallying*) Father, this creature –

ORGON: (*Roaring it out*) Hold your tongue, viper! (*Goes to* TARTUFFE) Oh, rise, brother, I beseech thee. (*Raising him up*) Oh, infamous, infamous!

DAMIS: But he's – it all –

ORGON: Silence!

(DAMIS *makes to speak.*)

ORGON: One word more, one word more – and I tear you limb from limb. With my own hands!

TARTUFFE: No, no, me! Tear *me* limb from limb, brother, with your own bare hands – but not your son, your only son – not

a scratch on your only son for my sake – my life rather –
(*Goes down on his knees again*) Forgive, forgive him, I
implore! (*Weeping.*)

ORGON: (*To* DAMIS) See – see what you have done? Are you
satisfied? (*Little pause*) Art thou satisfied? (*In a bellow,
moving threateningly towards him.*)

DAMIS: I – I – (*Stops himself as* ORGON *comes closer.*)
(ORGON *and* DAMIS *are eyeball to eyeball. There is a pause.*)
Father.

ORGON: I know you now. All of you. My wife. My children. My
household. Know you for what you are. Jealous. Fearful.
Treacherous. Oh, wicked, wicked, wicked! But understand
– understand – my love for this – this man is stronger than
the lies and hatred; the more you struggle to harm him, the
more I shall crush you down with the full force of his
goodness.

TARTUFFE: (*As if in prayer*) His will be done.

ORGON: He enters into my family as my son. My *chosen* son.

DAMIS: You force Mariane to marry him?

ORGON: Tonight, tonight, this very night I – we – God completes
your humbling. Before heaven. I challenge you. All of you!
Who is the master? Whose will do you obey?

TARTUFFE: (*As before*) His will be done!
(*Pause.*)

ORGON: At his feet. (*Goes to* TARTUFFE, *raises him up*) At his feet!
Beg for mercy!

DAMIS: Beg for mercy! From that – that swindler! Hah!

ORGON: Do it!
(DAMIS, *after a pause, shakes his head.*)

DAMIS: (*Quietly*) But I am your son.

ORGON: A stick! A stick! I'll kill – I'll kill – (*Makes to throw
himself on* DAMIS.)

TARTUFFE: (*Holds him back*) Brother! Brother – for the love of
God! And for me, brother!

ORGON: (*Stops struggling*) Very well, very well, very well. (*Pause*)
Very well. But leave this house now, leave my house now,
never set foot in this house again. I disinherit, I curse, I – I –
this man replaces you. Your inheritance becomes his.

(DAMIS *looks at* ORGON *in horror, turns, runs off. There is a pause.* ORGON *stands in his rage. Then blinks, and slowly, as if in bewilderment turns, looks about him. Sees* TARTUFFE. *There is a pause.*)

ORGON: Tartuffe – Tartuffe – my Tartuffe. (*Goes to him.*)

(TARTUFFE *opens his arms.* TARTUFFE *enfolds* ORGON *in his arms.* ORGON *lets out a wail.* TARTUFFE *strokes* ORGON'S *head.* ORGON *sinks to his knees, clutching at* TARTUFFE. *On this tableau: curtain.*)

ACT TWO

ORGON *and* TARTUFFE *are kneeling in prayer, opposite each other, and very close.* TARTUFFE, *after a moment, raises his head, looks at* ORGON, *smiles.* ORGON *seems to go on praying. Suddenly lets out a cry.*

TARTUFFE: What is it? (*Goes to* ORGON *tenderly.*)

ORGON: (*Pathetically*) I – I – oh, it's you, thank God, I – for a moment – thought I was alone. Quite alone.

TARTUFFE: How can you be alone? I am here. God is in my thoughts.

ORGON: Thank you, thank you.

TARTUFFE: But, brother, have you the strength to be alone with God, knowing that you are in my thoughts?

ORGON: What (*Looking at* TARTUFFE *fearfully.*)

TARTUFFE: Brother?

ORGON: What do you mean, brother?

TARTUFFE: I leave you, brother.

    (ORGON *cries out.*)

    Yes, brother, yes, I must. I see it now. Whether with God's grace I know not, though I've just sought his guidance, but from my crying out, 'Oh, Lord! My Lord!' I received no answering, 'Son, my son!' Sometimes his silence is our greatest test. And I lack strength.

ORGON: You – no, no. Impossible!

TARTUFFE: Oh, not in my love of him, but through my love – for you. There. I have confessed to a true sin. My love for you! I can no longer endure to suffer the spectacle of your suffering. The suffering I myself – oh, bitter, bitter! – I myself bring on you. The lies, the hatred. The jealousy. You spoke the words yourself, to your own son. All, all caused by me. But if they see you alone with our God they will understand at last that their fear is of him, not me! Their hatred, their jealousy, of him, not me. And then you may find peace. And for that I would – most willingly in spite of my heart – leave you, brother. (*Looks at him*) I remain with you in God. (*Emotionally, turns to leave*)

ORGON: No! Please, Tartuffe. (*Runs after him.*)

TARTUFFE: But while I stay their battle against you will be relentless. And one day, in the despair of their cunning, they will surely find a way to turn your heart against me.

ORGON: Never!

TARTUFFE: Oh, but brother – if you had to choose. Between me and your dearest possession, the treasure of your heart?

ORGON: (*Confused, looks at him*) But – but *you* are – are –

TARTUFFE: I mean your wife. Madame Orgon herself, monsieur.

ORGON: Oh. Well, if she loves me – how can there be a choice? If she loves me. And if you love me, how can you leave? When my life itself is at stake? If you go I – I shall lose my faith. You gave it to me. At a time when I seemed to see nothing but – but my death before me – and then you brought me light and understanding and – and my faith. Don't take it away, Tartuffe –

TARTUFFE: But then what of your wife? Am I to live as a leper in the house of mine dearest brother, demeaning you, my love for you, and our love of God, by slinking about and about the house, afraid to see her, to talk to her, because she may try again to make you turn from me in loathing? Am I? Nay, nay. (*Shakes his head*) I may not. In God's name, I may not.

ORGON: But, Tartuffe – do you think I'd listen to what she says about you? Never! Never! I would not listen to her – to anyone – to listen to them, to believe them, would mean that I'd lost my faith in you, in God, in my life – I *want* you to see her, to speak to her, in private, in public, wherever you wish, whenever you wish – I want the whole world to accuse you, lie about you, try to force me to reject you – because how else can I show my love for you, how else will you know I've made my choice. A leper! You! You, who will be my son-in-law, my brother and my master – and, yes, my sole heir. Everything I own shall be yours, legally made over to you in due form as the world demands – and these – and these – you shall even have these. (*Taking papers out of pockets, stuffs them into Tartuffe's hands.*)

(TARTUFFE *looks at them, looks at* ORGON)

A sacred trust. Given me by my oldest friend, Argaz. He was

against the king, you see, a conspirator in the uprisings –
though I warned him, warned him to be loyal! Now he lives
in fear, he thinks they are coming to arrest him, to search his
house – so he sent for me, Tartuffe, that's why I had to leave
you – to give me these, his most secret papers, some of them
compromising – if they were revealed, he would be ruined,
imprisoned – perhaps executed. *Now* do you see?
(TARTUFFE *stares at him, to conceal that he doesn't.*)
Now you will have everything – everything! My wife's
honour, my son, my daughter, my family, my home and my
dearest friend – his fate is already in your hands – and then
when the world tries to reject you it also rejects me, all I am
and ever was – and still we shall be as one, Tartuffe,
Tartuffe, what do you say?
(TARTUFFE *turns, walks around the room, his head bent, as if in
prayer.* ORGON *watches him, as if in terror.* TARTUFFE *stops,
looks at* ORGON. *Pause.* TARTUFFE *puts the papers into his
shirt.* ORGON *lets out a cry of joy.*)

TARTUFFE: His will be done!

ORGON: Amen, amen! I shall do the rest now – legally – in due
form – this very minute – and then let the world defy us, eh,
Tartuffe? Eh? (*Hurries off.*) My lawyers – my lawyers – fetch
them now – now – instantly – (*Exits.*)
(TARTUFFE *stands for a moment, then spreads his arms out in
exultation.* CLEANTE *enters, stares at* TARTUFFE *in
amazement.* TARTUFFE, *seeing* CLEANTE, *crashes forward on
to the floor, his arms still spread wide. He lies there for a moment,
praying in a low mutter, then rises slowly, still praying, opens his
eyes, looks at* CLEANTE.)

CLEANTE: Excuse me. I didn't mean to disturb you, but –

TARTUFFE: At monsieur's service. You entered on an act of
mortification. Your witnessing it increased my mortification.
Perhaps that was our Lord's intention.

CLEANTE: Ah, well, as a matter of fact I have an intention of my
own. Which is to discuss with you, monsieur, if I may –

TARTUFFE: Monsieur.

CLEANTE: This business of Damis. His father throwing him out
of the house and – and talking of disinheriting him. Well, as

you can imagine, monsieur, it's all over town – everybody's talking about it. And most unfavourably, I regret to say, monsieur, to yourself. My own view, if I may offer it, is that whether people are being fair to you or not is really rather beside the point.

(TARTUFFE *makes a gesture signifying martyrdom.*)

I'm perfectly willing to concede – it's only too likely – that Damis has only himself to blame. You were doubtless the object of one of his characteristic outbursts – in which he quite improperly accused – indeed, is at this moment accusing you, all over town, as I've already mentioned – and not only improperly, but what is worse, imprudently. But what *is* clear, monsieur, is that he believes everything he says. Especially when saying it at the top of his voice. In the manner of the distinguished preacher who used to note in the margins of his sermons, 'Weak argument here, shout like hell,' eh?

(CLEANTE *laughs. Checks his laugh as* TARTUFFE *looks sorrowfully away.*)

Forgive me, monsieur. Unlike the distinguished preacher, I have a tendency to misjudge my audience. I was forgetting the – the rigorousness of your principles.

(TARTUFFE *gestures forgiveness.*)

Our concern is Damis. Whatever the shortcomings of his temper, he is, at heart, a most honourable young man. His slanders – as I take them to be – come from youthful impetuosity, monsieur, rather than from malice. He would never knowingly tell lies. (*Little pause*) You are a man of faith, monsieur. Famously so. Could you not see your way to – forgiving him? After all, for a Christian and an instructor in Christ's teachings to be – however unwittingly – the cause of a loving son being driven out of his home, must give you the greatest of pain. And to be the subject of gossip and scandal can only diminish the strength of your appeal to – your public. Congregation, rather. (*Little pause*) As at the moment you appear to be the only human being – I intend you no slight, monsieur – who has the influence to reconcile my brother-in-law to his son. (*Little pause*) You can't want it to continue as it is, surely? And another thing –

TARTUFFE: (*Raises a hand*) I have forgiven him. (*Slightly intoning.*)

CLEANTE: Really? Well, that's splendid, splendid. So I can take it you'll do your best to persuade his father to re-admit him to home, family, etc.

TARTUFFE: Alas, alas.

CLEANTE: Alas?

TARTUFFE: My forgiveness is for his affront to me. But for God's forgiveness for his affront to God in slandering one of his servants is for God to give.

CLEANTE: I see. You're not at one on the matter, then? You and – (*Gestures.*)

TARTUFFE: Who can say what is in God's heart?

CLEANTE: Certainly not I. Hence my suggestion, that you intercede with his father.

TARTUFFE: But it would seem as if God has chosen not to soften the father's heart. Perhaps (*Crossing himself*) the offence is too grave.

CLEANTE: But if you would undertake to try. Use all your influence – encourage my brother-in-law to share your own condition of forgiveness, which does you so much credit, monsieur. Teach him even how to attain it?

TARTUFFE: (*Distressed*) Ah!

CLEANTE: Monsieur?

TARTUFFE: That I have done, sir. Ceaselessly taught, ceaselessly shared – but my influence over my brother, your brother-in-law, has not met with much approval in certain quarters, I believe? (*Eyeing* CLEANTE.)

CLEANTE: It would meet with approval in the present circumstances, sir. In every quarter. If it led to Damis being restored to his rightful place in the family. (*A little pause*) Monsieur?

TARTUFFE: I fear you mistake, monsieur, the nature of forgiveness. It is not offered instead of punishment, or to soften punishment, especially where punishment has been earned. Forgiveness and punishment flow from different sources, but work together to the same end, sir. Damis is

twice blessed, in being both forgiven *and* punished for his
sin. If he is truly repentant, his soul must cry out – yea, sir,
cry out – for punishment. You and I may forgive him, and
even his father unto his God in heaven may forgive him, yet,
how – how can he forgive himself, monsieur? For his father
to cast him out of his home and his inheritance is for his
father to show him his love and the path to the love of the
father above, who is the father of all fathers, the fount of all
blessings, all forgiveness and all punishment. So let us send
Damis to his salvation – by the pathways of humility.

CLEANTE: And penury?

TARTUFFE: (*Bows his head*) His will be done!

CLEANTE: And what about yourself, sir?

TARTUFFE: My – *self*, sir?

CLEANTE: Yes. Do you lord it over the home that should be his,
the wealth that should be his – in righteousness? That is what
the world will ask, monsieur? Is already asking?

TARTUFFE: Alas, poor world! Poor, poor world! (*Shakes his head*)
And what would it say if he were to return here, sir? It would
say that either he can have committed no offence, or worse –
that the offence was mine! That his lies are truth and my
truth – before heaven! – lies. That I am afraid of him, that he
has a hold on me, that he *forced* me to have his father recall
him. That would be the gossip and scandal then, monsieur,
with good turned into evil, evil good, strength into
weakness, weakness strength – and how would my –
congregation look upon me then, sir?

CLEANTE: You'd prefer it thought you a swindler and thief.

TARTUFFE: His will be done. I accept whatever disguises God in
heaven dresses me in. But whether I seem beggar, thief or
saint, I am his servant. He knows – as I know, as you
yourself know, of course, monsieur – that I accept the gift of
the son's inheritance from the father out of my love for our
God.

CLEANTE: (*After a little pause, nods*) And when you have it, you
will renounce it. By passing it on to the poor and the
imprisoned. As you have with all his other gifts?

TARTUFFE: Ah, monsieur, the distribution of our worldly goods

– what temptations, spiritual as well as temporal! I shall have to guard myself and pray for guidance, monsieur, not to try to buy heaven's blessings by scattering away the things of the earth – which he has delivered unto me. (*Looks at* CLEANTE, *a slight smile on his lips.*)

CLEANTE: And I shall pray to God – for *justice*, sir! And decency! And retribution for vicious – scoundrels, sir!

TARTUFFE: Well, you to your prayers, monsieur. And I to mine. Unless you join me in my little room? (*Makes an ingratiating gesture*) And we worship together?

(CLEANTE *turns away.* TARTUFFE *grins at his back, turns, goes out, mumbling, head bowed.* CLEANTE *whips around, stares after him as he does so, and* TARTUFFE *exits. There is a noise outside the other door.* DORINE *enters, followed by* ELMIRE, *who is half-supporting* MARIANE.)

DORINE: Oh, it's you, sir – thank God – she's in such a state – such a state – we're frightened for her. The master's up there with the solicitors working out the settlement for her marriage to Tartuffe – surely there's something we can do – oh, think of something, monsieur!

ORGON: (*Bursts in, clutching a sheaf of papers. Stops*) Where's Tartuffe?

CLEANTE: To his little room. To pray for guidance in disposing of your –

ORGON: But I wanted him to be here, when I – I – well, anyway, here it is! (*Laughs*) They wanted me to drag it out – but I insisted – a few sentences dashed down – their signatures – and here it is, child! A copy of your happiness, signed and sealed!

(MARIANE *says nothing.*)

Well, child. What do you say?

MARIANE: Nothing, Father.

ORGON: Nothing?

MARIANE: I am your daughter?

ORGON: Ah, and so?

MARIANE: The life I have you gave me.

ORGON: And so?

MARIANE: And is yours to command.

ORGON: (*After a pause*) Is this all?

MARIANE: Yes, Father.

> (*There is another pause.* ORGON *stands almost as if uncertain.*)

DORINE: No, it isn't all, how can it be all? Forbid her to marry the man she loves – force her to marry a man she loathes –

ORGON: Loathe him? Do you loathe him, child?

MARIANE: Yes, Father.

ORGON: Good. Very good. Excellent. Because the more you loathe him, the greater your virtue in surrendering to him, in obedience to me. God's will be –

DORINE: Unnatural! That's what it is –

ORGON: Hold your tongue, unless you want to follow her brother on to the street. I will purge my house. Purge it. (*Little pause*) Does anyone else wish to speak?

CLEANTE: If I may – may hazard a few words, brother –

ORGON: -in-law. Brother-in-law. Not by nature or by choice. An accident of marriage, sir. I hope that what you have to say is proper to our relationship. Otherwise – (*Gestures violently.*)

> (CLEANTE *makes to speak, doesn't.*)

ELMIRE: And me? What is proper to our relationship, monsieur?

ORGON: Your husband, madame? (*Bowing slightly.*)

ELMIRE: Your wife, monsieur, believes that you have been bewitched. By a man who attempted to dishonour her.

ORGON: Well, madame, wives are prone to enjoy certain – dramas. Even so they should make some pretence of being distressed, when they pretend to be assaulted. Out of courtesy to their husbands. Mine was too calm, madame.

ELMIRE: There are also wives, monsieur, who would pretend calm in order to save their husband's distress. Would you have believed yours more if she'd screeched like a demented prude, ravaged or otherwise? Yours thought you knew her, sir.

ORGON: He knows the man she slanders.

ELMIRE: But not the wife he married.

ORGON: I think I know them both, madame.

ELMIRE: Then test them both, monsieur, to be certain.

> (*There is a slight pause.*)

> Test them, monsieur. Your wife and your friend. To find out which is faithful to you.

ORGON: Hah! Ridiculous – what's the point? The affair is over –
I've forgiven you your part in my son's disgrace – you've a
soft heart – too lenient – but then, as a young step-mother,
only to be – be expected – so – so there's nothing more to be
said. Nothing.

ELMIRE: Are you afraid, then, monsieur?

ORGON: Afraid! What of?

ELMIRE: To risk your wife's virtue with your Tartuffe.

ORGON: Hah! Hah, hah!

ELMIRE: Then to risk your Tartuffe's virtue with your wife. You
must be afraid of risking one or the other, must you not,
monsieur? Or you would test us both. Or is it not proper to
our relationship that I be allowed to prove my innocence?

ORGON: Your innocence doesn't matter. As I've already chosen to
forgive you.

ELMIRE: But I choose not to be forgiven. As I have a right,
instead, to your trust and my own good name. You see,
monsieur, your Tartuffe is a liar, a hypocrite and a traitor.

ORGON: Madame –

ELMIRE: Or your wife is a hypocrite, a traitor and a liar. Which is
the truth, monsieur? Put us to the test.

ORGON: (*After a pause*) Hah! Very well. Hah! If it will satisfy you
to – renew your – your – but what sort of test? Eh? Some
trick that you and the rest have worked out – is that it?
Another of your conspiracies – and who'll be your witness
this time, do I call Damis back, hah! Or her? Or her? Or
him? Eh? Who?

ELMIRE: You, monsieur. And only you. Dorine, ask Monsieur
Tartuffe to come down, will you?

ORGON: He won't come if he's at his devotions. Not if I know my
Tartuffe.

ELMIRE: He'll come, monsieur, I stake my honour on it – if (*To*
DORINE) you tell him that his host's wife begs to see him.
(DORINE *exits.*)
(*To* MARIANE, CLEANTE) Now you must leave us, please.
This matter is now between Monsieur Tartuffe, monsieur
my husband, and myself.

CLEANTE: (*Takes* MARIANE) Come, my child. My brother-in-law has a wife, at least. (*Looks at* ELMIRE, *smiles at her, exeunt.*)

ELMIRE: Now, monsieur, if you'd help me with this table –

ORGON: What?

ELMIRE: The table – can we move it a little nearer – and adjust
the cloth – so. Thank you, monsieur.

ORGON: Hah! What nonsense –

ELMIRE: Could you get under it, please, monsieur?

ORGON: Under it! I? Under a table!

ELMIRE: But you must be in the room with us, monsieur, in case
I try to trick you and tell lies again.

(ORGON *looks at her, hesitates, gets under the table.*)

ORGON: As in a farce!

ELMIRE: Exactly, monsieur. A farce. (*Little pause*) Are you
comfortable?

(ORGON *grunts.*)

Good. Now, in order to make Monsieur Tartuffe reveal
himself, I shall have to be – not myself, monsieur. I trust that
nothing I say will shock you. Or if it does, that you wait until
Monsieur Tartuffe has had a chance to respond, before
interrupting us. After all, if he is what you know him to be,
his virtue and his love for you will protect him from me.
Agreed, sir?

ORGON: Oh, agreed – agreed, madame – but if he is what you
know him to be – what will protect you from him? Hah!

ELMIRE: (*After a little pause*) If not my virtue, monsieur, then
perhaps – my love for you.

(*A slight pause.* TARTUFFE *enters, accompanied by* DORINE.)

DORINE: It's all right, madame, I didn't disturb Monsieur
Tartuffe at his prayers, he was with the master's solicitors.

TARTUFFE: Urgent business of your husband's, madame, they
wanted to conclude with important papers to be transferred.
There is no situation, girl, in which the heart cannot speak
peacefully to God.

ELMIRE: You may go, Dorine.

(DORINE *curtsies and withdraws. There is a pause.*)

TARTUFFE: You sent for me, madame, I believe.

ELMIRE: Yes. Oh, yes. You see, monsieur, I confess I – I want
to –

TARTUFFE: Madame?

ELMIRE: Oh, but, please – make sure no one is hiding in any of the rooms, listening – after what happened last time we were alone, monsieur, with Damis going into that dreadful frenzy. I was so frightened for you, monsieur, I couldn't think what to do except to try and calm him down. Of course I realized afterwards I should simply have denied everything, but it never occurred to me my husband would prefer to believe you rather than his own son – I underestimated you, monsieur (*Laughs*) and it doesn't matter now, does it? As long as no one else – are we safe then?

TARTUFFE: (*Who has been looking into the rooms, nods*) Madame?

ELMIRE: Oh, good. Then it's all worked out for the best, hasn't it? Damis giving us away like that means that my poor husband will have to go on believing in our – innocence, doesn't it? As long as we're careful. (*Little pause*) The answer, monsieur, is yes.

TARTUFFE: Yes?

ELMIRE: Surely you haven't forgotten, monsieur, that just before we were – interrupted, you asked me a question?

TARTUFFE: Ah.

ELMIRE: As to whether I returned your – feelings, monsieur? Have you forgotten then? Oh!

TARTUFFE: Excuse me, madame, I remember a conversation between us. But its nature was rather different from the one you appear to be describing. Certainly its conclusion –

ELMIRE: I hesitated, you mean?

TARTUFFE: You were very practical, madame. There was no hesitation.

ELMIRE: No, you're right, monsieur. Not hesitation. Prevarication. We use them equally, without conscience, when we – oh, monsieur, how little you understand a woman's heart! It wasn't my – my hesitation, prevarication, denial you should have listened to, but the shame that forced me to it.

TARTUFFE: The shame?

ELMIRE: That forced me to it. Of my – my – feelings, monsieur. I intend my refusal to be a – a promised, oh, monsieur, now

you are forcing me to speak too freely, your expression, your
silence, cruel, cruel. Is this how you reward me, monsieur,
for listening to you with such eagerness before, thinking of
you ever since – what did I say, monsieur, what did I say to
deserve this, except to beg you to renounce a marriage with
my step-daughter that – would have been a knife in my
heart, monsieur. I was – jealous, monsieur. Is that to be
condemned? I wanted you to be solely mine. Should you
punish me for that? Oh, monsieur – speak – speak. For the
love of God!

TARTUFFE: (*After a pause*) Forgive me, madame, but my heart,
which is entirely yours, nevertheless – (*Hesitates.*)

ELMIRE: Nevertheless! Oh vile nevertheless!

TARTUFFE: – suffers still.

ELMIRE: Suffers? Your heart! Oh monsieur!

TARTUFFE: From the Devil's greatest weapon. From doubt,
madame. It yearns, my heart, for confirmation. You give it
hope, sweet hope. But not fulfilment. What your words have
aroused, only your – charms – can satisfy. So cries out my
heart, madame, yea!

ELMIRE: (*Coughing in response to a slight commotion under the table*)
But, monsieur, you – you proceed so quickly. I've already
gone too far, far further, than I intended – in telling you so
frankly my feelings, and now, already, you would have me,
oh, monsieur, have you no faith?

TARTUFFE: But how can I believe your words, though so
precious to me, unless we put them to the test? Talk of love
is talk, madame. While love itself is – (*Gestures.*)

ELMIRE: Oh, sir, sir – you have touched too much love in me, it
troubles me, throws me into, oh, confusion, such strange
confusion – oh, oh, give me time, I beseech you – time to
breathe, lead me by stages, gentle stages, to submission – do
not take advantage, sir, of a weakness you yourself have –
have caused. Have you no charity?

TARTUFFE: Charity? But it's not I who refuse to give, madame. It
is you. Why, if you love me? What are you afraid of?

ELMIRE: Of God, sir.

TARTUFFE: God?

ELMIRE: Our God in heaven, sir. About whom you've often offered to instruct me.

TARTUFFE: God in heaven will raise no serious objection to our love, madame. I assure you.

ELMIRE: But you make him sound so terrifying! When you talk of our sins and his punishment –

TARTUFFE: There will be no sin between *us*, madame, so how can there be punishment?

ELMIRE: No sin? When we betray my husband, your friend?

TARTUFFE: God looks into our intentions, madame, and, yes, our hearts! Our intentions are pure, our hearts so full of the love that flows from him, the first of all lovers, that he will look down upon us with blessings and praise. Trust me, madame, his will be done!

ELMIRE: (*Hesitantly*) But, monsieur, I don't understand –

TARTUFFE: But why do you think he gave us bodies, child, if not to join ourselves through each other in union with him? His desire is that we become one. In his name we will become one. In denying me you deny him. Oh, child, my child, you have not listened to *my* heart, or his heart, only to the false and easy sounds of entangling theologies and cursed pieties, that would take us away from the heaven given to us in our bodies by him who gives all things – that way lies blasphemy, the Devil himself, who can be reached by wrongful renunciation even more quickly than by – by – (*Gestures, looks up*) If there be sin, I take it on myself, oh Lord! Know thy son, yea! And smile on him and this your daughter in their delight. Thy will be done! (*Looks at* ELMIRE) So come, madame, come – he grows impatient! And so do I.
(ELMIRE, *as further commotions under the table, coughs.*)

TARTUFFE: This cough of yours, try some liquorice for it – here – (*Gives her some.*)

ELMIRE: I think it's too late for liquorice, monsieur. (*Stops coughing.*)

TARTUFFE: Now I've dealt with your fear of God in heaven –

ELMIRE: Yes, but – but (*Shyly*) – we live on earth, sir. In this world of scandal and gossip –

TARTUFFE: You've forgotten what I said to you before! (*Irritably*)

I shall not speak of our affair. Nor will you, will you, madame? And what the world doesn't know, the world can't condemn, can it, madame? No offence in this world without scandal, and as we'll make sure there's no scandal, we'll have committed no offence, madame! (*Little pause, gently*) So come, madame, come! You and I, my desire and yours, our hearts together, God and nature, all insist – that you yield, madame. So come, madame, come (*Almost crooning*) come, madame, come (*Taking her by the hand, raising her up, turning to face her*) – come, madame, come –

(ELMIRE *coughs again.*)

TARTUFFE: (*Starts with irritation and, more sharply*) Come, madame, come!

ELMIRE: Oh – oh – (*Recovering herself*) Well, monsieur, I see – I see I must. Wherever you take me, monsieur. How can I refuse you when you won't be satisfied with less than everything I can give? And yet it's hard – or so it seems – that the words of women mean so little to men who swear love to them, that we must either be distrusted or put to the test. But I am forced to this – this extremity, monsieur, am I not? The fault is not in me, sir, I pray?

TARTUFFE: What fault there is, madame, is mine alone. (*Taking her in his arms*) I've already said, I take it on myself –

ORGON: (*Coming out from under the table*) No, wretch, the fault is mine, you shall not rob me of that! (*To* ELMIRE) My fault, my lady, to have forced you to this – this extremity. (*Turns to* TARTUFFE) Well, my – my passionate swain, my loving shepherd! Marry my daughter and sleep with my wife, and *both* with God's blessing, eh? What a spoiled darling of heaven you are. Oh, traitor, villain, liar, oh! (*Stops, looks at him, and quite simply*) You were my brother, Tartuffe, I loved you.

TARTUFFE: I still am. You still do. This – lady here –

ORGON: Don't, don't, don't – speak!

TARTUFFE: I knew you were there. I was merely attempting to show – yes, before the eyes of the Lord –

ORGON: Don't!

(TARTUFFE *begins to mumble a prayer, eyes closed, head bowed.*) Stop. Stop! (*Almost strikes him*) Never! Never! Never again, never! Leave. Leave now. For your own sake, and without harm. To punish me for my folly – leave now.

TARTUFFE: (*Blandly*) Leave where, monsieur?

ORGON: My house.

TARTUFFE: Most willingly, monsieur. If you had a house for me to leave. But surely even you, monsieur, swollen with hypocrisy at the side of your (*Snarling, to* ELMIRE) – treacherous (*Back to* ORGON) – wife, monsieur, can scarcely order me off my own property, can he, madame? So (*Continuing to* ELMIRE) – you found a sin to commit after all? Well, punishment follows, just as you feared. (*To* ORGON) This will be done? (TARTUFFE *exits*.)

ELMIRE: What does he mean?

(ORGON *stares hopelessly after* TARTUFFE.)

Tell me (*Little pause*) – husband –

ORGON: The deed of gift.

CLEANTE: (*Enters*) Well, he's gone. (*Triumphantly*) So I take it – (*Stops, seeing their expressions*.)

ELMIRE: The deed of gift?

ORGON: The deed of gift. Signed, sealed and everything I – we – had is his.

CLEANTE: Everything?

ORGON: Everything.

CLEANTE: And he proved himself to be –

ORGON: Everything. Everything my – my wife – you said – you all said – ruined, ruined because of – because of – my – my –

CLEANTE: Yes, but still, we must keep calm. Calm above all. Now first, first, we find out whether this deed can be legally rescinded. And if it can't, reflect on consolations. You've rediscovered your wife and your wits in even less time than it took you to lose your home, your fortune and your son. Monsieur Tartuffe's connection with heaven certainly seems to give him the power to speed events along –

ORGON: Oh!

ELMIRE: Brother!

CLEANTE: Yes, I'm sorry. My tendency to misjudge –

ORGON: No, no, you're right – I deserve everything – everything – but, by God! The next time I clap eyes on some penniless vagabond in church I'll – I'll crush him, stamp on him, spit on him –

CLEANTE: In church? Well, don't reform yourself too zealously – you know, if you have a weakness – (*Catches* ELMIRE's *eye*) But the question is, remains, what to do to retrieve your property, and, incidentally, your son and your daughter – and I must say, given that you appear to have – have – I counsel prudence. Let's not go at him directly, we're bound to lose. So, brother, I suggest we – um – we –
(DAMIS *enters, followed by* MARIANE *and* DORINE.)

DAMIS: Is it true, Father, is it? That this – this scoundrel – this shameless and cowardly and – this – ungrateful –

ORGON: Yes.

DAMIS: What?

ORGON: True.

DAMIS: Ah. Ah! Then leave him to me! I'll deal with him, I'll get rid of him, I'll – I'll take him by the throat and I'll – I'll –
(*Gestures.*)

ORGON: (*Wryly*) *My* son.

DAMIS: Father, oh, Father –
(*They embrace.*)

ORGON: And my daughter.
(*They embrace.*)

CLEANTE: Well, you see, you've already recovered wife, son and daughter with no palpable effort –

MME PERNELLE: (*Enters*) What's all this?

ORGON: Mother?

MME PERNELLE: These stories going around.

ORGON: Ah! Well, Mother, I took him in out of (*Hesitates slightly*) – charity, clothed him, fed him, looked after him as if he were my own brother. Gave him my daughter's hand in marriage, threw my son out of the house for his sake, then made over to him everything I possess. His response has been to attempt to appropriate my wife, and when I object, to drive us all on to the streets. Are those the stories going around?

MME PERNELLE: Who?

ORGON: Monsieur Tartuffe, Mother.

DORINE: (*Sotto*) The poor chap.
(ORGON *turns, as if to glare at her, smiles instead*.)

MME PERNELLE: Nonsense!

ORGON: Thank you, Mother.

MME PERNELLE: They say it out of envy.

ORGON: Of whom, Mother?

MME PERNELLE: Of Monsieur Tartuffe, of course.

ORGON: Ah. And what do I say it out of? Although it's true I envy
him my house, my lands –

MME PERNELLE: When you were a child, my child, I told you
again and again that virtue is for ever persecuted in this
world, that though the wicked die, wickedness itself lives on,
flourishing always.

ORGON: And you were right, Mother. I've seen my wife's, my
son's and my daughter's persecution myself. And Monsieur
Tartuffe flourishes.

MME PERNELLE: Monsieur Tartuffe would never do anything
wicked.

ORGON: (*Bellowing*) Mother – Mother –

ELMIRE: (*Calming him with her hand*) Husband, husband.
(ORGON *looks at* ELMIRE, *controls himself*.)

MME PERNELLE: Earthly appearances are deceptive, good seems
like bad, bad like good – Monsieur Tartuffe has his motives.

ORGON: To own my property, marry my daughter, make love to
my wife – those are his motives, Mother! For God's sake –
(ELMIRE *again controls him with a touch*.)

CLEANTE: Can we get back to the main problem? How to deal
with him.

DAMIS: I agree.

CLEANTE: As I was suggesting before. We must compromise.

DAMIS: I disagree! Compromise with that – that – thief and – and
– (*Gestures*) Everybody knows what he's done, how he's
tricked and taken advantage of an (*Looks at his father*) – um,
us. They'll take our side, they're bound to! Aren't they?

CLEANTE: Some. Others will celebrate your disaster. Everybody
will enjoy the ensuing controversy. Nothing either party says
will affect the facts. We are the suppliants now. And as such,
I really do suggest we –

ORGON: Argaz!
(*There is a pause.*)
CLEANTE: What?
ORGON: (*Suddenly frantic*) Oh, my God, oh, my God, what have I
done, Argaz, what have I done to you?
(*Goes to* ELMIRE.)
You see, you see, even though I've got you back – all of you –
God is making a sacrifice, I am still to be an instrument of
destruction, but that it should be Argaz, my Argaz – oh, I
pray, I pray he hasn't thought –
(LOYAL *enters during this, coughs for attention.*)
What? Who is that man, send him away! Dorine –
DORINE: (*Going to* LOYAL) My master is in conference.
LOYAL: Then, mademoiselle, I've no desire to intrude. But
assure your master that my presence will not distress him.
On the contrary, I am here to discharge the responsibility of
telling him (*Pauses*) – something he will want to hear,
mademoiselle.
ORGON: (*Calling*) What?
DORINE: What? Who are you?
LOYAL: The embodiment of Monsieur Tartuffe's most generous
impulses. (*Bowing deeply.*)
DORINE: Master, he comes from Tartuffe. He says you'll want to
talk to him.
CLEANTE: See him! You must! Perhaps he's offering a
reconciliation –
(ORGON *hesitates, looks at* ELMIRE. ELMIRE *smiles, nods
support.*)
ORGON: Monsieur?
LOYAL: (*Sweeping himself forward*) Your servant, sir. And may
heaven strike down those who wish you harm. Furthermore,
may she favour you, sir, and those connected to you (*Bowing
in general direction of others*) – all the days of your life.
ORGON: Thank you. (*Bows slightly.*)
(LOYAL *offers himself for inspection and recognition.*)
(*Confused*) Um – well, please continue. If you have
something –
LOYAL: You don't recognize me, then?

ORGON: No. No, I'm afraid – um –

LOYAL: I was your father's servant, sir. This house has always been most dear to me.

ORGON: Oh, forgive me, monsieur, forgive me. Circumstances at the moment, you understand – and – and what is your name?

LOYAL: Loyal.

ORGON: Loyal. Well that's certainly a fine name, a fine name, eh? (*Looking around optimistically*.)

LOYAL: I'm a native of Normandy, monsieur, as perhaps your father mentioned. Since leaving his service I've risen somewhat in the world. (*Little pause*) I am now a tipstaff.

ORGON: What?

LOYAL: A tipstaff, monsieur. And now here I am, back in the old home of my dead master, to serve a writ on his son. Isn't that a consummate irony, monsieur?

ORGON: Did you hear – did you hear –

LOYAL: Now calm, sir, calm. My writ is merely a summons to have you and yours remove yourselves, from this house, along with such approved personal items to which you may still have claim, without delay or remission, as hereby decreed, to make way for the legally established owner. That's all, sir.

ORGON: To leave this house –

LOYAL: If you would be so kind, monsieur. At the moment you happen to be trespassing on the property of one Monsieur Tartuffe. I have the documents. They are in good order. As one would expect, monsieur, as they are signed by yourself, and witnessed by your own solicitors.

DAMIS: (*Laughs noisily*) Well, I must say, I admire his impudence. (*Advancing*) Good God man –

LOYAL: (*Sharply*) My business is not with you, boy! (*Turns to* ORGON) It is with you, sir. Whom I know to be – in as much as you resemble your father – a reasonable and civil man, with a reverence for the law and a strong sense of justice. This being the case, you'll allow me to discharge my responsibilities by delivering the papers, and clearing the premises. Nothing but the items currently in your pockets to go with you is, of course, understood, sir.

DORINE: And your name is Loyal, is it?

LOYAL: I sympathize with you, I need hardly say. I wouldn't have burdened myself with this melancholy duty if I hadn't feared the alternative might be a colleague with no sentimental attachment to – (*Gestures around.*)

CLEANTE: – the prospect of throwing us on to the streets.

LOYAL: Monsieur, there is no question of throwing you anywhere. I insist that you take your time. Indeed, I will suspend proceedings until tomorrow morning. During the night ten of my men will occupy the premises with the minimum of fuss and scandal, and in return for this concession you will deliver over – a formality, you understand, sir – the keys to all the doors of Monsieur Tartuffe's house before you go to bed. And then, after a good night's sleep – I shall personally see to it that you're not disturbed – you'll clear the house. I shall put my men at your disposal – strong fellows all, I chose them personally, with you in mind. Given so much consideration on my part, monsieur, I am sure you, on yours, will treat me as I deserve – (*Bowing.*)

ORGON: As you deserve! Yes, yes, I'll treat you as you deserve – a stick, a stick – where's my stick –

CLEANTE: Calm down, calm down –

DAMIS: No, no – the stick – get the stick – let me be the one –

DORINE: And me! I'll lay about you –

CLEANTE: Enough, enough of this! Monsieur Loyal, serve your writ, for God's sake, and leave us.

LOYAL: Thank you, monsieur. And please do not be embarrassed when you come to recollect your behaviour, monsieur. I assure you that the ability to endure such demonstrations is a chief qualification in my profession. (*Bows.*) May heaven preserve you all in happiness and health.

ORGON: (*As* LOYAL *exits*) May it confound you and him who sent you!

(*There is a long silence.*)

Ah, well – and what are your views now, Mother, on the deception of earthly appearances and good being bad and bad good? Which is this, Mother?

MME PERNELLE: I don't believe it! I can't believe it! I won't believe it!

CLEANTE: Then you have an advantage over the rest of us, madame.

DORINE: Perhaps madame thinks that Monsieur Tartuffe is concerned for our souls. Riches corrupt. Out of charity he taketh them away from us. Salvation is ours – yes!

ORGON: Yes, thank you, Dorine, enough – enough –
(ELMIRE *goes to him to comfort him. There is a pause.*)

DAMIS: If only – if only – (*Subsides.*)
(*There is a pause.*)

CLEANTE: Well –
(*There is a pause.*)

VALÈRE: (*Enters*) Excuse me, monsieur – madame – (*Looks at* MARIANE) mademoiselle – excuse me – only a matter of the greatest urgency would have brought me here at such a time – and knowing myself to be so unwelcome.

ORGON: In other words, more bad news.

VALÈRE: A close friend, a member of the court, trusted by the king and privy to the affairs of state has just warned me that you are in danger, sir.

ORGON: Yes.

VALÈRE: Your friend – Tartuffe – has just brought charges against you. He has in his possession the private papers of a most compromising kind belonging to –

ORGON: Oh, God, have I betrayed Argaz, then?

VALÈRE: And Tartuffe claims that you assisted in the concealment of these papers. He says he obtained them from you by means of a trick – in the king's name. It would seem that your friend will be arrested, monsieur. And that there is a warrant out against you. Tartuffe himself has undertaken to place you in custody. He is on his way now, with a police officer from the king himself following. They'll be here any minute, monsieur.

ORGON: Thank you.

VALÈRE: My coach is at the door. I've brought a thousand louis. Take them – please, please – (*Forcing them into* ORGON's *hands*) We must leave now, at once.

ORGON: We?

VALÈRE: I can help you –

ORGON: Valère – my son, as I believe you once wished to be. Here (*Takes him by the arm*) is my daughter, Mariane. Here, my child, is Valère. Whatever plans you have, make them between you. Here is your journey –

CLEANTE: Yes, but the carriage for yours is outside. Could you get into it –

ORGON: For what? My journey? But I've made my journey. When I began I had a wife and family, on my way I met Tartuffe and tried to give my wife and family away. Instead I gave away my home, betrayed my dearest friend and will lose my freedom – my journey is complete when I join Argaz in prison. I owe him that. His will be done.

ELMIRE: Husband, please! You must escape. For all of us.

ORGON: (*Looks at her, nods, turns to* VALÈRE) Well –

TARTUFFE: (*Enters with* LAURENT. *To* ORGON, ELMIRE, MARIANE, DAMIS, VALÈRE, CLEANTE, DORINE) Ah, monsieur, madame, mademoiselle, monsieur, monsieur, monsieur, mademoiselle – Take up your position, Laurent. (LAURENT *goes to stand by* ORGON) I bring greetings and blessings from our king, long may he reign over us in wisdom and power – but you appear a little restrained, monsieur, not your usual warm, excitable self – is it perhaps because you've been turned out of your lodgings? Well, don't worry, our royal majesty, who has the interests of all his subjects at heart, has enabled me, through his mercy, to place at your disposal – a small room, in one of his jails. There to rest while waiting his judgement. Ah – (POLICE OFFICER *enters, accompanied by several men.*)

TARTUFFE: Here is one of his officers, to escort you to your new accommodation. Execute your warrant, monsieur. His will be done. His will be done.

POLICE OFFICER: His will be done. This warrant has been too long in the execution. Justice awaits you. Seize him, Laurent. (LAURENT *seizes* TARTUFFE.)

TARTUFFE: Monsieur? (*Struggling*) Sir? Me, sir?

POLICE OFFICER: You, sir.

TARTUFFE: Hah? And why, sir?

POLICE OFFICER: Do you not know me?

TARTUFFE: Know you? An officer sent to do his duty? What more should I know of you?

POLICE OFFICER: That I am the law.

TARTUFFE: Then do the duty of the law.

POLICE OFFICER: The law is doing its duty. (*Steps forward. His cloak falls open*)

(*There is music.* TARTUFFE *stands in the grip of* LAURENT, *staring at the* POLICE OFFICER, *who is, of course, King Louis XIV. All the others kneel.* POLICE OFFICER *extends his hand.* ORGON *kisses it.* TARTUFFE *is forced to his knees. Throws back his head in a grimace, as if in a silent howl. Music continues. Curtain.*)

A Month in the Country

A Month in the Country was first shown at the Warner West End Cinema in November 1987. The cast was as follows:

BIRKIN	Colin Firth
MOON	Kenneth Branagh
MRS KEACH	Natasha Richardson
REVEREND KEACH	Patrick Malahide
DOUTHWAITE	Tony Haygarth
ELLERBECK	Jim Carter
COLONEL HEBRON	Richard Vernon
Director of Photography	Ken MacMillan
Production Designer	Leo Austin
Costumes	Judy Moorcroft
Editor	John Victor Smith
Producer	Kenith Trodd
Director	Pat O'Connor

A Pennies From Heaven Production.

ACT ONE

EXT. NO MAN'S LAND. DAY
A wasteland of mud. Rain. A SOLDIER *lies huddled alone, transmitter by his side, hands clamped around his head. The terrible sounds of war pushing him into the slime. We track slowly in to* BIRKIN.

INT. LONDON BEDROOM. NIGHT
BIRKIN'*s face in the middle of a nightmare. Suddenly he wakes up with a howl, sits up in bed sweating, twitching.*

BIRKIN: V–, Vi, Vinny, Vinny.

INT. TRAIN COMPARTMENT. DAY
BIRKIN *among Southerners. Cut to* BIRKIN'*s face. His cheek begins to twitch uncontrollably. He takes out of his pocket a packet of ten Woodbine, opens it. There are five inside. Takes one out, lights it. His hand is trembling slightly. Sits smoking as twitch subsides. Becomes aware of man in corner, watching him. Puts his hand up over his twitch, sits smoking.*

EXT. LOCAL STATION, NORTH COUNTRY. DAY
Overcast. BIRKIN *on the platform by himself at one end with baggage. A few other people gathered at the other end. Beside him the local train clatters up.*

INT. TRAIN COMPARTMENT. DAY
BIRKIN *sitting in corner. We see from his point of view other faces in the compartment, all of them dour. An old man by the window staring at him with what seems like hostility. Rain sliding down the window beside him.* BIRKIN *takes out a cigarette packet. A half-cigarette left, he takes it out, looks at it, is about to light it when the train stops. He hears over a voice shouting what could be 'Oxgodby'. He peers through the window and just distinguishes the sign* OXGODBY. BIRKIN, *putting the cigarette back in the packet, gets up, struggles out on to the platform with his kitbag, etc., eliciting a few grunts as he treads on toes, seeming almost deliberately.*

EXT. LOCAL STATION PLATFORM. DAY
Rain. BIRKIN *shuts the door, taking a last look at the dour faces as he does so. He is about to turn away. The* OLD MAN *in the compartment raps on the window, opens it.*

OLD MAN: Thoo's ga-ing ti git rare an' soaked reet down ti skin, maister.
> (*Cut to* BIRKIN's *face staring at him uncomprehendingly. Then he turns. He trudges down the platform in the rain. Cut to a girl of twelve, standing watching him from the station-house window.*)

ELLERBECK: (*Stationmaster*) Ticket, please.
> (BIRKIN *fumbles for ticket, gives it to him.*)
> (*Grimly*) Too can borrah me ombrella if that wantst.
> (*It's almost incomprehensible.* BIRKIN *twitches slightly.*)

BIRKIN: What?

ELLERBECK: (*Enunciating carefully*) I said you can borrow my umbrella.

BIRKIN: Th-thank you. But I'm not g-g-g- (*Stops. Then, making an effort*) Going far.

ELLERBECK: A cup of tea then. In station house.
> (ELLERBECK *nods towards station house, and we take in the girl — * KATHY — *still watching from window, now joined by a small boy —* EDGAR.)

BIRKIN: Th-th-th-thank you. But I have an appointment.

ELLERBECK: Aye. (*Nods.*) I know, you've come to the church, haven't you?
> (BIRKIN *looks at him, nods.*)
> (*Out of shot, shouting*) Well, if you don't find what you're looking for there, come see us other lot up at chapel.

BIRKIN: Th – thank you.
> (ELLERBECK *nods at* BIRKIN. BIRKIN *turns, goes on.*)

ELLERBECK: I hope it is there though, mind.

EXT. COUNTRY LANE. DAY
BIRKIN *trudging through the rain. The handle of his Fish-Bass gives way. He consults his map. He has reached the end of the lane, stops, stares.*

EXT. CHURCH. DAY
The church is isolated among fields. Cut to BIRKIN *staring at it. He smiles slightly as if in appreciation. Begins to walk towards it. Then, as if realizing something, he breaks into a run. He reaches the graveyard gate, fumbles loose the loop on it and begins to run around the building. As he does so, a man,* KEACH, *approaches up laneway, carrying an umbrella, stares incredulously towards* BIRKIN. BIRKIN *stares up at gutters and pipes around the church, anxiously. He finally smiles with relief, turns, goes towards the portico.*

INT. CHURCH. DAY
BIRKIN *enters church, stands breathing heavily, stares around him, then moves towards scaffolding.*

EXT. CHURCH. DAY
KEACH *enters portico, folds his umbrella and goes into the church.*

INT. CHURCH. DAY
KEACH: What were you doing?
BIRKIN: Um . . . um?
KEACH: Just now. Outside.
BIRKIN: Oh. Ch-ch-ch-checking the rain g-g-g-gutters. The
　　down pipes.
KEACH: Why?
BIRKIN: Because if they were no g-g-good, there'll be no p-p-p-
　　-point my bothering to come in. It would have been d-d-d-
　　destroyed, you see.
KEACH: Oh. Well, if you had waited to ask me I could have told
　　you that they're all functioning perfectly. You could have
　　saved yourself a run in the rain.
　　(KEACH *closes door behind him. It squeals.*)
　　(*Out of shot*) I'm Keach by the way. (*Little pause.*) Of course.
BIRKIN: Mmmmm?
　　(BIRKIN *turns and sees* KEACH.)
KEACH: The Reverend J. G. Keach. I'm the one who wrote to
　　you. If you're Mr Birkin, that is. I take it you are.
BIRKIN: Oh, yes.
　　(*They shake hands.*)

KEACH: At what time . . . ah . . . did you leave London?

BIRKIN: At Te-te-te- Eleven o'clock.

(KEACH *looks at Birkin's belongings, which he has put on the floor.*)

KEACH: I see that in your – your anxiety to look at the gutters you didn't take time to drop your things off. Where have you decided to stay?

BIRKIN: Well, I th-th-thought – here.

KEACH: Here! (*Looking around*) Where here?

BIRKIN: Wh-what about the belfry?

KEACH: The belfry?

(BIRKIN *nods. His cheek begins to twitch. Obviously trying not to look at* BIRKIN's *twitch.*) Well . . . (*Gives a little laugh.*) I can't say that appeals to me. Having someone live in the belfry. Can't you take lodgings? Or a room at the Shepherd's Arms?

BIRKIN: I'm short of m-m-m- (*Stops.*) A bit short, you see.

KEACH: Oh. Well, I suppose in that case – but I should warn you that Mossop rings the bell for Sunday Service and the rope passes through a hole in the belfry floor.

BIRKIN: Th-th-th-th-th-

(BIRKIN *gets caught in hideous and prolonged stammer.* KEACH's *face during this.* BIRKIN *stops himself. Pause. Silence between them.*)

I don't mind.

KEACH: Very well, then. Now, what period do you suppose it to be?

BIRKIN: P-p-period?

KEACH: The mural. The wall-painting.

BIRKIN: Oh. (*Looking towards the scaffolding, taking it in*) I would g-g-guess about 1430 because of the Black Death. Survivors avoided hell fire by d-d-donating wall-paintings to churches. But I won't be able to say for sure until I've unc-c-covered some of it. The c-c-clothes will give an indication, of course. Whether they're wearing snoods, which were later, or k-k-k-k- (*Stops. Little pause.*) Kirtles.

KEACH: Kirtles. So anyway about 1430. We shan't entertain any extras.

BIRKIN: There won't be any.

KEACH: There *mustn't* be any. You agreed to twenty-five guineas. Twelve pounds ten shillings to be paid halfway and thirteen pounds fifteen shillings when finished and approved by the executors.

BIRKIN: B-b-but not you?

KEACH: Mmmm?

BIRKIN: Not ap-ap-ap- I don't need your approval then?

KEACH: Miss Hebron omitted my name from the form of bequest. An oversight, of course. However, to all intents and purposes, I represent the executors. So you answer to them through me. I shan't mind if you touch it up. Any faint areas or even bits which may have disappeared. You can fill them in. So long as it's appropriate and tones in with the rest.

(BIRKIN's *face is controlled, except for slight twitch.*)

BIRKIN: (*Incredulously*) T-t-touch up?

KEACH: Yes.

BIRKIN: So that it t-t-tones in?

(BIRKIN *stares at* KEACH, *laughs. Checks his laugh.*)

Of course, it isn't absolutely sure there's anything there.

KEACH: Of course there's something there. I may have a certain reservation – which I'm not prepared to discuss – about Miss Hebron but she was no fool. She went up a ladder and scraped a patch until she found something.

(BIRKIN's *face begins to twitch.*)

BIRKIN: (*Even more incredulous*) Sc-sc-sc-scraped? How b-b-big a patch?

KEACH: One head, I believe. Certainly no more than two.

(BIRKIN *looks towards the wall.*)

Then she whitewashed it over again. You might as well know here and now that your employment doesn't have my support. But as the solicitors refuse to pay out her one-thousand-pound bequest to our fabric fund until you've done your job, I have no choice. (*Little pause.*) When the painting's uncovered it will be in full view of the congregation. It will distract from worship.

BIRKIN: After a t-t-t-t-time they won't notice it.

(KEACH *thinks, shakes his head.*)

KEACH: It will distract.

(KEACH *stares at* BIRKIN. BIRKIN *stares back.*)

Well, Mr Birkin, I'll leave you to settle into your quarters. Good night.

(KEACH *goes to the door, opens it. It squeals. He closes it. It squeals.* BIRKIN *smiles to himself. He turns and looks at the scaffolding and above it the blank white wall. He goes to his belongings, picks them up and we follow him up the stairs of the belfry.*)

INT. BELFRY. DUSK

BIRKIN *puts his belongings down, goes to the window. He takes out of his pocket a cigarette packet, extracts a half-cigarette, lights it. We see from his point of view rain still falling. Late evening, countryside dim and grey. Pick out, from his point of view a bell tent, in fact Moon's tent, in the field opposite. Beyond the field, the village. A man –* MOON – *emerges from the tent, stares up at the sky briefly, goes back into tent. Stay on tent, field, etc., then mix into shot of same point of view, night. Lights from the village very sparse. The light goes out in the bell tent.* BIRKIN *pulls his coat across the window, which is glassless. His oil lamp is on. He lies on his bed, smoking, calm.*

BIRKIN: (*Quietly*) Oxgodby.

(BIRKIN *smiles. Fade into* BIRKIN *asleep, restless, turning. He jerks up, lets out a howl. We stay on his face, fear-stricken.*)

INT. BELFRY. MORNING

BIRKIN *tottering to the window in the semi-darkness. He pulls his coat away from the window. Sunlight explodes into the room.* BIRKIN *recoils. Adjusting to the light, he looks out.*

EXT. MEADOW. MORNING

A marvellous morning, landscape, field, bell tent, etc. MOON *smoking a pipe, staring happily up at the sky.* BIRKIN *turns away.*

EXT. TOMBSTONE. MORNING

Mug and water on tombstone. BIRKIN *finishing shaving in the sun. His hand is trembling slightly.*

EXT. VILLAGE STREET. DAY

BIRKIN *walks up the street, passes* DOUTHWAITE *working in his blacksmith's forge. He nods to* BIRKIN, *who nods back. A* MAN *on crutches walks past him.* BIRKIN *enters small Post Office, which is also the local store. In the corner a young man, blind, (obviously from the war) is sitting.*

Several people talking in there fall silent, at the stranger's arrival.

BIRKIN *picks up the* Daily Mail, *takes money from his pocket, looks anxiously at how little he has, decides to buy cigarettes.*

BIRKIN: (*To the woman behind the counter*) A pa-pa-pa-packet of ci-ci-ci-
    (BIRKIN *can't finish the word. He stops, defeated, amid glances. Pays for the newspaper.*)
    Th-th-th-thank you.
    (BIRKIN *leaves.*)

INT. CHURCH. MORNING

BIRKIN *climbing scaffolding, carrying workcase, putting the case down.* BIRKIN *looks at the wall, runs his hand like a blind man across it. He stands for a moment, then opens the case. We see bottles, containing alcoholic solution of hydrochloric acid, distilled water, also brushes, dry colours, a lancet, various clothes.* BIRKIN *extracts a cloth, takes out bottle of hydrochloric acid. Pours liquid on to cloth, and makes to swab at wall. Looks at his hand. It is shaking slightly. Sound of the door squealing open, footsteps.* BIRKIN *turns, sees* MOON *below, pulling squashed hat off head.*

MOON: Good morning, good morning, I'm Charles Moon. I'm the chap in the bell tent in the field opposite. I'd meant to let you settle in but I felt I *had* to come and have a look at you. Well, partly that, but really because I get so stiff in the night my legs force me up, so I stump across most mornings to see if Laetitia's managed to climb out during the night.
    (MOON *looks towards her catafalque. We see Cojugam Optima Amantissima et delectissima.*)
Oh, most loving and delightful wife. I can never make out

if that is grief or relief. (*Laughs*.) Do you mind if I come up
for a moment?
(BIRKIN *hesitates*.)
I won't if you think I'm invading.
BIRKIN: C-come up.
(MOON *climbs the scaffold, stands beside* BIRKIN.)
MOON: You think there's something there?
BIRKIN: I hope so.
MOON: Good. We live by hope. And what do you think you'll
find?
BIRKIN: A Judgement, I expect.
MOON: Ah, yes, a Judgement, that's what it would be, wouldn't
it? Judgements always got the plum spots. So the whole
parish could see the God-awful things that happened to them
if they didn't fork out their tithes or marry the girls they'd
got with child. St Michael weighing souls, Christ in Majesty
refereeing and, down below, the Fire that flameth evermore,
eh? Look, why don't you come over and have a cup of tea
before you start?
(BIRKIN *looks towards the cloth, the wall-painting. Checks his
hand.* MOON *sees this.*)
(*Grinning*) Come on. You've got the whole summer. Spin out
the anticipation another half an hour, why don't you?
(BIRKIN *smiles, nods. Puts down cloth, etc.*)

EXT. MEADOW. DAY
MOON *and* BIRKIN *walking across the meadows, turning towards
the tent.*

MOON: . . . so officially I'm looking for the grave of Miss
Hebron's forebear, one Piers Hebron, born 1373. He was
excommunicated. Buried somewhere outside the graveyard.
Miss Hebron set aside fifty pounds in her will for a chap like
me to find out where, and get him back into consecrated
ground. All I have to do is spend three or four weeks digging
for his bones, and if I don't find them – (MOON *gestures.*)
BIRKIN: You'll have wasted your t-t-t-time.
(MOON *stops, looks at* BIRKIN.)

MOON: Wasted my time? Good God, man, can't you see? (*Sweeps an arm around the meadow*.) I'm not here for Piers's bones, I'm here for a major discovery. My dear chap, we're standing on top of a basilica. A Saxon chapel. Probably goes back to 600. I spotted it the moment I got here. I've already come across a couple of cremation jars. There must be hundreds of them. You'll keep quiet about it, though, won't you? I don't want anyone to tumble to what I'm up to until I've got all I want and written it up.

BIRKIN: So you're be-be-being paid for one job and doing another?

MOON: That's right. Why not, if it's money well spent? And I'll leave a bit of time to prod around for the bones before I leave. I'll find them, don't you worry.

(*They have reached the tent.* MOON *pulls open the flap. It is pitched over a deep pit.* BIRKIN *almost falls into it.* MOON *catches him.*)

You were over there too. (*Pause*.) I can tell. That's where you developed your twitch and tremor and stammer, eh? Well, I developed a great affection for holes.

(MOON *jumps down. As* BIRKIN *follows he sees an open trunk with Moon's clothes and personal effects jumbled inside. Among them* BIRKIN *spots a Military Cross.*)

They make me feel safe, and they keep me insulated.

(*Pulls away a piece of sacking to expose an object.*) Here you are. My latest cremation jar. Come and have a look.

(BIRKIN *gets down as the tent flap opens.* COLONEL *appears,* MOSSOP *slightly behind him at his shoulder.*)

COLONEL: Ah, Moon.

(MOON *turns quickly and stands to conceal the cremation jar, which is nevertheless glimpsed by* MOSSOP.)

MOON: Morning, Colonel. Morning, Mossop. (*Directed at* BIRKIN) Colonel Hebron, Miss Hebron's brother. Mossop looks after the church. This is Mr Birkin who's come to uncover the painting.

COLONEL: Ah. Good. Well done. And what about you, Moon? Making progress? Any sign of old Piers's bones yet?

(MOSSOP *looks around.*)

MOON: Not yet, Colonel.

COLONEL: Found anything out of the ordinary, gold or silver, jugs and jars, etc.?

MOON: Wish I had.

COLONEL: Well, press on. Let me know.

(*Directed at* BIRKIN) Stay as long as you like. Care to umpire for us on Saturdays? Mossop here says he can't do it any more, on account of his legs. Well, would have liked to loiter with you. Another morning perhaps. Must be on my way. Things – (*His face goes blank.*) Things to do. So, Mossop, there's your umpiring taken care of. (*Directed at* BIRKIN) Very civil of you. (*The* COLONEL *shambles off.* MOSSOP *fixes his eyes on the jar suspiciously, just visible behind* MOON.)

MOSSOP: Th'a found some'at then.

MOON: Oh, just the usual artefact, I'm afraid, Mossop.

(MOON *is blocking* MOSSOP's *view.* MOSSOP *tries to peer around him. Turns and plods off to church.* MOON *and* BIRKIN *exchange smiles.*)

INT. CHURCH. DAY

We come in on BIRKIN's *hand. Slight tremor. Cut to* BIRKIN's *face concentrating on steadying his hand. He is on the scaffolding at the apex of the roof. He takes a deep breath. Begins work.* MOSSOP *sweeping around the floor, grimly.* BIRKIN's *face concentrating. Cut to wall: we see the head of Christ gradually emerging. Cut to* BIRKIN's *face staring in concentration and take in his hand, now controlled. Cut back to the head of Christ.* BIRKIN *stops work.*

INT. CHURCH. DAY

Several days later. MOON *and* BIRKIN. *Christ's face is now distinct, sharp beard, drooping moustache, heavily lidded eyes visible through the whitewash. Cut to* BIRKIN, *his face intense, leaning forward. Cut dramatically to face fully present and vivid. Cut to* MOON *staring at it.*

MOON: Yes, well he isn't out of the usual catalogue, is he? He's a wintry hard-liner, your Christ. All justice and no mercy.

(*Cut to* BIRKIN *staring at the Christ.*)

No, I wouldn't fancy being in the dock, if he was the beak.

'And he shal com with wondes rede to deme the quikke and
the ded – '
(*Bell tolls over the image of Christ.*)

INT. BELFRY. DAY
Rope being pulled through the floor, bells very loud. BIRKIN *lying in
bed, eyes open, staring.*

INT. CHURCH. DAY
BIRKIN, *half dressed, looking down on congregation, from whom a
hymn thinly rises.*

KEACH: (*Voice over, from below, just audible*) Let us pray.
    (*The congregation kneels and* BIRKIN'*s eye travels along past*
    KEACH *and up to take in the wall, the image of Christ.*)
BIRKIN: (*Aloud as* KEACH'*s voice drones on*) Look behind you,
    Keach. That's what you're praying to but he doesn't want
    your prayers, he wants some answers. Did you f-f-fede the
    hongry? Did you give d-d-drynke to the thirsty? Did you
    c-c-clothe the naked and nedye, h-h-herbowre the houseless,
    comfort the s-s-seke, visit the prisoners? And what about
    me, eh? Did any of you offer me bed and board?
    (*The congregation rises. Organ sound over. The hymn begins.*)
    Yes, you smug Yorkshire lot. I'll have a word with Him
    about the way you've treated me. He'll g-g-g-et you yet.
    (*Grins.*) And so will I.
    (BIRKIN *looks down, notices* MRS KEACH *in her pew, with hat,
    half profile.* BIRKIN *doesn't see her full face. She doesn't see
    him. Hymn weedily continues.*)

INT. CHURCH. DAY
BIRKIN *on scaffold, working. Sound over of door squealing, shutting,
footsteps.*

KATHY: (*Out of shot*) Hello there, Mr Birkin.
    (BIRKIN *turns, and sees from his point of view* KATHY *and*
    EDGAR.)
BIRKIN: Hello.

(BIRKIN *returns to his work, paying no attention to the two below.* KATHY *is carrying packages of food.* EDGAR, *with great difficulty, a gramophone and records.* EDGAR *puts them down.* KATHY *puts on a record: 'Angels ever bright and fair / Take, O take me to your care'.* BIRKIN *turns and looks down in surprise.*)

KATHY: I'm Kathy Ellerbeck. And this is my brother, Edgar. Our dad's the stationmaster. We've brought you a rabbit pie. Our mam says you'll need the nourishment.

BIRKIN: Thank you.

EDGAR: Our dad says you must be miserable working all day on your own up there, so he said we could play you some records. (*Directed at* KATHY) Didn't he?
(*Cut to* BIRKIN *working as record, at various stages, comes scratching to a halt.*)

KATHY: Can we come up now?

BIRKIN: Sorry. No one's allowed up. That's an ab-ab-absolute rule.

KATHY: What about Mr Moon? Mr Mossop says you let him up.

BIRKIN: Ah, well. We have a re-re-reciprocal agreement. He looks at my work and I look at his.

KATHY: Can we stay down here then?

BIRKIN: As long as you don't mind my t-t-turning my back on you. But why do you want to?

KATHY: My dad said you were an opportunity that mightn't come again in a little spot like this – watching an artist at work.

BIRKIN: Ah, but I'm not an artist. I'm the labourer who cleans up after artists.

EDGAR: We have a picture painted on our chapel wall. Behind the pulpit.

KATHY: Three big arum lilies. It's very beautiful.

BIRKIN: Why?

KATHY: Why what?

BIRKIN: Why is it lilies? Why just lilies? Why not lilies and roses or just roses? Or roses and d-d-daisies?

KATHY: Because underneath it says, 'Consider the lilies' in old-fashioned lettering. It's a text. 'Consider the lilies how they grow. They toil not –' You know.

BIRKIN: I do. It's in support of malingering. I wouldn't have thought you Ch-ch-chapelers would agree with that.

KATHY: (*After a little pause*) Mam wanted one of roses, with 'By cool Siloam's shady rill' under it. But in the end Dad and Mr Douthwaite decided on the lilies. Because of the congregation.

BIRKIN: But why? Why couldn't they look at roses or d-d-daisies?

KATHY: (*Savagely*) Oh, I don't know!

(KATHY *seizes the record, turns it over and winds up the gramophone. She listens for a moment, watching* BIRKIN. *Cut to* BIRKIN, *working, over 'O for the Wings of a Dove'.*)

EXT. CHURCH GRAVEYARD. NOON
Pies, scones, bread, etc. Take in MOON *and* BIRKIN *eating contentedly in the graveyard.*

MOON: From the stationmaster's wife, eh?

BIRKIN: That's right, her children brought it.

(MOON *takes a large bite out of the pie, savouring it.*)

MOON: And what has the Rev J. G. Keach brought you?

BIRKIN: Nothing.

MOON: No money yet?

(BIRKIN *shakes his head.* MOON *takes out his pipe and looks at* BIRKIN.)

(*Shyly*) Oh, by the way, you said the other day something about longing for a Woodbine. Well – (*Takes out of his pocket a packet of Woodbines.*) Look what I dug up this morning.

(MOON *hands the packet to* BIRKIN.)

BIRKIN: (*Taking it*) Thanks.

(*They smoke contentedly as we watch from the point of view of the belfry window.* MOON *gets up and walks towards the field. Cut back to* BIRKIN *still sitting, smoking. We see from his point of view as if hazily, close to sleep,* MOON'S *retreating figure.* BIRKIN *gets up slowly, goes to box tomb, lies down on it, puts his handkerchief over his eyes. Long shot of the graveyard with* BIRKIN *asleep, on tomb.*)

EXT. GRAVEYARD. EARLY AFTERNOON

ALICE KEACH's *face, hazy, slightly out of focus.* BIRKIN, *blinking, staring at her, the handkerchief slipped down.* MRS KEACH *wearing a wide-brimmed straw hat that casts a shadow across her face.*

MRS KEACH: Oh, I'm sorry, did I wake you?

BIRKIN: That depends on wh-wh-whether I'm awake. (*Sits up.*) Have you been here long?

MRS KEACH: Maybe ten minutes. I'm not sure. I'm Alice Keach. I just wanted to find out if you were all right in the bell loft, or if there's anything you needed. It seems so – so inhospitable, we in our beds and you up there on the floorboards. We've got a travelling rug.

BIRKIN: No, I'm all right, thank you. At the end of the day I'm so tired I sleep like the d-d-dead. And d-d-during the day too, sometimes.

(BIRKIN *laughs, gesturing to the box tomb.*)

MRS KEACH: Oh. Well then –

(*Vaguely, she looks around, sees* MOON, *in the meadow, doing an odd dance. She watches puzzled.*)

BIRKIN: He's working off his cramp.

MRS KEACH: Oh.

(MRS KEACH *steps forward.* BIRKIN *sees her face properly for the first time.*)

The painting. When will we be able to see all of it?

BIRKIN: Well, I don't know really. It's a bit like a jigsaw. A face, a shoe, here a bit, there a bit.

MRS KEACH: Oh.

BIRKIN: It comes together very slowly. If it comes together at all. But of course after f-f-f-f-

(MRS KEACH's *face. Cut back to* BIRKIN. *Slight pause.*)

(*Desperately*) F-f-five hundred years I can't be sure what I'll f-f-f-f-

MRS KEACH: But that's the exciting part, isn't it? Not knowing what's around the corner. Like opening a parcel at Christmas. (*Laughs.*) So you must let me see it, Mr Birkin, because Christmas is for everybody. Anyway, I'll haunt you a little until you do.

(MRS KEACH *begins to move away.*)

BIRKIN: Are you by any chance related to the Reverend J. G. K-Keach, the vicar?

MRS KEACH: I'm his wife.

BIRKIN: Oh.

(BIRKIN *smiles and nods.* MRS KEACH *turns, walks across the meadow, passes* MOON, *who lifts his hat.* MRS KEACH *nods, smiles.* BIRKIN *watches.* MOON *comes up to him.*)

MOON: A stunner, isn't she?

BIRKIN: Is she?

MOON: Of course she is. And you know it. Come on, admit you do.

(*Cut to* MRS KEACH *from their point of view walking across meadow.*)

BIRKIN: Oh, I admit it. But per-per-perhaps she wouldn't. Perhaps she doesn't even know it.

MOON: Rubbish! Every woman knows if she's beautiful. And think of Keach catching her. Of all people. You're married too, aren't you?

BIRKIN: Sort of. (*Pause.*) She went off with another chap. Not for the first time. Can't really blame her, I suppose. Her name's Vinny.

MOON: Thought it might be something like that. As for me, never met the right woman. Luckily for her.

(MOON *laughs. Turns to* BIRKIN *but there's something uneasy in his eyes.* MRS KEACH *walks away in the distance.* BIRKIN *looks away from* MOON, *looks after* MRS KEACH.)

INT. CHURCH. DAY

Some days later. Cut to BIRKIN *working on painting, uncovering particularly ugly devil-like face as, over, 'O for the Wings of a Dove' coming to an end. The record whirrs to a stop.*

KATHY: (*Out of shot*) That's all for today, Mr Birkin.

BIRKIN: (*Abstractedly*) Oh, right.

KATHY: (*Out of shot*) Oh Mam and Dad say you've got to come to lunch on Sunday.

BIRKIN: What?

(BIRKIN *turns, looks down. We see* KATHY *and* EDGAR *from his point of view.*)

EDGAR: You're coming to lunch on Sunday.

BIRKIN: Oh, well, thank you.

KATHY: Oh, Mr Douthwaite will be coming too, the blacksmith. He comes most Sundays.

BIRKIN: Right. Well, thank you.

(KATHY *nods. She and* EDGAR *turn to leave.*)

Oh, but what time?

KATHY: Eleven o'clock, of course.

BIRKIN: Eleven o'clock?

KATHY: Yes, at the chapel. It starts at eleven.

(*Cut to* BIRKIN'*s face.*)

EXT./INT. CHAPEL. DAY

We come in on ELLERBECK, *in the pulpit, staring ferociously out.*

ELLERBECK: (*Bellowing*) Brethren and fellow sinners!

(*He slams his fist down on the pulpit; the water decanter leaps.*)

Yea, sinners, I say 'sinners', for are we all not hereunto sinners?

(*Cut to* MRS ELLERBECK *sitting, head lowered,* KATHY *and* EDGAR *staring up at* ELLERBECK.)

Is there one among you here who can't say he isn't a sinner? Is there? If so, I challenge him to come forward and speak.

(*He gazes around. Finally settles his gaze on* BIRKIN. *Cut to* BIRKIN'*s face.*)

INT. ELLERBECK KITCHEN. DAY

Later. We come in on the kitchen table. ELLERBECK, MRS ELLERBECK, DOUTHWAITE, KATHY, EDGAR *and* BIRKIN *standing, heads lowered around it. There is a pause.* DOUTHWAITE *is thinking. He is in fact in the middle of Grace.*

DOUTHWAITE: So what it comes to, Lord, is that we accept with thanks all the provisions you provided for Mr and Mrs Ellerbeck, Kathy, Edgar, Mr Birkin and myself, and would like you to know that as we settle down to our meal we are holding you with love in our hearts because we know, Lord, that if it weren't for you, we wouldn't have a meal and furthermore we wouldn't be here in the first place. (*Thinks again*.) So thank you, Lord.

INT. ELLERBECK KITCHEN. DAY
Later. Close on ELLERBECK's *hands sharpening a knife, a virtuoso performance, steel crashing together, up to* ELLERBECK's *face, back to knife and steel, as he comes to a flourishing conclusion.*

ELLERBECK: My father was a butcher, Mr Birkin.
(*Cut to* BIRKIN *sitting with* MRS ELLERBECK, KATHY *and* EDGAR *as they sit around a huge Sunday joint*.)

INT. ELLERBECK FRONT ROOM. DAY
After lunch. ELLERBECK *asleep in chair.* DOUTHWAITE *asleep in chair.* MRS ELLERBECK *sewing,* BIRKIN *sitting drowsy.* KATHY *at the table, reading.* EDGAR *drawing. Silence, except for sleeping noises from* ELLERBECK. BIRKIN *looks at* ELLERBECK, *then* MRS ELLERBECK, *who smiles at him, then he looks vaguely ahead.* ELLERBECK *wakes up with a start.*

ELLERBECK: Well, it's Barton Terry for me this afternoon, Mother.
MRS ELLERBECK: Does it have to be you? You're tired out. At your age you should be having a lie-down, not doing that long walk in the sun.
KATHY: And the last time you went you came back all faint, didn't he, Mam?
DOUTHWAITE: I'd do it for you, William, except that I promised I'd go and help out at Grimsley Sunday School.
ELLERBECK: No, that's all right, George, I'll manage.
KATHY: Mr Birkin here will go for you, won't you, Mr Birkin?
BIRKIN: (*Blinking*) What? Go where?
KATHY: We'll show you.
MRS ELLERBECK: (*Directed at* MR ELLERBECK.) Well, what do you say?
ELLERBECK: Well, there's no denying that Mr Birkin's legs are younger than mine.
MRS ELLERBECK: You wouldn't mind going, would you, Mr Birkin?

BIRKIN: But to do what?

ELLERBECK: Oh, just a bit of preaching.

BIRKIN: But I've never p-p-preached in my life.

ELLERBECK: (*Comfortably*) Well, you heard me this morning.
Just do that.

KATHY: (*Grinning*) Yes, just do what Dad does.

EDGAR: Yes.

INT. BARTON TERRY CHAPEL. AFTERNOON

We come in on BIRKIN *in the most enormous pulpit and take in from
his point of view* LUCY SYKES *at the organ and a congregation
consisting of several old men, an old lady, a few farm lads and* KATHY
and EDGAR. *Cut back to* BIRKIN.

BIRKIN: Brethren and – and (*feebly*) fellow sinners um – let us –
um – p-p-p-pray.
(*He lowers his head, mutters vaguely, lifts his head, pats the front
of pulpit, looks around.*)
My sermon today derives – derives – (*Little pause.*) Oh, look
here, I only came in place of Mr Ellerbeck because he's – he's
indisposed. I can't preach. (*Little pause. Swallows.*) All I can
talk to you about is what I'm up to in Oxgodby. In the
church there. And – and if you want to leave or nod off that's
all right by me.
(*The congregation stares up at* BIRKIN *with curiosity.*)
You see, I'm cleaning the wall there. The one above the
nave. Because behind the dirt and the layers of paint is a
p-p-picture. So there I am, you see, up there on my s-
scaffolding, cleaning away until I get back to the painting
itself. It's like – like prising open a window in a filthy wall.
Every day or so I open it a square foot or so wider. It's really
all patience, you see, my sort of work. But I don't get any
second chances. That's what makes it so exciting. One dab
too few and some poor chap won't get back from five centuries
ago. One dab too many and I'll have wiped him out for ever.
Oh, that makes me sound rather like God, doesn't it?
(*The congregation stares up at him, expressionlessly. Cut back to*
BIRKIN.)

But really I'm just a servant like every one of us. Except that
I'm the servant of the painter. I hope I'm good enough to
serve him because this painter deserves the best of servants.
(*Little pause.*) Now I'll tell you about my tools. What I
basically use is a lancet – that's for lifting off the limewash.
Then I have alcoholic solution of hydrochloric acid –

EXT. OUTSIDE CHAPEL. AFTERNOON
*We come in on the elderly from the congregation, the old man in front.
Pause on his face. Cut to* BIRKIN's *face, apprehensive, and cut back
to the old man's face. The old man nods acknowledgement, turns
away, the others following him.* BIRKIN *stares after them, then turns
to* KATHY *and* EDGAR *as* LUCY SYKES, *in shot, locks the chapel door.*

KATHY: (*To* EDGAR) They liked it, didn't they?
EDGAR: But our Dad's louder.
    (LUCY SYKES *approaches. Little pause.*)
LUCY: You could come and have your tea.
BIRKIN: Well, I – I came with these two.
LUCY: They can come too.

INT. SYKES PARLOUR. AFTERNOON
MR SYKES, MRS SYKES, LUCY SYKES, KATHY *and* EDGAR *and*
BIRKIN *in the farmhouse parlour. Window open, butterflies visible,
drowsy heat without. Within, they are eating tea. A piano, a
photograph on top of it.*

SYKES: (*After a pause*) You're from London then, Mr Birkin?
BIRKIN: Yes. (*Little pause.*) London. That's right.
MRS SYKES: We've never met a Londoner before.
SYKES: You're our first, Mr Birkin.
BIRKIN: Oh.
    (*Pause.* LUCY *glances at him shyly, smiles.* BIRKIN *smiles
    tentatively back. This is observed by* KATHY.)
SYKES: (*Out of shot*) You were over there, were you, Mr Birkin?
    In France?
    (BIRKIN *nods.*)
MRS SYKES: So was our Perce.

(MRS SYKES *nods towards the photograph of a young man on the piano.* BIRKIN *looks at the photograph. The young man is stocky, smiling.*)

(*Out of shot*) He had it taken on his last leave. His nineteenth birthday.

SYKES: (*Out of shot*) He was a right good lad, Perce. A real worker. Would give anybody a hand. They all liked him.

(BIRKIN'S *face staring at the photograph.* SYKES, MRS SYKES, *staring at him.* LUCY'S *face, very quickly turning slightly away.*)

(*Attempting joviality*) Well, would you like to see the farm, Mr Birkin?

MRS SYKES: Yes. Lucy, why don't you show Mr Birkin around the farm?

LUCY: (*To* KATHY *and* EDGAR) Would you like to see around?

KATHY: We can't. We've got to visit Emily Clough. (*To* BIRKIN) We promised her and we told our Sunday School teacher we'd take her her star card.

BIRKIN: Emily Clough?

KATHY: We said we'd bring you too. She's expecting you. (*To* EDGAR) Isn't she?

EDGAR: Yes.

(*There is an uncertain pause.* BIRKIN *clearly at sea.* KATHY *obviously determined.*)

MRS SYKES: Oh well, perhaps another Sunday.

(LUCY *smiles at* BIRKIN.)

EXT. CLOUGH COTTAGE. AFTERNOON
The cottage door open.

INT. CLOUGH COTTAGE: HALLWAY. AFTERNOON
KATHY *in the hall,* BIRKIN *and* EDGAR *behind her.*

KATHY: Mrs Clough, Mrs Clough, we've come to bring Emily some flowers.

(MRS CLOUGH *appears at the door of the kitchen at the end of hallway.*)

MRS CLOUGH: Go on up. On your way out you can have a jam tart.

(*She looks at* BIRKIN *as he pauses at bottom of stairs. She is grief-stricken and turns away quickly.* BIRKIN *understands.*)

INT. EMILY CLOUGH'S BEDROOM. DAY
Cut to an apple tree, seen through the window, a sense of oppressive heat. Then drift to Edgar's flowers, in a jar beside a bed, to which we drift next, and EMILY'*s face, luminously pale.*

KATHY: (*Out of shot*) I've brought your star card, Emily. Mr Douthwaite stamped it S for sick. S's count the same as stars.
(*Cut to* EMILY)
You only need six more stars for a prize.
EDGAR: Or S's for sick.
EMILY: I've been thinking about my prize. I like *The Forgotten Garden*. Can Mr Douthwaite get me one by the same author? What are you having?
KATHY: *The Coral Island*. And Edgar's having *Children of the New Forest*.
BIRKIN: Isn't that a bit beyond him?
KATHY: He'll grow to like it later. I've heard it's a good story with two girls in it. Mr Birkin's the man living in the church, Emily.
EMILY: I've heard about you. I hope you'll still be there when I'm up, Mr Birkin. I like your straw hat, Kathy. Can I try it on?
(KATHY *takes off the straw hat, hands it to* EMILY. EMILY *puts the hat on, turns to the mirror. She is suddenly racked by a tubercular cough. She presses a handkerchief to her mouth on which spots of blood appear. She recovers and smiles weakly.*) I think it suits me. I like hats. Wearing a hat's part of the fun at Sunday School.
EDGAR: When you come next you can wear it, can't she, Kathy?
(EMILY *looks at* BIRKIN. *Their eyes meet.*)

EXT. CLOUGH COTTAGE. AFTERNOON
BIRKIN *and* KATHY *walking down the road,* EDGAR *to one side, picking flowers.*

KATHY: (*Out of shot*) She knows she's dying, doesn't she?
(*Fade on them receding down the road.*)

INT. ELLERBECK FRONT PARLOUR. LATER
We come in on BIRKIN *sitting, remote. He has his hand covering his
cheek. Very slight tremble in the hand.* ELLERBECK, MRS
ELLERBECK, KATHY *and* EDGAR *with cups of tea.*

MRS ELLERBECK: Are you all right, Mr Birkin? You haven't
touched your tea.
KATHY: (*Smiling slightly unpleasantly*) He had his tea at Lucy
Sykes'. She asked us in.
MRS ELLERBECK: She's a fine strong girl, Lucy Sykes.
ELLERBECK: That's right. Good Christian upbringing too.
MRS ELLERBECK: Time we asked her along to the Sunday School
outing, eh, Father?
ELLERBECK: Aye. I meant to last year –
(BIRKIN, *clearly not taking this in, suddenly gets up,
interrupting, his face twitching slightly.*)
BIRKIN: P-p-please excuse me. I have a g-g-g-g- must get back.
(*He puts his hand to his face.*)
KATHY: (*As* BIRKIN *leaves; out of shot, confidentially*) It's that
Lucy Sykes. He's been funny ever since he saw her.

EXT. VILLAGE. LATER
Cut to BIRKIN *walking through the village. As he does so, he passes
the blind young man sitting on the doorstep.* BIRKIN, *glancing at him,
continues walking, his face set.*

EXT. MOON'S FIELD. EVENING
BIRKIN *walking past Moon's tent towards the church. From the
church suddenly sound of hymn thinly: 'O God our Help in Ages
Past'. Evensong.* BIRKIN *stops. Stares at the church.*

BIRKIN: (*Screaming suddenly*) God? What God? There is no God.
(*Behind him,* MOON *comes out of his tent.* BIRKIN, *as if
suddenly aware, turns. He and* MOON *look at each other.*)

INT. CHURCH. DAY
BIRKIN *at work*. MRS KEACH *arrives in the church*.

BIRKIN: I don't really want 'Angels Bright and Fair' this morning,
    if you don't mind.
MRS KEACH: Well, will you accept my travelling rug?
BIRKIN: I'm sorry. I thought you were someone else.
MRS KEACH: Yes, I know. Kathy Ellerbeck and her gramophone.
    (MRS KEACH *puts the rug down on Laetitia's tomb*.)
    Now you'll have to let me come up. That's our agreement.
    (*Pause*.) May I? (*Starts to climb*.) Mr Moon said he was sure
    you wouldn't let me, that you wanted to keep it all to yourself.
    (MRS KEACH, *her face upturned, seen from* BIRKIN's *point of
    view. He holds out his hand tentatively. She takes it, steps off the
    ladder. Just for a second their eyes meet. She turns to the painting.
    We see her expression change. Cut to painting.* BIRKIN *watches
    her. She is clearly shocked by the Bosch-like images of hell and
    suffering*.)
    Why, it's a sort of – a sort of hell. Horrible.
BIRKIN: Well, probably not so horrible if you believed in it.
MRS KEACH: And do you believe in it, Mr Birkin?
BIRKIN: When I look at it – when I'm working on it I believe in his
    belief. Impossible not to really.
MRS KEACH: But otherwise you don't believe there is a hell?
BIRKIN: Well, I suppose hell means different things to different
    people.
MRS KEACH: What does it mean to you?
BIRKIN: (*Slight smile*.) Hell on earth, I think.
MRS KEACH: (*Thinks; realizes*.) Yes, of course. Although I don't
    understand really, how could I?
BIRKIN: Why should you?
MRS KEACH: I suppose one should try.
BIRKIN: (*Suddenly blurting out*) No, you shouldn't. I'd rather you
    didn't.
    (*There is a pause.* MRS KEACH *makes to say something, says
    instead*:)
MRS KEACH: Were you always in the cleaning business, Mr Birkin?
    (BIRKIN *nods*.)

How did you come by it?

BIRKIN: It's in the f-family. My father travelled in s-s-soap.

(*He looks at her seriously. She looks back, then begins to laugh.* BIRKIN *smiles. She goes to the ladder. Begins to go down it.* BIRKIN *makes to say something, obviously to offer to accompany her, checks himself.*)

MRS KEACH: Thank you.

(BIRKIN *is puzzled.*)

For letting me see.

(*We see* MRS KEACH *walking across the church from* BIRKIN's *point of view. The door squealing as she goes out.*)

EXT. VILLAGE PUB. DAY

Later. Opposite the pub is the chapel. BIRKIN *and* MOON *are sitting on the bench outside the Shepherd's Arms. As they talk,* PEOPLE *are entering the chapel. Among them the* ELLERBECKS, *who don't see* BIRKIN *and* MOON.

MOON: (*With an expression of strain, in the pause of a painful speech*) I half wanted it to happen. There were times when I'd had enough. Well, you know that. I mean – when I was sure my nerve would give way and I'd lie down before I was hit. Or worse. Wouldn't be able to drive myself over the top, ever again. So many had gone. Chaps I cared for. Sometimes it seemed they were the lucky ones. (*Pause.*) The night's the bad time. Well, I expect you've heard me. I still wake up screaming. I can still see . . . still see . . . (*pause*) but I tell myself it'll be better as time passes and it sinks further back. But it's got nowhere to sink to, has it? We'll always be different, won't we, the whole lot of us? (*Little pause.*) All the millions of us that survived. If millions did. Different, I mean, from the generations before us who had no idea that anything like that could ever happen. I don't know if it's worse not having something to show for it. Like a lost limb or two or blindness. I mean, people like you and me, the intact ones. The worse part for me was the last part when I was kept away from the fighting. Went for months without seeing a single corpse. The faces I did see – (*stops*) – but I'm a

little round the bend, you know. Always will be, I expect.
(*Suddenly cheerful*) Still, there's no point in letting it get one
down. One's got a life to lead anyway. (*Grins.*) 'And then he
shal come with wondes rede to deme the quikke and the
dede.'
BIRKIN: But you got the Military Cross, didn't you? I saw it in
your tent.
MOON: Medals!
(*From the chapel the sudden crashing of an out-of-tune organ.
Voices raised in a cheerful hymn.*)
Ah, there go the chapel lot. I wish they'd get themselves a
new organ.
BIRKIN: (*Standing up*) I'll get us another –
(BIRKIN *begins to go into the pub. Puts his hand into his pocket,
takes out a few coins, looks down at them, stops.*) I'm sorry, I
can't.
MOON: Keach still hasn't coughed up, eh? Then you'll just have
to go and get it from him, won't you? Like a good soldier.
Tell him you need it to drink a toast to that lost beauty, his
wife. Tonight's on me. (*Gets up, then turns back.*) Did she get
you to show her the painting? I saw her going into the
church.
BIRKIN: Yes.
MOON: I told her you wouldn't, but I was sure you would.
(BIRKIN *stands, looks towards the chapel, from which comes the
discordant hymn, voices even louder. He suddenly smiles.*)
BIRKIN: That's more like it.

EXT. VICARAGE. DAY
Seen from BIRKIN's *point of view at the edge of the clearing.* BIRKIN
*walks across, knocks on the door. Knocks again. Seen in long shot,
then we come in closer as he spots the bell. Pulls it out. Nothing. He
pulls again, more savagely. From within the house a remote tinkle.*
BIRKIN *pulls again. Tinkle continues.* BIRKIN *turns angrily, and cut
to* MRS KEACH *standing on the drive by the porch, staring at him.*

BIRKIN: I've come to see your hus-hus-husband. But he isn't . . .
(*He gestures.*)

MRS KEACH: Oh, he wouldn't be able to hear you. He's playing.
Right at the end of the house.
(*They go to the house up steps.*)

INT. VICARAGE: CORRIDOR. DAY
A long shot from inside the hallway of MRS KEACH *and* BIRKIN *as*
MRS KEACH *opens the door.*

MRS KEACH: You haven't been here before, have you? We have it
all to ourselves. (*Gives an odd little laugh.*) Of course it's
much too big.
(*They begin to walk down the corridor. Faintly, the sound of a
violin, playing a melancholy air. It gets stronger as they proceed
towards it.*)
Most of the rooms are empty, you see. This one . . .
(*Touches the door as she passes.*) And this one – and this one –
completely empty – this one . . .
(*They approach the room at end of the corridor, from which,
evidently, the violin.* MRS KEACH *stops.*)
It can be quite oppressive. It gives me nightmares
sometimes. Well, the same nightmare really. Of the trees
outside closing in, and only the walls – these walls – to stop
them.

INT. VICARAGE: LIVING ROOM. DAY
At the end of the room, sparsely furnished, KEACH *is playing a fiddle
in front of a music stand. He continues playing, not seeing* BIRKIN,
*his eyes closed, an expression of concentrated rapture on his face. He
plays rather badly. Then he opens eyes, sees them. Stops.*

MRS KEACH: I found Mr Birkin on the doorstep. But you couldn't
hear the bell.
KEACH: No, I suppose not. At least I didn't hear it.
MRS KEACH: We don't have many visitors, you see.
KEACH: Yes, one gets out of the habit of listening for them.
MRS KEACH: And I was just saying to Mr Birkin, such a big
house, isn't it, for just the two of us?
KEACH: Yes, it is, really.

MRS KEACH: And all the rooms – we don't know what to put in them, do we?

(MRS KEACH *gestures around the room.*)

KEACH: No, that's true.

(BIRKIN *looks, nothing on the walls, the windows curtainless. His eyes take in the vacancy, then come to rest on a massive unidentifiable piece of furniture.*)

MRS KEACH: Except for that. At least it's big enough. But we don't know what it is or does. It seems to be part of something else. My husband's father bought it at an auction sale because no one else wanted it. To help fill the room, didn't he?

KEACH: That's right. He did.

(BIRKIN *nods, hesitates.*)

BIRKIN: I just came to sort out the qu-qu-question of my mon-mon-mon-money.

(KEACH *and* MRS KEACH *appear to be staring at him in horror. There is a pause, as the situation is held, then* BIRKIN *turns. At the window, glaring in, a large cat, with a bloody songbird in its mouth. The cat leaps off the window.* BIRKIN *turns back.* KEACH *looks at* BIRKIN *blankly. Then realizes.*)

KEACH: Oh, yes, the money. I suppose you brought the receipt, Mr Birkin.

BIRKIN: The receipt?

KEACH: For the money.

BIRKIN: The mon-money?

KEACH: Yes, I sent Mossop with your first instalment this morning. Didn't he give it to you?

BIRKIN: We must have passed each other. Thank you.

(KEACH *nods. Slight pause.*)

KEACH: Well, perhaps some refreshment.

BIRKIN: No, thank you, I'd better get back to work.

MRS KEACH: Did you come by the wood?

BIRKIN: No. The road.

MRS KEACH: I'll show you the way through the wood.

KEACH: When are you going to show my wife the painting? She's very anxious to see it.

MRS KEACH: Oh, I've already seen it.

KEACH: Have you? I hadn't realized.

INT. VICARAGE: CORRIDOR. DAY
MRS KEACH *and* BIRKIN *walking down the corridor.* BIRKIN
opening the door as, over, sound of KEACH *on his violin.* BIRKIN
glances back and we see from his point of view the door of room open,
KEACH *playing his violin.* BIRKIN *closes the door on this image.*

EXT. VICARAGE: GARDEN. DAY
BIRKIN *and* MRS KEACH *walk along the garden path towards the*
woods.

MRS KEACH: Do you like my roses, Mr Birkin? I spend a lot of
    time on them. Though there isn't really anyone else to look
    at them but me. This one's a Sarah van Fleet. It's a very old
    variety.
    (BIRKIN *looks, makes to pick one, hesitates.*)
BIRKIN: May I?
MRS KEACH: Mind. It has sharp thorns. (*Picks one.*) They keep on
    blooming into autumn. So you'll know when summer's
    ended because I always wear one of the last in my hat.
    (MRS KEACH *hands the rose to* BIRKIN. BIRKIN *takes the rose.*)

EXT. WOODS. DAY
A wood, almost unreal in its loveliness. BIRKIN *and* MRS KEACH
walking through it. Birds flying. BIRKIN *stops.*

BIRKIN: But this is beautiful. A kind of paradise.
MRS KEACH: (*Excited*) Look!
    (BIRKIN *looks. Just visible, a hare bounding.* BIRKIN *smiles.*)
BIRKIN: I think you're b-b-beau . . .
    (*Sudden sound of shot loud and close. The hare leaps and bounds*
    off at great speed. Cut to BIRKIN's *face. It is in spasm. His hand*
    to his face, shaking. The COLONEL *appears with a gun. Greets*
    them cheerfully and walks on. BIRKIN *brings himself under*
    control. Slight pause. BIRKIN *attempts a smile.*) Well, I
    suppose that's what comes of believing in paradise. (*He*
    smiles. MRS KEACH *smiles back. They part.*)

INT. BELFRY. NIGHT
Seemingly the same shot, though the light comes from an oil lamp.
BIRKIN *is sitting on the camp bed, but we come directly in on his hand holding the rose. He puts it between the pages of a book. Closes the book, and presses hard. Take in the cover: Scott-Bradshaw: A* History of Church Architecture. *Continues to press hard, puts book down beside the bed. Turns off the lamp. Holding the book, crosses to the window, looks out.*

EXT. COUNTRYSIDE. NIGHT
Darkness. Lights twinkling in the village and in Moon's tent. BIRKIN *stands at window, gazing out.*

EXT. GRAVEYARD/MOON'S TENT. NIGHT
Moonlight. Later. A sudden cry from Moon's tent.

INT. BELFRY. NIGHT
BIRKIN'S *face, sympathetic.*

EXT. MOON'S TENT. NIGHT
Lights go on in the tent, shot of MOON *in silhouette, sitting bent, clutching his hands. Stay on Moon's tent, fading into shot of him standing in silhouette, putting out lamp. Cut to darkness. Fading into misty dawn. And cut to* BIRKIN'S *face, still at window, looking out.*

INT./EXT. BELFRY/MEADOW. DAY
The landscape is radiant. MOON *emerges from his tent, looks up to belfry. Salutes* BIRKIN *cheerily.* BIRKIN *in long shot seen from* MOON'S *point of view.*

INT. CHURCH. DAY
BIRKIN *on the scaffold. He is cleaning the last stages of the whole image of the falling man. We see him working on a detail, not clear what it is. He steps back and takes in the whole image. His face expresses controlled excitement. Cut to image. A crescent-shaped scar on his brow, bright hair streaming like a torch (a second Simon Magus), plunging headlong down the wall. Two demons with*

delicately furred legs clutching him, one snapping his right wrist while his mate splits him with shears.

BIRKIN: (*Mutters*) I wonder what you did then.
    (*The sound of footsteps below.* BIRKIN *is unaware.*)
MOSSOP: (*Out of shot*) Mr Birkin.
BIRKIN: (*Still engrossed*) Mmmmm?
MOSSOP: (*Out of shot*) Don't forget tha't standing umpire again
    this Sunday, Mr Birkin.
BIRKIN: What?
    (BIRKIN *turns and sees* MOSSOP.)
    Oh, no, I'm afraid I can't, Mossop, I've got an important
    engagement. (*Slightly maliciously*) You'll have to do it, I'm
    afraid.
MOSSOP: I can't neither, Mr Birkin. I'm busy too.
BIRKIN: Then it'll have to be the Colonel.
    (BIRKIN *turns back to the painting and we see again the falling
    man.*)

EXT. CROSSROADS. MORNING
Shot of crossroads, hot. Absolute stillness. BIRKIN *standing at it, his
coat slung over his shoulder.* MOON *stands nearby. Their faces
expectant, turning to look down one road, and then the next, and cut
back to the crossroads. Then, almost inaudible at first, a clip-clop of
horses' hoofs, growing louder and louder, cut back to their faces. Then,
locating where sound is coming from, they look down the road, and
there suddenly appear two flat-wheeled carts.* BIRKIN *and* MOON *are
delighted. The horses glint with farthingales. The horses stop beside
them. They climb into the first cart, which is less full.*

EDGAR: Mr Birkin, Mr Birkin!
    (BIRKIN *pauses, turns.*)
    You're with us.
    (KATHY *nods in agreement.* BIRKIN *moves to the second cart, sits
    between* KATHY *and* EDGAR, *across from the* ELLERBECKS *and
    others. In Moon's cart,* DOUTHWAITE, *his fingers in plaster, the
    blind man from the Post Office and several maimed men and
    LUCY SYKES. MOON sits next to LUCY SYKES. On the bench,*

the adults, the children sitting with their legs over the side of cart.
BIRKIN *squeezes in between the adults on the bench, then takes in*
MOSSOP *sitting beside him, and evidently* MRS MOSSOP *beside*
MOSSOP. MOSSOP *greets him with a nod.*)

BIRKIN: What are you doing with the chapel lot? You're church,
aren't you?

MOSSOP: Nay. Ay've me fee at i'beath camps. The lot of 'em ha'
git ti come at t'finish to let me put 'em ti bed.

EDGAR: (*Out of shot*) There she is, Mr Birkin.
(*Cut to* EDGAR's *face, serious, beside it* KATHY's *grinning not
entirely pleasantly.* EDGAR *pointing to the front cart, and as*
BIRKIN *turns, sees at back of front cart,* LUCY SYKES *among the
maimed men and next to* MOON, *who gestures triumphantly back
at* BIRKIN. LUCY SYKES *from* BIRKIN's *point of view, and then
we see her cart, Birkin's cart, trundling through the countryside,
idyllic.*)

EXT. FIELD BESIDE RIVER. DAY
Fire burning, kettle on it, and scattered around, the company, the
ELLERBECKS, *the* MOSSOPS, *and then* LUCY SYKES, *all from*
BIRKIN's *point of view as* DOUTHWAITE *by fire leads them in the
doxology as: men without jackets larking around, younger men and
women in pairs talking, sidling off,* EDGAR *off with other* BOYS
*collecting sticks, the women sitting around talking, among them, to one
side* LUCY SYKES *watching* MOON *as he demonstrates in mime how he
intends with his rod to locate Piers's grave. The men begin to leapfrog
in background.* BIRKIN *turns his head suddenly; we see beside him*
KATHY. KATHY *is looking towards* LUCY SYKES.

KATHY: What are you going to do now, Mr Birkin?
(BIRKIN *sees* LUCY SYKES *glancing towards him. The men
playing leapfrog in the background begin to divert* MOON's
attention.)

BIRKIN: Why, talk to you of course, Miss Ellerbeck.
(*Pause.*)

KATHY: What about?

BIRKIN: I don't know. But you usually have something to say
about things.

KATHY: You'll be leaving soon, won't you?

BIRKIN: Well, as soon as I've finished.

KATHY: Why?

BIRKIN: Well, I'll have to go somewhere else where I can make a living.

(BIRKIN *sees* MOON *say something to* LUCY SYKES *and with a self-deprecating laugh run over to the leapfroggers and join in.* KATHY, *taking in that* LUCY SYKES *is now alone, more urgently pursues her conversation with* BIRKIN. LUCY *watches* MOON *leapfrogging, clearly aware of* BIRKIN.)

KATHY: My mam says she doesn't see how you *can* make a living at your job. She says there can't be all that many pictures hidden on walls.

BIRKIN: (*Grins.*) Well, it's true I don't make much of one.

KATHY: Well then, why don't you change your job and stay on at Oxgodby?

BIRKIN: Why?

KATHY: What?

BIRKIN: Why should I stay on in Oxgodby?

KATHY: My mam and dad have taken a liking to you, for one thing.

BIRKIN: What about you, do you think I should stay on?

KATHY: Lots of my friends would miss you. They like to think of you at your work. From the way I tell them about it. And I've told them about your roughing it up in the belfry, they like that too.

BIRKIN: But you still haven't answered for yourself. Why do *you* want me to stay?

KATHY: Anyway you're too late.

(BIRKIN *follows* KATHY's *gaze. Cut and see from his point of view and* KATHY's *a young man bending over* LUCY SYKES, *saying something.* LUCY SYKES *rises, goes off with the young man.* BIRKIN *turns to* KATHY, *who is grinning.* KATHY *runs off towards* EDGAR. *From* BIRKIN's *point of view we see* KATHY *running towards* EDGAR. *She turns, looks towards* LUCY SYKES *and the young man, who are walking off.* MOON, *in a state of great exhilaration, catches* BIRKIN's *eye and laughs wildly.* BIRKIN *smiles back. We take in* KATHY *and* EDGAR *watching, amazed.*)

EXT. COUNTRY ROADS. LATE AFTERNOON
Shot of the carriage returning in the dusk. LUCY SYKES *and the young man in first carriage. Also* MOON, *expression reflective, almost sad.* KATHY, EDGAR, MR *and* MRS ELLERBECK *in the second carriage with* BIRKIN *sitting opposite them.* ELLERBECK *asleep.* MRS ELLERBECK *with her arm around* EDGAR, *who is asleep.* KATHY, *her face set, seen from* BIRKIN's *point of view, clearly avoiding his gaze.* BIRKIN *continues to look at* KATHY, *who stares gravely back at him.* BIRKIN *smiles.* KATHY, *suddenly unable to help herself, grins, as the carriages come to a halt. Voices from the first carriage.* KATHY, *in an attempt to retrieve her dignity, looks away from* BIRKIN. *She looks serious as* MOSSOP *approaches the carriage.*

MOSSOP: It's Emily Clough. She died this afternoon.
    (*Cut to* BIRKIN's *face, he looks towards* KATHY. *Cut to* KATHY's *face.* BIRKIN *looks towards* KATHY *as carriages start up. Cut to shot of carriages continuing down the road, around the bend, in the twilight. Fade on carriages disappearing.*)

INT. CHURCH. DAY
The COLONEL's *face as he stands in nave looking at the mural.* BIRKIN *on the scaffold.* MOON *is with him. Both looking down. They both wait for the* COLONEL's *response. He nods in approval and leaves.*

MOON: (*Turning to* BIRKIN) You're quite right. It's a masterpiece. I feel terribly smug, just the two of us knowing about it, before the *Times* art critic tips off the academic parasites. For the moment it's just ours – (MOON's *face, cheerful.*)
BIRKIN: Look at this. (*Points to falling man.*) Have you ever seen a detail like it, in a medieval painting? It anticipates the Bruegels by a hundred years. And the face meant something to him. It's a portrait. It must be. And he was covered over years before the rest.
MOON: Yes, I see what you mean. The crescent scar. One could swear he was meant to be identifiable. But would he have dared, your painter? What was he like? You must know him pretty well by now.

BIRKIN: I can't even put a name to him, as he hasn't signed it.
But then why would he? Our idea of personal f-f-fame meant
nothing to him. (*Little pause.*) But he was fair-haired. I know
that from hairs that keep turning up where his beard
prodded into the paint. He was right-handed, about your
build – he had to use some sort of stool to get up to six feet.
He probably lived in a monastery, because – well, look at the
hands –
(*Cut to montage of hands.*)
– they talk to each other. Like monks' hands must have,
during the long silences.
(*Montage of feet casually done.*)
The weird thing is he didn't finish the job himself. See this
last bit –
(*Cut to corner of hell.*)
You can see it's a rough job. A fill-in. Probably done by his
apprentice. I can't imagine why – just when his nose was past
the finishing post. And he knew that this was his great work.
You can feel it, can't you?
(MOON *nods.*)
Whatever he'd been on before was only a run-up to this.
He'd sweated here, tossed in his bed, g-g-groaned, howled
over it –
(*Cut to Christ, his hands torn, fingers bent as if in agony.*)
Those hands, those fingers.
(*Cut to* MOON.)

MOON: And he shal come with wondes rede, eh?
(MOON *turns away to leave. Cut to* BIRKIN'*s face as he turns
back to the painting. Cut to the falling man. Sound over of*
MOON'*s feet to which* BIRKIN *is oblivious. Sound of door
squealing open.* BIRKIN *turns, suddenly realizing that* MOON *has
gone. Then an expression of sudden realization as he looks down,
and cut to the floor rising at him dizzyingly.* BIRKIN *looks
towards the door,* MOON *just about to close it.*)

BIRKIN: (*Shouting*) Moon! Moon!
(MOON *turns.*)
He fell! (*Shouting*) That's why he didn't finish. It was his last
job. He fell!

(MOON, *after a pause, grins.*)

MOON: OK. Mind your own step then.

(MOON *exits. Closes door.*)

EXT. TRAIN. DAY
Trains racing across countryside.

INT. TRAIN COMPARTMENT. DAY
BIRKIN, ELLERBECK, KATHY, DOUTHWAITE, *all at their most respectably dressed,* KATHY *with a package on her lap.*

ELLERBECK: Ah, but, Mr Birkin. You've a real eye for quality. That anybody can tell. And we want the best. Well, put it this way (*nods*) we want the best we can afford.

EXT. TRAIN. DAY
Train hurtling along.

EXT. STREET. DAY
Market stalls up and down the street. BIRKIN, ELLERBECK, DOUTHWAITE *and* KATHY *crossing through stalls towards a shop, in long shot, entering.*

INT. SHOP: BACKROOM. DAY
Directly in on a YOUNG MAN.

YOUNG MAN: You'd better have a look behind that lot over there. (*Gestures.*) We took them in part exchange.

DOUTHWAITE: I suppose it's in order to try one or two out?
(*The sound of the door opening; the bell rings. The* YOUNG MAN *turns towards it, as we hear the sound of people entering.*)

INT. SHOP. LATER. DAY

ELLERBECK: That's settled then. One of these three. Kathy lass, try them out.
(KATHY, *sitting at an organ, playing 'All People that on Earth do Dwell' and cut to her at another organ playing 'All People*

that on Earth do Dwell' and to the third organ playing 'All
People that on Earth do Dwell'; on each occasion
DOUTHWAITE *listening with his head to the organ's back*.)
DOUTHWAITE: (*As the third organ comes to silence*) I'm no
musician, Mr Birkin. That I freely admit to. But wind, that
I do understand.
ELLERBECK: What do you think, Mr Birkin?
BIRKIN: Well, um – that one vibrates. And that one smells odd.
ELLERBECK: (*Indicating the third organ*) Then this is the one we
test. To the limit. Kathy, lass.
(KATHY *arranges herself at the organ, raises her hands to start.
Sudden peals of thunder, fanfares from the front of the shop.*)
KATHY: Go inquire how long he's going to make that din for,
Mr Birkin.
(BIRKIN *hesitates, turns, and as the music from front continues,
goes through the aisle of organs to the front of shop.*)

INT. SHOP FRONT. DAY
As BIRKIN *reaches the front, the shop door opens and* YOUNG
WOMAN *holds it open for young man who enters on crutches –*
MILBURN. *He has only one leg. The organ music stops. Cut to*
YOUNG MAN, MR *and* MRS KEACH *around the organ, and then
focus on* MRS KEACH *listening to the* YOUNG MAN, *his voice
murmuring politely, over, seen from* BIRKIN's *point of view. In
periphery* MILBURN *and* YOUNG WOMAN *have gone over to inspect
some flutes.* BIRKIN, *transfixed, and then to* MRS KEACH, *stay on
her face, bending to listen, as, abruptly over, the voices of* KATHY,
ELLERBECK, DOUTHWAITE *raised in hymn, organ playing:
'Worthy is the Lamb / Worthy is the Lamb / Worthy is the Lamb for
sinners slain'.* MRS KEACH, *smiling looks towards the sound, sees*
BIRKIN. KEACH *looks up bewildered. The* YOUNG MAN *looks up in
irritation.* MILBURN *and* YOUNG WOMAN *look first bewildered,
then laugh.*

VOICES: (*Out of shot*) For Sinners slai-i-i-in / Worthy is the
Lamb for sinners slai-i-i-in.
(BIRKIN *stands in the room as the hymn continues, then
suddenly stops. There is a pause.*)

MILBURN: (*To the* YOUNG WOMAN) I must say I much prefer the jolly hymns.

(ELLERBECK *and* DOUTHWAITE *enter the front,* KATHY *following.*)

ELLERBECK: (*As he enters, to the* YOUNG MAN) That's it then, we'll have the Auberdech.

DOUTHWAITE: Any discount for cash? (*Taking out a heap of cash*) Let's say a couple of pounds off, cash down, shall we?

(MILBURN *and the* YOUNG WOMAN *obviously enjoying this.* MILBURN *suddenly becoming slightly aware of* BIRKIN.)

ELLERBECK: And to include delivery, of course.

YOUNG MAN: Where to?

DOUTHWAITE: Oxgodby.

(*Throughout this* BIRKIN *is conscious of* MRS KEACH.)

EXT. MARKET. DAY

KATHY, ELLERBECK, DOUTHWAITE, BIRKIN, *emerging from the shop.* BIRKIN *glancing into the shop at* MRS KEACH, *her face half turned towards him, but noticing that* MILBURN *is watching him.*

DOUTHWAITE: Well, that's a neat little bit of business neatly done. Four pounds off plus delivery.

ELLERBECK: We'll have to move a bit if we're going to catch the four seven.

KATHY: That's Mrs Keach, you know, with the vicar. (*To* BIRKIN) Have you met her yet?

DOUTHWAITE: Come on then. Let's get going.

BIRKIN: Actually I'd quite like to have a look at the church as I'm here.

(*Cut to* KATHY's *face looking at him suspiciously as* BIRKIN *glances back into the window and we see from his point of view* MRS KEACH. *He is still not really aware of* MILBURN *who is watching him.*)

INT./EXT. TEASHOP/ORGAN SHOP/MARKET. DAY

BIRKIN *has a cup of tea before him, but is staring through the teashop window into the organ-shop window, through which he can make out the shapes of* KEACH *and* MRS KEACH, *and the* YOUNG MAN *in conference. We see him first, then them from his point of view.* MR *and* MRS KEACH *come through shop door, on to the pavement, confer briefly. They separate,* MRS KEACH *going to a stall to the left of* BIRKIN's *vision, but staying in vision.* KEACH *going to stalls on right of* BIRKIN's *vision. Cut to shot of* MRS KEACH *selecting apples. Cut to shot of* KEACH *bent over, studying the fish. See his face in relation to the fish, fastidiously selecting some plaice. During this* MILBURN *comes out on the pavement with the* YOUNG WOMAN. *Spots* BIRKIN *in the teashop. Stands on the pavement, explaining something to the* YOUNG WOMAN. *Cut back to* MRS KEACH, *a bag of apples in her hand.* MRS KEACH *takes an apple out, bites it. As she does so, she sees* BIRKIN. *She smiles. Cut to* BIRKIN's *face, smiling back at her. Cut back to* MRS KEACH. *She makes as if to move towards him.* KEACH *appears beside her, carrying fish wrapped.* MILBURN *says something to the* YOUNG WOMAN, *touches her on the arm, heads towards the shop, unnoticed by* BIRKIN. KEACH *says something to* MRS KEACH, *looks down at the fish.* MRS KEACH *looks over towards* BIRKIN *as sound of the teashop door opening, over.*

MILBURN: Excuse me.
  (BIRKIN *looks up.*)
  You're from Oxgodby.
BIRKIN: Yes, well, just visiting.
MILBURN: Have you bumped into a chap called Moon over there.
  Charles Moon. Digging up some field or something.
BIRKIN: Yes. I have.
MILBURN: And is he a short, round-faced, curly-haired pink sort
  of chap? Smiles a lot?
BIRKIN: (*Smiling*) That's pretty well him, yes.
MILBURN: A Captain in the Eighteenth Norfolk Artillery?
BIRKIN: Yes.
MILBURN: Well, that clinches it, doesn't it? Must be the same
  chap. Would you give him a salute from me?
BIRKIN: Of course.
MILBURN: And from all the other officers of the Eighteenth
  Norfolk. The ones who didn't sit out the last six months in
  the glasshouse. For buggering their batman.
  (MILBURN, *nods, turns, limps out.*)

INT./EXT. TENT. DAY
MOON *and* BIRKIN *sitting outside the tent drinking tea. Cut to* MOON
glancing at BIRKIN. BIRKIN *abstracted.* MOON *smiles affectionately.*

MOON: It agrees with you, doesn't it?
BIRKIN: What does?
MOON: Oxgodby. Since you've been here they've almost gone,
    your ticks and twitch and stammer.
BIRKIN: Yes, I suppose they have. I hadn't noticed.
MOON: And what about the vicar's lovely lady? Have you seen
    anything of her?
BIRKIN: No, not really.
MOON: A pity.
BIRKIN: Is it?
MOON: (*Laughs.*) No, probably not. Much better off without it,
    aren't we? If we want an easy life.
    (BIRKIN *lifts his mug, smiles at* MOON.)
BIRKIN: Well, here's to an easy life.

EXT./INT. LANDSCAPES/PAINTING. MONTAGE
*Sweeping shots of village, meadow, graveyard, etc. Mingling shots of
above with shots of paradise from the painting, to make up an actual
and an ideal landscape into one, but ending on paradise section in
picture.*

> *Wide shot of landscape near church, in sun/rain/dawn/dusk*
> *Fields in heat haze*
> *Tent in the meadow in heat haze*
> *Dew on the meadow*
> *Rain on the leaves*
> *Birds/bees/butterflies*
> *Sheep*
> *Horses*
> *Trees*
> *Threshing machine/work*
> *Headstones in the moonlight*
> *Sound: moorland before sunset; dawn chorus*

INT. CHURCH. DAY

The face of MR KEACH, *on the scaffold, observing the finished picture and faces of the saved. The sound of the door squealing open, footsteps. Cut to* BIRKIN *below, seen from* KEACH'S *point of view on the scaffold. Cut to* KEACH *climbing the ladder.*

KEACH: Mossop told me you'd finished. And I can see you have. Very good. In accordance with the executors' wishes, here is the final payment from Miss Hebron's estate. (*At the bottom,* KEACH *hands* BIRKIN *an envelope.*) Thirteen pounds fifteen shillings, as was agreed.

BIRKIN: What do you think of it?

KEACH: (*Vaguely*) Mmmm?

BIRKIN: The painting. What do you think of it?

(KEACH *looks vaguely towards it.*)

KEACH: Well, it's there. So you've done the job you were contracted for. And now you've been paid.

BIRKIN: (*After a slight pause*) Thank you. Of course I'll need the scaffolding for several more days.

KEACH: Why?

BIRKIN: Because I haven't finished.

KEACH: What remains to be done?

BIRKIN: That's for me to decide.

KEACH: I shall have the scaffolding removed.

BIRKIN: Oh, will you? Then I shall inform the executors that you've prevented me from completing my work, which will relieve them of the obligation to contribute the thousand pounds to your fabric fund, won't it?

KEACH: (*After a slight pause*) I should not wish to quarrel with you, Mr Birkin.

(BIRKIN *nods.* KEACH *turns to go, then turns back, looks at* BIRKIN. BIRKIN *waits.*)

Oh, I know how you see me, Mr Birkin. The way you want to. You and Mr Moon. And all the people in this parish. My parish. You've never thought what it's like for a man like me, have you? The English are not a deeply religious people. Most of those who attend divine service do so only from habit. Their acceptance of the sacrament is perfunctory. I have yet to meet the man whose hair rose at the nape of his neck because he was about to taste the blood of his dying Lord. Would I find such a man in Oxgodby? When they come to my church in large numbers, at Harvest Thanksgiving or the Christmas Midnight Mass, it's no more than a pagan salute to the passing of the seasons. They do not need me, they merely find me useful at baptisms, weddings, funerals. Chiefly funerals. Because I help see to the orderly disposal of their dead. (*Laughs bitterly*.) But I'm embarrassing you, Mr Birkin. And embarrassing people is a real sin, isn't it? For one thing it makes them see us slightly differently. (*Makes to say something else, checks himself*.) If you could let me know when I may have the scaffolding dismantled.

(*Cut to* BIRKIN's *face, as, over, the sound of* KEACH's *footsteps, the door squealing*.)

EXT. GRAVEYARD WALL. MORNING
At the subsidence by the graveyard wall, by them a bag, a shovel, an old wooden box, a camera, MOON *holding a long steel shaft.*

MOON: Oh, come off it, Birkin, of course Keach is right. You have finished. If one couldn't tell by looking at the wall, one can tell by looking at your face. You can't keep munching at this piece of cake for ever. Here. (*Hands diviner to* BIRKIN.) Excommunicate or not my Piers was important enough to rate a stone box. Push it into the earth. There. Do you feel it?

BIRKIN: (*Pushing it in*) No.

MOON: Well, then – do it again a few inches further on. And so forth. Until you hit it. (*Little pause, grins*.) Off you go. I'll take over when we'll need a professional touch.
(*Cut to* MOON *some time later, further on, probing delicately. Cut to* BIRKIN *watching him. Cut back to* MOON, *stopping suddenly*.)

BIRKIN: What is it?

MOON: Either a boulder deeper than it ought to be, or the lid of a stone coffin perhaps.

(MOON *puts down diviner, picks up shovel, slight pause, hands it to* BIRKIN.)
Do you know what this is for?

EXT. HEBRON'S GRAVE. DAY
Montage. Cut to BIRKIN *digging in the heat. Twelve inches down and sweating.* MOON *sitting on the box watching.* BIRKIN, *shirt off, two feet down. Low up to wall.* MOSSOP *and scythe leaning against it. School bell ringing.* MOSSOP *eating his lunch off the wall. Low up to* MOON *sitting smoking his pipe. A crescent of school children, including* KATHY, *around them. They gradually disperse.*

MOON: A true-blue British workman, eh? Mr Mossop?
(MOSSOP, *lunch finished, sitting on the wall. He looks dour and sceptical as he moves away, muttering.* BIRKIN *digging in the heat as the hole gets deeper.*)
(*Out of shot*) Doesn't it excite you? Digging where someone dug five, six hundred years ago?
(BIRKIN, *sweating profusely, glances towards him.*)
Oh, well, you're spoiled. You clean a wall and find a masterpiece. You turn over the earth and expect to find a pot of gold. But we diggers keep our palates fresh. A mild deviation of tinge is all we need – (*moving towards* BIRKIN) – to stir the adrenalin. (*Holds out his hand for the spade.*)
Haven't you noticed that you're throwing up soil that should have been three spits deeper?
(MOON *is trowelling earth into the bag almost full. Signals.* BIRKIN *draws it up, dumps it. Cut to* MOON *holding up an object.*)
Horn button. Fifteenth century.
(MOON *tosses it up.* BIRKIN *catches it.*)
(*Out of shot*) Right on target.
(*Cut to* MOON. *He is brushing away with his hands with rapid strokes, barefooted. Cut back to* BIRKIN *watching him, crouching. Moon's socks and shoes beside him, and then back to* MOON, *close in on his hands brushing the earth, then back to* BIRKIN *his face expressing excitement, and then back to* MOON's *hands, uncovering the stone so that it swims into sight. A carved*

shaft branching gracefully into whorls of stone raised upon a convex lid. At its head a hand holding a sacramental cup. Wafer poised at its rim. MOON *stops brushing when it's completely revealed, peers. Cut to* BIRKIN.)

BIRKIN: Well? Come on. Is it Piers or isn't it?

(*Cut to* MOON *peering down.*)

MOON: Just 'Miserisimus'. I of all men the most wretched. They really had it in for the poor devil. (*Looking up, his face dirty.*) Didn't they? I wonder why. Ah well, I suppose we'll never know.

(*Cut to* MOON *taking photographs from different angles, succession of shots.*)

For publication. Against the day when I need a university job. (*Putting down camera*) They don't want to know if you've been anywhere, seen or done anything, just what you've published. (*Turns. Grinning*) Shall we have a peep inside?

(*Cut to* MOON, BIRKIN *in the pit.* BIRKIN *pushing,* MOON *pulling at lid, then cut to shot of the coffin, seen from above as lid swivels slowly off. Revealed, a skeleton, full length. Stay on it.*)

(*Out of shot*) Look – see it. Third rib down.

(*Close in on something metal swinging glintingly behind the rib cage. Cut to golden crescent, on a chain, in* MOON'*s hand. Cut to* MOON'*s face, looking down, then to* BIRKIN'*s looking down, then back to crescent.*)

Miserisimus.

INT. CHURCH. DAY

BIRKIN *and* MOON *on scaffold. Cut to face of falling man on wall, crescent of forehead evident.*

MOON: He was a converted Muslim. Caught on some Christian Crusade, I suppose, and converted to save his skin. Imagine the ructions in Oxgodby when he turned up again and was still worshipping to the East.

(*Little pause as we take in the two demons clutching him, one snapping his right wrist, one splitting him with shears, his face in torment.*)

Both our mysteries solved.
BIRKIN: Well, it was the same mystery, wasn't it?

INT. BELFRY. AFTERNOON
MRS KEACH *appears at the trapdoor. In her hat a rose, a Sarah van Fleet. We see her from* BIRKIN'S *point of view then cut to him looking at her. He is sitting, smoking on the bed.*

MRS KEACH: I hear you've finished.
BIRKIN: Yes.
MRS KEACH: I've brought you a bag of apples. To say goodbye with.
(*She holds out bag.* BIRKIN *takes it.*)
BIRKIN: Thank you.
MRS KEACH: They're Ribston Pippins. They do well up here. Exactly the right soil and climate. Lots of other varieties don't take, though.
BIRKIN: You're an expert in apples, then, are you?
MRS KEACH: I am. My father taught me. Before he bit into one he'd sniff it, roll it around his cupped palms, then smell his hands. Then he'd tap and finger it like a blind man. Sometimes he made me close my eyes and when I'd had a bite he'd ask me to say which apple. So this is where you've been living all this time.
(MRS KEACH *looking around, observed by* BIRKIN, *as she takes in lamp, kitbag, camp bed. She picks up Scott-Bradshaw's* A History of Church Architecture, *glances at cover, makes to open it, doesn't. A pause between them.* MRS KEACH *still holding the book. She crosses to window, looks out.* BIRKIN *watches her.*)
(*Looking out of the window*) And there's Mr Moon.
BIRKIN: (*Watching her*) Yes.
(*As if coming to a decision,* BIRKIN *walks over to the window beside her. They are pressing against each other, side against side.* MOON, *seen from their point of view sitting outside his tent, scribbling and drawing.* BIRKIN *turns towards* MRS KEACH. *She turns towards* BIRKIN. *They straighten. They stand staring at each other.*)

He's dug up the bones he was commissioned to dig up. And turned up an Anglo-Saxon basilica in the process. The basilica is what he really came for. He knew it was here.

MRS KEACH: Oh. Bones and a basilica.

BIRKIN: Yes.

MRS KEACH: (*Nods*) So you've both found what you came to find?
(*Cut from her face to his. He makes to say something, doesn't. There is a pause.*)
I'm glad.
(*Little pause. She turns to go. Cut to* MRS KEACH's *face. Hat. Sarah van Fleet rose. Cut from rose to* MRS KEACH *walking across the steps. Begins to go down. Stops. Smiles.*)
Your book.

BIRKIN: Oh.
(*He goes over, takes it from her.*)

INT. BELFRY STEPS. DAY
MRS KEACH *descending the steps.*

INT. BELFRY. DAY
BIRKIN *standing, holding book. Sound of footsteps below, the door squealing open, squealing shut.*

INT. BELFRY/NAVE. EVENING
BIRKIN *sitting with his back against the wall. The book beside him, open. See rose. Twilight through the window. Below, distantly and over, the sound of the door squealing open. Footsteps.* BIRKIN *rises, goes to steps, looks down. From his point of view the nave empty. Sound of footsteps approaching beneath.* KATHY *appears. Turns her face up towards him.*

KATHY: (*Calling upwards*) Mr Birkin – Mr Birkin –
(*Stay on* KATHY *as she looks around, from* BIRKIN's *point of view then she turns, walks away. Sound of footsteps, door opening with a squeal, closing.*)

INT. BELFRY. EVENING
Later. BIRKIN *gets up, leaves belfry.*

EXT. VICARAGE. NIGHT
BIRKIN *approaches, looks at the lit windows, hears the violin, turns and goes.*

INT. CHURCH. MORNING
BIRKIN *finishes packing his tools with great energy.* MOON *arrives at the door, dressed for departure.*

MOON: (*Cheerfully*) A letter. The postman asked me to drop it 'up'.
BIRKIN: Thank you. (*Looks at it.*) From Vinny. My wife.
    Probably wanting us to start over again. She usually does.
MOON: And will you?
BIRKIN: (*Wryly*) I usually do.
    (BIRKIN *looks at* MOON.)
    And where are you off to.
    (*He grins.*)
MOON: Basra – Baghdad. There's a big dig going on there. I'd like to get in on it.
BIRKIN: Right.
MOON: What about you?
BIRKIN: Don't know. Wait for another church, I suppose.
MOON: You'll never get another one like this.
BIRKIN: I know. (*Little pause.*) It's been a summer, hasn't it?
    (MOON *nods. There is a pause.*)
MOON: So.
    (MOON *looks vaguely around, then back towards* BIRKIN. *Cut to* BIRKIN'*s face. Cut back to* MOON. *Slight pause.*)
    Well.
    (*He holds out his hand.* BIRKIN *takes it. They shake hands. Cut to* MOON, *from* BIRKIN'*s point of view at the belfry window, walking jauntily across and out of frame, carrying bags, etc.* BIRKIN *turns away, takes coat off hook.*)

INT. CHURCH NAVE. MORNING
BIRKIN *stopping at the catafalque. Laetitia, and the lettering: 'Conjugam Optimam Amantissima et Delectissima –' Cut to* BIRKIN'*s face, smiling slightly. He places* MRS KEACH'*s rug on the*

tomb. BIRKIN, *take him in full shot. He is turning away from the catafalque and is as when he arrived, carrying his kit, etc., but with his coat over his arm. He turns, looks towards the wall-painting. The scaffolding is still up,* BIRKIN's *view of the painting obscured. He hesitates, as if about to go towards it. Turns, walks down the nave towards door, his footsteps clapping. Open door. It squeals.*

EXT. MEADOW/GRAVEYARD. DAY
BIRKIN *walking across the meadow. He reaches into one of his bags, takes out an apple, bites on it. Eats.* MOON, *his tent, all sign of his occupancy gone. The day is almost sunless, windy. Horse and cart labouring across a corner of the meadow. Stay on* BIRKIN *walking away, eating an apple as suddenly the sound of a hymn 'As Pants the Heart' thinly but distinctly.* BIRKIN *stops, turns, the apple halfway to his mouth, looking towards church.*

EXT./INT. CHURCH. DAY
The church from BIRKIN's *point of view, cars parked, modern. An* OLD MAN, *carrying a book, walking with a stick, approaches church door. The hymn continues. The* OLD MAN *watches the sparse, singing congregation. He is standing at the back. In his hand, an old book, possibly the Scott-Bradshaw* A History of Church Architecture, *but the title is not distinct. The* OLD MAN *lifts his eyes from the congregation to the wall-painting, which slowly fills the screen as the hymn is replaced by magnificent music.* BIRKIN *crossing field, eating apple, and back again to wall-painting, back to* BIRKIN, *as music continues and finally fading from* BIRKIN *to the wall-painting.*